# Motorcycle Basics TechBook

## by Matthew Coombs
*incorporating material from the Haynes Motorcycle Basics Manual by Pete Shoemark*

*(3515-224)*

© Haynes Publishing 2002

ABCDE
FG

A book in the **Haynes TechBook Series**

ISBN **978 0 85733 998 0**

**British Library Cataloguing in Publication Data**
A catalogue record for this book is available from the British Library

**Library of Congress Catalog Card Number 2001131367**

Printed by **J H Haynes & Co Ltd, Sparkford, Nr Yeovil, Somerset BA22 7JJ, England**

**Haynes Publishing**
Sparkford, Nr Yeovil, Somerset BA22 7JJ, England

**Haynes North America, Inc**
861 Lawrence Drive, Newbury Park, California 91320, USA

**Haynes Publishing Nordiska AB**
Box 1504, 751 45 UPPSALA, Sweden

*Printed using 33-lb Resolute Book 65 4.0 from Resolute Forest Products Calhoun, TN mill. Resolute is a member of World Wildlife Fund's Climate Savers programme committed to significantly reducing GHG emissions. This paper uses 50% less wood fibre than traditional offset. The Calhoun Mill is certified to the following sustainable forest management and chain of custody standards: SFI, PEFC and FSC Controlled Wood.*

# Contents

# Introduction

Quite a large number of motorcycles and scooters in everyday use are ridden by owners who have little understanding of how their machine works. Many are quite content to remain in this state of blissful ignorance, having their machine serviced at regular intervals as and when the need occurs, or repairs carried out when problems necessitate. Not everyone has the ability or inclination to look after these matters themselves and it is as well that they are aware of their own limitations.

Unfortunately, roadside breakdowns are likely to occur without warning, and always at a bad time. They can range from something mildly irritating, such as the refusal to start one morning, to a complete breakdown in some remote spot on a dark wet night. It is on occasions like these that most people begin to have some regret at not having even a basic understanding of how their machines work so that they could, perhaps, have taken precautionary measures, or, at the very least, have an idea of where the fault lies.

No book, however well written, can turn an unskilled amateur into a skilled mechanic. What it can do is to explain in simple terms how each major component of a motorcycle or scooter functions and the role it plays in ensuring the machine remains in good running order. No previous understanding of the subject is assumed and all technical terminology used is explained in a glossary at the end of the book.

Today's motorcycles are the end product of many years' continual development work, becoming both complicated and sophisticated in the quest for improved performance. Although the use of electronics is increasing, especially for the control of fuelling and ignition, many components on the motorcycle are still of mechanical operation and it will often be found that a complicated looking assembly is nothing more than a number of relatively simple basic units bolted together to make up a single, compact unit.

This book is also aimed at students on Further Education courses in Motorcycle Engineering.

# About this book

The text in each chapter is arranged in numbered section order and will correspond with the contents list at the beginning of the chapter. If a section in another chapter is referred to, a typical instruction 'see Chapter 4, Section 8' will be found.

All illustrations are keyed into the text with their chapter number and section number. Where several illustrations relate to a single section, they carry an alphabetical code, e.g. 5.3b relates to Chapter 5, Section 3, 2nd illustration.

It has been our objective to present the information given in this book in as simple a form as possible, using line drawings wherever possible to illustrate components and systems in their basic form. Technical terms have been kept to a minimum, and to help further, a basic glossary of technical terminology can be found immediately before the index.

**Whilst every attempt is made to ensure that the information in this book is correct, no liability can be accepted by the authors or publishers for loss, damage or injury caused by any errors in, or omissions from, the information given.**

# Acknowledgements

Our thanks are due to the following companies who provided many of the illustrations used throughout this book:

Cooper-Avon Tyres Ltd, Burmah Castrol Ltd, Ducati Meccanica SpA, Dwek International Ltd, Heron Suzuki (GB) Ltd, Kawasaki Motors (UK) Ltd, Mitsui Machinery Sales (UK) Ltd, NGK Spark Plugs Ltd, NVT Motorcycles Ltd, Robin Chan of Contact Developments and Vespa (UK) Ltd.

We would also like to thank Tony Tranter who gave permission to use line drawings from his book *The Motorcycle Electrical TechBook*.

Professional mechanics are trained in safe working procedures. However enthusiastic you may be about getting on with the job at hand, take the time to ensure that your safety is not put at risk. A moment's lack of attention can result in an accident, as can failure to observe simple precautions.

There will always be new ways of having accidents, and the following is not a comprehensive list of all dangers; it is intended rather to make you aware of the risks and to encourage a safe approach to all work you carry out on your bike.

## Asbestos

● Certain friction, insulating, sealing and other products - such as brake pads, clutch linings, gaskets, etc. - contain asbestos. Extreme care must be taken to avoid inhalation of dust from such products since it is hazardous to health. If in doubt, assume that they do contain asbestos.

## Fire

● Remember at all times that petrol is highly flammable. Never smoke or have any kind of naked flame around, when working on the vehicle. But the risk does not end there - a spark caused by an electrical short-circuit, by two metal surfaces contacting each other, by careless use of tools, or even by static electricity built up in your body under certain conditions, can ignite petrol vapour, which in a confined space is highly explosive. Never use petrol as a cleaning solvent. Use an approved safety solvent.

● Always disconnect the battery earth terminal before working on any part of the fuel or electrical system, and never risk spilling fuel on to a hot engine or exhaust.

● It is recommended that a fire extinguisher of a type suitable for fuel and electrical fires is kept handy in the garage or workplace at all times. Never try to extinguish a fuel or electrical fire with water.

## Fumes

● Certain fumes are highly toxic and can quickly cause unconsciousness and even death if inhaled to any extent. Petrol vapour comes into this category, as do the vapours from certain solvents such as trichloro-ethylene. Any draining or pouring of such volatile fluids should be done in a well ventilated area.

● When using cleaning fluids and solvents, read the instructions carefully. Never use materials from unmarked containers - they may give off poisonous vapours.

● Never run the engine of a motor vehicle in an enclosed space such as a garage. Exhaust fumes contain carbon monoxide which is extremely poisonous; if you need to run the engine, always do so in the open air or at least have the rear of the vehicle outside the workplace.

## The battery

● Never cause a spark, or allow a naked light near the vehicle's battery. It will normally be giving off a certain amount of hydrogen gas, which is highly explosive.

● Always disconnect the battery ground (earth) terminal before working on the fuel or electrical systems (except where noted).

● If possible, loosen the filler plugs or cover when charging the battery from an external source. Do not charge at an excessive rate or the battery may burst.

● Take care when topping up, cleaning or carrying the battery. The acid electrolyte, evenwhen diluted, is very corrosive and should not be allowed to contact the eyes or skin. Always wear rubber gloves and goggles or a face shield. If you ever need to prepare electrolyte yourself, always add the acid slowly to the water; never add the water to the acid.

## Electricity

● When using an electric power tool, inspection light etc., always ensure that the appliance is correctly connected to its plug and that, where necessary, it is properly grounded (earthed). Do not use such appliances in damp conditions and, again, beware of creating a spark or applying excessive heat in the vicinity of fuel or fuel vapour. Also ensure that the appliances meet national safety standards.

● A severe electric shock can result from touching certain parts of the electrical system, such as the spark plug wires (HT leads), when the engine is running or being cranked, particularly if components are damp or the insulation is defective. Where an electronic ignition system is used, the secondary (HT) voltage is much higher and could prove fatal.

# Remember...

✗ **Don't** start the engine without first ascertaining that the transmission is in neutral.

✗ **Don't** suddenly remove the pressure cap from a hot cooling system - cover it with a cloth and release the pressure gradually first, or you may get scalded by escaping coolant.

✗ **Don't** attempt to drain oil until you are sure it has cooled sufficiently to avoid scalding you.

✗ **Don't** grasp any part of the engine or exhaust system without first ascertaining that it is cool enough not to burn you.

✗ **Don't** allow brake fluid or antifreeze to contact the machine's paintwork or plastic components.

✗ **Don't** siphon toxic liquids such as fuel, hydraulic fluid or antifreeze by mouth, or allow them to remain on your skin.

✗ **Don't** inhale dust - it may be injurious to health (see Asbestos heading).

✗ **Don't** allow any spilled oil or grease to remain on the floor - wipe it up right away, before someone slips on it.

✗ **Don't** use ill-fitting spanners or other tools which may slip and cause injury.

✗ **Don't** lift a heavy component which may be beyond your capability - get assistance.

✗ **Don't** rush to finish a job or take unverified short cuts.

✗ **Don't** allow children or animals in or around an unattended vehicle.

✗ **Don't** inflate a tyre above the recommended pressure. Apart from over-stressing the carcass, in extreme cases the tyre may blow off forcibly.

✔ **Do** ensure that the machine is supported securely at all times. This is especially important when the machine is blocked up to aid wheel or fork removal.

✔ **Do** take care when attempting to loosen a stubborn nut or bolt. It is generally better to pull on a spanner, rather than push, so that if you slip, you fall away from the machine rather than onto it.

✔ **Do** wear eye protection when using power tools such as drill, sander, bench grinder etc.

✔ **Do** use a barrier cream on your hands prior to undertaking dirty jobs - it will protect your skin from infection as well as making the dirt easier to remove afterwards; but make sure your hands aren't left slippery. Note that long-term contact with used engine oil can be a health hazard.

✔ **Do** keep loose clothing (cuffs, ties etc. and long hair) well out of the way of moving mechanical parts.

✔ **Do** remove rings, wristwatch etc., before working on the vehicle - especially the electrical system.

✔ **Do** keep your work area tidy - it is only too easy to fall over articles left lying around.

✔ **Do** exercise caution when compressing springs for removal or installation. Ensure that the tension is applied and released in a controlled manner, using suitable tools which preclude the possibility of the spring escaping violently.

✔ **Do** ensure that any lifting tackle used has a safe working load rating adequate for the job.

✔ **Do** get someone to check periodically that all is well, when working alone on the vehicle.

✔ **Do** carry out work in a logical sequence and check that everything is correctly assembled and tightened afterwards.

✔ **Do** remember that your vehicle's safety affects that of yourself and others. If in doubt on any point, get professional advice.

● If in spite of following these precautions, you are unfortunate enough to injure yourself, seek medical attention as soon as possible.

# Chapter 1
# Engine

# Contents

## 1 Introduction

All powered two-wheelers share a number of similarities, even though at first glance a 50 cc scooter seems far removed from a large-capacity sports motorcycle. Each has two wheels, an engine and a transmission system, which are all held together by a framework, usually with some form of suspension between that and the wheels. In this chapter we will be looking at the various types of engine to try to establish how they work and why they come in so many diverse shapes and sizes.

The engine produces the power necessary for the motorcycle to move. The principle components and assemblies we are concerned with in this chapter are the cylinder head, the cylinder(s) and piston(s), the connecting rod(s) and the crankshaft. With the exception of the rotary engine design, all engines have these components, the main difference between them being in the number of cylinders and pistons, and their arrangement.

On almost every modern design, the engine components are housed in or bolted onto cast alloy cases. These cases are almost universally called crankcases, even though they contain rather more than just the crankshaft. On many early British designs, and until recently certain American motorcycles, the engine was entirely separate

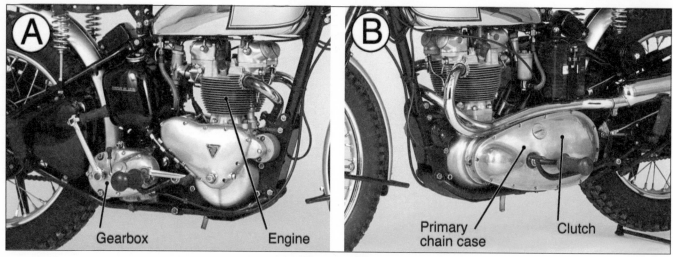

1.1a The 'pre-unit' engine

A   The right-hand side view shows the separate engine and gearbox units
B   The left-hand side view shows the primary chaincase which links the engine and gearbox and also houses the clutch

from the transmission, and they were linked by a chain or belt **(see illustration 1.1a)**. Modern designs almost universally house all the transmission components within the crankcases, and are normally referred to as being of 'unit construction' **(see illustration 1.1b)**. This has led to the earlier arrangement being called 'pre-unit', for obvious reasons.

There are a few exceptions to the pre-unit or unit engines, which fall somewhere between the two, where the transmission is housed in its own case rather than the crankcase, with the case being bolted directly onto the crankcase rather than mounted separately on the frame **(see illustration 1.1c)**. The most notable of these engine types are the long-running and well-proven designs from BMW and Moto Guzzi, and it is of course the arrangement used in the majority of car engines.

## 2   Which engine?

### The purpose of an engine

The purpose of an engine is to convert fuel into work (power). All motorcycles use internal combustion engines, and these burn fuel inside a cylinder. The energy created by the burning fuel causes the piston to move, and this turns the crankshaft. The reason it is called an internal combustion engine is that the fuel is burned inside the engine. In an external combustion engine, such as a steam engine, the fuel is burned externally and heats water, which creates steam pressure to move the piston.

### The engine cycle

All internal combustion engines must arrange for four events to occur to complete one engine cycle. These are the induction, the compression, the ignition, and the exhaust of the fuel/air mixture.

The majority of motorcycles will have either a two-stroke engine or a four-stroke engine, both known as 'reciprocating' engines, and having much in common. In both types, a mixture of fuel and air is compressed inside the cylinder and then ignited by a spark. The mixture burns very quickly, and in doing so it expands, pushing the piston down the cylinder bore. The piston is connected to the crankshaft by a connecting rod, and its up and down (or reciprocating) movement is converted at the crankshaft into the rotary motion required to turn the rear wheel and

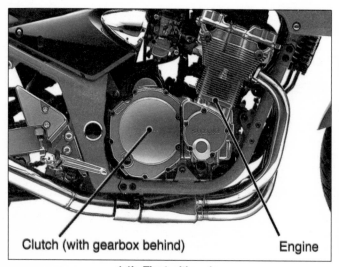

1.1b The 'unit' engine

1.1c Engine, clutch and gearbox positions as used by Moto Guzzi

thus drive the machine (see Section 3). The difference in the engines is that a two-stroke will perform the four events within two strokes of the piston (one up, one down), while a four-stroke performs the events over four strokes of the piston.

The exception to the established two- and four-stroke designs is the rotary engine. This is also an internal combustion engine, but it works on a rather different principle to conventional two- and four-stroke designs. Further details of the rotary engine can be found in Section 23.

### Two-stroke or four-stroke?

Having set aside the rotary engine, there remains the choice of two-stroke or four-stroke units. Each has its own advantages and disadvantages, and this is why neither has ever managed to oust the other. In its simplest form the two-stroke unit is by far the less complicated of the two, and is thus cheaper to manufacture. In the past this has been the main reason for its widespread use in scooters and lightweight motorcycles. The simple two-stroke does have its drawbacks, though, and at one stage its disappearance seemed possible because of the insurmountable problems of high noise and pollution levels. In fact it has actually been banned from road use in certain parts of the world for those reasons.

In recent years the two-stroke engine has become an altogether more sophisticated device, and the advances are such that it remains a popular choice for many applications. But with the exception of scooters and commuter-type motorcycles, the 'low-cost' aspect has largely disappeared, and the modern performance two-stroke is now used primarily in sports or racing machines because of its light weight and the power it produces when highly tuned. It is worth noting that certain major car manufacturers have been testing two-stroke engines in small cars.

The four-stroke engine was traditionally chosen for larger machines because of its superior spread of power and fuel economy. Its main drawback was the higher manufacturing cost and relative complexity, and this made it a bad choice for smaller capacity engines. Just as the two-stroke became more refined, however, so did the four-stroke, and over the years the distinction between the role of each type blurred; small four-strokes became just as good a proposition as large two-strokes.

In the end, two-stroke and four-stroke engines can be viewed as two means to the same end, namely a way of propelling a vehicle. Each has its supporters and detractors, and this is reflected in manufacturers' catalogues, which for certain categories often offer very similar models with two- and four-stroke engine alternatives, leaving the choice in the hands of the prospective owner. Until recently it was quite easy to look at a particular engine type and see clearly its good and bad points. The level of technology now applied to engine design and manufacture has led to a situation where almost any drawback can be engineered out of the design, though often at the expense of simplicity. Later in this Chapter we will examine the two-stroke and four-stroke engines in greater detail, but before looking at the differences between them, let us deal with their similarities.

### 3   Basic principles

### The cylinder and piston

All reciprocating engines have a number of basic parts in common, and these are recognisably similar even between the extreme examples of a two-stroke scooter and a four-stroke tourer. Two of these are the cylinder and the piston.

To convert the fuel/air mixture into useful work it must be burnt in a carefully controlled manner and the resulting energy changed into movement. The combustion takes place in the cylinder and the energy produced causes the piston to move **(see illustration 1.3a)**.

1) A mixture of fuel together with the necessary amount of air is introduced into the cylinder, above the piston. The piston, with piston rings that fit around it so that it is a tight fit in the cylinder bore to prevent leakage, is pushed upwards and the mixture is compressed.

2) The fuel air mixture now occupies a much smaller space than it did at atmospheric pressure. This effectively concentrates the energy contained in the fuel, allowing the maximum amount of power to be extracted when it is burnt.

3) At the appropriate moment a spark jumps across the spark plug electrodes, igniting the mixture. This burns very quickly, and can be considered almost a controlled explosion. The resulting hot gases rapidly increase the pressure in the cylinder, forcing the piston down with far more energy than was required to compress the mixture originally.

### The crankshaft

The controlled combustion of fuel in air can be used to produce power. This process is repeated many times every minute (up to sixteen thousand on some engines) to produce a relatively continuous source of motive power. In the present form, however, it is of little use in driving a motorcycle; we must first convert it to rotary motion.

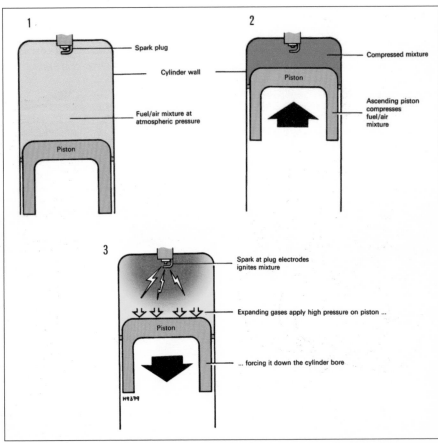

**1.3a  Compression and ignition of the fuel/air mixture in the combustion chamber**

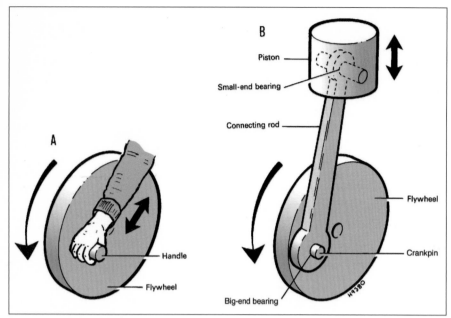

**1.3b How the crankshaft converts linear motion into the rotary motion required to turn the rear wheel**

A   *By alternately pushing and pulling on the handle, the flywheel can be made to revolve. At the two extremes of the stroke there will be no significant force applied to the flywheel, but stored energy, or momentum, will carry it through these dead points.*

B   *Compare this with (A). The pushing force applied by arm and hand through the handle has been replaced by the piston and connecting rod assembly through the big-end bearing and crankpin.*

The principle of the crankshaft is well known and is employed by many people every day. When you ride a bicycle or wind down a car window, you are converting a more or less linear movement into a rotary one, and you can see the comparison between a hand-operating a flywheel and a piston turning a crankshaft in an engine **(see illustration 1.3b)**. The flywheel performs a very important role; as the piston is pushed down the cylinder bore and turns the crankshaft, the flywheel picks up momentum and this is used to carry the piston back up the cylinder for the process to continue. Similarly, if in the hand-operated version we assume that the wheel is turned only by pushing in one direction (rather than pulling in the other as well), the momentum created will keep the flywheel turning until it is in the right position to be pushed round again.

To allow our example crankshaft to work, one or two refinements are needed. Firstly, there has to be some sort of bearing between the lower or big-end of the rod that connects the piston and the flywheel, to reduce friction. This can be a bush, or a ball or needle roller bearing, fitted into the big-end eye and engaging over the crankpin. Similarly, at the upper or small-end of the connecting rod, it will be necessary to allow the piston to rock in relation to the connecting rod. Again, a bush or bearing is used in the small-end eye, and the piston is located by a short pin, known as a gudgeon pin, piston pin or wrist pin.

In a working example of an engine there is normally a flywheel on each side of the connecting rod big-end, and they are connected by the crankpin, which the connecting rod runs on **(see illustration 1.3c)**. The flywheels are carried by a central shaft that runs in bearings on each side, these being fitted into a light alloy casing, or crankcase. The cylinder is held in the correct position by being bolted to the crankcase, or on many modern sports bikes by being part of the crankcase, in which the crankshaft runs.

**Note:** *Crankshaft flywheels are commonly known as 'webs', and are often not round (for reasons that will be covered later).*

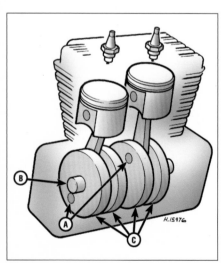

**1.3c  The crankshaft, connecting rod and piston assembly from a 'parallel' twin cylinder engine**

*A Crankpin    B Shaft    C Flywheels*

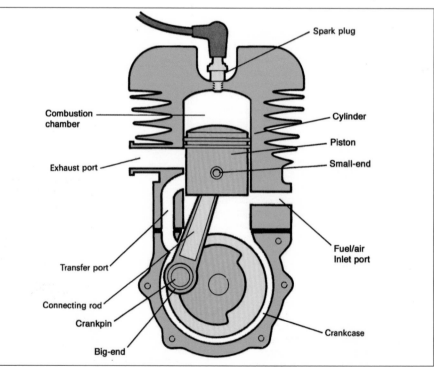

**1.4a  The two-stroke engine in its simplest form**

## 4 The two-stroke engine

Having established the mechanical requirements of a simple internal combustion engine we can now look at ways of making it run as a suitable power source for a motorcycle. The simplest of these in mechanical terms is the piston-ported two-stroke (see illustration 1.4a). The drawing shows the engine in section, and you should be able to identify the engine components shown in the previous illustrations.

You will notice that the cylinder bore has gained a few holes in its surface. These are known as ports and are fundamental to two-stroke operation. The inlet and exhaust ports are obvious enough – the inlet port allows the fuel/air mixture into the engine to be burnt, and the exhaust port allows the resulting burnt gases to be expelled from the engine. The function of the transfer port is to allow the mixture to be passed from the crankcase, into which it was initially drawn, to the combustion chamber, where it is burnt. This raises the question of what the mixture is doing being drawn into the crankcase below the piston, rather than directly into the combustion chamber above the piston.

To understand this it should be noted that the crankcase fulfils an important secondary role in a two-stroke engine, acting as a sort of pump for the mixture. It forms a sealed chamber, closed at the top by the piston, and it follows that the volume of this chamber, and therefore the pressure inside it, varies as the piston rises and falls in the cylinder (as the piston rises, the volume increases, and so the pressure falls below that outside the crankcase, creating a vacuum; conversely as the piston falls, the volume decreases and so the pressure rises above that outside the crankcase).

The inlet port in the cylinder wall is kept closed for much of the time by the piston 'skirt', but is uncovered as the piston nears the top of its stroke. The vacuum created draws a fresh charge of mixture into the cylinder, then as the piston falls and creates pressure in the crankcase this mixture is pushed into the combustion chamber via the transfer port. The sequence is described and illustrated below (see illustrations 1.4b and c).

A) *The piston is nearing the top of its stroke, and the blue shaded area above it indicates that the fuel/air mixture is being compressed ready for combustion. As the piston has been rising the crankcase volume has been increasing, but since it is sealed a partial vacuum has been created. The piston has now passed the inlet port and fresh fuel/air mixture (indicated by the blue arrows) is drawn into the crankcase from the carburettor.*

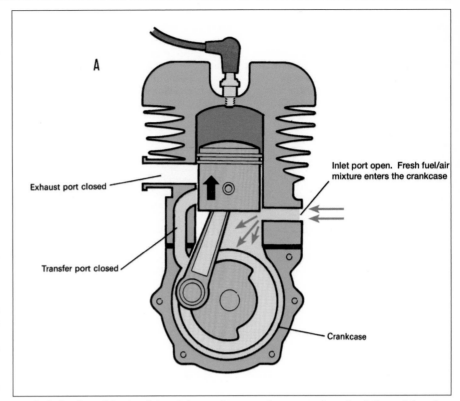

Exhaust port closed

Transfer port closed

Inlet port open. Fresh fuel/air mixture enters the crankcase

Crankcase

**1.4b  Induction of fresh mixture into crankcase and compression of existing mixture in combustion chamber**

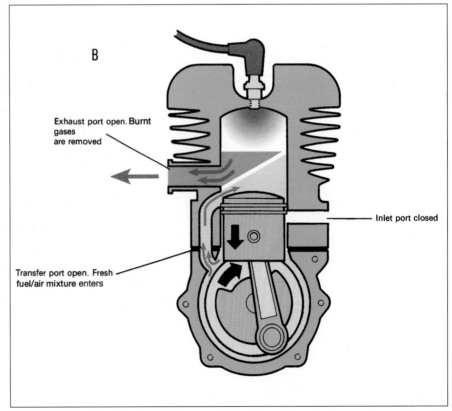

Exhaust port open. Burnt gases are removed

Inlet port closed

Transfer port open. Fresh fuel/air mixture enters

**1.4c  Ignition and exhaust of existing mixture in combustion chamber, and transfer of fresh mixture to combustion chamber**

*The large black arrow indicates piston movement.*

B) *The spark plug ignites the compressed mixture and the expanding gases force the piston downwards. The piston covers the transfer and inlet ports and begins to compress the fresh mixture trapped below it in the crankcase. As the top of the piston passes the exhaust port, the gases in the combustion chamber (indicated by the red arrows), which are still under some pressure (though most of the useful energy has been used to move the piston), rush out through the exhaust port. The top of the piston then passes the transfer port, and the fresh mixture is now able to pass from the crankcase into the combustion chamber. Note that the transfer port directs the incoming mixture upwards, where it helps to displace the burnt gases. If this were not done, the incoming mixture would tend to rush (or 'short-circuit' as it is known) straight out of the exhaust port, wasting fuel and leaving some of the burnt mixture from the last power stroke in the cylinder. The piston reaches the bottom of its stroke and begins to rise again. The transfer and exhaust ports close and the mixture in the combustion chamber is compressed. As the piston continues to rise, creating vacuum in the crankcase, the inlet port is uncovered and thus the cycle is completed and repeated.*

This design, known as a 'piston-ported' two-stroke for obvious reasons, is the simplest form of two-stroke engine, and has very few moving parts. Whilst this is a considerable advantage in many respects, it leaves a lot to be desired in terms of efficiency. At one time almost every two-stroke engine was of the piston-ported type, but on current designs it has been abandoned in favour of more sophisticated and efficient arrangements.

## 5 Improved two-stroke engine designs – influencing gas flow

One of the causes of inefficiency in the simple piston-ported two-stroke engine is the incomplete scavenging of the exhaust gases. If these remain in the cylinder they prevent the full amount of fresh mixture from entering, and thus the power output is reduced. There is also the related problem of the fresh mixture passing from the transfer port and straight out of the exhaust port, and as has been mentioned in the previous section, the transfer port directs the mixture upwards to minimise this.

### Deflector pistons

Scavenging efficiency and fuel consumption can be improved by creating a more efficient gas flow inside the cylinder, and in the early days of two-stroke development this was achieved by fitting a piston shaped on the top to deflect the mixture up towards the top of the cylinder and away from the exhaust port – this was known as a deflector piston **(see illustration 1.5a)**.

However the use of deflector pistons in two-stroke engines was short-lived due to the problem of piston expansion. The heat generated in the combustion chamber tends to be higher than in a four-stroke engine because there are twice as many detonations, and it is also hotter at the top than elsewhere. This causes problems with piston expansion. Pistons are actually shaped to be slightly out-of-round and tapered at the top, so that when they expand with the varying heat, they become round and cylindrical. Adding an irregularly shaped lump of metal in the form of a deflector to the top of the piston changes its expansion characteristics (if a piston expands too much in the wrong direction, it will seize in the cylinder), and also makes them heavier, with the weight offset from the centre. This drawback becomes much more evident as engines are developed to run at much higher speeds.

### Loop scavenging

As the deflector piston had too many drawbacks, and a flat or slightly rounded piston crown does little to influence the flow of the incoming mixture or the escaping exhaust gases, an alternative method was required. This was developed in the 1930s by using two transfer ports instead of one, and the principle was known as 'Schneurle loop scavenging', after Dr. E. Schneurle, who invented and patented it (though admittedly he did design it originally for a two-stroke diesel engine). The transfer ports are situated opposite each other on the sides of the cylinder, and are angled upwards and backwards **(see illustration 1.5b)**. The incoming mixture therefore hits the back wall of the cylinder and is forced up, then loops over at the top to come down on the burnt exhaust gases, helping to push them out through the exhaust port. By careful positioning of the transfer ports good scavenging can be obtained in this way.

The size and shape of ports has to be considered very carefully. If a port is too wide, the piston ring may expand into it as it passes and catch, causing damage. As a result, ports are sized and shaped to ensure smooth feeding of the rings past it, and some wide ports are bridged in the middle to provide support for the rings. Alternatively, a larger number of smaller ports can be used.

There are many variations of port size, arrangement and number in current use, and these have increased the efficiency of the

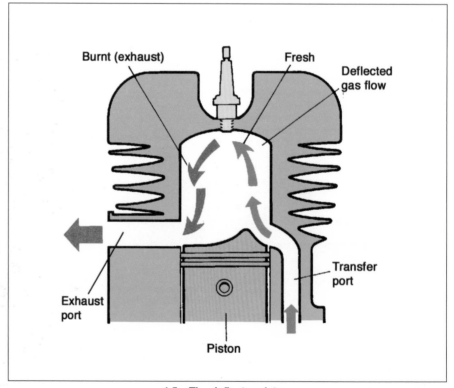

**1.5a The deflector piston**

*The incoming mixture (blue arrows) is directed up towards the top of the combustion chamber where it helps to displace the exhaust gases (red arrows) from the previous power stroke. This helps to prevent the incoming mixture and the burnt gases from mixing, and from the fresh mixture going straight out the exhaust port.*

two-stroke engine a great deal **(see illustration 1.5c overleaf)**. Some engines have transfer ports whose sole purpose is to maximise scavenging, and these open slightly before the main transfer ports which carry the bulk of the fresh mixture.

But there is only so far you can go to improve gas flow without making the components expensive to produce. To improve performance further it is necessary to control the induction timing more precisely.

## Engine timing

Engine timing can be defined as the point in a revolution of the engine at which an event (i.e. induction, compression, ignition, exhaust) occurs. Timing is most commonly referred to in degrees of rotation of the crankshaft, related to the position of the piston within the cylinder and whether it is moving up or down. When the piston is at its highest point in the cylinder and is neither moving up nor down, it is at top dead centre (TDC). When the piston is at its lowest point in the cylinder and is neither moving up nor down, it is at bottom dead centre (BDC). When it is either side of these positions, it is known as being so many degrees before or after TDC or BDC, and these acronyms become BTDC, ATDC, BBDC, and ABDC.

When the piston is either ATDC or BBDC, it is on a downward stroke. When the piston is ABDC or BTDC, it is on the upward stroke. From this it can be seen that if an engine is at 90°ATDC, it is also at 90°BBDC. Similarly, an engine which is at 180°BTDC is actually at BDC. To avoid confusion though, for timing purposes one revolution of the engine is split into four 90° sections rather than two of 180° or one of 360°. The first 90° of a revolution (from 1 to 90°) is 1 to 90°ATDC, the second 90° (91 to 180°) is 1 to 90° BBDC, the third 90° (181 to 270°) is 1 to 90° ABDC, the fourth 90° (271 to 360°) is 1 to 90° BTDC.

In a two-stroke engine, induction and exhaust are controlled by port timing, which is covered in the following two-stroke sections. In a four-stroke engine, induction and exhaust are controlled by valve timing, which is covered in Section 15. In all engines, ignition, the point at which the spark plug ignites the fuel/air mixture, is controlled by ignition timing, which is covered in Chapter 3.

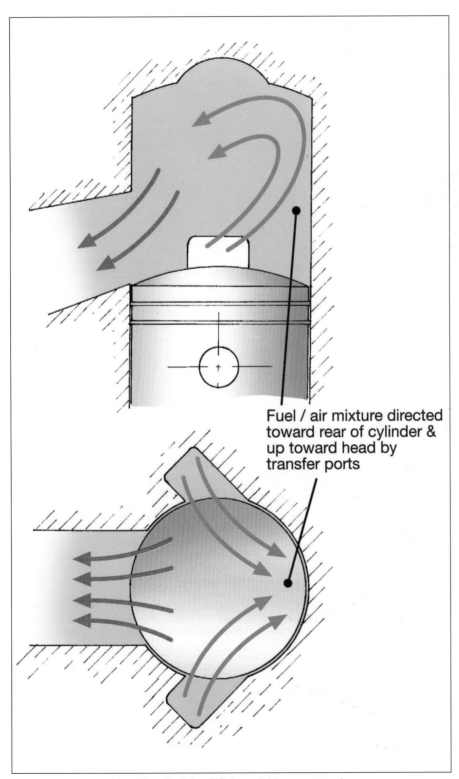

Fuel / air mixture directed toward rear of cylinder & up toward head by transfer ports

**1.5b The principle of 'Schneurle' loop scavenging**

## 6 Improved two-stroke engine designs – reed valves

With any two-stroke design, improving performance and fuel economy means the engine has to do its job more efficiently, and that entails burning the maximum amount of fuel (and thus extracting the maximum amount of power) on each power stroke. There remains the problem of trying to expel all of the exhaust gas and filling the cylinder

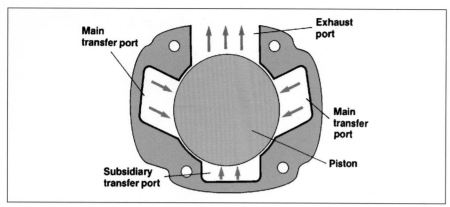

**1.5c Transfer port positions on a typical modern two-stroke engine**

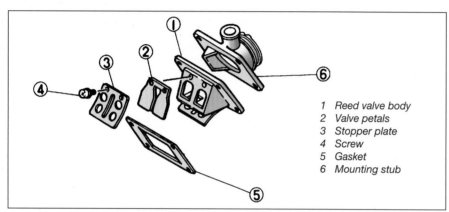

1  *Reed valve body*
2  *Valve petals*
3  *Stopper plate*
4  *Screw*
5  *Gasket*
6  *Mounting stub*

**1.6a Typical reed valve unit**

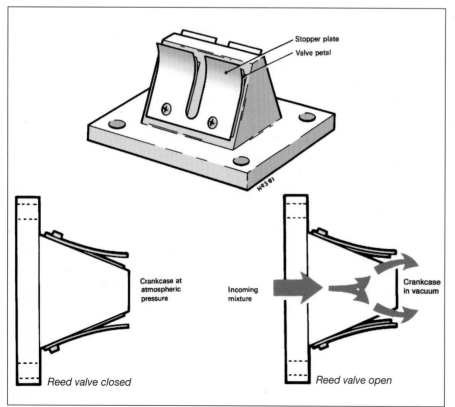

**1.6b Sectioned view of reed valve in operation**

with as much fresh mixture as possible. Whilst improved gas flow helps to improve the basic piston-ported engine, it cannot prevent a little of the exhaust gas remaining in the cylinder, nor can it increase the volume of incoming mixture to help force the exhaust gases out.

The answer could be to draw more mixture into the crankcase by increasing its volume, but in practice this means that the pumping action is made less effective (due to the relationship between volume and pressure, as mentioned earlier). Increasing pumping efficiency means reducing the crankcase volume, and thus restricting the space available to contain the mixture. So the best compromise is used, and other methods of improving efficiency must be found.

In the case of a piston-ported two-stroke it is inevitable that some of the fuel/air mixture drawn into the crankcase will be lost as the piston begins to move down during combustion. This mixture is pushed back out of the inlet port and is wasted. To prevent this happening, a more efficient way of controlling the incoming mixture is required. This can be achieved by using either a reed valve or a disc (or rotary) valve, or a combination of them.

A reed valve consists of a metal valve case with a synthetic rubber sealing lip bonded to its face **(see illustration 1.6a)**. Two or more valve 'petals' are attached to the valve case and under normal atmospheric conditions these petals are closed. Also fitted are stopper plates, one for each valve petal, whose purpose is to limit the petal movement and thus prevent breakage. The thin valve petals are normally made of flexible steel, though more exotic materials such as phenolic resin or glass reinforced epoxy resin are becoming popular.

The petals open by bending out against the stopper plates, and are designed to open readily when there is a positive pressure difference between the atmosphere and the crankcase, and this happens when the rising piston creates a vacuum in the crankcase **(see illustration 1.6b)**. As the mixture enters and the piston falls, the pressure inside the crankcase climbs to that of the surrounding atmosphere and the petals close, sealing the valve. In this way, the maximum amount of mixture is admitted and any back-leakage is prevented. The additional mixture fills the cylinder much more completely and scavenging is more effective.

To start with, reed valves were adapted for use on existing piston-ported engines, and they made a significant improvement to engine efficiency. In some cases manufacturers chose a combination of the two designs, with piston-porting being supplemented by a reed valve to allow induction to continue via sub-ports into the crankcase after the piston had closed the main port, if crankcase pressure conditions

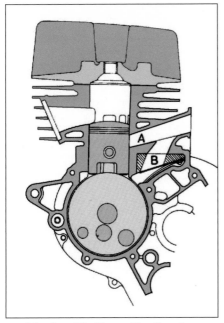

**1.6c Suzuki's 'Power Reed' system**

*A sectioned view of the TS125ER engine unit, showing how conventional piston porting (A) has been combined with reed valve induction directly into the crankcase (B).*

allowed it **(see illustration 1.6c)**. In other cases, windows were cut out of the piston skirt to effectively do away with the control the piston has over the port, which was then opened and closed purely by the reed valve.

This development meant the position of the valve and the inlet port could be moved from the cylinder to the crankcase. The dire warnings that reed petals would fracture and be drawn into the engine proved to be largely groundless.

Re-siting the inlet port provides a number of advantages, the main one being that the gas flow into the crankcase area is more direct, and so more mixture can be drawn in. This is aided to some extent by the momentum (the speed and weight) of the incoming mixture. With the inlet port removed from the cylinder, efficiency can be further improved by relocating the transfer port(s) to the best possible position for scavenging. Inevitably, the basic reed valve arrangement has been subjected to a good deal of research in recent years and sophisticated designs employing two-stage petals and multi-reed cages have appeared. Recent development in reed valves has been in the materials used for the petals, and in the siting and size of the valves.

## 7 Improved two-stroke engine designs – disc valves

In the preceding sections we have seen how the basic piston-ported two-stroke engine relies on the inlet port being uncovered by the rising piston to admit fresh mixture, and how this tends to reduce the efficiency of the engine. The reed valve is one way of side-stepping the limitations of piston-porting, but it is by no means the only one. The disc (or rotary) valve provides another alternative to piston-porting, and in some respects it is a better arrangement than the reed valve, though they have also been used in conjunction to good effect.

A disc valve consists of a thin steel disc secured to the crankshaft by a key or splines so that they turn together. It is positioned over the inlet port between the carburettor and the crankcase cover, so that the port is normally closed off by the disc. To permit induction at the correct part of the engine cycle, part of the disc is cut away. With the rotation of the crankshaft and the disc valve, the inlet port is uncovered as the cutaway section passes the port, allowing mixture to be drawn directly into the crankcase **(see illustration 1.7a)**. The port is then sealed off by the disc, preventing back-leakage into the carburettor as the piston starts to fall.

### Merits

The obvious advantages of using a disc valve are closer control of the induction timing (i.e. when the cutaway section passes the port), and the induction duration (i.e. how large the cutaway is, and so how long the port stays open). Also, a disc valve allows a large inlet port diameter to be chosen, and ensures an unobstructed passage for the mixture entering the crankcase.

Unlike the reed valve with its rather bulky valve case, the disc valve presents no obstruction in the inlet port, and thus the gas flow into the engine tends to be better.

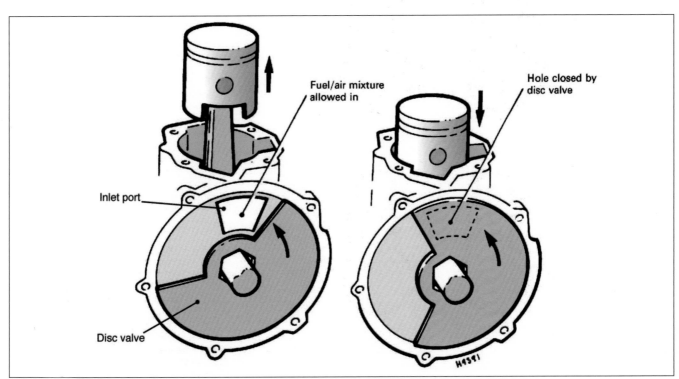

**1.7a Disc valve operation**

Another advantage of a disc valve, especially when used in racing, is the speed at which it can be changed, so that the performance characteristics of the engine can be easily adapted to suit different circuits. Its main disadvantages are mechanical complexity requiring fine manufacturing tolerances, and the valve's inability to respond to varying engine demands like a reed valve. In addition, all disc valves are vulnerable to damage from debris drawn into the engine, the particles of dust becoming trapped in the valve sealing faces and scoring the disc. Despite these, the disc valve works very well in practice and will usually produce a

respectable amount of power at low engine speeds, unlike the basic piston-ported engine **(see illustration 1.7b)**.

## Combining reeds and discs

The disc valve's inability to respond to varying engine demands has led to some manufacturers using a combination of the disc valve and the reed valve to provide greater engine flexibility. Therefore, when conditions demand it, crankcase pressure will close the reed valves, thereby closing the crankcase end of the inlet port, even though the cutaway section of the disc may still be leaving the carburettor end of the port open.

## An alternative disc

An interesting variation of the disc valve has been used for some years on certain Vespa scooter engines. Instead of fitting an entirely separate valve assembly, the manufacturers have adapted the standard crankshaft to perform a similar function. The edge of the right-hand flywheel is machined to a very fine tolerance so that it runs a few thousandths of an inch from the crankcase. The inlet port is directly above the flywheel (the cylinder is arranged horizontally on these engines) and thus is blocked off by the flywheel edge.

By machining a recess in part of the flywheel it is possible to uncover the port at the required point in the engine cycle in exactly the same way as a conventional disc valve. Although the resulting inlet passage has to be less straight than would otherwise be the case, the system works very well in practice. As a result the engine produces useful power over a wide range of engine speeds, and yet remains mechanically uncomplicated.

### 8 Improved two-stroke engine designs – exhaust port position

Although exhaust systems are covered in detail in Chapter 2, it is only fair to mention them here, if only to underline the importance of exhaust port design to the efficient running of a two-stroke engine. Indeed, in many respects the induction and exhaust systems on a two-stroke are very closely linked. In the previous sections we have discussed ways of getting mixture into the cylinder and exhaust gases out. The exhaust system has a profound effect on both of these areas, and it is recommended that the relevant parts of Chapter 2 are read in conjunction with the above and the following.

Over the years designers and tuners alike have discovered that the timing of the flow of the gases into the exhaust can have as significant an effect on performance as can the timing of induction. Exhaust timing is controlled by the height of the exhaust port in the cylinder wall, i.e. when it is covered and uncovered by the piston as it moves up and down. Of course, as with all other aspects, there is no one best position that covers all engine conditions. It depends firstly on what the engine is to be used for, and secondly the way in which that engine is used. For example, for the same engine, the ideal height for the exhaust port is different at low engine speeds to that at high engine speeds, and to complicate matters, so is the size of the port, and the size of the exhaust pipe itself.

As a result, manufactures have designed various systems to alter the characteristics of the exhaust while the engine is running to suit varying engine speeds. Systems have appeared from Yamaha (YPVS), Honda

**1.7b Two-stroke induction systems compared**

*The illustrations show the principle of each system, and do not attempt to exactly resemble the layout of an engine*

A Piston porting     B Reed valve     C Disc valve, or rotary valve

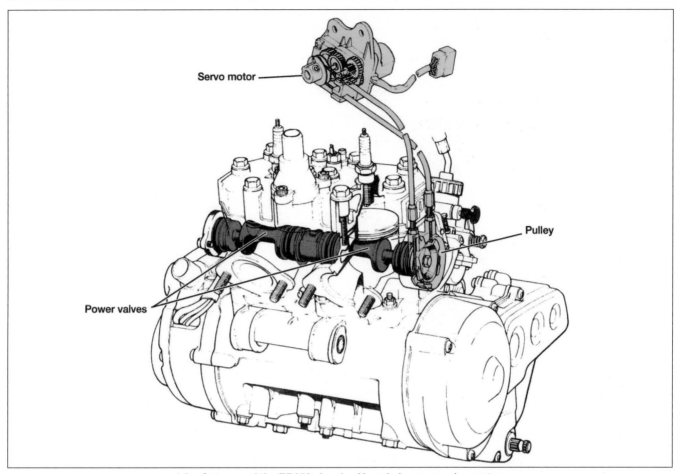

**1.8a  Cutaway of the RD350 showing Yamaha's power valve system**

(ATAC), Kawasaki (KIPS), Suzuki (SAPC), Cagiva (CTS) and Aprilia (RAVE). The Yamaha, Kawasaki and Honda systems are described below.

### Yamaha Power Valve System – YPVS

At the heart of Yamaha's system is the power valve itself, which is essentially a rotary valve set in the cylinder barrel so that its bottom edge forms the top of the exhaust port **(see illustration 1.8a)**.

At low engine speeds the valve is closed, effectively reducing the height of the top of the port, which improves low and mid-range performance. When the engine speed reaches a pre-set level, the valve opens, effectively raising the height of the port, which improves high speed performance.

The power valve is operated by a cable and pulley arrangement from the servomotor. The YPVS control unit receives information on the angle of valve opening from a potentiometer on the servomotor and engine rpm information from the ignition control unit; this data is used to provide the correct signal to the drive mechanism of the servomotor **(see illustration 1.8b)**.

Note that Yamaha's off-road models use a

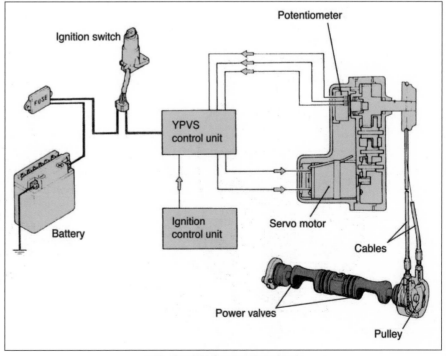

**1.8b  The YPVS operating circuit**

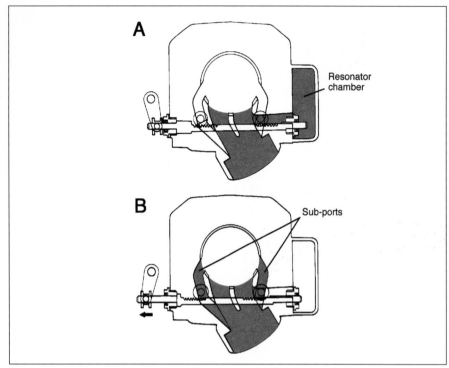

**1.8c Kawasaki's integrated powervalve system**

A At low engine speeds the sub-ports are closed, but the duct from the main port to the resonator chamber is open

B At a certain engine speed the valves open the sub-ports, which are situated higher than the main port, and simultaneously close the resonator chamber

slightly different version of the system because of their lack of battery power; the power valve is operated by a centrifugal mechanism on the crankshaft.

### Kawasaki Integrated Powervalve System – KIPS

Kawasaki's system is mechanically operated via a crankshaft-driven ball and ramp governor. A vertical operating rod links the drive mechanism with the power valve operating rod set in the cylinder barrel.

The two power valves are located in sub-ports each side of the main exhaust port, and connect to the operating rod via a rack and pinion arrangement. As the operating rod is moved from side-to-side the valves rotate to open and close sub-ports in the cylinder and a resonator chamber on the left-hand side **(see illustration 1.8c)**.

The system is timed so that at low speed the sub-ports are closed by the valves to give a short port duration. The left-hand valve opens the resonator chamber to the escaping exhaust gases, thus increasing the volume of the expansion chamber **(see illustration 1.8d)**.

At high speed the valves rotate to open both sub-ports and increase the port duration and provide more top-end power **(see illustration 1.8e)**. The resonator chamber is closed off by the left-hand valve, thereby reducing the overall volume of the exhaust pipe.

The KIPS system therefore gives the benefit to low and mid-range performance of lower port height and greater exhaust volume, and the benefit to high speed performance of a higher exhaust port and smaller volume. The system has been further refined with the introduction of an idle gear between the operating rod and one of the valves to allow the valves to turn in opposite directions, and by the introduction of a flat power valve at the front edge of the exhaust port. On larger capacity models starting and low speed running have been improved by incorporating bleed cut-outs in the tops of the valves.

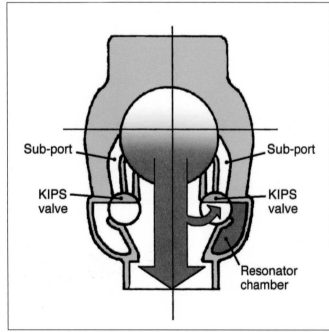

**1.8d KIPS valve position at low speed**

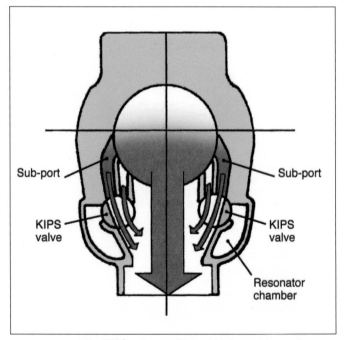

**1.8e KIPS valve position at high speed**

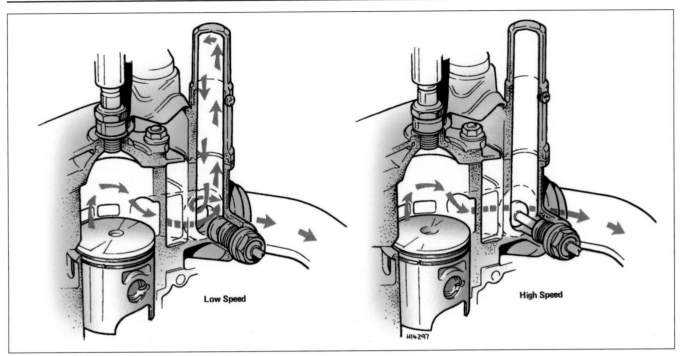

**1.8f ATAC operation**

### Honda Automatically-controlled Torque Amplification Chamber – ATAC

Honda's system is controlled automatically by a centrifugal mechanical governor on the crankshaft. A rack and spindle mechanism transmit the drive from the crankcase to the ATAC valve housed in the cylinder barrel.

The HERP (Honda Energy Resonance Pipe) chamber is opened by the ATAC valve at low speeds and closed at high engine speed **(see illustration 1.8f)**.

### 9  Improved two-stroke engine designs – fuel injection

The seemingly obvious way to eliminate all problems surrounding the induction of fuel and air into the combustion chamber of a two-stroke engine, not to mention the problems of high fuel consumption and emissions, is to use fuel injection. However, unless the fuel is injected directly into the combustion chamber, the inherent problems of induction timing and efficiency all still occur.

The problem with injecting fuel directly into the combustion chamber is that it can only be injected after the exhaust port has closed, which leaves little time for the fuel to be atomised and thoroughly mixed with the air in the cylinder (which is drawn in via the crankcase as with conventional two-stroke engines). This creates another problem, in that the pressure inside the combustion chamber after the exhaust port has closed is high and rapidly increasing, so the fuel has to be injected at an even higher pressure otherwise it simply won't come out of the injector. This requires a fairly substantial fuel pump, which adds problems of weight, space and cost.

Aprilia have addressed these problems using a system called DITECH **(see illustration 1.9)**, based on the design of an Australian company, and Peugeot and Kymco have designed a similar system. The injector sprays fuel into a separate closed auxiliary chamber containing compressed air (sourced either from a separate compressor or via one-way ducts from the cylinder), and this is done early on in the engine cycle. After the exhaust port has closed, the auxiliary chamber opens to the combustion chamber via a valve or nozzle, and the mixture enters close to the spark plug. The principles involved in the system are actually quite

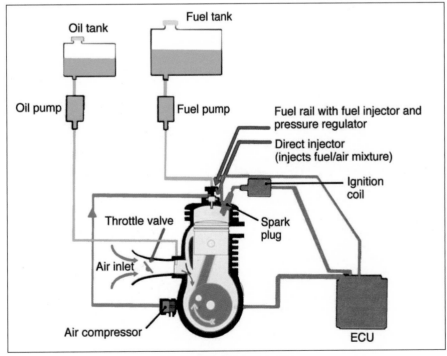

**1.9 Aprilia's DITECH engine**

complicated, involving stratified charge combustion, and are beyond the scope of this book. They are covered in greater detail in the Haynes *Fuel Systems Techbook*.

However the benefits of the system are easy to understand. Aprilia claim an 80% reduction in emissions, achieved through a 60% reduction in oil consumption and a 50% reduction in fuel consumption. Not only that, but it is 15% quicker than the same scooter with the standard carburettor.

The main benefit of using direct injection is that it gets away from the normal two-stroke necessity of pre-mixing the fuel with oil for engine lubrication (see Chapter 5). Lubrication is improved as the oil does not get washed off the bearings by the fuel, and so less oil is needed, thus reducing emissions. The fuel also burns better, and there is less carbon build-up on pistons, piston rings and in the exhaust. Air is still drawn in via the crankcase (metered by a butterfly valve connected to the throttle twistgrip), which still means that oil is going to be burnt and that lubrication will not be as efficient as it could be, but that aside the test results speak for themselves. All that is needed now is a way of getting all the air that is needed without having to get it via the crankcase.

## 10 The four-stroke engine

In the preceding Sections describing the operation of the two-stroke engine it will have become obvious that whilst the mechanical principles of the engine are simple enough, the need to burn carefully calculated amounts of fuel at the right time, and disposing of the burnt gases that result, pose more of a problem.

As discussed in Section 2, the alternative to the two-stroke engine is the four-stroke. But while the four-stroke engine can eliminate many of the problems inherent in two-strokes, in doing so it creates problems of its own, with the end result that neither can be said to be better than other as an engine – it depends on its purpose. Each has its place in the world of motorcycles, and where one does its job very well and is ideally suited, the other will not be so, and vice versa.

Whilst you cannot argue against the fact that four-stroke engines are much more efficient in terms of fuel consumption and levels of emission, their increased complexity means they are much more expensive to produce. This has led to a happy medium, whereby two-stroke engines are ideal for small mass-produced motorcycles and scooters which are cheap to buy (though they still have their place as high performance racing machines, for the time being at least), while four-stroke engines are ideal for the vast majority of motorcycles from 125 cc and upwards, from learner bikes and commuter bikes, to large capacity high performance sports machines, and everything in between.

While there was a time when medium capacity (250 to 750 cc) two-stroke engines had their place and were very much a challenge to four-stroke engines of similar or larger capacity, those days have passed, and now two-strokes larger than 250 cc are quite rare on the road.

### Suck, squeeze, bang, blow

While the four events of the internal combustion engine (induction, compression, ignition, exhaust, or suck, squeeze, bang, blow as they are sometimes endearingly referred to) become inter-mixed over the cycle of a two-stroke engine, in a four-stroke engine each event is more defined, and in principal is assigned its own stroke in the cycle (though in practice, as will be seen later in Section 15, this is not quite so).

Mechanically, the four-stroke engine is fairly similar to the two-stroke, and shares the basic components, namely the piston, cylinder, connecting rod and crankshaft. It does, however, have a number of extra components, known collectively as the valve train, and these are all concerned with the control and timing of induction and exhaust. Induction is controlled by the inlet valve, and exhaust by the exhaust valve. In a way they are the four-stroke's equivalent of the piston and reed or disc valve. There are a number of different arrangements to examine, but they are all different approaches to the same end.

The accompanying illustration shows the operation of a typical four-stroke engine **(see illustration 1.10a)**. Note the differences in the cylinder head to that of a two-stroke, and that

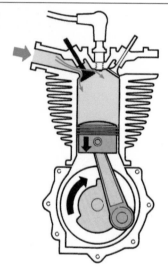

*Induction: As the piston descends the inlet valve opens, allowing the fuel/air mixture to be drawn directly into the combustion chamber.*

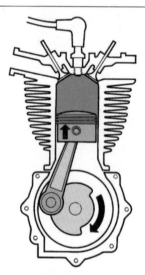

*Compression: The piston starts to ascend and the inlet valve closes. The mixture is compressed as the piston rises.*

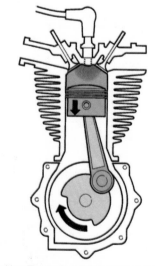

*Ignition: The spark plug ignites the compressed mixture, forcing the piston down the bore.*

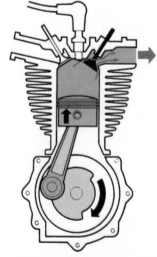

*Exhaust: The exhaust valve opens to allow the burnt gases to be expelled through the exhaust port as the piston rises.*

**1.10a The four-stroke cycle in principle**

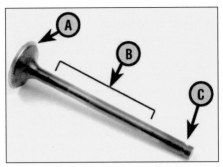

**1.10b The 'poppet' valve**

A  *Valve face*        C  *Collet groove*
B  *Valve stem*

the ports in the cylinder itself have gone. Also, with the incoming mixture arriving directly in the combustion chamber, the crankcase no longer plays a part in the induction cycle. Despite the increased mechanical complexity and the halving of the number of power strokes, the induction and exhaust stages can now be more carefully controlled and thus the engine is relatively efficient.

## Valves

All four-stroke engines feature valves, more correctly known as poppet valves, through which mixture is admitted to the combustion chamber and exhaust gases are expelled. On all modern engine designs the valves project down from the cylinder head. Until the 1950s there were many machines which used valves that projected upwards into an extension of the combustion chamber on the side of the cylinder, and these were known as side-valve engines. Although cheaper to produce, they are less efficient than overhead valves.

The poppet valve consists of a circular head attached to a long stem rather like a large-headed nail **(see illustration 1.10b)**. The valve head has a tapered seating face ground on the stem side which is designed to seal against a corresponding face on the valve seat, which is incorporated in the cylinder head (or in the combustion chamber extension on side valve engines). The valve stem passes through a guide in the cylinder head and emerges through its upper surface.

The valve is automatically closed and held shut by a strong spring (sometimes two springs are used), which is/are held by the spring retainer, which itself is locked into a groove in the top of the valve stem by a pair of collets **(see illustration 1.10c)**. The valves can be opened in a number of ways – the principal is the same whichever way is chosen, but the components used differ, with the exception of the camshaft.

## Camshafts

The camshaft is found on all conventional poppet-valved four-stroke engines and is used, either directly or indirectly, to open and close each valve at the correct point in the four-stroke cycle. Bearing in mind that the cycle lasts for four strokes of the piston

1  *Collets*
2  *Spring retainer*
3  *Outer spring*
4  *Inner spring*
5  *Valve stem oil seal*
6  *Inner spring seat*
7  *Outer spring seat*
8  *Valve guide*
9  *Cylinder head*
10 *Valve*

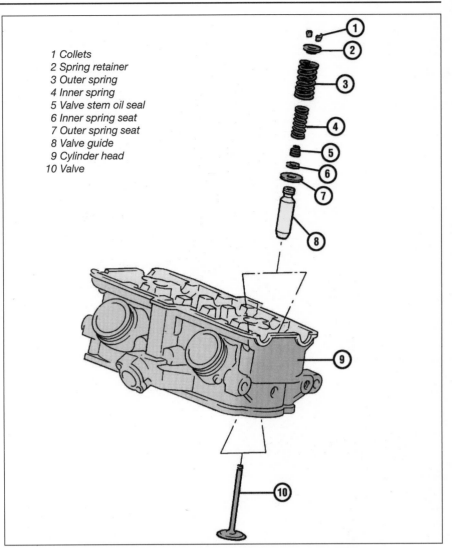

**1.10c  Exploded view of the valve assembly components**

(which equates to two complete revolutions of the crankshaft) and that each valve is required to open once in that cycle, the camshaft is arranged to run at half crankshaft speed. This means that the camshaft completes one revolution for the crankshaft's two, and this is accomplished by the simple arrangement of a gear, chain or belt drive between the two

shafts in which the crankshaft gear or sprocket has exactly half the number of teeth of its counterpart on the camshaft.

Along the camshaft are projections known as cams or lobes, whose purpose is to actuate the components in the valve train to push open the appropriate valve at the required moment **(see illustration 1.10d)**.

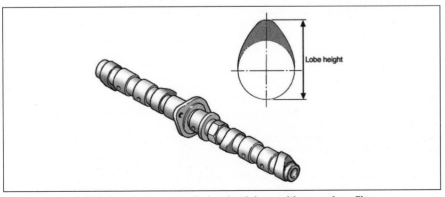

**1.10d  A typical camshaft showing lobe positions and profile**

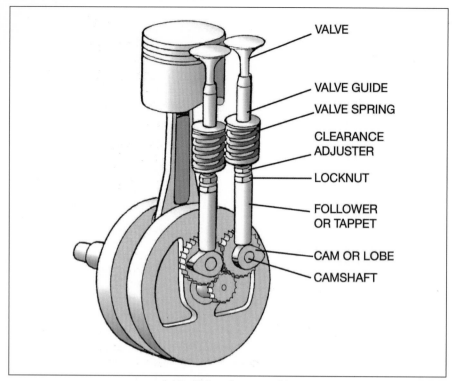

VALVE

VALVE GUIDE

VALVE SPRING

CLEARANCE
ADJUSTER

LOCKNUT

FOLLOWER
OR TAPPET

CAM OR LOBE

CAMSHAFT

**1.11a Side-valve assembly**

## 11 Four-stroke engine designs
– valve train arrangements

All four-stroke engines are similar in principle, differing only in the way the inlet and exhaust valves are arranged and operated. As with most things on a motorcycle, sophistication tends to lead to complexity, and in achieving higher speeds and power outputs the four-stroke engine has been improved a great deal over the years. The various principles are discussed below, starting with the side-valve, which, though largely obsolete, serves to show the modern overhead camshaft designs in their true perspective.

### Side-valve (SV)

The side-valve engine is a relatively simple application of the four-stroke principle, using a minimum of mechanical parts to convey movement from the camshaft to the valve. The camshaft, driven either by gear or chain, is located close to the crankshaft. The cams or lobes bear upon the followers or tappets, which are in the form of short rods running vertically up towards the cylinder **(see illustration 1.11a)**. These rods incorporate screw and locknut adjusters which alter their length so that the correct 'valve clearance' can be maintained between the follower and the end of the valve stem. The vertical position of the valves means that they are contained in an

extension of the combustion chamber on the side of the cylinder, rather than in the cylinder head as in other four-stroke designs.

The side-valve is probably the easiest and cheapest four-stroke engine to manufacture, and most of the British and US companies made extensive use of it at one time, often powering the utility or economy models of their range. The awkward shape of the combustion chamber, dictated by the position of the valves which were set to one side of the cylinder bore, limited the efficiency of the engine, which produced less power and used more fuel than a comparable overhead valve unit.

The inefficiency became more pronounced at higher engine speeds, so the traditional side-valve evolved as a large capacity single of relatively low power output. Fitted with large flywheels, it produced a good deal of torque or 'pulling power' at low engine speeds, and thus was a popular choice with devotees of sidecars. These softly-tuned and simple engines were outstandingly reliable, and were very easy to work on if problems did arise.

The demise of the side valve engine came about after the second World War, with the advent of improved materials and manufacturing techniques. Faced with far more competition from OHV designs, the side-valve faded away in the motorcycle world, but can still be found on lawnmowers and in similar applications where simplicity and cheapness outweigh any performance considerations.

## Valve clearance

The small gap that exists between the end of the valve stem and the component that bears upon it on all four stroke engines (with the exception of those with hydraulically damped tappets, covered later) is known as the 'valve clearance' (see illustration 1.11c). Checking and if necessary re-setting or adjusting the valve clearance is a normal maintenance task on all four-stroke engines. The clearance is necessary to allow for expansion in components as they heat up, and it needs to be adjustable to allow for wear. Because the exhaust valve is subjected to higher temperatures than the inlet valve, its clearance is usually slightly greater.

## Valve train terminology

The projections on the camshaft which actuate the valve train are known as either cams or lobes. Cam is the most technically correct and logical, but you may find that lobe is more commonly used, particularly in specifications where a 'lobe height' is given (and also because camshaft is often shortened to cam). Throughout this book they will be referred to as lobes.

The component which the lobe bears on is known as the follower or tappet (note that they are often referred to as cam followers). Throughout this book it will be referred to as a follower. One particular type of follower is also commonly known as a 'bucket', because of its shape, and in this book will be referred to as a bucket-type follower. However, where hydraulics are used in the valve train, the hydraulically operated components are known as hydraulic tappets, and not hydraulic followers. Where a cam or lobe bears on a rocker arm, the portion of the arm that is borne on (basically a hardened pad) is known as the 'slipper'.

### Overhead valve (OHV)

Strictly speaking, the overhead valve engine describes all non side-valve four-stroke engines, but is usually used to indicate pushrod-operated overhead valve engines, rather than overhead camshaft (SOHC or DOHC) engines.

The overhead valve engine has long pushrods running up through a tunnel in the cylinder barrel and cylinder head which emerge above the cylinder head casting, close to the valve stems **(see**

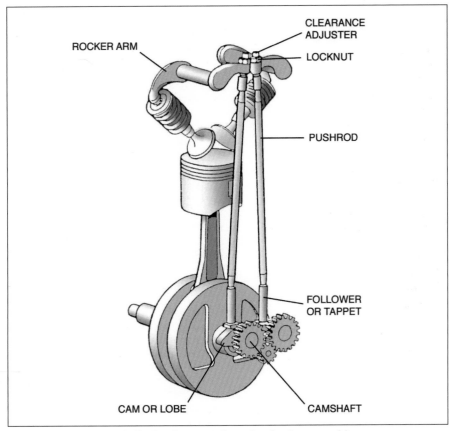

ROCKER ARM

CLEARANCE
ADJUSTER

LOCKNUT

PUSHROD

FOLLOWER
OR TAPPET

CAM OR LOBE

CAMSHAFT

**1.11b Pushrod-operated overhead valve assembly**

illustration 1.11b). The pushrods and the ends of the valve stems are linked by short rocker arms which pivot on a shaft. Valve clearance adjustment is achieved either by a screw and locknut type adjuster in one end of the rocker arm, or by a telescopic type adjuster in the pushrod which alters its length.

The layout of the overhead valve engine is very similar to that of the side-valve, although its design has a number of major advantages over the latter, the main one being the freedom to design an efficient combustion chamber shape. In most respects a hemispherical (a half sphere) combustion chamber is ideal, and the overhead valve design with the valves angled from vertical produces a combustion chamber shape which works very well indeed. This positioning of the valves allows an efficient gas flow through the engine and more even combustion of the fuel/air mixture. This basic layout of the OHV engine proved perfectly adequate for several decades, but apart from a few examples still in production has now been superseded by overhead cam designs.

Inevitably, the search for more usable power has brought to light the limitations of the design, at first in racing engines and later in road-going versions. Given an efficient combustion chamber design, one way to extract more power from the engine is to raise its operating speed, and thus the number of revolutions, and therefore power strokes, per

minute. As the engine speed rises a number of mechanical limitations start to cause problems, notably in the valve train components. With the engine running at high speed the followers, pushrods and rocker arms have to be strong enough to withstand the loads imposed on them. Unfortunately, increased strength invariably leads to increased weight, and this brings problems of its own.

As the lobe on the camshaft begins to lift the follower and pushrod, and to open the valve via the rocker, these components gradually accelerate. Up to a certain speed there is no problem, but beyond this the weight of the valve train components is such that they are unable to respond quickly enough as the lobe passes the follower and begins to fall away again. At this point the valves begin to 'float' despite pressure from the return springs. Not only is the engine speed restricted by this, but the onset of valve float brings with it the risk of the pushrods bending or dislocating, and in severe cases of the inlet and exhaust valves getting tangled inside the combustion chamber. If this occurs, the next time the piston reaches the top of its stroke it smashes into the valves, causing extensive damage. Fitting stronger valve springs is one solution, but this causes more drag, and thus less power, and leads to accelerated wear. Not only that, but it can also lead to valve 'bounce'. The valve train

components can be lightened, but this also weakens them. The alternative is to use specialist materials to manufacture the components, but although they will be lighter and stronger, they will also be a lot more expensive.

From the above you will appreciate that the pushrod-operated OHV engine is an efficient design for most purposes, but where very high power outputs and engine speeds are required it has a definite limitation. Where they are used, such as in Honda's robust and long-running CG125 single, and in Moto Guzzi's range of V-twin engines, the resulting machine is a simple and reliable workhorse if an undistinguished performer. The advantage in a V-configured engine is that you only have to use one camshaft, which are expensive items, and, as many V-twins are used in custom and cruiser type machines, the restriction in performance is not a problem. In many ways the pushrod-operated OHV engine is the current equivalent of the now abandoned side-valve.

## Valve 'float' and 'bounce'

**Valve float** – Condition where the valve is being opened again before the spring has had a chance to close it, and is caused by too weak a valve spring, too heavy a valve, incorrect lobe profile, or simply by running the engine at higher speeds than it was designed for.

**Valve bounce** – Condition where the valve is hitting the valve seat and is bouncing back off it, rather than being held shut by the spring. This can be caused by too strong a valve spring, too light a valve, incorrect lobe profile, spring surge (whereby the spring starts to vibrate as it reaches its resonant frequency), or simply by running the engine at higher speeds than it was designed for.

### Single overhead camshaft (SOHC)

To overcome the problems caused by increasing the weight of the valve train components it is desirable to eliminate as many of the reciprocating parts as possible. These include the camshaft follower, the pushrod, the rocker arm and the valve itself. In the case of the follower and the valve little can be done, other than to reduce their weight as far as possible by careful design and the choice of a strong, durable but lightweight material.

In racing engines, where manufacturing costs are not important, exotic materials such as titanium can be employed, but this is not really practical for mass production. What can be done is to move the camshaft to the cylinder head, thus eliminating the pushrod, and have the lobes contact the rocker arm on a hardened pad (or slipper as it is known),

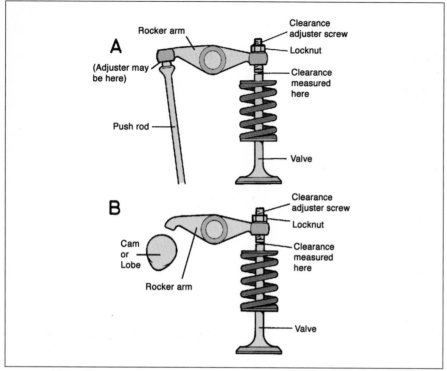

A
B

1.11c Comparison of overhead valve and overhead camshaft operation

A *The valve is opened by a pushrod and rocker arrangement. In this example, the adjuster is incorporated in the rocker arm, though some incorporate it in the pushrod. The clearance is measured between the top of the valve stem and the component that bears on it.*

B *In this version, the camshaft has been relocated in the cylinder head (hence overhead camshaft, or OHC). The cam or lobe bears directly on the rocker arm. The follower or tappet and pushrod have thus been eliminated.*

thus eliminating the follower **(see illustration 1.11c)**. The idea is by no means a new one, and there are many examples of pre-war four-stroke engines with overhead camshafts.

In a typical single overhead camshaft (SOHC) engine the camshaft is housed in the centre of the cylinder head, between the inlet and exhaust valves. On early racing engines the camshaft was driven by bevel gears off a shaft running up the side of the cylinder barrel **(see illustration 1.11d)**. The normal arrangement is chain drive, via a sprocket either in the middle or on the end of the crankshaft which the cam chain is looped around, which in turn drives a sprocket on the camshaft **(see illustration 1.11e)**.

The camshaft lobes bear on short rocker arms which in turn operate the valves, in a similar fashion to the pushrod-operated OHV engine. The only remaining reciprocating parts are the rockers and valves, so the design is still not perfect, but a good deal better than coping with the extra weight of pushrods and followers as well. Valve clearance adjustment is achieved by the screw and locknut type adjuster in one end of the rocker arm. Many modern four-stroke engines are based on SOHC operation, and this explains why they are able to operate comfortably at speeds that would have blown a pushrod engine apart.

## Double overhead camshaft (DOHC)

The DOHC four-stroke engine represents the refinement of the SOHC, designed to eliminate the only remaining avoidable

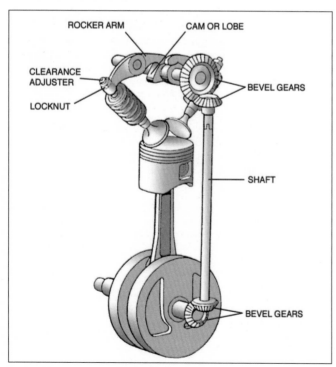

1.11d Single overhead camshaft (SOHC) valve operation driven by shaft and bevel gears

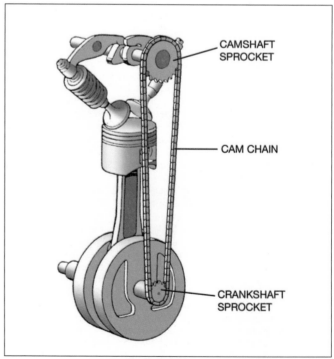

1.11e Single overhead camshaft (SOHC) valve operation driven by cam chain and sprockets

reciprocating weight; the rocker arms (though in doing so, followers must be brought back in). Instead of the single central camshaft, two are used, positioned directly above the valve stems **(see illustration 1.11f)**.

A cam chain and sprocket arrangement is by far the most common way of driving the camshafts and the cheapest to manufacture, though a notable (but not yet widely used) development, following on from trends in the car industry, has been to use a toothed belt and pulley arrangement instead. Examples of this include Honda's Goldwing and Pan European, Moto Guzzi's Daytona and Centauro and Ducati's current range. The advantages of a belt are that they are quieter, they do not stretch like chains, and the pulleys that they run on don't wear like sprockets, though they do have to be changed more regularly. Another method of driving the camshafts, as used on Honda's VFR range, is via a gear train driven off the crankshaft **(see illustration 1.11g)**. This eliminates having to use a tensioner, and they also run quieter than a chain, though the gear shafts can be prone to wear.

The camshaft followers are in the form of 'buckets' due to their shape, which run in bores in the cylinder head. When bucket-type followers are used, the valve clearance is set using a small round disc, known as a shim. While the shims themselves are not adjustable, they can be replaced by one of a different thickness to restore the correct clearance. On some engines, the shim is almost as wide as the bucket itself and fits

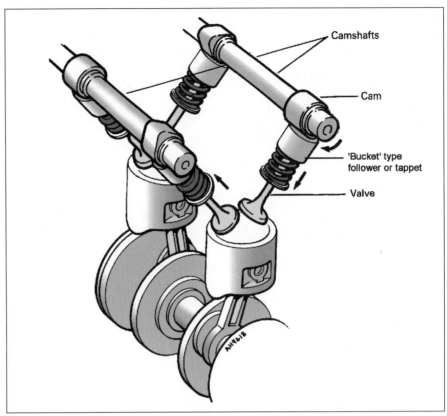

**1.11f Typical double overhead camshaft (DOHC) arrangement**

*In this arrangement two camshafts are used, one above each valve or bank of valves. The valves are opened via bucket cam followers or tappets, and the clearance is adjusted using shims. This arrangement eliminates all but the essential elements of the valve train.*

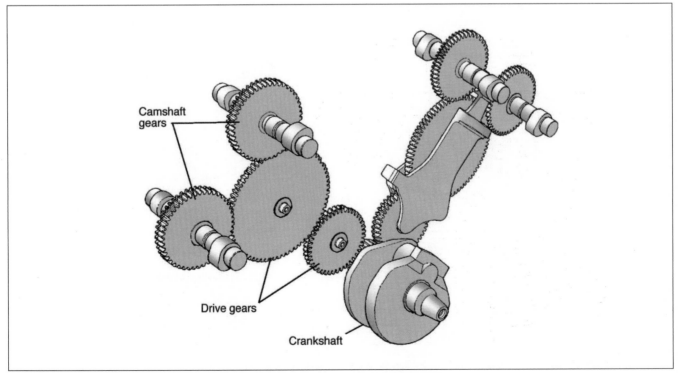

**1.11g Gear driven camshaft arrangement**

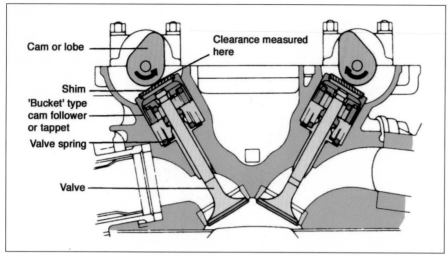

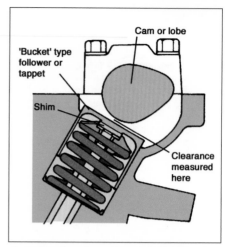

**1.11h Section through typical DOHC valve train showing shim-on-top buckets**

**1.11i Section through typical DOHC valve train showing shim-under buckets**

into a seat in the top of the bucket, and these are known as shim-on-top buckets **(see illustration 1.11h)**. The shim can be changed by holding the bucket down using a special tool so there is enough clearance between it and the camshaft to slip the shim out of the top.

On other engines the shim is much smaller and sits under the bucket in the middle of the valve spring retainer, and bears directly on the top of the valve stem, and these are known as shim-under buckets **(see illustration 1.11i)**. Reciprocating weight is reduced further by having a small shim, but it becomes necessary to remove a camshaft every time a valve clearance needs to adjusted, and this adds to the cost and complexity of servicing.

To avoid having to use either a special tool or remove the camshaft, some DOHC engines use small lightweight rockers instead of the bucket-type follower **(see illustration 1.11j)**.

On some of the engines using this arrangement, the rockers have the standard screw and locknut type adjuster. On others the rockers bear on a small shim, which sits in the middle of the valve spring retainer, and the rockers themselves are on shafts which are longer than the rocker is wide, with a spring over the shaft to hold the rocker in place above the valve. To replace a shim, the rocker is slid aside against the spring so the shim can be lifted out.

The DOHC arrangement allows higher engine speeds than SOHC, but even so valve

bounce or float can still be a problem. To eliminate this, performance engines often have two valve springs instead of one, with a narrower spring fitting inside a wider spring **(see illustration 1.10c)**. There are two advantages of this, firstly a greater spring force to close the valves, and secondly, because the springs have different resonant frequencies, the possibility of surge can be reduced. Variable pitch springs can also be used, whereby springs are closer wound at one end than the other, again giving a variable resonant frequency within one spring. A combination of both these ideas, using two variable pitch springs per valve, is now common. Variable pitch springs should be fitted with the closer wound coils at the bottom, to minimise reciprocating weight.

To sum up, the overhead camshaft engine represents the most common design in four-stroke motorcycles today. That is not to say that development has ceased, though it is unlikely that this basic principle will be supplanted in the foreseeable future. Further development has been confined to refining existing layouts using improved techniques and new materials. The most exciting development in four-stroke motorcycle engines is variable valve timing (see Section 15), which is already in use in the automobile industry and now starting to appear on motorcycle engines.

### Using hydraulics in the valve train

Hydraulics are sometimes used in the valve train to take up valve clearance, thereby creating self-adjusting (or 'zero-lash' as it's known in the USA) valves. Honda used an hydraulic valve system on their CBX750 of the 1980s, Kawasaki use it on their VN1500 and Harley-Davidson use it across a range of their engines.

There are two main advantages: variations in valve clearance due to heat expansion and contraction, and due to wear, are automatically compensated for, and noise is

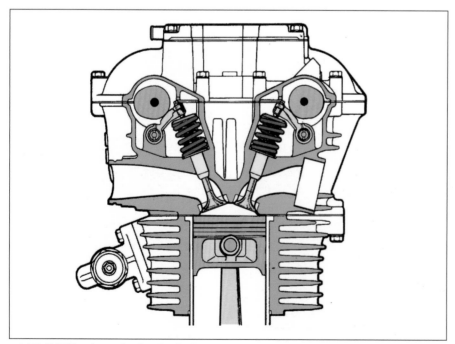

**1.11j DOHC valve train showing indirect valve operation by short rocker arms to allow simplified valve adjustment**

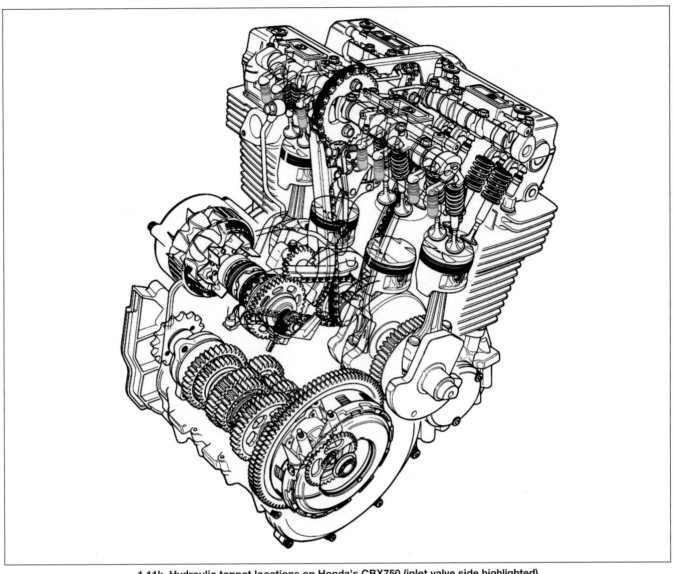

**1.11k Hydraulic tappet locations on Honda's CBX750 (inlet valve side highlighted)**

reduced. Also, by keeping a zero clearance between the parts that would otherwise would be hitting each other, wear and inertia are both reduced.

The way the system works is to take up any clearance between the cam or lobe and the follower by using oil pressure to move a telescoping tappet. The engine that Honda have fitted the system to is a DOHC engine using rocker arms. The hydraulic tappet forms the pivot for the rocker, and keeps the rocker in constant contact with the cam or lobe. Harley-Davidson have placed their hydraulic tappet in between the camshaft lobe and the pushrod.

Honda's hydraulic tappet consists of the tappet body, a plunger which fits inside the body, a spring that fits between the plunger and the body, and a check valve sealed by a ball. The bore of the plunger acts as a reservoir for the oil **(see illustrations 1.11k and l)**.

As the camshaft turns and the lobe bears on the slipper on the rocker arm, the plunger moves down the body and compresses the spring. This compresses the oil in the high pressure chamber, which forces the check valve ball against its seat, sealing the chamber. As the lobe continues its action on the slipper, the pressure in the chamber prevents any further movement between the plunger and the tappet, and so the movement is transferred to the valve, which opens.

As the tip of the lobe reaches the slipper, the pressure increases to its maximum and at this point a tiny amount of the oil is forced out of the sides between the plunger and the tappet body, which not only lubricates their mating surfaces, but also helps absorb some of the shock at maximum valve lift. As the lobe bears off the slipper and the valve closes, the pressure on the plunger is reduced, allowing the spring to push it up in the tappet body. As it does so, the oil pressure in the

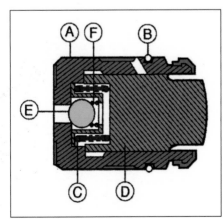

**1.11l Cross-section through an hydraulic tappet**

A Tappet body
B O-ring
C Spring
D Plunger
E Check valve ball
F Spring

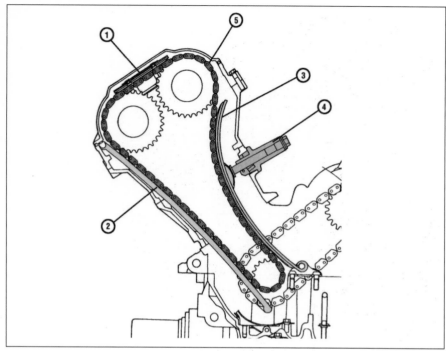

**1.11m  Cam chain tensioner and blades on a DOHC engine**

*1  Top guide blade    2  Front guide blade    3  Tensioner blade    4  Tensioner    5  Cam chain*

chamber reduces, allowing the check valve to open, and oil from the reservoir flows into the chamber to completely fill it. The plunger raises, taking up all clearance between the components in the train, until equilibrium is reached.

### Cam chains and tensioners

The advantage in using a chain driven camshaft over a belt or gear train is in the cost of manufacture. However chains stretch with use, and without a method of maintaining the correct tension the valve timing would become inaccurate and the chain would become noisy in operation. So all cam chains are run with a tensioner, which presses against the slack run of the chain via a tensioner 'blade' **(see illustration 1.11m)**. There is also a guide blade fitted to the tight run of the chain, and often on DOHC engines there is a guide for the top run, between the camshaft sprockets.

Having a certain amount of slack built into the chain even before it stretches is very useful though, as it makes removing camshafts a much easier task. It used to be common to have to periodically manually reset the tensioner to take up any increase in slack, but nowadays the majority of tensioners are self-adjusting, using a spring pressing against a plunger on a ratchet or spiral mechanism.

Belt drive arrangements still require a tensioner, but this is used in set-up and servicing to achieve the correct tension for the belt to run at and is not usually self-adjusting.

### 12  Improved four-stroke engine designs – multi-valve heads

The main aim of any engine designer is to improve volumetric efficiency. This means getting more out of an engine without increasing its capacity. To do this you have to get more fuel/air mixture into the combustion chamber, burn it more efficiently so that every joule of energy is extracted from the fuel, and then get rid of all the waste gasses. Bigger carburettors and a freer flow of air into the engine is one way of doing it, but only so much mixture can pass a valve of a given size in a given time. So the obvious solution is to increase the size of the valves. The problem is that there is only so much room in the cylinder head, and sooner or later a point is reached where the valves would touch if enlarged further.

To get round the problem, designers decided to use two smaller inlet valves instead of one big one, creating a three-valve head. The two valves have a combined area greater than that of the large single valve they replace, and though individually they are smaller and lighter, collectively the overall extra reciprocating weight does not outweigh the benefits in terms of gains in efficiency. The added advantage of using valves that are individually smaller and lighter is that they can run at higher speeds with less risk of bounce or float.

This system was a definite improvement, so manufacturers decided to try an extra exhaust valve as well, and so the four-valve head was introduced, though it is worth noting that the inlet valves are usually slightly larger than the exhaust valves. The only change necessary to the way the multiple valves are actuated on DOHC engines is to use a forked rocker arm that contacts two valves simultaneously, or to have twice as many lobes on the camshaft. But multi-valve heads do not have to follow the DOHC arrangement, and alternatives include Honda's SOHC four-valve engine (which uses forked rockers), and of course the CX500 V-twin which uses pushrods and forked rockers.

In addition to the immediate advantage of a bigger valve area, multi-valve heads have led to improved combustion chamber designs and the preferable central placing of the spark plug (giving better gas flow and more efficient combustion). A good original example of this

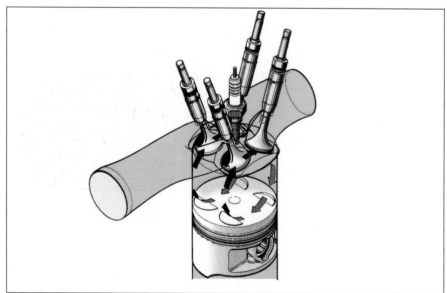

**1.12a  Suzuki's Twin Swirl Combustion Chamber (TSCC) head showing the four valves**

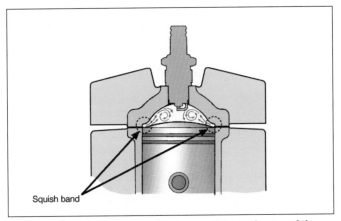

**1.12b  The shaped area or band around the perimeter of the combustion chamber 'squishes' the mixture as shown for improved combustion**

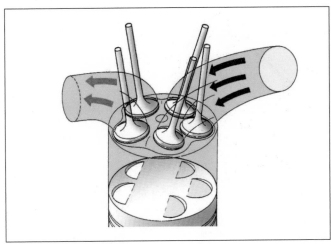

**1.12c  Yamaha's five valve combustion chamber**

is Suzuki's patented TSCC (Twin Swirl Combustion Chamber) **(see illustration 1.12a)**. The classical hemispherical cylinder head design is replaced by a more subtle shape where each valve seat area has its own miniature hemispherical recess. The incoming mixture is induced into a swirling motion inside the cylinder, speeding and aiding the rapid filling of the combustion space. To improve combustion, many engines incorporate a 'squish' band around the perimeter of the combustion chamber which squeezes the mixture inwards and upwards towards the spark plug as the piston rises, so that when the mixture is ignited the flame spreads rapidly, releasing energy from the fuel at the best point for obtaining maximum power from it **(see illustration 1.12b)**.

Another improvement has been in the design of the inlet tract, which becomes narrower as it gets closer to the valve. This creates a 'venturi effect', whereby the rate of flow of the mixture increases as the tract it flows in becomes narrower. But this is not necessarily good unless the shape of the valve around which the mixture must flow and the shape of the combustion chamber into which it flows all work hand-in-hand to produce an overall effect and achieve an overall end.

Yamaha have taken the concept one stage further in the development of a five-valve head, used on the FZR and YZF 750 and 1000 cc 20V Genesis engines **(see illustration 1.12c)**. By using five valves (three inlet and two exhaust), maximum use is made of the combustion chamber area given the limitations of working with round valves, thus achieving improved volumetric efficiency over a four-valve head design. The only disadvantage of this design is in the increased cost of manufacturing the cylinder heads and valve gear.

Using multi-valve heads goes hand-in-hand with the current trend for using cylinders with shorter strokes and wider bores to achieve greater engine speeds. A shorter stroke

means the piston has to travel less far before it reaches its next power stroke, and a wider bore means a wider combustion chamber, into which more valves can be squeezed. A wider bore also gives a piston with a larger top surface, so there is a greater area for the combusted fuel/air mixture to act on. This advantage can be demonstrated by the fact that a boat with a large sail will go faster than the same boat with a smaller sail, given the same wind.

## 13  Improved four-stroke engine designs – desmodromic valves

The imposingly-named desmodronic valve arrangement is perhaps the definitive answer

to the problem of valve bounce or float. In all conventional four-stroke arrangements the valve is pulled closed by one or two return springs. As has been mentioned, the springs can be changed to avoid surge or valve bounce or float problems, but any change is only ever a compromise, for there is normally a detrimental aspect to every benefit.

Desmodronic valves avoid this by using (originally) an extra camshaft to actuate extra rocker arms that positively close the valves in exactly the same way as they are used to open them **(see illustration 1.13a)**. The valve opens normally, with the opening rocker pressing down on the stem. As the lobe passes the highest point and the rocker begins to release the valve, the closing rocker pulls the valve shut. Later versions of the system use only one camshaft with all the

**1.13a  Desmodromic valve operation – early type**

*This three-cam arrangement was employed on the early Ducati works racers. The outer camshafts open the valves, whilst the single central camshaft pulls them closed.*

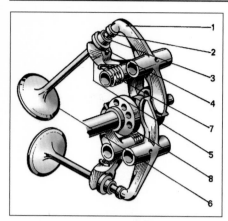

**1.13b Desmodromic valve operation –
later type**

*In this later design the valve opening and
closing rockers are all controlled by the lobes
on a single central camshaft*

1  *Opening (or upper) rocker*
2  *Upper rocker adjuster*
3  *Half-rings*
4  *Closing rocker adjuster*
5  *Closing (or lower) rocker*
6  *Valve*
7  *Closing rocker return spring*
8  *Camshaft*

relevant lobes machined onto it **(see
illustration 1.13b)**.

In practice, the desmodronic valve system
is rather exotic and too expensive for normal
mass production motorcycles. It is used only
by Ducati, but to good effect, particularly in
the case of their racing engines. Whether it is
necessary on road-going machines is open to
question, particularly in the case of the larger
models whose maximum engine speed is
limited by other considerations. What is
beyond dispute is the effectiveness with
which it eliminates the problem of valve
bounce and float.

## 14 Four-stroke induction systems – alternatives to the poppet valve

From the preceding sections it will be seen
that the trend in the development of the four-
stroke induction system has been to
eliminate, as far as possible, the reciprocating
parts in the valve train. Whilst the DOHC
design comes very close to this, the poppet
valve itself remains a limiting factor. That the
poppet valve works cannot be denied, but it
does have obvious limitations. Apart from the
problem of its reciprocating weight it presents
a considerable obstruction to the incoming
mixture, causing unwanted turbulence and
drag which impede cylinder filling. In most
current designs a lot of effort has been
directed towards compensating for these
drawbacks, but the fundamental problem
remains.

Over the years there have been
innumerable attempts to replace the poppet
valve with an alternative valve system, and
amongst these the Cross rotary valve design
looked the most promising **(see illustration
1.14a)**. This took the form of a hollow tube set
transversely across the cylinder head in a
special chamber. The tube was driven at half
engine speed and featured a slot in its wall
which aligned with the inlet and exhaust ports
at the appropriate point in the engine cycle.

The valve assembly thus operated in a similar
way to the two-stroke's disc valve and offered
an unobstructed gas flow into the combustion
chamber. Norton tried the valve on its racing
engines during the early 1950s, but beset by
sealing problems, reverted to poppet valves
soon afterwards.

Along with the Knight sleeve valve and the
Aspin valve **(see illustration 1.14b)**, the Cross
rotary valve was abandoned mostly because
of the inherent sealing problems, and the
poppet valve was sufficiently well established
to dissuade the manufacturers from further
development.

However the rotary valve concept has not
been forgotten, and there is a four-stroke
engine in existence which doesn't use poppet
valves. It features a rotating cylinder into
which ports are cut. The cylinder is gear
driven off the crankshaft and turns at half
crankshaft speed. The significant feature of
this engine is that the piston moves up and
down in the same cylinder, and sealing
problems are taken care of by a standard
piston and ring arrangement. It is essentially a
cross between the rotary type valves
mentioned above and the port system used in
a two-stroke engine.

## 15 Four-stroke engines – valve timing

It seems common sense that the inlet valve
should be open throughout the induction
stroke, and the exhaust valve should be open
throughout the exhaust stroke. In practice, an
engine that used such valve timing would be a
very poor performer.

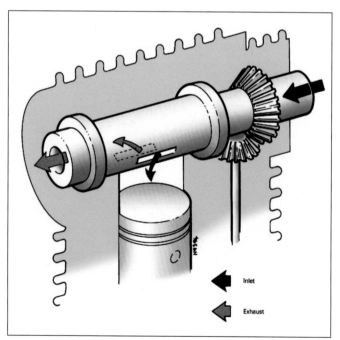

**1.14a  The Cross rotary valve**

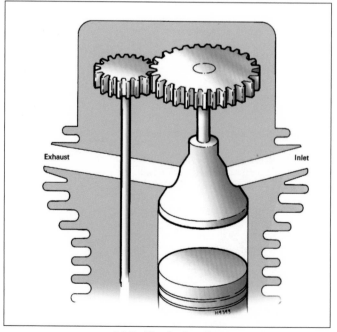

**1.14b  The Aspin valve**

## Inlet valve timing

An inlet valve is set to open before TDC, towards the end of the exhaust stroke, and close after BDC, at the beginning of the compression stroke **(see illustration 1.15a)**. There are very good reasons for this.

Firstly, a valve cannot open instantly, so if the inlet valve began opening at TDC, it would not be fully open until the piston had travelled a good way down the bore, and if was to be fully closed by the time it reached BDC, the actual time that the valve would spend fully open would be minimal, and the amount of lift (how far into the cylinder the valve projects when full open) would have to be small, to reduce the time taken to open and close. This would reduce the amount of mixture drawn into the cylinder, and so would reduce the engine's volumetric efficiency.

Secondly, the incoming mixture has a mass, and once it starts moving into the cylinder it tries to keep on moving. Leaving the inlet valve open after BDC means that the momentum of the mixture causes more to be packed in, even though the piston has started to rise. The number of degrees that the crankshaft turns between BDC and the inlet valve closing is called 'inlet valve lag'.

## Exhaust valve timing

Similarly, an exhaust valve is set to open before BDC, towards the end of the ignition stroke, and close after TDC, at the beginning of the induction stroke **(see illustration 1.15a)**. Apart from ensuring that the valve is fully open at the start of the exhaust stroke (for the same reasons as above), opening the valve early prevents the exhaust gas forming a high pressure cushion to impede the piston as it rises up the bore.

Closing the valve after TDC ensures the cylinder is thoroughly scavenged, and,

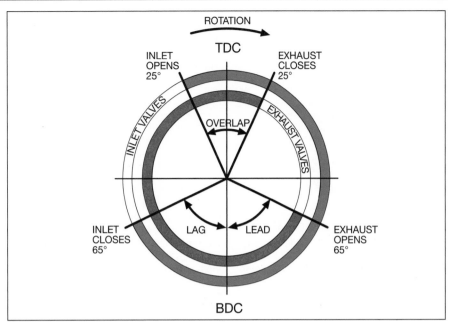

**1.15a  Typical valve timing diagram for the average four-stroke engine**

remembering that the inlet valve opens before TDC on the induction stroke (meaning that both valves are open at the same time), the exhaust gas rushing out creates suction in the inlet tract which helps draw the fresh mixture in. Once the fresh mixture is entering the cylinder, it helps to push the exhaust gas out.

The number of degrees that the crankshaft turns between the exhaust valve opening and BDC is called 'exhaust valve lead'. The number of degrees that the crankshaft turns while the inlet and exhaust valves are open together around TDC is called 'valve overlap'. The number of degrees that a particular valve is open for is called 'duration'.

## Lead, lag and overlap

The amount of lead, lag and overlap determines the performance characteristics of the engine, and the intended use of the engine will determine how the valve timing is set. For example, a low revving long-stroke twin cylinder engine as used in a 'custom cruiser' is expected to have lots of low down 'grunt' in the form of torque, and will have completely different valve timing to a high revving multi-cylinder short-stroke engine as used in a sports bike requiring a power band high in the rev range **(see illustrations 1.15b and c)**. This is because valve timing

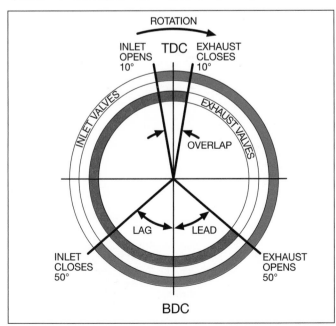

**1.15b  Typical valve timing for a low revving engine**

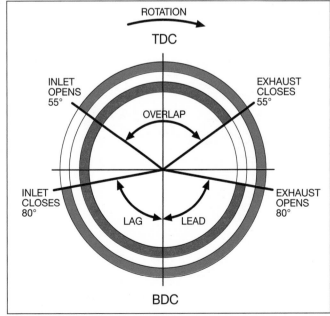

**1.15c  Typical valve timing diagram for a high revving engine**

affects where peak torque and power occur in the rev range.

As engine speed rises, there is less time available for the engine events to occur, so high revving engines with a power band high in the rev range need more valve overlap and lead and lag than low revving engines to allow in large amounts of mixture in a small amount of time. However, when valve overlap is large, poor low speed performance results as the incoming fresh mixture has time to short circuit straight out of the exhaust, leaving the cylinder poorly filled. Similarly on a low revving engine there is more time for the events to occur, so smaller valve overlap and angles of lead and lag are required, giving efficient induction and scavenging at low engine speeds. This however means that there is not enough time to allow enough mixture to enter to give any high speed performance. There is a half-way point

between the extremes of sports bike and custom cruiser, and it is possible to obtain a good spread of power over the rev range, though neither low down grunt or peak power will be very special.

This means that in effect every engine with static valve timing is a compromise. Every bit of extra power gained high in the rev range through hotter valve timing will result in a loss of torque and power low down in the range, and vice versa. Which begs the question, why not have variable valve timing to achieve the best of both worlds?

### Variable valve timing

Variable valve timing means that for any given engine speed, the amount of overlap, lead, lag and duration can be optimised.

In the early 1980s Honda developed a system for a 16 valve engine which used a duplex-rocker to operate only two of the four

valves per cylinder at low engine speeds, but locked in the extra rocker arm at a pre-set speed to operate all four valves. The system was developed further by using three camshaft lobes per duplex-rocker arm, the central one of which had higher lift and longer duration than the outer two. This allowed all four valves to be used with mild lift and duration at low engine speeds, then at a pre-set speed the third lobe locked in to actuate the rockers, operating all the valves with hotter lift and duration.

The latest development from Honda is their Hyper V-TEC system, introduced on the Japan-only CB400 Super Four in 1999 and used on the 2002 VFR800 **(see illustration 1.15d)**. It reverts to the two valves at low speeds, four valves at high speeds principle, but does away with the complex rocker arm set-ups that all added reciprocating mass.

Two of the valves per cylinder (one inlet, one exhaust) are actuated by conventional bucket-type followers, and are in use all of the time. The other two valves per cylinder have bucket-type followers that are also actuated all the time, but in each follower there is a pin with a hole in it that sits between the bucket and the valve stem, with the hole aligned at low speeds so that the contact point of the bucket fits into it, so no contact is made with the valves and they remain closed. At a pre-set speed, an oil-way opens, and oil pressure forces the pin across so that the hole is no longer aligned with the follower contact, which instead contacts the pin and opens the valve.

Suzuki developed a variable valve timing system for their Japan-only GSF400 Bandit and RF400 models. This system is controlled electrically by a servomotor mounted on the engine valve cover. At a pre-determined engine speed the servomotor brings additional valves into operation via a rack and pinion mechanism.

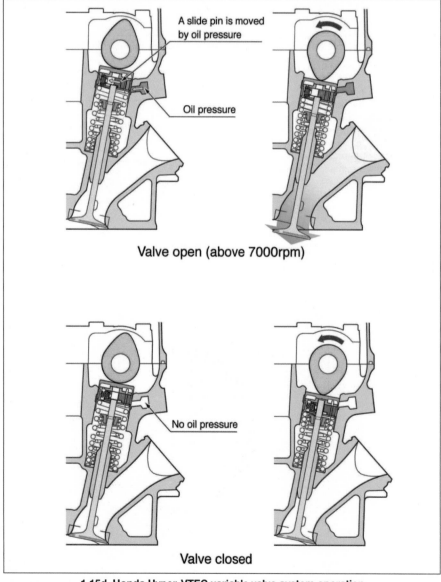

A slide pin is moved by oil pressure

Oil pressure

**Valve open (above 7000rpm)**

No oil pressure

**Valve closed**

**1.15d Honda Hyper-VTEC variable valve system operation**

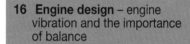

**16 Engine design** – engine vibration and the importance of balance

With the exception of the rotary engine, all motorcycle engines have some parts which rotate, and other parts which go up and down, or reciprocate.

### Vibration

The problem of engine vibration is caused by the crankshaft, connecting rod and piston assembly. If you start with the bare flywheels, these can be spun quite easily in their bearings and cause no vibration problems. As soon as you start to add more rotating components to the flywheel, namely the crankpin, big-end bearing and bottom part of the connecting rod, you introduce a vibration problem created by out-of-balance rotational or centrifugal forces.

But when it comes to adding reciprocating

components such as the top half of the connecting rod and the piston, things are less straightforward. The explanation is no less involved. As the piston reaches the top of its stroke (TDC) it has to decelerate rapidly, stop, and then accelerate rapidly in the opposite direction. It reaches its maximum speed roughly half-way to the bottom, then it has to decelerate, stop at BDC, and then accelerate again, and so on. Every time the piston is at TDC or BDC the rapid deceleration causes a pulse of vibration through the engine. The forces involved are known as reciprocating or inertia forces, which are at a maximum at TDC and BDC and zero half-way between when the piston is at its maximum speed.

### Balance

Rotational or centrifugal forces can be dealt with quite easily either by removing some of the flywheel material next to the crankpin or adding a similar amount of weight directly opposite to it, and the assembly is back in balance.

To compensate for reciprocating or inertia forces, a further amount of weight could be added to the flywheels opposite the crankpin, so that the total weight of the reciprocating components was balanced out. This is termed a 100% balance factor. By creating a second set of out of balance forces we have effectively cancelled out completely the imbalance at the top and bottom of the piston's stroke, and thus have removed the vibration problem entirely – or have we?

Unfortunately not. The trouble is that this arrangement does not work between TDC and BDC, because the added (balance) weight on the flywheels is still creating a constant rotational force while the reciprocating force moves from maximum to zero and back again. The result is horizontal vibration.

The trouble is that the piston and connecting rod do not remain in the same position in relation to the flywheels, and so the out of balance forces are constantly changing as the crankshaft turns. Even though the overall weight of the crankshaft remains constant, part of that weight is constantly changing position, and so there are varying rotational forces to deal with.

There is no real solution to this problem; the only course of action open to the engine designer is compromise. What has to be done is to reduce the reciprocating balance factor so that the rotational imbalance is also reduced, but without the reciprocating imbalance becoming intolerable. The final balance factor is decided by the maximum designed speed of the finished engine, the type of frame and numerous other considerations, and so it varies between one engine and another, but a balance factor of around 60% to 70% is common.

The forces we have looked at so far are called primary balance forces, but the plot thickens as there are also secondary forces to be dealt with, and this is where things start to

get even more complicated. We have so far assumed that the amount of reciprocating force is the same at TDC as it is at BDC. Unfortunately this is not the case. Because of the angling of the connecting rod, maximum piston speed is actually reached slightly closer to TDC than the mid-stroke position. This means that, for a given engine speed, it takes less time for the piston to decelerate from maximum speed, stop, change direction and then accelerate to maximum speed around TDC than it does to do the same around BDC. And because reciprocating force (or inertia) is related to acceleration and deceleration as well as mass, it follows that the reciprocating force at TDC is greater than at BDC.

The problem of engine balance and how to deal with it starts to become very mathematically complicated and beyond the scope of this book. Suffice to say that there are ways, but each is a compromise to an ideal situation. But as long as the principle of balance can be appreciated, it can be seen why engine designers have tried many different engine configurations and crankshaft layouts (the positional relationship of one piston to another on multi-cylinder engines) to try and eliminate, or at least minimise, the inherent problems.

If we look at a few engine examples it is immediately obvious that the problem becomes greater as the engine size increases. On a moped engine the out of balance forces may be quite high, but because the piston and connecting rod are so small the vibration is evident only as a slight buzz felt at the handlebars; hardly a serious problem and barely noticeable in use. On bigger machines

the vibration becomes more noticeable to the point where it starts to impose limitations on the practical maximum engine size. Although there are many other considerations, this in part explains why there are no 1000 cc singles. The vibration problem allied to possible structural aspects of the engine internals have effectively limited singles to a maximum of 650 cc or so, and also explains why big singles are traditionally slow-revving engines; by keeping the engine speed down, both wear and vibration are kept to a minimum. More power means more displacement and/or higher engine speeds, and so the need arises for more cylinders.

### Hiding the effects of vibration

There are a few ways of hiding the effects of vibration, without having to take the difficult route of eliminating the cause. The design of the frame and accessories is important, because these can either dampen or encourage the vibration. A good example of this is in the handlebars fitted to some machines where sympathetic vibration at the bar ends reaches finger-numbing proportions in use. The answer is simply to weight the ends of the handlebars. This alters the resonant frequency of the bar and thus dampens out the vibration. Similar techniques are employed to stop rear-view mirrors blurring, and even to prevent recurrent fractures in mounting brackets.

Another approach is to isolate the engine unit from the frame by fitting bonded rubber engine mountings and this can absorb much of the vibration, making the machine feel more comfortable to ride (see illustration 1.16a). There are attendant problems due to the need

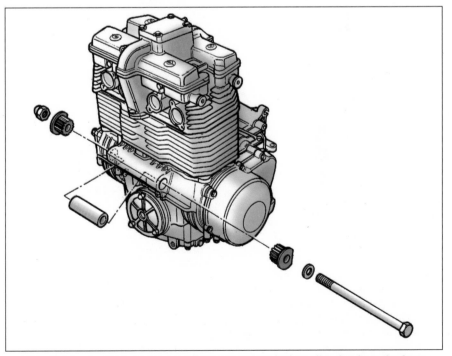

**1.16a Rubber bushed engine mountings can help to isolate vibration from the frame**

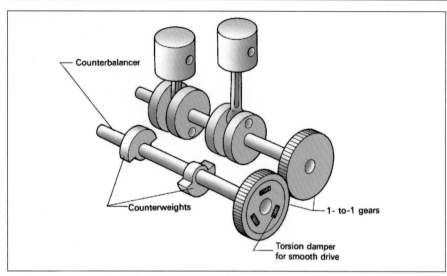

1.16b Typical twin-cylinder balancing system

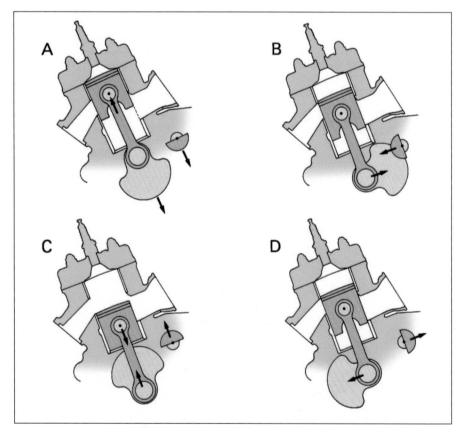

1.16c Operation of a balancer mechanism

**A** *The piston is at top dead centre (TDC) and the crankshaft balance weight, aided by the balancer shaft weight, compensates for the mass of the piston and part of the connecting rod*

**B** *As the piston descends to the mid-point of its stroke the crankshaft balance weight creates an unwanted out-of balance force at right angles to the bore. The counter-rotating balance shaft weight cancels this out with a corresponding force in the opposite direction*

**C** *At bottom dead centre (BDC) the downward thrust of the piston is offset by the combined upward forces of the crankshaft and balancer shaft weights*

**D** *The piston arrives at mid-stroke once more, and the out-of-balance force of the crankshaft weight is cancelled by that of the balance shaft weight*

for the engine to be mounted securely in the frame to ensure that the final drive is kept in alignment, and this leads to difficulties on all but the smallest engines.

Hiding the effects of vibration is all very well on machines that do not vibrate very much, or where an increase in weight is a greater concern (and on such machines methods of hiding can be used), but as will be seen in the following sections, there are some engine configurations that create a lot more vibration than others. In such cases where comfort and ease of use are more important than weight and performance, it is necessary to tackle the cause further, not the effect.

As it is not possible to eliminate the original forces that cause the problem, it is necessary to produce further equal but opposite forces to cancel out those that already exist. The most common method is to use one or more balancer shafts driven off the crankshaft, but in the opposite direction of rotation **(see illustration 1.16b)**. On the shaft there are carefully positioned and calculated weights. As the accompanying illustration shows, the forces produced by the weights on the balancer shaft offset the normal vibration produced by the crankshaft and piston **(see illustration 1.16c)**. If a shaft is used to counteract primary forces, it is driven at the same speed as the crankshaft and in the opposite direction. If a shaft is used to counteract secondary forces, it will be driven at twice engine speed, and again in the opposite direction to the crankshaft.

## 17 Engine arrangements – single-cylinder engines

The simplest arrangement of all is the single-cylinder engine **(see illustrations 1.17a and b)**. Its main virtues are mechanical simplicity and small size, which means that it is easy and cheap to build and generally less demanding to maintain and service. As such it is ideal for mopeds, scooters and small commuter bikes, and indeed there are few

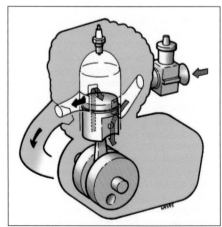

1.17a Typical single cylinder two-stroke

**1.17b Typical single cylinder four-stroke**

machines in this category which do not use a single cylinder engine. In off-road sporting applications too, the single combines simplicity with the essential lack of weight and bulk, and thus is universally popular. But it does have many limitations as well, in terms of performance.

Because a single-cylinder four-stroke fires once every 720° of crankshaft rotation, large flywheels are needed to keep the engine turning until it reaches the next power stroke. To avoid an excessive amount of weight the flywheels have to be thin and of large diameter. Given the need to keep the piston as light as possible, and the necessity of a long connecting rod, the resulting engine is a so-called long-stroke design. The characteristics of such an engine are good up to a point; it is economical, has a very wide spread of power and can pull with relative ease from low engine speeds. The gear ratios can be widely spread to make use of this generous power band and the machine has a relaxed feel to it. Indeed, the effects of engine vibration are to some extent subjective, and as a rule, quite high levels of low frequency 'thumping' are preferable to a less intense but more irritating 'buzz'.

As soon as you try to make it go faster, however, the drawbacks become apparent. The massive flywheels mean a lot of stored up energy, or inertia, and thus acceleration is confined to a gentle gathering of speed by today's standards. The small bore and long stroke mean high piston speeds and a high rate of wear in these components. As soon as you try to reduce the stroke significantly, the smoothing effect of the large flywheels is lost and the out of balance forces are increased, so the easy-going single becomes more like a mobile road drill.

Another problem with large capacity single cylinder engines is that they can be difficult to start, even with an electric start. But as many of the large capacity singles are used for off-road competition, they are not fitted with electric starts, and so it is necessary to set the engine up at just before TDC on the compression stroke and to give it a hefty boot to get the crankshaft moving. Then there is the problem of kickback, which is when the engine is not positioned correctly, and/or is not kicked over hard enough, so that there is not enough force to get the piston past the compression stroke, and it effectively bounces back under the compression. At this point the kickstart lever is sent back upwards, either launching you over the handlebars, or possibly breaking your leg. Some singles are fitted with a decompression facility which is designed to alleviate both starting and kickback problems. Honda have a system whereby, when the engine is kicked over, a small cam acts on the exhaust valve to leave it very slightly open at TDC on the compression stroke. This reduces the force necessary to turn the engine over. A second cam comes into operation if kickback occurs, again opening the exhaust valve slightly so that the force is reduced.

## 18 Engine arrangements – twin cylinder engines

### The 360° parallel twin four-stroke

Historically, the parallel twin was surprisingly like a single-cylinder engine that had been modified to accept two cylinders, pistons and connecting rods **(see illustration 1.18a)**. To be a little less obscure about it, the traditional British four-stroke parallel twin had pistons which moved up and down in unison, but with each cylinder firing on alternate revolutions of the engine, or at 360° intervals; thus it became known as a 360° parallel twin.

At first sight, the choice of a 360° crankshaft may seem a little hard to explain, because it retains the balance problems of the single, but it is an improvement in some respects. The crankshaft assembly has an increased weight because it is wider to accommodate the extra crankpin and connecting rod, though this is offset to some extent by reducing its diameter. The out of balance forces can be reduced somewhat by employing relatively large diameter pistons with a shorter stroke, so the balance problem, though still there, is reduced. More significantly, the traditional 'thump' caused by the power stroke of a large single is smoothed out by having the two smaller power pulses spread evenly across two revolutions of the engine.

The 360° parallel twin was not without its disadvantages, but offered a number of improvements over the single in the search for more power. The main advantage does not relate directly to the balance problem but rather to the physical limitations of the single.

### The 180° parallel twin four-stroke

An alternative to the 360° crankshaft parallel twin is to arrange the crankpins so that they are spaced 180° apart **(see illustration 1.18b)**. With this arrangement the primary out of balance forces are minimised. At first sight this is a much better choice than the 360° type, and most recent designs have opted for it. One disadvantage of the 180° crankshaft is that it has uneven power strokes, and another is that it creates what is known as a 'rocking couple'.

This curious-sounding effect is evident in all engine designs using more than one cylinder, with the exception of the V-twin, of which more later. Imagine the effect as one cylinder fires; as the piston is pushed downward the pressure on that end of the crankshaft is increased and there is a tendency for it to try to 'rock' to one side. When the next cylinder fires the effect is repeated with the crankshaft rocking the other way. The only way to eliminate this is to have both crankpins on the same plane, but this is physically impossible with a parallel twin. If you compare the two arrangements you will find that both the 360° and 180° designs have

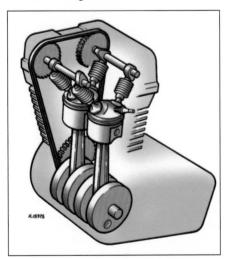

**1.18a 360° parallel twin four-stroke**

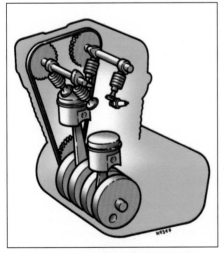

**1.18b 180° parallel twin four-stroke**

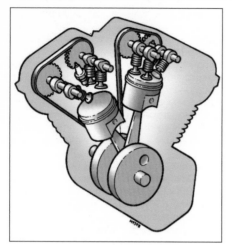

**1.18c Four-stroke V-twin**

**1.18d Two-stroke V-twin**

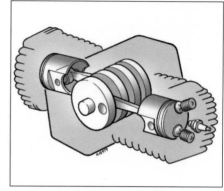

**1.18e Horizontally-opposed four-stroke twin**

their own particular advantages and drawbacks, making it impossible to say that one is better than the other. To reduce the balance problem further you need (you've guessed it!) more cylinders.

### Two-stroke parallel twins

These are almost invariably built using a 180° crankshaft, and being a two-stroke they show fewer disadvantages when compared to a four-stroke of similar layout. This is because each cylinder fires after every complete revolution of the crankshaft, and thus the firing irregularity found in the four-stroke is no longer a source of vibration.

The dreaded 'rocking couple' effect is still at large, however, and given the higher engine speeds normally found on two-stroke engines, the out of balance forces can result in fairly obtrusive vibration levels. This problem is made worse by the need for the two cylinders to have separate crankcases; this means having a central main bearing and oil seals with the result that the crankshaft has to be wider than on a similar four-stroke. With the added leverage thus obtained at the crankpins, the effect of the rocking couple is magnified.

### The four-stroke V-twin

The V-twin engine is almost as old in concept as the motorcycle itself, and the fact that it is still used today is indicative of its basic soundness **(see illustration 1.18c)**. The original arrangement of two splayed cylinders sharing a common crankpin avoids the rocking couple problem of the parallel twin, particularly where one normal connecting rod is straddled by the forked rod end of the second rod. With the two rods in line, no rocking couple exists, and even where two conventional rods are positioned side-by-side on a wider crankpin the offset is so small as to make the effect insignificant.

In terms of balance, the best angle between the cylinders is 90°. If the reciprocating weight of the pistons and connecting rods is perfectly

balanced (a 100% balance factor) the inevitable out of balance forces of one cylinder are offset by the opposing mid-stroke forces of the other. There is still a residual problem of the forces which combine to shake the engine in a horizontal plane, but these are mild compared to the vibration levels so far discussed. In practice, if the engine is mounted in-line, the vibration levels are relatively insignificant, and are mostly due to the 'thump' on each power stroke (firing intervals are 270° and 450°). With a transversely mounted engine the forces are more noticeable as a side-to-side shuddering at low engine speeds, but again, far less obtrusive than the parallel twin.

Whilst the in-line 90° V-twin seems an ideal motorcycle engine, its widely-splayed cylinders make it rather bulky and thus difficult to incorporate in a motorcycle frame. Whilst it can be done, as in the case of the Ducati range, it is still relatively uncommon, though becoming more popular in Sports models due to the success of Ducati in World Superbike racing. Most in-line V-twin designs exhibit a compromise between optimum balance and compactness by having a smaller angle between the cylinders, as in the case of Harley Davidson (though this does affect the firing intervals, becoming more unevenly spaced). In-line V-twins do have an advantage of being narrow, but unless liquid-cooling is used, the rear cylinder can run hotter than the front.

The transversely mounted V-twin, as used to good effect for many years by Moto Guzzi, slots easily into a frame, and has excellent cooling as both heads are stuck out in the wind. It also provides the perfect set-up for using shaft drive.

### The two-stroke V-twin

The two-stroke V-twin is very much a rarity, but there was an example in the Japan-only Honda NS250 **(see illustration 1.18d)**. Because it is a two-stroke and each cylinder needs a separate crankcase it is impossible to employ the normal shared crankpin of the four-stroke V-twin, and so inevitably it suffers from the rocking-couple effect common to all

two-stroke twins. Even so, the normal out of balance forces of the parallel twin are largely cancelled out.

### The horizontally-opposed twin

The horizontally-opposed twin, or 'flat twin' as it is sometimes known, offers an almost perfect solution to the out of balance forces which have affected the designs examined so far. By having both pistons moving simultaneously in opposite directions, the primary imbalance of one piston and connecting rod perfectly offsets the other **(see illustration 1.18e)**. But because this necessitates having two crankpins as opposed to one, the rocking couple effect between the two cylinders is introduced, but the vibration levels that result are not normally very obtrusive.

A more practical consideration is how to fit the unavoidably awkward unit into a motorcycle frame. A few examples of fore-and-aft mounting exist, as illustrated by pre-war Douglas models. This does make for a long machine though and leads to problems when trying to find a suitable location for the transmission components. Another problem is the tendency for the rear cylinder, which is masked by the main bulk of the engine, to overheat.

The best-known example of the horizontally-opposed engine in a modern motorcycle is the BMW. These, like most other flat twin designs, employ a transverse mounting arrangement which again makes it a simple matter to adopt shaft final drive.

### 19 Engine arrangements – three cylinder engines ('triples')

### The in-line triple

The transversely mounted in-line three cylinder engine is really an extension of the parallel twin in an attempt to strike a compromise between the vibration problems of the latter and the width of a four **(see**

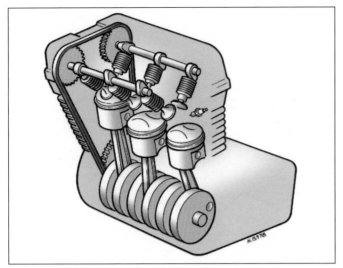

**1.19a 120° in-line four-stroke triple**

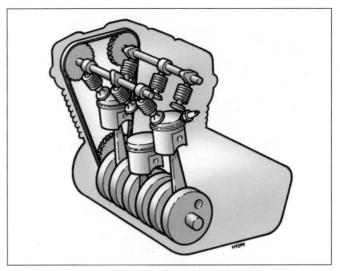

**1.19b 180/360° in-line four-stroke triple**

**illustration 1.19a)**. This is particularly true of two-strokes whose crankcases begin to grow uncomfortably wide as a triple, and would be positively unwieldy as a four.

The two-stroke triple was a firm favourite in the 1970s, with various examples from Suzuki and Kawasaki. Both these manufacturers went as far as producing a 750 cc two-stroke; the water-cooled GT750 from Suzuki and the KH750 from Kawasaki. With their 120° crankshafts the primary forces were quite well balanced, but the complicated rocking couple (rocking triple?) effect gave them a reputation for a fairly high level of high-frequency vibration, especially where the unit was not well insulated from the frame with rubber mountings.

The four-strokes are well represented too, from the BSA Rocket Three and Triumph Trident of the late 1960s, through to Yamaha's XS750 and 850 shaft-drive tourers and the Laverda triples of the seventies and eighties. For many years Laverda used a 180/360 degree crankshaft (when the middle piston reaches TDC, the remaining pair are at BDC and vice versa) **(see illustration 1.19b)**, but later adopted a 120° crankshaft and the resulting engine has become far smoother.

Triumph has stayed loyal to the triple, with many models from the Hinckley Triumph company featuring a transversely mounted in-line triple engine. In the opinion of most manufacturers, however, the triple has little advantage over the in-line four, however it does offer a superb compromise between the low revving grunt of a twin and the peaky power of a four.

### The horizontal in-line triple

BMW came up with an interesting variation of the above in their K75, which has the cylinders lying horizontally and the crankshaft running in line with the frame; it was essentially a development of their earlier flat four cylinder engine **(see illustration 1.20b)**.

**1.19c Two-stroke V-three**

Though a little odd at first sight with its cylinder head running down one side and its crankcase on the other, it is quite a narrow and compact unit which gives a low centre of gravity and is suited to the use of shaft drive.

### The V-three two-stroke

By any standards, the V-three two-stroke is an oddity and seems unlikely to become a popular engine configuration **(see illustration 1.19c)**. Initially, the engine appeared as a 500 cc GP power unit, the strange layout of the cylinders being chosen to avoid the width problem associated with a two-stroke in-line triple; having reduced the crankshaft width to the minimum possible with separate crankcase compartments, the engine would still have been bulky by virtue of the wide barrels and their transfer ports. By displacing the centre cylinder they would be allowed to overlap somewhat, and the engine width was thus reduced. After racing successes, Honda produced a road-going derivative, the

NS400R.

### 20 Engine arrangements – four cylinder engines

### The in-line four

When Honda introduced its CB750 Four in 1969 it gave the motorcycling public hitherto undreamed of sophistication, and in so doing laid down the basic arrangement for medium to large capacity motorcycle engines for well over a decade. Of course there was nothing new about the in-line four – car manufacturers had settled on it decades ago as the best compromise between smoothness and compactness for their purposes – but most small capacity four cylinder car engines would have been far too large and heavy for a motorcycle. However Honda had some four cylinder car engines in the sixties that had

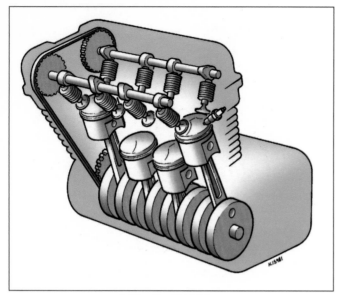

**1.20a The in-line four**

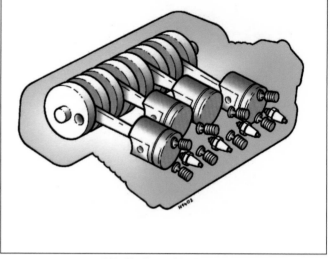

**1.20b Horizontal in-line four**

been made much more compact than those of other manufacturers, for use in small sports cars, and so they adapted them further for use in motorcycles, the result being a unit not too much wider than the parallel twin it was to displace, though still wide enough.

The transversely mounted in-line four is basically two 180° twins joined together in a common crankcase **(see illustration 1.20a)**. In most engines of this type the crankshaft is arranged so that the two inner pistons move up and down together, and 180° apart from the outer pistons. The crankshaft, although necessarily long to accommodate the four connecting rods and the main bearing journals, does not need to be of large diameter. This is because the relatively frequent power strokes, one at every half-revolution of the crankshaft, obviate the need for large flywheels to maintain momentum.

Also of importance is the small size and weight of the pistons and connecting rods, resulting in low primary forces on each individual cylinder, and the forces are spread more evenly than on single, twin or three

cylinder units. With a good degree of crankshaft balance and relatively small diameter flywheels, the four has a relatively short stroke and is therefore responsive and can be designed to run at relatively high engine speeds. As such it has found considerable favour from the public and manufacturer alike.

The only real problems, apart from the consideration of its sheer mechanical complexity, is the width of the crankshaft and the inevitable buzzing vibration caused by the secondary and rocking couple forces. Although this is inevitable, the forces involved are not great and the problem is really little more than an irritation that in most applications can be ironed out through careful design of the frame, engine mounts and everything else around the engine.

To reduce the crankcase width, some manufacturers who had previously mounted the alternator on one end of the crankshaft have resorted to mounting it on the top of the crankcase, and driving it off the crankshaft via a chain or gears, thus allowing the crankcases to be made as narrow as possible. And now

that small electronic ignition components have replaced larger contact breaker units with mechanical advance and retard mechanisms (which were usually mounted on the opposite end of the crankshaft to the alternator), the crankcase width is now narrower on some engines than the width of the cylinder block.

Another possibility is to mount the engine in line with the frame rather than across it, much like a conventional rear wheel drive car. There have been examples from Brough Superior, Wilkinson, Henderson and Indian, but the additional length of the engine unit and resultant long wheelbase are not feasible for most purposes.

As for the two-stroke, four separate crankcase compartments are really too unwieldy to be a practical proposition, so the two-stroke in-line four has always been considered a non-starter.

### The horizontal in-line four

As with their version of an in-line triple, BMW's in-line four, as used on the K100, has the engine lying horizontally, with the cylinders running across the frame and the crankshaft in line with it **(see illustration 1.20b)**. By normal 'four' standards its engine unit is quite narrow, and its height is less of a problem than a vertically mounted four. It also has the advantages of a low centre of gravity and the ease with which shaft drive can be applied.

### The horizontally-opposed four

Just as the parallel twin was enhanced to form the in-line four, two cylinders were also added to the horizontally-opposed twin to produce the horizontally opposed four **(see illustration 1.20c)**. The resulting engine, also known as a 'flat four', is exemplified by the 1000, 1100 and 1200 cc Honda Gold Wing

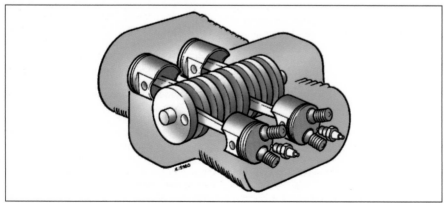

**1.20c Horizontally-opposed four**

**1.20d The square four**

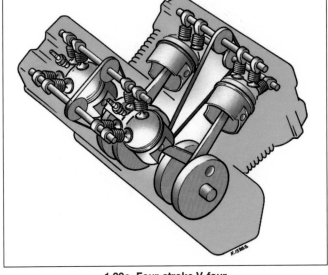

**1.20e Four-stroke V-four**

models, just about the only modern example of this arrangement in the motorcycle world.

The unit is superbly smooth and gives the Gold Wing excellent stability by having a low centre of gravity. The main drawback is the sheer width of the engine, making it unsuitable for anything other than a large tourer or cruiser. Engine width is a constant problem confronting the motorcycle designer, and although the 'flat four' is almost ideal in every other respect, this one factor is sufficiently important to prevent its extensive use.

### The square four

The square four represents another way of doubling the parallel twin to make a four-cylinder unit, this time with two separate crankshafts arranged one behind the other and connected by gears or chain **(see illustration 1.20d)**. This arrangement allows the engine width to be kept to that of a twin cylinder unit, with only a small increase in its length, and so provides the advantages of an in-line four without the problem of width.

The most common application of this arrangement was in the Ariel Square Four models. These were all four-stroke engines, and in their final form offered the then remarkable capacity of 1000 cc. Much more recently, the square four arrangement has been used very successfully in two-stroke racing engines to permit rotary valve induction, and found its way onto the roads in the form of the Suzuki RG500.

The main problem of the square four is that of cooling the rear cylinders. If air-cooled, the front pair of cylinders effectively mask those at the rear, and even with carefully designed finning, overheating tends to become evident in traffic. Liquid-cooling is one way to resolve the problem, but this means additional weight and complexity.

### The V-four

Yet another way of arranging four cylinders, the V-four offers an alternative to the square four in terms of compactness, but avoids some of its overheating problems by having the rear cylinders slightly more exposed to the airstream (though again liquid-cooling is the only really efficient way of running them) **(see illustration 1.20e)**.

In general, the V-four is no more than a doubled-up V-twin, and thus most of the remarks applicable to the latter can also be applied here. It is possible to arrange the crankshaft with the two crankpins lying parallel (forming a 360° crankshaft), and this is the best arrangement in terms of minimising vibration and eliminating rocking couple. Another approach is to arrange the crankpins at 180° to each other. Whilst the resulting vibration is higher, this is offset by the more regular firing of the four cylinders (every 180°). As with V-twins, the optimum angle for the cylinders is 90°, but reduced angles can work as well.

Though a complex engine in terms of maintenance and a costly one in terms of manufacturing, the V-four has become popular through its extensive use in Honda's VFR range, and has achieved racing success in the forms of the RC30 and RC45. Other notable uses of the V-four have been in Yamaha's 1200 cc V-Max and their two-stroke RD500, and of course the two-stroke V-fours used in GP racing.

Surely the most technologically advanced V-four must be Honda's limited edition NR750. Using build technology and materials from the aircraft industry Honda designed a 32 valve oval-pistoned engine in the V-four configuration.

### 21 Engine arrangements – more than four cylinders

In the preceding Sections we have seen the various ways in which engine designers have improved on the basic single cylinder unit in terms of power output and vibration levels in an attempt to build the perfect engine. But long ago they discovered that an improvement in one area usually means a drawback in another, what is good for one type of motorcycle is no good for another. This is a limitation of the reciprocating engine and demands careful choices and compromises to be made at the design stage if the desired characteristics for the particular machine are to be obtained.

If you stop to think about it, the sheer variety of engine arrangements is itself indicative of the designers' dilemma; there is no ideal engine. If there were, it is safe to assume that all manufacturers would use it exclusively, but in reality the best that can be achieved is to select the one which comes closest to fulfilling the requirements of a particular application, and then to incorporate those modifications or improvements that offset the more significant drawbacks. This approach has led to the major motorcycle engine designs discussed previously, and has also generated some less common alternatives.

In the main, these have had too few advantages over existing arrangements to gain wide acceptance, or have suffered the motorcyclist's traditional distrust of change. In the examples below, some, like the V-three two-stroke previously mentioned, may disappear without trace in the coming years, while others, like the new V-five four-stroke,

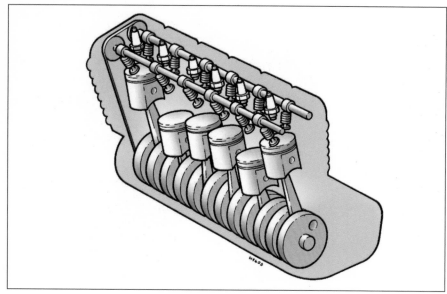

**1.21 The in-line six**

could offer the first real challenge to the in-line four, the V-four and the V-twin.

### The V-five

With the introduction of four-strokes into GP racing in 2002, manufacturers have turned their attention to developing machines to comply with the various engine size and weight restrictions. Honda have concluded that the ideal arrangement, given those restrictions, is a V-five. With three cylinders at the front and two at the back and the crankshaft running across the frame, it mimics the old V-three two-stroke and is an extremely compact unit.

It is not the first five cylinder motorcycle engine to have been built, even though they are very popular in the car world. In 1965 Honda (again) built an in-line five two-stroke that was capable of revving to 20,000 rpm.

### The in-line six

One way of reducing still further the vibration of the in-line four is to add yet more cylinders **(see illustration 1.21)**. With careful design most of the primary and secondary forces can be balanced out, making the six a notably smooth unit. The six's relatively tiny pistons produce a smooth flow of power and thus it is not necessary to employ large and unresponsive flywheels. The price for this smoothness is mechanical complexity, cost and the sheer and unavoidable width of the engine unit.

The most well known of the six-cylinder motorcycles must be Honda's CBX1000 models. Kawasaki have also tried an in-line six in the shape of their Z1300, which was conceived at the outset as a fast touring machine, and featured liquid-cooling and shaft drive in its specification. Of the European manufacturers, only Benelli saw fit to explore the potential of the in-line six with

their 750 cc Sei and were the first to market a production model.

### The horizontally-opposed six

In 1988 Honda further developed their 1200 cc horizontally-opposed four cylinder engine by added two more cylinders and an extra 300 cc. The resulting 1500 cc engine, also known as a 'flat six', is the engine used in their Gold Wing models up to 2001 when its capacity was increased once again to become an 1800 cc unit. Like its predecessor, it is just about the only example of this arrangement in the motorcycle world.

### The V-8

The V-eight, surely the ultimate engine, has been extremely popular for years as a smooth and powerful car engine, but due to its size and complexity has rarely been found on mass production motorcycles. The Norton V-8 Nemesis represents the latest venture in this direction.

Like most things, the V-eight has already been tried in a motorcycle and one of the most successful was from Moto Guzzi, who in 1955 produced a 500 cc V-8 engine that was way ahead of its time. It even had magnesium crankcases. Unfortunately the frame and tyres were never good enough for the engine and the bike suffered from poor handling. It had its best racing successes in 1957, and was clocked at an unbelievable 178 mph along the Masta straight at Spa in Belgium.

## 22 The search for more power – bore and stroke

In looking at the various common engine arrangements we have seen how there has always been a dilemma facing the engine

designer. Essentially, the engine should be as simple as possible, and thus cheap to manufacture and reliable in use. This approach was most evident in the post-war years where cost effectiveness was a major requirement of any successful motorcycle, and is a major reason for the popularity of the single cylinder engine for many years. Whilst the same requirements remain today in the moped and commuter bike markets, the purpose of the motorcycle in a general sense has evolved. Although it is still used by many as basic transport, it is no longer the case that the main requirement is cheapness and reliability; performance is the main criteria of today's average motorcyclist.

The most obvious way to obtain more power from any engine is to increase its capacity, bearing in mind the considerations discussed in the preceding Sections. Traditionally, however, there have also been very good reasons to concentrate on extracting more power from an engine of a given size. The main one of these in many countries is legislation which often dictates a capacity limit for riders of a certain age or ability. Even where legislation is less restrictive, the cost of insurance increases with a machine's capacity, providing a self-imposed capacity limit for many people. Equally important is the manufacturer's problem of convincing you that his 600 cc four is better than all the others, and the best way to do this is to make it go faster/accelerate quicker/look better than its rivals.

We have already seen some of the modifications to the basic two-stroke and four-stroke designs which attempt to make them more efficient in use. Additionally, there are factors which influence the way in which the engine's power is delivered, notably the choice of bore size and the length of the piston's stroke. For any given cylinder capacity there are a number of bore and stroke combinations which may be chosen **(see illustration 1.22)**. In our theoretical engine we could arrange to have the bore diameter equal to the length of the piston stroke, an arrangement known as 'square'. If we increase the stroke and reduce the bore size the engine becomes under-square, or long-stroke, whilst at the other extreme a large bore size could be used in combination with a short stroke to produce an 'over-square' or short-stroke engine.

Before we go any further, two more essential pieces of terminology, bhp and torque, must be considered. Bhp (brake horsepower) is the unit used to measure the power produced by an engine at any given speed. Torque can be interpreted most easily as the 'pulling power' of the engine. These two values are established by testing the engine on a device known as a dynamometer over a wide range of engine speeds; from the readings thus obtained the bhp and torque outputs can be plotted as a graph. Without going into the complex mathematics involved,

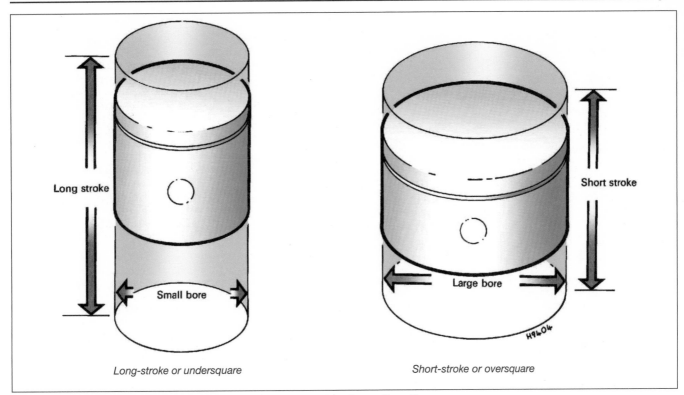

Long stroke

Small bore

*Long-stroke or undersquare*

Short stroke

Large bore

H9604

*Short-stroke or oversquare*

**1.22 Bore and stroke configurations**

the advantages and disadvantages of the various arrangements can be summarised as follows.

### Long-stroke

The long-stroke engine is characterised by its flat spread of torque across a wide range of engine speeds. The torque is the result of the relatively high leverage exerted on the long connecting rod and is what allows a long-stroke engine to pull strongly from low speeds. The torque curve, if plotted, would show a gentle increase as the engine speed rises, reaching a peak after which it begins to reduce. Given that the engine is at its most efficient when maximum torque is being produced it is obviously desirable to have as flat a torque curve as possible, and in this respect the long-stroke engine excels.

Where the long-stroke engine loses out is in the overall power available, measured in brake horsepower (bhp). This is very low at low engine speeds, rising in a steep curve and tailing off only at very high speeds. In this respect we need the engine to turn as fast as possible to obtain the maximum amount of power from it, and it is here that the long-stroke is less than convenient; the high piston speed imposes a limitation above which rapid engine wear or damage would result, so this in turn restricts the amount of power available.

### Short-stroke

The short stroke engine can run at higher speeds than can a long-stroke design of

similar capacity, and so it is possible to extract more power strokes (and thus more power) in a given time. The drawback is that the shorter stroke means less leverage on the crankshaft, and this in turn dictates a steeper torque curve. In this way the short-stroke is more powerful, but over a narrower band of engine speeds.

As you will no doubt have guessed, the answer is a compromise between the two extremes, namely the 'square' engine described above. In practice, many modern motorcycle engines are nearly square in arrangement with slight variations to suit particular applications, though with sports bikes being so popular, short-stroke engines have increased in number to give buyers as much power as they need on paper, even though, on machines above 600 cc, they are unlikely to be able to use it all on the roads.

## 23 The rotary engine

### History

The simplest example of a rotary engine is the turbine. This is an excellent engine for ships, aeroplanes and helicopters, but isn't well suited to the varying speed requirement of motorcycles (though having said that, there is currently a motorcycle being produced which uses the engine form a helicopter - it is

capable of ridiculous speeds and ticks over at around 20,000 rpm!).

In the 1920's Dr. Felix Wankel propounded the theory of the engine that now bears his name. The first practical use of the idea came in the 1950's when a supercharger working on the Wankel principle was used to boost the power of a 125 cc four-stroke engine fitted in an N.S.U. record breaking motorcycle. The N.S.U. company held the patents on Wankel designs, and fitted the first production engine in a small sports car in the mid 1960's. This was followed by the N.S.U. Ro80 car, an ambitious project which effectively bankrupted the company. N.S.U. sold licenses for Wankel engine production to many firms world-wide, and the fruits of these licensing agreements of the late 1960's and early 1970's are the series of Mazda sports cars and the motorcycles and industrial engines made by Norton. Other Wankel engined motorcycles have been made by Suzuki (the RE5), DKW/Hercules (the W2000) and Van Veen.

### How it works

The engine works because of the shape of the rotor and the chamber in which it rotates. The rotor shape is a 'trochoid' and the chamber is an 'epi-trochoid'. When the rotor traces a circular orbit in the chamber, its corners are in contact with the chamber wall all the time. This means that, while rotating, the rotor divides the space within the chamber into three parts, each expanding

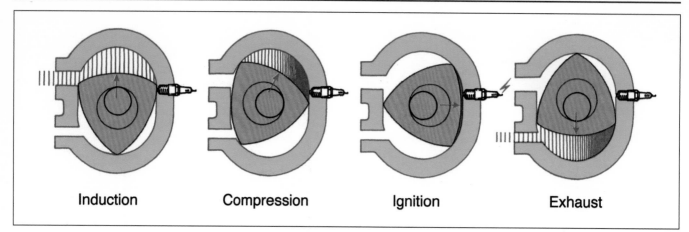

**Induction**     **Compression**     **Ignition**     **Exhaust**

**1.23 Rotary engine cycles**

and contracting in volume as the rotor turns, and each face of the rotor acting like a piston.

The rotation is controlled by an internal gear in the side face of the rotor, which meshes with a smaller gear on the plate that forms the side of the chamber. These gears permit the rotor to turn in a circular orbit, centred on the engine shaft. A circular lobe mounted eccentrically on the engine shaft fits in a bearing in the centre of the rotor. The movement of the rotor pulls the shaft round.

The four essential events (induction, compression, ignition, and exhaust) of the internal combustion engine must also occur in a rotary engine. But instead of being spread over two or four strokes, they all occur within one revolution of the rotor **(see illustration 1.23)**. As the rotor has three sides, each acting like a piston, three complete cycles occur and so three power strokes are produced for every revolution of the rotor.

Holes cut in the chamber wall act as inlet and exhaust ports, similar to those in a two-stroke engine. The mixture drawn in travels around the chamber with the rotor, being compressed and ignited by the spark plug. The high pressure gas produced presses on the rotor face and turns the engine shaft via the eccentric, but during this time the gearing between rotor and casing causes the shaft to make three revolutions.

The rotary engine eliminates the reciprocating movement of components that create out of balance forces. Consequently it is easy to balance, having only centrifugal forces to deal with, and can be built light as there is less stress imparted on it. The end result is an extremely smooth engine. The drawbacks with them are the poor combustion chamber shape which inhibits flame spread, the need for special spark plugs, and high rotor tip seal wear (the tips seal the combustion chamber, so wear causes loss of compression and gas blowby).

# Chapter 2
## Fuel system and exhaust

## Contents

### 1 Introduction

Chapter 1 covered the basic mechanical components of the internal combustion engine and the ways in which these could be arranged to suit various motorcycle applications. Common to all of these designs is the need to control precisely and accurately the flow of the fuel/air mixture through the engine. This Chapter covers the process of mixing the fuel and air in the correct proportions, delivering this mixture to the cylinder(s) in the correct volume for the required engine speed, and disposing of the residual gases after combustion has been completed.

Though it is common to separate the functions of induction and exhaust, it is valuable to consider them as a single process in which the energy in the fuel is extracted and turned into useful work, and its by-products, heat and noise, are then removed.

This Chapter tackles the basic theories, principles and methods of fuelling. The subject is covered in greater detail and depth in the *Haynes Motorcycle Fuel Systems Techbook*.

### Fuel

The universal choice of fuel for road-going motorcycles is petrol (gasoline), although diesel-fuelled motorcycle engines have been developed. There are a number of other possibilities which we might use instead, but these are either more expensive or less efficient. Petrol is a fraction of crude oil, that internationally important and finite commodity found in deposits below the earth's surface. The crude oil is broken down in refineries by distillation, a process involving heating the crude oil and condensing various fractions as they rise up through a tower divided into temperature-controlled galleries.

The choice of petrol as a fuel is governed by a compromise of two qualities, its calorific value (CV) and its volatility. The CV of a fuel is the amount of heat energy, and thus the useful work, that can be obtained from a given quantity. The volatility of a fuel is a measure of how easily it will evaporate at low temperatures. Ideally an internal combustion engine requires a reasonably volatile fuel with a high CV. However as the CV rises, so the volatility falls, and the lower the volatility of the fuel the more difficult it is to burn, and hence the need for a compromise.

Having chosen a fuel it is necessary to find out in what ratio it must be mixed with air to ensure complete and efficient combustion; too little air means unburnt fuel will be expelled with the exhaust gases, whilst too much air means valuable energy (in the form of fuel) will be excluded from the cylinder.

Complete combustion requires air and fuel in the ratio 14.7:1, and this is known as the Stoichiometric air/fuel ratio, though greatest power is developed with a 0 to 10% air deficiency (a slightly 'rich' mixture), and greatest economy is obtained at a 0 to 10% air surplus (a slightly 'lean' mixture). In practice though, the design of the engine and its combustion characteristics have an influence on the optimum ratio, as do atmospheric conditions.

The car world is seeing the introduction of 'lean burn' engines that can run at a relatively high air/fuel ratio, and unbelievable fuel economy is being achieved. In general, the practical limits for successful combustion are between 12:1 and 18:1. Now all we need is a reliable method of delivering this mixture to the engine.

### The fuel system

The fuel system is responsible for storing the fuel and delivering it to the carburettors or injectors.

The fuel is stored in a tank, and is fed either by gravity or under pressure using a pump, via a strainer and a filter, down the fuel pipes to the carburettors or injectors. If a fuel pump is used, it is either housed inside the tank itself or fitted in the fuel line outside the tank. Similarly, although the fuel strainer is always inside the tank, the filter could be either inside or outside in the fuel line.

In most cases a fuel tap is used to allow or stop the flow of fuel from the tank, and this is either manually operated or actuated by a vacuum acting on a diaphragm. Some modern systems using fuel injection do not have a tap as such, and flow is controlled only by the pump. The fuel system components are covered in greater detail in Section 9.

### Mixing fuel and air

Carburation is the process of charging air with a spray of liquid hydrocarbon fuel. The carburettor is still the most common method of mixing and controlling the fuel and air in motorcycles, although is beginning to give way to fuel injection systems. The Sections

which follow look at how the carburettor mixes the fuel in the correct proportions, how it is used to control the speed of the engine and how it can adjust to the varying loads imposed on the engine, and how these and other demands have lead to the development or different types of carburettor.

Fuel injection, is now commonplace on many new motorcycles, where carburettor development has been unable to keep pace with engine design and the demand for more powerful engines. Additionally fuel injection provides an easier means of complying with stringent emission regulations. Refer to Section 7 for details of the fuel injection system types and operation.

### The intake system

This rather broad description covers the various components, other than the carburettor or fuel injector, which are concerned with the intake side of the process. These include the air filter, the function of which needs little explanation, and the casing in which it is housed, known as the airbox.

Whereas the airbox used to be nothing more than a housing for the filter, nowadays it often now takes the form of a carefully shaped container known as a Plenum Chamber, and in conjunction with intake or 'ram air' ducts performs the additional job of silencing, controlling and pressurising the incoming air. We should not forget the intake port itself in the cylinder head. Although this is part of the engine, its diameter, shape and length are influential in controlling the incoming mixture, and so it must work in conjunction with the carburettor or injector.

On performance machines, carburettors are often mounted almost horizontally so that the

intake duct can be as straight as possible, meaning it has to be almost vertical, giving the added advantage that the fuel/air mixture is not as affected by gravity as it would be travelling along a horizontal duct.

The airbox, air filter and air induction systems are covered in Section 10.

### The exhaust system

The exhaust system, as its name implies, conducts the spent gases from the combustion chamber to the outside world. In addition to this, the explosive exhaust pulses must be subdued to a tolerable level by the silencer.

Another function of the exhaust system is to improve the scavenging efficiency, and this is obviously of great significance in two-stroke engines. Since this in turn affects the intake system and carburation we should view all the above components and systems as part of one overall system which starts at the air intake and finishes at the exhaust silencer.

### 2  How carburettors work

### The basic principle

The basic operating principle of any carburettor is the 'venturi' effect. A venturi is little more than a specially-shaped tube, and it works in the following way. If air is drawn through a normal tube with parallel walls it will remain at a constant pressure and velocity along its length, as might be expected. If we now make a reduction in size somewhere in the tube, the air-flow characteristics will be modified; at the point of maximum reduction in size the air-flow will increase in speed, and at the same time its pressure will fall. Thus at the smallest point in the tube there exists a slight vacuum. A venturi is precisely this; a tube with a restriction. In the interests of good gas flow, the restriction becomes progressively greater to its maximum point and then gradually opens out again.

In the accompanying line drawing is a simple venturi in cross-section **(see illustration 2.2a)**. You will note that at the point of maximum restriction we have added a small drilling with a tube in it going into a reservoir of fuel. A combination of the low pressure area (or vacuum) in the venturi and the higher atmospheric pressure which is maintained in the fuel reservoir moves the fuel up and out of the drilling, where it disperses into the airstream in tiny droplets. If the drilling is fitted with a nozzle (known as a 'jet') of such a size that one part of fuel enters for every fourteen of air we have a very crude but effective carburettor. Fit this device to an engine, which will draw the air through the venturi as the piston moves down, and the mixture necessary for combustion will be provided. Easy isn't it?

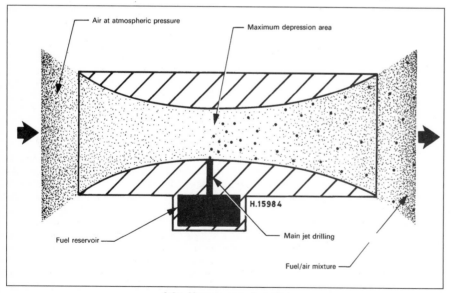

Air at atmospheric pressure

Maximum depression area

H.15984

Fuel reservoir

Main jet drilling

Fuel/air mixture

**2.2a  How a venturi works**

*As air flows through the venturi, the restriction causes it to speed up and so its pressure is reduced. This low pressure area, in conjunction with the higher atmospheric pressure in the fuel reservoir, is used to draw fuel through the tube in the drilling at the centre of the venturi, and the emerging fuel is atomised as it mixes in the airstream.*

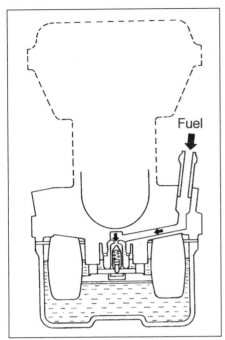

**2.2b  The float assembly maintains a constant level of fuel in the chamber**

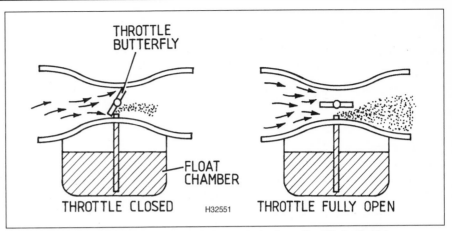

**2.2c  Varying air flow through the venturi using a throttle 'butterfly'**

So why aren't all motorcycles fitted with this pleasantly simple and foolproof device? The answer is that it cannot do all that we require of a carburettor; it would be quite sufficient for a simple engine running at constant speed and loading, but for most applications we need a more sophisticated device.

### The float assembly

To ensure consistent operation a carburettor needs a constant supply of fuel kept at a constant level in the reservoir. This job is done by the float assembly, housed in the float chamber (previously referred to as the fuel reservoir, and also known as the float 'bowl') below the main jet drilling.

If you want to see an example of how the float system works, go into the bathroom and take the top off the WC cistern. Inside you will see the float, an arm connecting it to a valve and a cistern full of water. Flush the WC and the water level falls and with it the float. This opens the valve and the cistern fills with water until the rising float closes the valve again. The carburettor float valve assembly does exactly the same job, keeping the fuel level constant **(see illustration 2.2b)**.

### The throttle

To be able to control the speed of the engine we need some sort of movable obstruction to vary the amount of fuel/air mixture entering the engine. This can be achieved using a circular plate (known as a 'butterfly'), supported on a movable spindle, in the venturi **(see illustration 2.2c)**. If the plate is turned so that it blocks the venturi, the air-flow is stopped (and with it the engine).

Turn the spindle and the plate will allow air to pass until, when it is at right-angles, it offers little restriction. This arrangement is known as a butterfly throttle, and is used on fixed venturi carburettors (Section 3).

Another method is to have a movable throttle valve (or slide) housed in a vertical extension of the venturi **(see illustration 2.2d)**. The slide is able to rise or fall so that it partially or completely blocks the airflow through the carburettor, effectively varying the size of the venturi and so controlling the opening of the carburettor. This arrangement is known as a slide throttle, and is used on slide carburettors (Section 4).

A combination of the two is used on CV carburettors (Section 5). Slide and CV carburettors are known collectively as variable venturi carburettors.

Control of the throttle is achieved by having a cable which links the butterfly or slide to the throttle pulley (known as a 'twistgrip') on the handlebar. A return spring is fitted so that the throttle automatically closes when the twistgrip is released.

### Starter circuit (cold starting)

The fuel in the incoming mixture needs to be in a finely vaporised form for successful combustion. When the engine is cold, the fuel condenses on the cold metal in the engine, so that it is no longer vaporised, and consequently the engine will be very difficult to start. To compensate for this we have to make the incoming mixture very much richer in fuel than normal.

This can be achieved in three ways: firstly by manually depressing (or 'tickling') the float to get more fuel in the chamber, secondly by cutting off (or 'choking') the venturi, and thirdly by supplying more fuel through a separate cold-start (or 'enrichment') circuit. All systems tend to be known as 'chokes', but

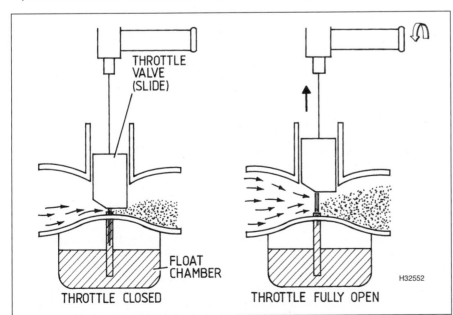

**2.2d  Varying the size of the venturi using a throttle slide**

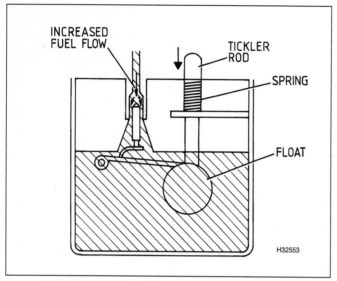

2.2e The 'tickler' system for cold-start enrichment

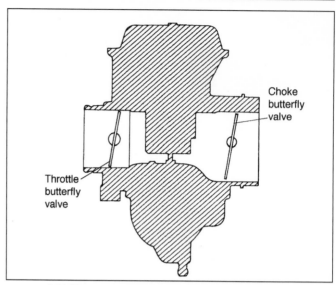

2.2f The 'choke' system for cold start enrichment

strictly speaking it is only the second system that works by 'choking' the venturi.

Once the engine has started it will begin to warm up, and eventually it will be necessary to turn off the cold start device to prevent the engine being flooded by the excess fuel.

### The tickler

A spring loaded rod is in direct contact with the float **(see illustration 2.2e)**. When the rod is manually depressed, more fuel is allowed into the float chamber, and so the fuel level rises above its normal level. This means that less vacuum is needed to draw up the normal amount of fuel. However as the vacuum

created has not changed, more fuel than normal is drawn into the venturi, and so the mixture becomes richer.

The tickler is a fairly crude method of enriching the mixture, and though it was once widely used on motorcycles, nowadays it is only seen on basic lawnmower engines.

### The choke

A butterfly valve in the mouth of the venturi is used to stop most of the air getting in, so that when the engine is turned over the pressure in the venturi becomes much lower than normal, thus increasing the proportion of fuel that is drawn up **(see illustration 2.2f)**.

### The enrichment circuit

This system works on the same principle as the choke, but uses a separate circuit within the carburettor to provide the rich fuel/air mixture. A 'choke' lever or knob is connected, usually by cable but sometimes by a linkage, to a plunger which opens and closes the enrichment circuit **(see illustration 2.2g)**. When the circuit is open and the engine is turned over (with the throttle closed), air is drawn in via a passage in the mouth of the carburettor that by-passes the main venturi, and this picks up fuel from the float chamber via a starter jet. The fuel/air mixture is then

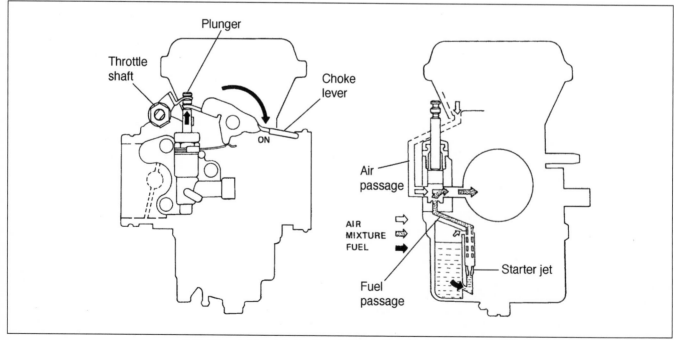

2.2g The enrichment circuit as used on all modern carburettors

discharged into the throat of the carburettor via a port situated beyond the venturi and the throttle.

On the illustration you will notice that the plunger is linked to the throttle shaft (though on other types it may be linked to the throttle stop), meaning that when the enrichment circuit is opened, the throttle also opens a little. This is mainly because an engine will idle very poorly with a rich mixture unless the engine speed is raised to between 2000 and 3000 rpm, and also because it helps to get the lubricating oil circulated quicker. Early and crude versions do not have the direct link with the throttle, and so the throttle has to be opened manually if the enrichment circuit is left open while the engine warms up.

### The automatic choke

Though not essential to the operation of the carburettor, an automatic choke is an increasingly common feature on mopeds and scooters.

In its simplest form, some moped carburettors have a small cam arrangement which shuts off the choke lever if the throttle is opened beyond a certain point.

On more sophisticated models a temperature-sensitive choke unit is fitted, but it works off the temperature of the choke unit itself, which has an electric heater, rather than the temperature of the engine. When the choke unit itself is cold, the enrichment circuit is always open, allowing a rich mixture (see illustrations 2.2h and i). When the engine is started, a current is supplied to a heater element in the choke unit. The unit has either a bi-metallic strip which bends when heated, or a wax-filled chamber which expands when heated, and this acts on a plunger which gradually closes off the enrichment circuit as the choke unit and the engine warm up.

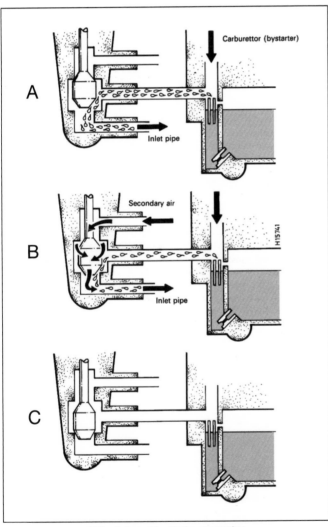

**2.2h Automatic choke operation**

**A** *When the engine is started from cold, an enriched-mixture is drawn through the by-starter chamber and supplements the mixture from the carburettor. At the same time, a current is supplied to the choke unit.*

**B** *As the engine begins to warm up, the bimetal strip bends or the wax expands and so begins to open the valve, allowing extra or secondary air to enter the system. This means that the enriched mixture is diluted with air, giving a semi-rich mixture.*

**C** *When the engine is warm, the valve opens fully, closing off the cold start circuit.*

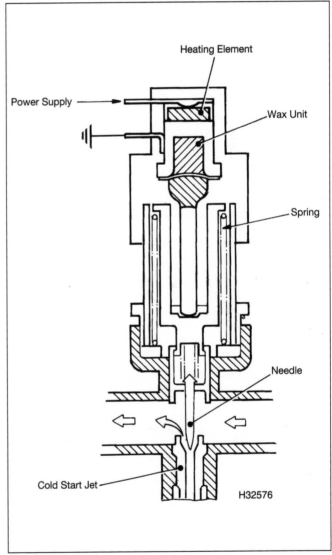

**2.2i Automatic choke operation**

*In this example, the needle is fully retracted when cold, allowing a full amount of fuel out of the cold-start jet to mix with the air and the fuel from the normal running jets, creating a rich mixture. As the engine warms and the wax heats up and expands, the needle slowly drops, progressively reducing the amount of fuel out of the cold-start jet, thereby progressively weakening the mixture, until the jet is completely cut out by the needle when the engine is warm.*

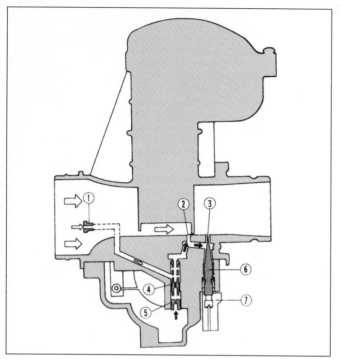

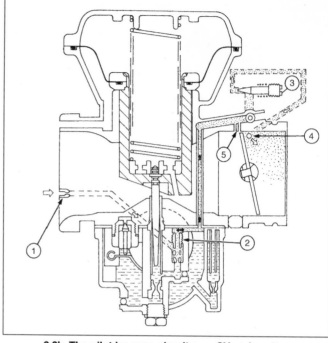

**2.2j Cross-section of a slide carburettor showing the pilot circuit**

1  Pilot air jet
2  Air bypass outlet
3  Pilot outlet
4  Secondary pilot jet
5  Primary pilot jet
6  Pilot screw
7  Limiter cap (fitted to prevent tampering)

**2.2k The pilot by-pass circuit on a CV carburettor**

1  Pilot air jet
2  Pilot jet
3  Pilot screw
4  Pilot outlet port
5  Pilot bypass ports

## The pilot circuit

For a carburettor to operate over a wide range of engine speeds a single running circuit using one jet size will not be adequate.

At very low speeds, the depression (the partial vacuum) in the venturi is not enough to lift the correct amount of fuel through the jet, so the engine will falter and die. To compensate for this a separate circuit for running the engine at low speeds (from closed to 1/8 throttle) is incorporated, and is known most commonly as the pilot circuit, but also as the slow-running or idle circuit **(see illustration 2.2j)**.

In much the same way as the enrichment circuit described above, air is drawn in via a passage in the mouth of the carburettor that by-passes the main venturi, and this mixes with fuel from the float chamber which is drawn up via a pilot jet. The fuel/air mixture is then discharged into the throat of the carburettor via a port situated beyond the venturi and the throttle. As there is always a small amount of opening left in the venturi even with the throttle shut there is a localised venturi effect which is used to draw in the pilot mixture. As the throttle opens this effect is lost and the other circuits take over.

## The cutaway circuit (slide carburettors)

If the bottom of the slide were left flat there would be an interval between the influence of the pilot circuit and that of the main circuits. To avoid this, the leading edge of the slide is machined at an angle, emphasising the venturi effect between the slide and the venturi at intermediate (1/8 to 1/4) throttle openings.

## The pilot bypass circuit (fixed venturi and CV carburettors)

This is the equivalent of the cutaway circuit on the slide carburettor in that it meters fuel from off-idle to a small throttle opening **(see illustration 2.2k)**. The pilot circuit has two extra discharge ports, known as bypass ports, positioned so they are just inside the butterfly when it is fully closed. When the throttle is opened a little way, the rim of the butterfly passes each port in turn, allowing airflow past which draws out the fuel.

## The needle circuit (slide and CV carburettors)

To provide variable fuel/air metering between 1/4 and 3/4 throttle openings, a tapered needle hangs from the bottom of the throttle slide and passes down into the needle jet. The needle jet is sometimes positioned so that it is flush with the venturi, though more often it projects slightly into it. The reason it projects is to create localised disturbance which helps to diffuse and atomise the fuel in the air.

The main jet, which is chosen so that it is of the correct size at full throttle, screws into the bottom of the needle jet. At 1/4 to 3/4 throttle openings, while the needle is in the jet, the gap between the needle and the wall of the jet is considerably less than the size of the main jet, and so the fuel flow is controlled by the needle jet **(see illustration 2.2l)**. As the throttle is opened and the needle rises, the gap widens due to the taper of the needle and the needle jet allows more fuel to pass through it, and is thus able to adjust to the increased demand.

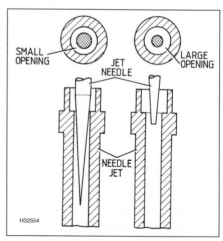

**2.2l As the needle rises it constantly increases the amount of fuel it lets past**

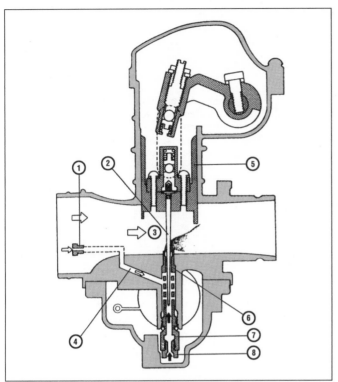

**2.2m Cross-section of a typical slide carburettor showing all basic circuits**

| 1 | Main air jet | 5 | Throttle slide |
|---|---|---|---|
| 2 | Jet needle | 6 | Needle jet |
| 3 | Venturi | 7 | Air bleed pipe |
| 4 | Air passage | 8 | Main jet |

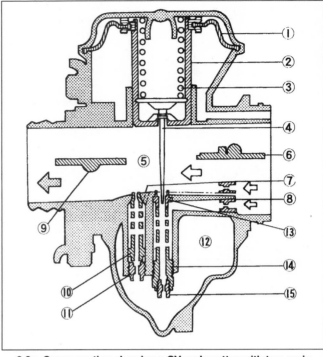

**2.2n Cross-section showing a CV carburettor with two main circuits**

| 1 | Diaphragm | 7 | Primary main air jet | 11 | Primary main jet |
|---|---|---|---|---|---|
| 2 | Throttle piston | | | 12 | Float chamber |
| 3 | Spring | 8 | Secondary main air jet | 13 | Needle jet |
| 4 | Jet needle | | | 14 | Needle jet holder |
| 5 | Venturi | 9 | Throttle valve | 15 | Secondary main jet |
| 6 | Choke valve | 10 | Bleed pipe | | |

## The main circuit

On slide and CV carburettors, from about 3/4 to full throttle, the needle tapers off and the gap between it and the jet exceeds that of the main jet, and so control is passed to the main jet (see illustration 2.2m). On some carburettors, where it is advantageous, there are two main circuits, a primary and a secondary (see illustration 2.2n). The primary main circuit is operating from the moment the slide or piston rises, whereas the secondary main circuit is governed by the needle rising out of it in the same way as the main circuit on a standard carburettor.

On fixed venturi carburettors, as there is no needle circuit, there are often two or more main circuits, and there are a few CV carburettors that also have two main circuits. Sometimes an extra main circuit is achieved using what is known as a 'power jet' (see illustration 2.2o). This is simply an extra main jet in a tube from the float chamber, but the tube is positioned upstream from the throttle slide and projects significantly into the venturi so that the venturi effect only reaches the discharge nozzle when the throttle slide is high enough to allow it.

## The emulsion tube

On many (but not all) carburettors, if you study a needle jet closely, you will see that the

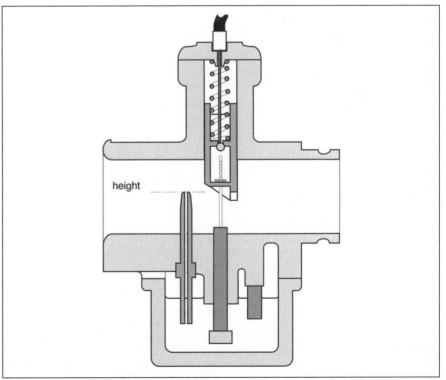

height

**2.2o Cross-section showing the positioning of a power or high speed jet**

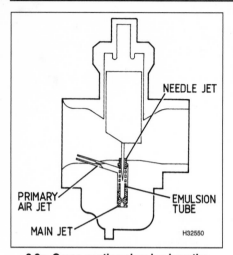

**2.2p Cross-section showing how the emulsion tube pre-mixes the fuel with a small amount of air**

wall of the jet is perforated with many small holes, and that there is a space between the wall of the jet and the drilling which houses it **(see illustration 2.2p)**. This portion of the needle jet is known as the emulsion tube.

There is also a narrow air passage, known as the primary air circuit, in the mouth of the carburettor which directs a small amount of air (metered by an air jet) into the chamber created by the space. The small holes allow the fuel and air to pre-mix (or emulsify) so that the process of atomising the fuel is made more efficient. Many pilot circuits incorporate the same system.

### The accelerator pump (fixed venturi and slide carburettors)

Fitting an accelerator pump overcomes the inherent problem of a sudden weak mixture when the throttle is snapped open. The pump enriches the mixture at the required moment and by the right amount, which is dictated by how far the throttle is opened.

On some carburettors, the pump is operated by the throttle slide acting on a lever **(see illustration 2.2q)**, while on others a cam on the throttle shaft acts on a rod **(see illustration 2.2r)**. In both cases, the lever or rod then acts on a diaphragm pump which squirts or sprays a measure of fuel into the venturi.

### The air cut-off valve (slide and CV carburettors)

Many carburettors are fitted with an air-cut off valve, which prevents after-burn, the popping through the exhaust that sometimes occurs under engine braking after the throttle has been closed **(see illustration 2.5b)**. This occurs because when the throttle is closed, the mixture becomes weak.

### Carburettor warming systems (slide and CV carburettors)

Many carburettors are fitted with a warming device to prevent carburettor 'icing'. Icing can occur in conditions of high humidity and low air temperatures (around 4 to 5°C), and happens because of the refrigeration effect on the water in the air when the fuel vaporises. It can lead to ice forming in the throat of the carburettor, which could cover the pilot circuit outlets, causing stalling or poor performance, and could cause the throttle butterfly to stick on CV carburettors.

Oil companies put anti-icing additives into petrol (gasoline), but this is not always enough to prevent it. To make sure some manufactures incorporate a warming system, either by fitting a small electrical heating element in each carburettor, or by circulating engine coolant around the carburettor. The heating elements have the advantage of being effective when the engine is cold.

### Throttle position sensor (slide and CV carburettors)

Many modern bikes now have a throttle position sensor (TPS). These have no effect on the fuel metering process, but are used

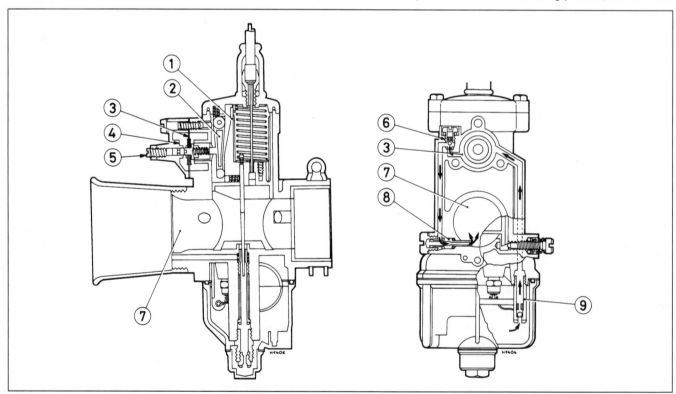

**2.2q Accelerator pump operation**

*In this example of a Dell'Orto PHF accelerator pump, the rising throttle slide (1) presses the lever (2), pushing the pump diaphragm (3). Fuel in the diaphragm chamber (4) is forced past the non-return valve (6) and is sprayed into the venturi (7) via a discharge nozzle (8). The amount of diaphragm movement and hence the amount of fuel is controlled by the adjusting screw (5). When the throttle is closed, the diaphragm returns under spring pressure and the non-return valve closes. The movement of the diaphragm creates a suction which opens the inlet valve (9), allowing fuel from the float chamber to fill the diaphragm chamber.*

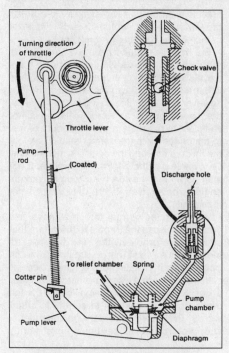

**2.2r Accelerator pump operation**

*In this example of an accelerator pump the pump rod attached to the throttle lever acts on a diaphragm via the pump lever. Otherwise the principle of operation is the same as with the Dell'Orto.*

instead to provide the control unit for the electronic ignition system with information regarding throttle position, movement (i.e. opening or closing) and rate of movement (i.e. how quickly the throttle is being opened) to optimise ignition timing. Ignition systems and ignition timing are covered in Chapter 3.

## 3 Carburettor design – the fixed venturi carburettor

As mentioned earlier there are three types of carburettor used in motorcycles, of which the fixed venturi is the least common. Harley-Davidson used them across their range for a while, and Suzuki fitted one to the rotary-engined RE5, and apart from a few other exceptions, they were mainly found on car engines (until fuel injection took over). It is known as a fixed venturi type, simply because the profile of the venturi remains constant at all times, even though the throttle butterfly varies the amount of air allowed through it **(see illustration 2.2c)**.

Fixed venturi carburettors incorporate a choke type cold start circuit, which uses a second butterfly valve in the mouth of the carburettor to cut off the air, and a pilot circuit, much the same as other carburettors **(see illustration 2.3)**. But due to the limitations of the butterfly in varying the

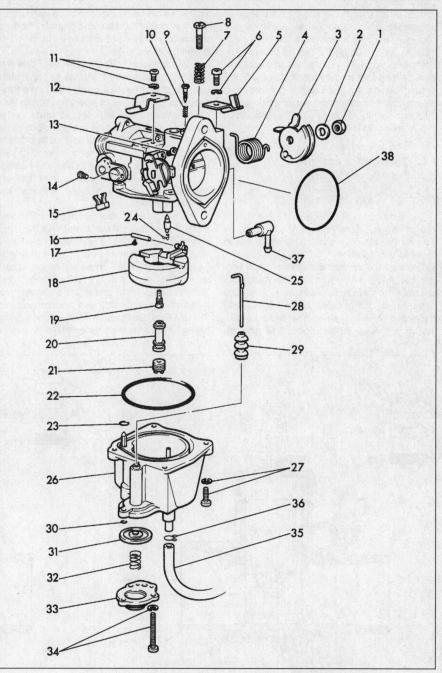

**2.3 Exploded view of a Keihin fixed venturi carburettor**

| | | |
|---|---|---|
| 1 Nut | 14 Screw | 27 Screw/washer |
| 2 Washer | 15 Spacer clip | 28 Accelerator pump rod |
| 3 Throttle pulley | 16 Float pivot pin | 29 Rubber boot |
| 4 Return spring | 17 Grub screw | 30 O-ring |
| 5 Throttle cable bracket | 18 Float | 31 Accelerator pump |
| 6 Screw/washer | 19 Pilot jet | diaphragm |
| 7 Spring | 20 Main nozzle | 32 Spring |
| 8 Throttle stop screw | 21 Main jet | 33 Accelerator pump cover |
| 9 Idle mixture screw | 22 O-ring | 34 Screw/washer |
| 10 Spring | 23 O-ring | 35 Overflow hose |
| 11 Screw/washer | 24 Float needle valve clip | 36 Clip |
| 12 Choke cable bracket | 25 Float needle valve | 37 Hose union |
| 13 Accelerator pump | 26 Float chamber | 38 O-ring |
| adjustment screw | | |

venturi effect, and because of the lack of needle jet, it is usually necessary to have a pilot by-pass circuit and more than one main circuit jet (usually called secondary or compensating jets) positioned and sized to provide a correct mixture for all speeds. There is also usually an accelerator pump circuit which compensates for rapid changes in throttle opening which would otherwise result in a weak mixture.

## 4 Carburettor design – the slide carburettor

The slide carburettor tackles the problem of the changing demands of the engine by varying the effective size of the venturi **(see illustrations 2.2d)**.

The variable venturi, coupled with the way the rate of fuel delivery through the main jet is controlled by the needle circuit, reduces the need for a complicated array of jets and passages which typifies the fixed venturi instrument **(see illustrations 2.4a and b)**.

This in turn means that the slide carburettor can be made smaller and lighter, both of which are important considerations when building motorcycles.

A less obvious advantage is the subtle way in which the various stages of operation overlap and influence each other. We have seen that the stages of operation of the slide carburettor are pilot jet, throttle valve cutaway, needle jet and main jet, but these are really only arbitrary divisions; in practice the transition between each stage is quite gradual, and so the careful choice of settings can be used to produce a very smooth response at widely varying speeds and throttle openings.

The slide carburettor proved to be so well suited to motorcycle use that it was the usual choice for around half a century. In this time it evolved quite considerably, and in its later years developed into a much more sophisticated device to comply with increasingly stringent demands of performance, economy and pollution control. There aren't as many new production bikes being fitted with them these days, though a

notable example was Kawasaki's ZXR750R of the early 90s which used flat-slide carburettors **(see illustration 2.4c)**.

But there has always been one fundamental problem with basic slide carburettors: if the throttle is snapped open from tickover, a large volume of air is drawn into the carburettor; however as the engine speed is still very low, the speed of the air across the jet is not sufficient to draw the required amount of fuel to match the air in the correct ratio. Therefore the mixture entering the engine is momentarily very weak and the engine will hesitate, if not stall. Opening the throttle progressively as engine speed rises is the only way to get round this.

Whilst under normal circumstances few riders will misuse the throttle to the extent that stalling is a problem, the real drawback is more subtle. Just as a gross mismatch between throttle setting and engine speed will cause stalling, so a lesser mismatch will cause a less severe but equally significant variation of the correct mixture strength. In other words, unless you are very conscientious, your motorcycle will be running inefficiently

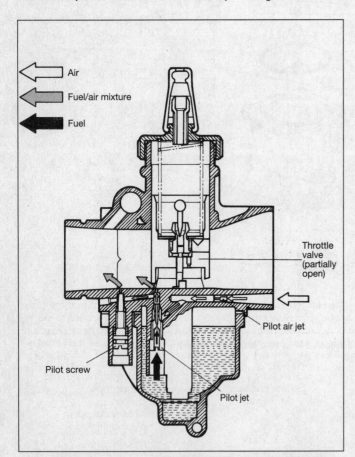

**2.4a  The pilot, or slow running circuit – simple slide carburettor**

*In this example, air is drawn through an inlet passage and is regulated by the pilot air jet. Fuel is drawn up through the pilot jet and mixes with the air, the resulting mixture entering the main bore at the pilot outlet, just below the edge of the throttle valve. The strength of the pilot mixture can be varied via the pilot screw and its outlet.*

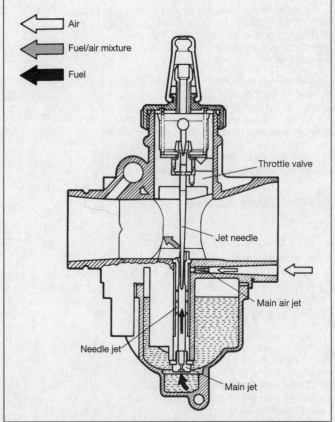

**2.4b  The main jet circuit – simple slide carburettor**

*As the throttle is opened, the mixture strength is controlled by the main air jet and main jet. Through intermediate throttle openings, the volume of mixture entering the main bore is controlled by the needle and needle jet. Note the air bleed holes in the latter – these help to atomise the fuel using air drawn from the main air jet.*

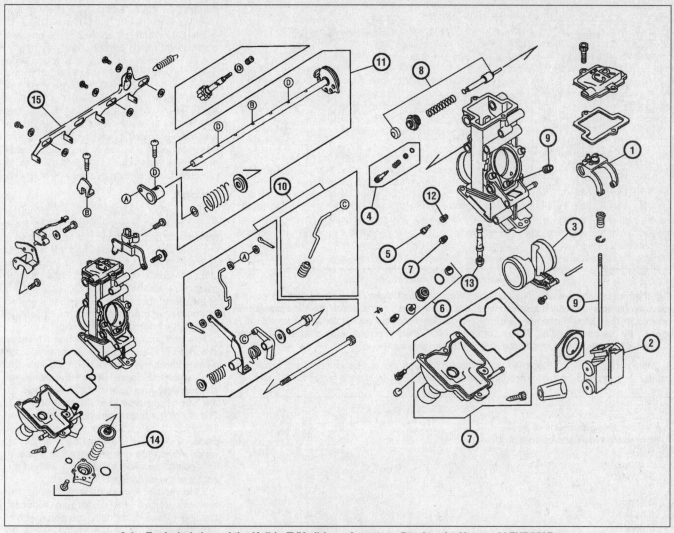

**2.4c Exploded view of the Keihin FVK slide carburettors fitted to the Kawasaki ZXR750R**

| | | | |
|---|---|---|---|
| 1 Throttle slide lever | 5 Pilot jet | 9 Air jet | 12 Starter jet |
| 2 Throttle slide | 6 Float needle valve | 10 Accelerator pump | 13 Main nozzle |
| 3 Float | 7 Float chamber |     mechanism | 14 Accelerator pump |
| 4 Pilot screw | 8 Choke plunger | 11 Throttle pulley | 15 Choke operating rod |

for much of the time, and both performance and fuel economy will suffer.

Slide carburettors on performance machines compensate for this by using an accelerator pump, as on the fixed venturi carburettor. But it was the introduction of the CV carburettor that resolved the problem.

## 5  Carburettor design – the constant velocity carburettor

The constant velocity or CV carburettor (also known as a constant vacuum (CV) or constant depression (CD) carburettor) is another example of the variable venturi, and has much in common with the slide carburettor described above.

It differs in that the throttle slide is replaced by a piston, similar in shape to a slide but without the cutaway, and its position in the venturi is no longer controlled by the throttle twistgrip, but by the difference in pressure between the air in the venturi and that in the atmosphere. The overall airflow through the carburettor, and thus the engine speed is now regulated by a butterfly valve, much like that of a fixed venturi carburettor, positioned after the piston in the throat of the carburettor, and linked to the throttle twistgrip by cable.

### How it works

The significant element of the carburettor is the piston, and how it works: imagine a tin can fitting snugly inside a tube, which is closed at one end. A spring is fitted between the top of the can and the closed end of the tube. There

is an air hose going into the top of the tube above the can. If a suction is applied to the air hose, it draws the air out, thereby reducing the pressure above the can. As the air below the can is at normal atmospheric pressure, the can is sucked up the tube against the pressure of the spring. If the suction is removed, the can slides down under the pressure of the spring, and air is drawn back in above the can.

When this principle is applied to a carburettor in which the venturi is linked by a narrow air passage or by a hole in the piston to a closed chamber above the piston, and there is air at atmospheric pressure supplied below the piston, it can be seen that as the low pressure area in the venturi, and therefore the chamber, varies with engine load, the height of the piston will vary accordingly **(see**

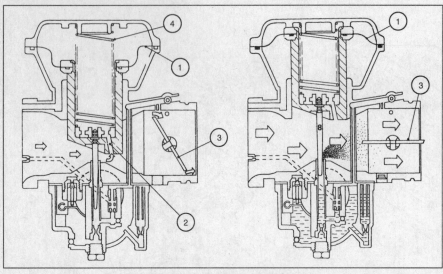

**2.5a  Vacuum piston operation**

*Air, at atmospheric pressure, fills the area below the diaphragm (1). Air is routed up into the vacuum chamber (above the diaphragm) via a hole in the base of the piston (2). A low pressure is created in the vacuum chamber and the piston begins to rise as the throttle butterfly (3) is opened by the throttle cable. The return spring (4) inside the piston helps stabilise the piston position so that the pressure on each side of the diaphragm is equal.*

*As the throttle butterfly (3) opens fully, air speed through the venturi is increased, creating a greater drop in pressure in the vacuum chamber; in so doing this lifts the piston fully.*

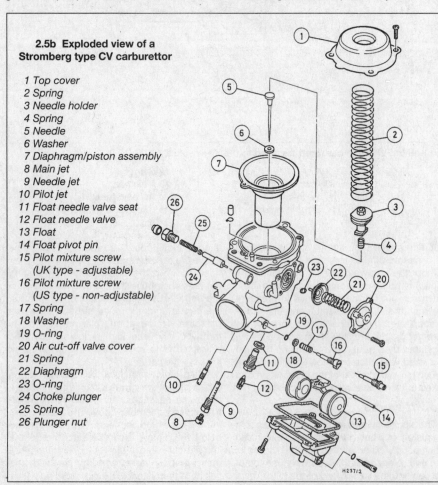

**2.5b  Exploded view of a Stromberg type CV carburettor**

1 Top cover
2 Spring
3 Needle holder
4 Spring
5 Needle
6 Washer
7 Diaphragm/piston assembly
8 Main jet
9 Needle jet
10 Pilot jet
11 Float needle valve seat
12 Float needle valve
13 Float
14 Float pivot pin
15 Pilot mixture screw
   (UK type - adjustable)
16 Pilot mixture screw
   (US type - non-adjustable)
17 Spring
18 Washer
19 O-ring
20 Air cut-off valve cover
21 Spring
22 Diaphragm
23 O-ring
24 Choke plunger
25 Spring
26 Plunger nut

illustration 2.5a). Basically, if there is low pressure in the venturi, the piston will rise.

The CV carburettor addresses the problem outlined with slide carburettors very nicely: even if the throttle butterfly is snapped wide open, the venturi itself is still closed off by the piston, and the piston will only rise when the engine speed has increased the air flow sufficiently to reduce the venturi pressure, and then it rises in direct proportion to the rate at which the pressure is reducing, so the mixture does not become suddenly very weak. Overall this means that the fuel is metered much more precisely to the air than in a slide carburettor.

### Design

The early approach, used on some motorcycles but mainly on cars, was to use a piston with a close fitting rim on its top in a chamber above the venturi, and this is known as the SU type. Low pressure air reaches the chamber above the piston via an air hole or passage, while the area directly below the rim of the piston (but above the venturi) is vented at atmospheric pressure by an air passage through the body of the carburettor.

This design was improved when advances in synthetic materials allowed an elastomer (synthetic rubber) diaphragm to separate the low pressure area from the one at atmospheric pressure, and this is known as the Stromberg type **(see illustration 2.5b)**. The rim of the diaphragm locates in a groove in the top of the carburettor body and the low pressure chamber is formed by a top cover, which sits on the rim, securing it in place. A light plastic piston is bonded to a hole in the centre of the diaphragm.

If the vacuum level in the venturi is high the pressure above the diaphragm reduces, drawing it upwards, bringing the piston with it, until the pressure of the spring exerts an opposite force and a state of equilibrium is reached. The level of the piston at which equilibrium is reached depends on the amount of vacuum in the venturi. The strength of the spring and the weight of the piston are designed in conjunction with all other components (jets, needle, float height etc.) so that the piston is always in the correct position for the requirements of the engine. When the vacuum reduces, the pressure above the diaphragm increases and the piston moves down again **(see illustrations 2.5c and d)**.

The CV carburettor therefore controls the mixture strength in response to the demands of the engine, the rider merely signalling the required change of engine speed via the butterfly valve. The mixture strength is kept much closer to the correct proportions at all times, and the engine is kept running efficiently, irrespective of a rider's over-enthusiasm in operating the throttle twistgrip.

### Slide or CV?

The CV carburettor offers a number of clear advantages over the slide type, and both

H237/2

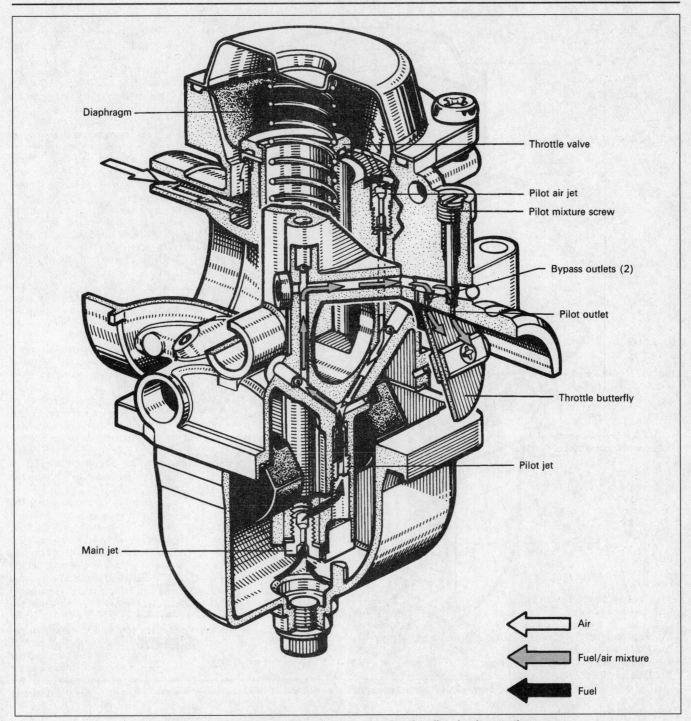

Diaphragm

Throttle valve

Pilot air jet

Pilot mixture screw

Bypass outlets (2)

Pilot outlet

Throttle butterfly

Pilot jet

Main jet

Air

Fuel/air mixture

Fuel

**2.5c Cut-away view of a CV carburettor showing the pilot circuit operation**

variable venturi types are better suited to motorcycle use than the fixed venturi types. The difference between the slide and CV carburettor is not so great as might be thought however, and in practice the two types are used according to the type of engine and the overall cost of the machine.

In many cases the extra cost of a CV carburettor is felt to outweigh its advantages, and on some more sporting machines, the

simplicity and responsiveness (when used correctly) of the slide type are felt to be more important than improved efficiency. In consequence, both types may be encountered in a wide range of applications. And so will hybrids, for example a CV carburettor with primary and secondary main circuits has been used where it has proved has advantageous, as has a twin venturi carburettor, one with a slide, the other with a CV piston.

## 6 Slide and CV carburettors – basic adjustments

All carburettors have some provision for adjustment to allow them to be set up for particular operating conditions, and also to allow for some tuning by the owner.

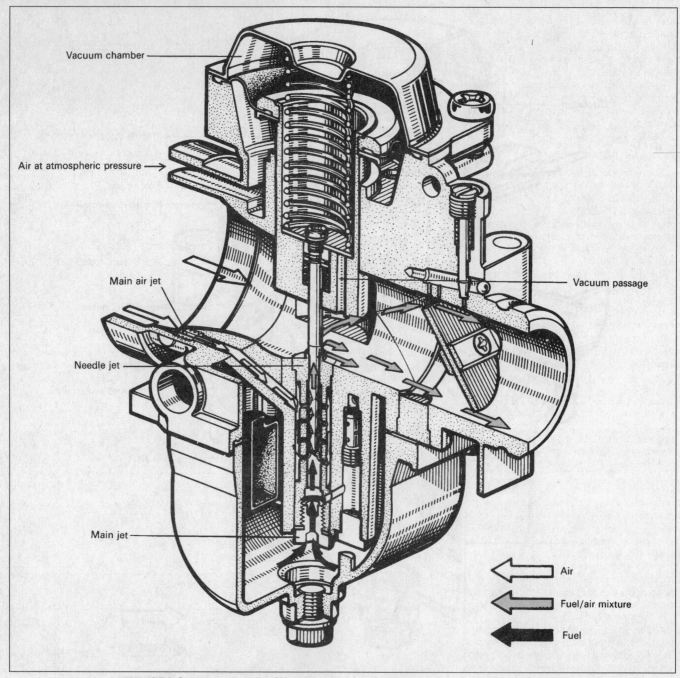

**Vacuum chamber**

**Air at atmospheric pressure**

**Main air jet**

**Needle jet**

**Main jet**

**Vacuum passage**

Air

Fuel/air mixture

Fuel

**2.5d Cut-away view of a CV carburettor showing the main jet circuit operation**

### Idle speed

The most obvious need is for some method of controlling the idle speed, and this is normally provided by an adjustable 'throttle stop' which sets the minimum opening of the throttle slide or butterfly at the desired point. In most cases this takes the form of a knurled screw on the side of the carburettor, though on multi-cylinder motorcycles with linked carburettors a single throttle stop screw (also known as an idle speed adjuster) controls all instruments via a linkage. Only on a few mopeds is this control omitted on the grounds of economy, and they rely on adjustment of the throttle cable to achieve the same result.

### Pilot mixture

To fine-tune the mixture at idle speed it is necessary to provide some method of controlling the pilot mixture. This can be done by adjusting the amount of air entering the pilot circuit using a pilot air screw **(see illustration 2.6a)**; fuel is metered by a pilot jet. The other method is to control the overall volume of the mixture with a pilot mixture screw **(see illustration 2.2j)**; fuel and air are both metered by jets. Both arrangements are widely used.

### Float adjustment

The level of the fuel in relation to the jets in the carburettor must be set accurately or the mixture strength of all circuits will be affected at all engine speeds.

Most manufacturers specify either a float

height, which can be measured with a ruler after the float chamber has been removed **(see illustration 2.6b)**, or a fuel level, which can be measured using a graduated tube connected to the float chamber drain screw **(see illustration 2.6c)**.

The float height can be adjusted by bending the small tang which carries the float needle valve. It is worth noting that an incorrect fuel level can create baffling problems, especially on multi-cylinder engines.

### Jet selection

The various jet sizes do not normally require alteration once the size has been chosen by the manufacturer, but if conditions dictate a change it is possible to fit jets of a slightly larger or smaller size. Also, the jet needle can be changed to one of a different profile. This allows the effect of the needle jet to be altered quite subtly.

On many machines, one or more air correction jets may be encountered in the carburettor's air inlet drillings. These are normally fitted by the carburettor manufacturer to allow a single basic carburettor casting to be used to produce a number of types, and they should not be altered.

### Tuning

Some owners attempt to improve the performance of their engine by 'tuning' the carburettors. But changing carburettor jets alone is a pointless task that will achieve negative results unless other systems are also changed, so that the overall system works in harmony.

There is no doubt that increasing jet sizes will allow more fuel into the combustion chamber, but unless the mixture was weak to begin with, or you are looking only to achieve a minimum increase in the fuel/air ratio to get the 0-10% above the 14.7:1 that gives most power (and uses more fuel), there is no point in sending loads more fuel into the combustion chamber unless there is more air to go with it, and that means changing your air filter for a freer flowing one.

Additionally, there is no point in sending a greater volume of fuel/air into the combustion chamber if the exhaust is incapable of getting rid of it, and that means changing your exhaust system for a freer flowing one. And even then there is a limit to the extra volume that can be packed into and scavenged from the combustion chamber, and here the limit is on the valves; since it is impractical to actually increase the size of the valves, the only solution is to fit different camshafts with lobes that give a higher valve lift and a longer duration, which would certainly boost top-end power, but of course low and mid-range would suffer for it.

The other problem with tuning is knowing which air filter to fit with which exhaust, and how much larger your jets need to be to make best use of other 'performance' parts. Trying

1  Pilot air screw
2  Spring
3  Pilot outlet
   passage
4  Pilot jet passage
5  Pilot jet

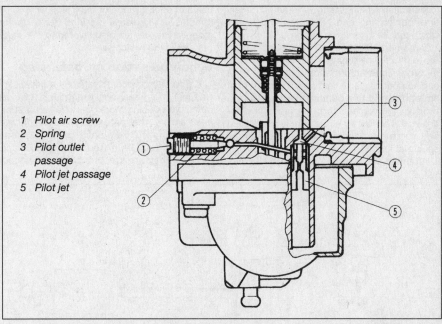

**2.6a  The pilot air screw adjusts the volume of air entering the pilot circuit**

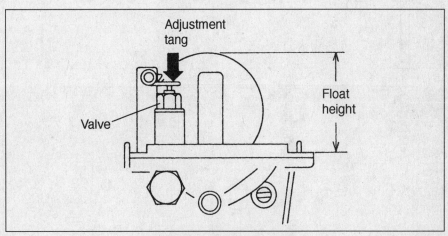

**2.6b  Checking the float height**

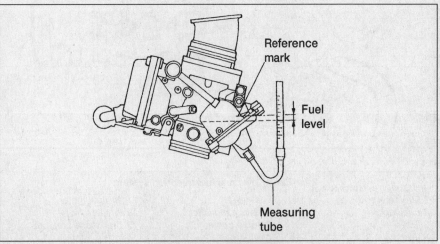

**2.6c  Checking the fuel level**

to establish which jets to fit is an extremely time consuming and hit-and-miss process which requires extensive testing.

Dynamometer testing offers a solution to the difficulty of tuning. The system's data recorder logs information collected from engine speed, rear wheel speed and exhaust emissions and this data can be exported to produce power and torque graphs and for analysis. The testing equipment is specialised and interpretation of the results requires specialist knowledge and skill.

Aftermarket tuning kits are available for DIY use and offer a range of main jets, air jets, jet needles and piston springs for popular models. The kits are also tailored to the 'state of tune' of the motorcycle.

### Synchronisation or 'balancing'

Carburettor synchronisation is a necessary routine maintenance procedure on all motorcycles using more than one carburettor. It is simply the process of adjusting the carburettors so they each pass the same amount of fuel/air mixture to their cylinder, meaning they are synchronised or balanced.

Essentially it is making sure that for any given throttle opening, the height of the throttle slide or angle of the throttle butterfly (according to carburettor type) is exactly the same on each carburettor.

This is done by measuring the vacuum produced in each cylinder, using a set of vacuum gauges or a manometer. Carburettors that are out of synchronisation will result in increased fuel consumption, increased engine temperature, less than ideal throttle response and higher vibration levels that will lead to premature wear of engine internals.

## 7  Fuel injection

### Introduction

Fuel injection in one form or another has been around, believe it or not, since 1898, which is almost as long as the internal combustion engine itself. Mechanical systems were in widespread use by 1940 in both the car and aviation industries. Although the first full electronic fuel injection system was introduced by Bendix as far back as 1950, the carburettor has over the years been the most widely used fuel supply system.

Kawasaki were the first to introduce fuel injection on a production motorcycle, the Z1000-H1 in 1980, and Honda, Kawasaki and Suzuki all used fuel injection on their turbo-charged bikes in the early and mid-eighties **(see illustration 2.7a)**. BMW utilised fuel injection on their 1983 K100 with the Bosch LE-Jetronic system and later fitted the Bosch Motronic system to all their models. Since the mid 1990s many engine management systems have appeared on production motorcycles, some of the most common are manufactured by Bosch, Marelli, Denso and Sagem, plus Honda's PGM-FI system.

The quest to meet demands for improved engine performance and rideability as well as increased fuel economy, together with the need to meet the standards that legislation demands regarding the control of exhaust emissions, has now forced motorcycle manufacturers to abandon the carburettor in favour of fuel injection for many of their models. This has been helped by the development of cheaper and more sophisticated electronic control systems, which are suited for motorcycle use where size and weight are important factors.

Regulations limiting the concentration of noxious constituents of exhaust gases emitted from internal combustion engines are constantly becoming more stringent. This dictates the need for increasingly accurate measurement of the fuel/ air mixture. With carburettors there are many operating conditions under which it is difficult to ensure that the correct mixture is delivered to the engine's cylinders for combustion. These

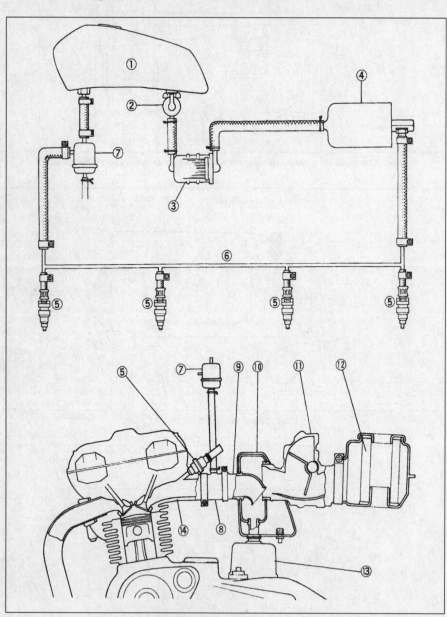

**2.7a  Early Kawasaki fuel injection system**

| | | |
|---|---|---|
| 1 Fuel tank | 6 Fuel rail | 11 Air flow meter |
| 2 Fuel tap | 7 Pressure regulator | 12 Air filter |
| 3 Filter | 8 Throttle bodies | 13 Crankcase breather |
| 4 Pump | 9 Air ducts | 14 Intake tract |
| 5 Injectors | 10 Surge tank | |

include cold starting and warm-up, where low operating temperatures diminish fuel vaporisation; low idling speeds; conditions of rapid acceleration and full load running. Once the best air/fuel ratio, or mixture setting, has been established, it is important to maintain accurate control of it under all operating conditions. Through its sensors and operating principles, an electronic fuel injection system ensures that the necessary close control is always achieved and maintained, thus ensuring the optimum balance between performance, economy and levels of exhaust emissions.

## Principles of operation

The term fuel injection is used to describe any system in which the fuel is pumped out under pressure to mix with the air supply. An ideal injection system must supply to the engine a quantity of vaporised fuel which is correct to suit the engine speed, the engine load, its operating temperature, and atmospheric conditions. The system must vary this quantity, to allow for any changes in these operating conditions, to ensure optimum performance.

An electronic fuel injection system is able to achieve this by the rapid and accurate assessment of information received from various sensors fitted to the engine, and by responding automatically to the slightest change. Information concerning engine load (air flow into the engine), engine speed, crankshaft angle, air temperature, engine temperature, throttle position and air density is collected by the sensors and relayed to the electronic control unit. The control unit uses this information to calculate the required opening time of the fuel injectors and thus the quantity of fuel supplied, and sends the equivalent electrical pulse to each injector. As the injector opens, pressurised fuel is sprayed around the inlet valve, where it mixes with air and vaporises, before entering the cylinder where it is compressed and ignited.

Of all the information collected by the sensors, the air flow into the engine cylinders is the major controlling parameter for fuel metering.

An electronically controlled fuel injection system consists of two main component groups, namely the fuel circuit and the electronic control circuit **(see illustration 2.7b)**.

The fuel circuit consists of a tank, pump, filter, pressure regulator and injectors. The function of the circuit is to store, deliver, clean and inject the fuel.

The electronic control circuit consists of detecting elements, called sensors, and an electronic control unit (ECU). The sensors collect all the engine operating information necessary for calculation of the fuel requirement, and the control unit processes the information, determines the amount of fuel needed, and controls the injectors.

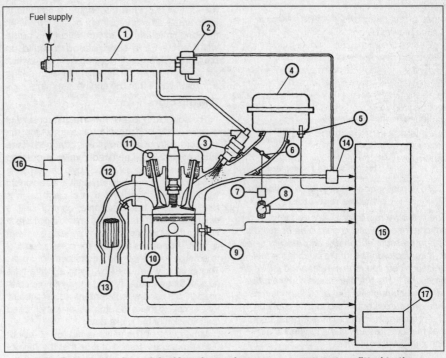

**2.7b Schematic view of the Yamaha engine management system fitted to the GTS1000 model**

| | | |
|---|---|---|
| 1 Fuel rail | 8 Throttle position sensor | 14 Intake air pressure sensor |
| 2 Fuel pressure regulator | 9 Engine or coolant temperature sensor | 15 Electronic control unit (ECU) |
| 3 Fuel injector | 10 Crankshaft position sensor | 16 Ignition coil |
| 4 Air box | 11 Camshaft position sensor | 17 Atmospheric pressure sensor |
| 5 Air temperature sensor | 12 Oxygen (Lambda) sensor | |
| 6 Throttle body butterfly | 13 Catalytic converter | |
| 7 Fast idle system | | |

## The fuel circuit

Fuel is supplied from the tank and pumped by an electric pump through a filter to the fuel distributor rail, from which the individual injectors are fed **(see illustrations 2.7a and b)**. Operating pressure is generated by the pump and is maintained and controlled by the pressure regulator, which usually consists of a spring-loaded diaphragm and ball valve.

### The pump

The pump delivers more fuel than is required by the engine so there is sufficient pressure in the fuel system at all normal operating times **(see illustration 2.7c)**. A

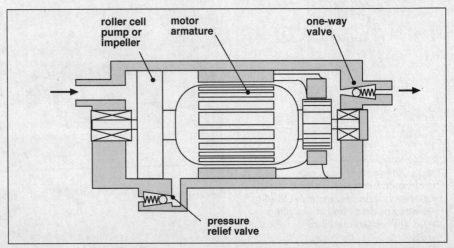

**2.7c Pumps are usually immersed in fuel, with either a roller cell rotor or impellers (or a combination of the two) to move the fuel through them**

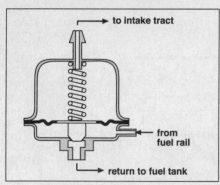

**2.7d Cross-section through a typical fuel pressure regulator**

*The pressure regulator is a sealed unit in which a needle valve is held onto its seat by spring pressure and intake air pressure close to the injector in the intake duct. If the fuel pressure gets too high in relation to intake air pressure, it lifts the diaphragm, opening the valve which releases fuel back into the tank until pressure is equalised in the regulator. The regulator is linked to intake pressure so that the fuel pressure is maintained at a constant level above it*

pressure relief valve protects the system from too high a fuel pressure by releasing excess fuel back into the fuel inlet side **(see illustration 2.7d)**. A non-return valve prevents fuel draining back when the ignition is switched off.

A safety circuit switches the pump off when

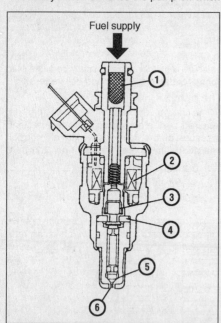

**2.7e All injectors work on the same solenoid/needle valve principal, but different nozzle designs give different spray patterns and atomisation characteristics**

| | |
|---|---|
| 1 *Filter* | 4 *Seat* |
| 2 *Solenoid coil* | 5 *Needle valve* |
| 3 *Plunger* | 6 *Pintle* |

the ignition is on but the engine is stationary, for example after an accident or stalling. When the ignition is initially switched on the pump will operate for a short period to build up pressure in the fuel lines, but will then switch off and not operate again until a cranking signal indicates that the engine is turning.

### The injectors

The solenoid operated fuel injector consists of a valve body and needle valve to which the solenoid plunger is rigidly attached **(see illustration 2.7e)**. The needle valve is pressed against a seat in the valve body by a helical spring to keep the valve closed until the solenoid winding is energised. When a current pulse is received from the electronic control unit a magnetic field builds up in the solenoid coil which attracts the plunger and lifts the needle valve from its seat. This opens the path for pressurised fuel to emerge as a finely vaporised cone of spray. This is usually obtained by using a Pintle-type nozzle, though other types, and even multiple-nozzles, are used when it proves advantageous, for example to make the atomisation better suited to the design of the intake duct.

Movement of the valve is limited to about 0.15 mm and the period of time that the valve is open varies from about 1.5 to 10 milliseconds, the actual amount depending on the injection pulse duration from the control unit. This variation in opening times dictates the amount of fuel that is supplied, and is determined by the requirements indicated to the electronic control unit by the sensors in the engine.

Injection systems can be divided into two main groups, single-point and multi-point. This classification is based on the number and positions of injectors.

### The throttle body assembly

The throttle bodies house the throttle butterfly valves, the throttle position sensor and the fast idle unit. The individual throttle bodies link together in a similar manner to a bank of carburettors and usually have some means of adjustment in their joining links to

enable synchronisation of the butterfly valves. On certain designs the fuel rail and pressure regulator may be integral with the throttle body assembly **(see illustration 2.7f)**.

### System types

Motorcycle systems are termed 'indirect injection (IDI)', where the injector is housed in the intake duct just before the inlet valve of each cylinder, or in the throttle body. Other systems are termed 'direct injection (DI)' and have applications on diesel engines and a few petrol car engines; on a DI engine the injector sprays the fuel directly into the combustion chamber.

Single point injection systems (used mainly on cars) have a single injector mounted on an inlet manifold just before the throttle valve, in the same position as a conventional carburettor would be. The air/fuel mixture is then split between the individual manifold ducts as it is drawn into each cylinder.

Multi-point injection systems (used on motorcycles and a few cars) have a separate injector for each cylinder of the engine, ensuring even distribution of the fuel, and some racing motorcycles have two or even three injectors per cylinder.

There are three types of injector: simultaneous, where all injectors fire at the same time; grouped, where say on a four cylinder engine fire together in groups of two; and sequential, where each injector is timed to fire just before the intake stroke of it's cylinder. The sequential system is used for motorcycles and offers the most control over fuelling and emissions.

### *The electronic control circuit*

The electronic control circuit consists of the electronic control unit (ECU) which assesses information received from various sensors in the engine. These sensors provide information on engine speed, crankshaft position, air temperature, air pressure, engine temperature, and throttle position.

The control unit uses this information to

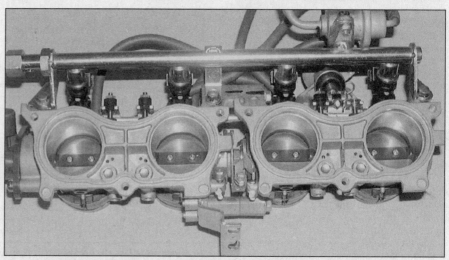

**2.7f Throttle body assembly with fuel rail and injectors (CBR600F-1)**

calculate the required opening time of the fuel injectors and thus the quantity of fuel supplied, and sends the equivalent electrical pulse to each injector. As the injector opens, pressurised fuel is sprayed around the inlet valve, where it mixes with air and vaporises, before entering the cylinder where it is compressed and ignited.

### Air sensors

Air pressure and temperature sensors analyse the air flowing into the engine and take account of air density and temperature of the air. Thus compensations in the air/fuel mixture are made for variations in atmospheric temperature and pressure. This feature is especially significant for vehicles that operate at varying altitudes.

Air flow sensors were also used at one time, but due to their reliance on non-electronic components that were constantly exposed to fast flowing air, and the fact that air flow could be calculated accurately using information from other sensors, they became obsolete.

### Position sensors

Camshaft and/or crankshaft sensors are used to provide information on the engine speed and crankshaft position. Engine speed data is assessed in conjunction with information from the other sensors enabling the control unit to determine exact fuel requirements. Crankshaft angle determines the timing of the pulse sent by the control unit to initiate injector opening and engine speed determines the frequency of the pulse.

### Temperature sensor

The engine temperature (or coolant temperature on liquid-cooled engines) is used to assess fuel enrichment requirements for cold start conditions and engine warm up.

### Throttle position sensor

The throttle position sensor (TPS) provides the control unit with data on idling, over-run, acceleration, and full-load running. A potentiometer (variable resistor) is used to sense the throttle butterfly position and movement and thus provide information to the control unit, which signals for fuel enrichment for acceleration and full load conditions, and fuel cut-off when the engine is in over-run. The TPS is also influential in ECU decisions regarding ignition timing, and this is covered in Chapter 3.

### Oxygen sensor

Some systems also incorporate an oxygen sensor (known as a lambda sensor) in the exhaust system. The exhaust will also incorporate a catalytic converter.

The oxygen sensor samples the gas content of the exhaust gases and sends a signal to the ECU when lambda exceeds a certain value, enabling the ECU to adjust the mixture if emissions are too high. Systems using an oxygen sensor are termed 'closed-loop' systems, because the results of previous decisions are used to determine the next decisions, i.e. by analysing the exhaust content the ECU is able to determine whether the decisions previously made regarding fuelling were correct, and if not change them. Systems without an oxygen sensor are termed 'open-loop' systems.

The advantage of closed loop systems is that they take account of wear on the engine and components such as throttle slides (which affect air flow) as mileage increases and by analysing exhaust content can compensate for this in the fuelling. An open loop system assumes the engine will always be in the same condition as when it was built.

### Safety and back-up circuits

The more sophisticated systems incorporate two safety circuits. When the ignition is switched ON, the fuel pump runs for a few seconds to pressurise the system. Thereafter the pump automatically switches off until the engine is started. The second circuit incorporates a tip-over sensor, which automatically switches off the fuel pump and cuts the ignition and injection circuits if the motorcycle falls over.

Most systems incorporate a self-diagnostic function, whereby any faults detected by the electronic control unit are stored in its memory as codes which can be downloaded for diagnosis via a dedicated code reader.

### Adjustments

Fuel injection systems are not as easy to tune as carburettors, especially in unskilled hands, however they can be re-programmed or re-chipped, if the necessary software, hardware and components are available.

The performance characteristics of all electronic systems are based on 'mapping'; a map is basically a three-dimensional graph showing the ideal amount of fuel for any given combination of conditions within sensible parameters (see illustration 2.7g). All the maps for a particular system are programmed into the electronic control unit.

On some systems, and with the right equipment, it is possible to re-map the ECU's Eprom chip, which basically involves changing the shape of the maps. On some other systems it is possible to simply remove the standard chip, on which all the maps are stored, and plug in an alternative chip which has revised maps.

Apart from that, throttle bodies need to be kept synchronised or balanced to ensure they all open at the same time and by the same amount.

### 8 Turbo-charging and supercharging

Turbo-charging and super-charging are two types of forced induction, which is the term applied to any engine that has the fuel/air mixture forcibly pushed into the engine (as opposed to sucking it in, termed normal aspiration). Forced induction is used to improve volumetric efficiency by cramming as much air into the engine as possible.

There are two ways of doing this, using a super-charger or a turbo-charger. A super-charger is a compressor that is mechanically driven directly off the engine, while a turbo-charger is a compressor that is driven by the exhaust gases. Super-chargers are not often found on standard motorcycles mainly because of the amount of room they take, and application is limited to sprint or drag-racing.

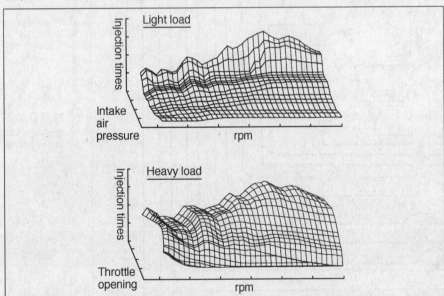

**2.7g Three-dimensional maps are a graphic way to show the data tables which the ECU uses to calculate the fuel injection quantity**

*Under light engine loading, the fuel injector time (and therefore quantity) is determined by the intake air pressure and engine rpm (upper map). Under heavy loading the throttle opening and engine rpm determine injector time (lower map).*

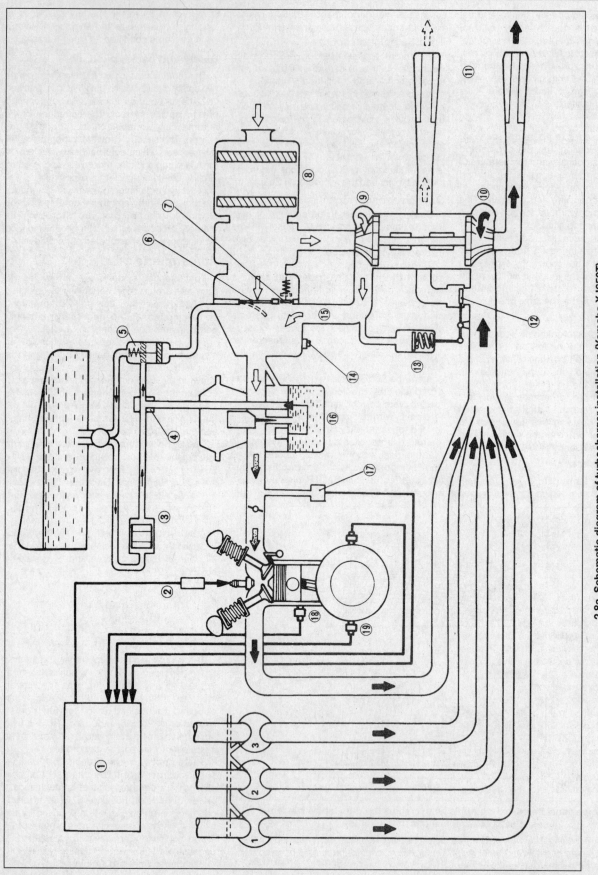

**2.8a Schematic diagram of turbocharger installation (Yamaha XJ650T)**

1 Ignitor
2 Ignition coil
3 Fuel pump
4 Check valve
5 Pressure regulator

6 Reed valve
7 Relief valve
8 Air filter
9 Compressor
10 Turbine

11 Exhaust pipes
12 Waste gate
13 Actuator
14 Drain valve
15 Surge tank

16 Carburettor
17 Boost sensor
18 Knock sensor
19 RPM sensor

During the eighties there was an upsurge in interest by the manufacturers in turbo-charging as a method of extracting more power from an engine of a given capacity. Models were produced by the Japanese manufacturers which ranged from 500 to 750 capacity, but they failed to set a trend and were never superseded by later developments **(see illustration 2.8a)**. Although there are no current production turbo motorcycles, the turbo-charging of normally aspirated engine remains a popular project for many people.

The turbocharger consists of a compact turbine unit driven by the exhaust gases and turning at very high speed (around 180,000 rpm) **(see illustrations 2.8b and c)**. At the other end of the turbine shaft is an impeller unit, and this is used to force air into the engine at well above atmospheric pressure. With a greater volume of air entering the combustion chamber during each induction stroke, a correspondingly greater amount of fuel can be admitted and burnt, thus producing more power. The turbo unit also incorporates a pressure-sensitive valve arrangement, known as a 'waste gate' to prevent manifold pressure rising above a certain limit; usually about 15 psi.

Most turbo designs use fuel injection to control the quantity of fuel delivered to the cylinder at any given engine speed and pressure. This arrangement avoids the technical problems of using carburettors at high pressures, and can ensure a degree of accuracy that would otherwise not be possible. An electronic control unit monitors engine speed, temperature and boost pressure to allow the fuel quantity to be constantly corrected.

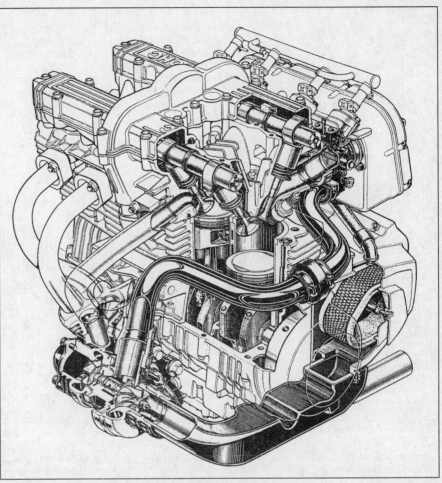

2.8b  Cutaway view of Kawasaki's ZX750T

## 9  The fuel tank, fuel tap and fuel pump

### Fuel tank

Most tanks are made of pressed steel, though other materials such as plastics are now being used because they are lighter. The tank incorporates a vent, usually in the filler cap, to allow air to enter as the fuel is leaving. There is also usually a breather hose to vent evaporative emissions (fumes) into the atmosphere or emission control system, and an overflow hose. A fuel level gauge sender unit or level sensing device is often housed in the base of the tank, and on certain models the tank is used to house the fuel pump (see below).

Fuel is fed from the tank either by gravity or by using a pump. It travels via a strainer and/or filter, a tap and hoses to the carburettors or the fuel rail and injectors.

### Fuel tap

The purpose of the fuel tap is to provide control over the flow of fuel from the tank to the fuel system, enabling the fuel flow to the turned off when removing the fuel tank for

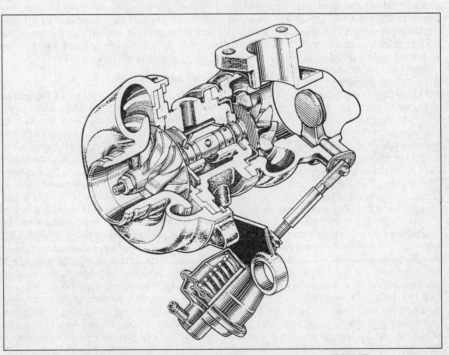

2.8c  Cutaway of the turbocharger and wastegate – ZX750T

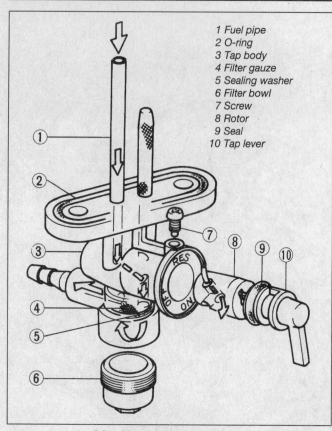

1 Fuel pipe
2 O-ring
3 Tap body
4 Filter gauze
5 Sealing washer
6 Filter bowl
7 Screw
8 Rotor
9 Seal
10 Tap lever

2.9a  Manual fuel tap operation

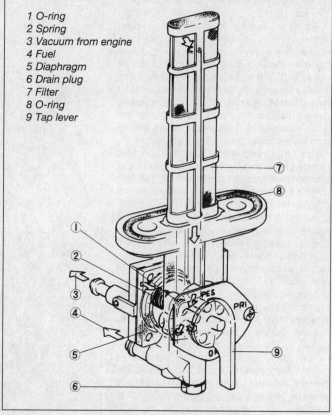

1 O-ring
2 Spring
3 Vacuum from engine
4 Fuel
5 Diaphragm
6 Drain plug
7 Filter
8 O-ring
9 Tap lever

2.9b  Automatic fuel tap operation

example. It is situated at the lowest point on the fuel tank and linked by flexible hoses to the fuel system.

On many machines the tap is manually operated, having a small lever on the side of the tap to select the OFF, ON or RES (reserve) positions as required (see illustration 2.9a). An internal rotor allows fuel to flow through the selected port to the fuel pipe. The RES setting switches to a second feed pipe that is set lower in the tank than the main one, gives access to the fuel in the bottom of the tank, and serves as a reminder that you are low on fuel. The transition from main to reserve must be made manually by turning the lever on the tap. Many motorcycles now incorporate a fuel gauge and/or low fuel warning light, which often means there is no reserve facility fitted in the tap.

An automatic vacuum-operated fuel tap is a common alternative to the manual type (see illustration 2.9b). The tap is operated by a flexible diaphragm inside the main body. This is connected by a synthetic rubber hose to the inlet port of the engine. The depression which exists in the inlet port when the engine is running opens the fuel tap, supplying fuel to the carburettor. As soon as the engine stops and the inlet port returns to atmospheric pressure, the tap closes.

On most vacuum-operated taps there is an additional manual reserve setting, and also a priming position, denoted by PRI. The latter allows the carburettor float bowls to be filled

after they have run dry or have been drained; without this facility it would be necessary to crank the engine for a long time until sufficient fuel had flowed through to allow it to start.

There have been examples of electrical switching for fuel taps. Yamaha's FZR1000 was fitted with an auxiliary control set in the fairing cockpit panels to ease the task of switching over to reserve.

## Fuel pump

In many cases the fuel flow from the tank to the carburettors is by gravity alone and a pump is not needed. However, with the use of straighter and almost vertical intake ducts the carburettors and air box sit much higher in the frame, and often occupy the space that would have previously been occupied by the fuel tank. The tank therefore has to fit around the airbox, and to maintain capacity much of the fuel is now stored in the rear of the tank, quite low down. This, coupled with the high position of the carburettors, means that a pump is required to feed the fuel from the tank to the carburettors.

Motorcycles with fuel injection require a pump to achieve the high fuel pressure required for the system. Typically a fuel pump used in an injection system would supply fuel at around 30 to 50 psi, compared to the pump pressure of 1.5 to 3 psi used for a carburettor system. Refer to Section 7 for more details.

The fuel pump is usually electrically operated and is controlled by the ECU or

engine management unit via a relay. Mechanical and vacuum-operated fuel pump designs have been used in the past, but have given way to more reliable and compact electrically powered pumps.

There are several types of fuel pump, the low pressure reciprocating plunger type and the high pressure roller cell, internal gear, peripheral channel and side channel types. The pump is either located in the fuel line from the tank, usually with a filter unit between them, or inside the fuel tank (see illustrations 2.9c and d). High pressure pumps are often immersed in fuel or have fuel running through them to cool the pump.

## 10 The air filter, airbox and air intake systems

### Air filter

The reasons for fitting an air filter to an engine need little explanation, but it is worth considering the ways in which a supply of clean air can be achieved. Like most other components on motorcycles, the air filter has become increasingly sophisticated over the years; the early wire mesh arrangements having been replaced by the far more effective oil-impregnated foam or pleated paper filters used today (see illustrations 2.10a and b).

2.9c  Fuel pump (A) and filter (B) are mounted in the fuel line from the tank to carburettors

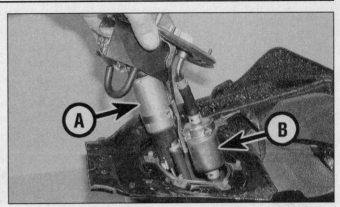

2.9d  Fuel pump (A) and filter (B) mounted inside the tank

2.10a  An impregnated foam type filter as used on Kawasaki's ZX6-R

2.10b  A pleated paper type filter as used on Yamaha's R1

Both types are effective methods of trapping the airborne dust which would otherwise enter the engine to wear away the various moving parts, and it follows running the engine with the filter missing or damaged will effectively shorten the engine's life. Also because a filter's flow rate is designed in conjunction with the fuel system so that the correct fuel/air mixture is achieved, to run a bike with a dirty or missing air filter will upset the carburation of the machine.

Most four-strokes and many two-strokes use a filter element of pleated resin-impregnated paper. The resin impregnation prevents the paper from becoming saturated by moisture and thus disintegrating. The pleated arrangement presents the maximum filter area within the limits imposed by the filter housing. This allows the pores in the paper to be kept as fine as possible to trap almost all of the incoming dust, and at the same time avoids restricting the air-flow to the engine. The oil-impregnated foam elements found on many smaller two-strokes are rather coarser in texture, and at first sight might seem less effective as filters. In practice, the oily surface presented to the incoming air catches a good deal of the dust.

All types of filter element require regular cleaning or renewal. The performance of the filter falls off gradually until it begins to affect the mixture strength or to allow dust to pass through it. In the case of the paper elements, the pores in the paper will become more and more clogged, air will pass through it less freely and the mixture will become excessively rich. With foam types, once the oily coating is covered by dust particles it will be unable to trap further dust until the filter element has been cleaned and re-oiled.

### The airbox

The airbox used to be nothing more than a housing for the air filter, and on many smaller commuter motorcycles that it still mainly what it does.

In recent years it has developed into an integral part of the overall fuel system on sports and performance machines, working in conjunction with air intake systems (see below) (see illustration 2.10c). It is designed

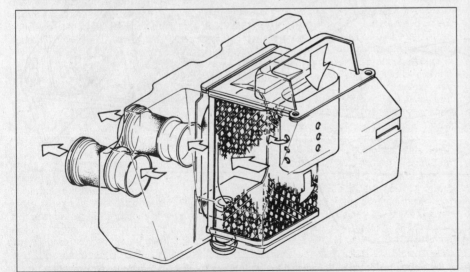

2.10c  Section view of typical air filter housing

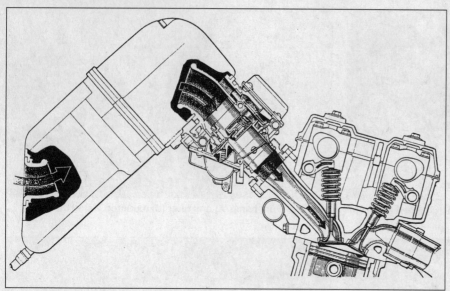

**2.10d This ZX10 airbox design illustrates the first use of the plenum chamber**

motorcycle to collect, direct and pressurise incoming air. Current designs use various scoop, port and duct systems, all with the aim of creating higher air pressure inside the airbox **(see illustration 2.10e)**.

A more recent development on sports models is a system that operates a flap in the air filter housing which regulates the air flow into it according to engine speed **(see illustration 2.10f)**. At low to medium engine speeds, the flap is closed. At medium to high engine speeds, the flap is open. The flap is activated by a rod connected to a diaphragm, which itself is activated by a vacuum taken from the intake manifold. The vacuum to the diaphragm is controlled by a solenoid valve, which is controlled by the electronic control unit. The idea of the system is to regulate air speed and pressure conditions so they are better suited for all engine speeds.

## 11 Emission control systems

The combustion process of a motorcycle engine produces hydrocarbons (HC), carbon monoxide (CO), and oxides of nitrogen ($NO_x$). HC emission consists of raw, unburned fuel that passes through the engine, indicating a significant ignition, carburation or mechanical fault. CO is partially burned fuel, and an excess indicates a rich mixture, due either to too much fuel or not enough air. $NO_x$ is caused by a very lean mixture (not enough fuel or too much air), or by very high engine temperatures.

to act as a plenum chamber; i.e. it holds a volume of air relatively still and at a relatively constant pressure, reducing air pressure differences that occur between low and high speeds so that fuelling is not upset **(see illustration 2.10d)**. On two-strokes in particular this is important, because the constantly varying air pressure and velocity around the engine would otherwise make it difficult to ensure constant mixture strength. It is not uncommon for racing two-strokes based on road machines to retain the original filter housing/plenum chamber to prevent any fall-off in performance. The effect is less significant on four-strokes where the air is drawn more positively into the combustion chamber, but still significant.

The airbox does another very important job, acting as a control for crankcase emissions (see Section 11).

### Air intake systems

The concept of Ram-Air was introduced by Suzuki in the 1970's, and the basic theory was 'to ram as much air into the intake as possible' by using the forward speed of the

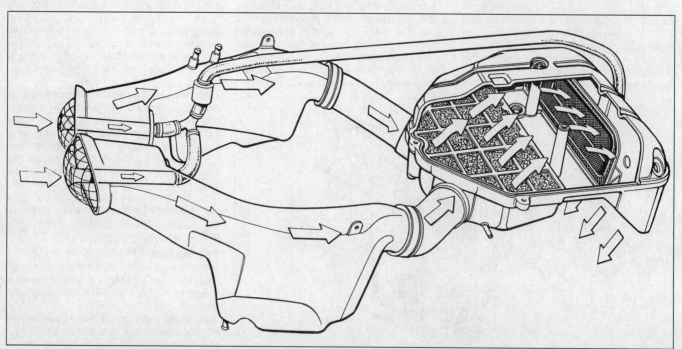

**2.10e Manufacturers now make full use of the airbox potential with forward facing intakes to pick up maximum air pressure (Kawasaki ZZ-R1100 shown)**

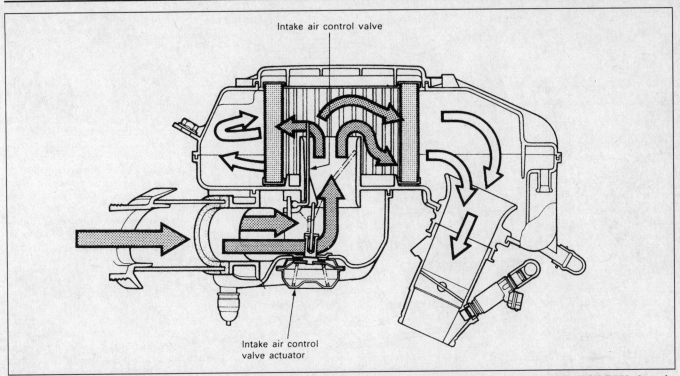

Intake air control valve

Intake air control
valve actuator

**2.10f  Some manufacturers use variable intake geometry to get the best power at both high and mid-range speeds (GSX-R750 shown). The central valve in the entrance to the air filter housing is fully open at high speeds and is closed at low engine speeds**

The world-wide need to reduce the amount of noxious exhaust emissions has led to the development of emission control systems on motor vehicles to ensure that they comply with the regulations in force. Although these regulations vary from country to country, generally this has led to a reduction of engine and exhaust noise and a reduction of fuel system and exhaust emissions. Stringent emission control laws have already been implemented in California and Switzerland and motorcycles destined for these markets are fitted with emission control systems. From 2006 mandatory emission limits will apply to EU member states for motorcycles over 150 cc.

Exhaust noise reduction has been achieved by improved silencer design and engine noise by liquid-cooling and sound damping materials. A reduction in the emission of noxious fumes has been achieved by incorporating systems which prevent the escape into the atmosphere of unburnt fuel (from the fuel tank vent) and crankcase vapours. Exhaust gas emissions have been reduced by the close control of fuelling provided by fuel injection, secondary air systems which improve the burning of exhaust gases, and catalytic converters.

### Crankcase emission control

As the engine reciprocates it is effectively pumping air around the crankcase, and so the pressure inside is constantly changing, necessitating some form of breather or vent. Additionally, blow-by gases from the combustion process pass from the combustion chamber to the crankcase.

On four-stroke engines, to prevent the air in the crankcase, which is heavily contaminated with oil and a certain amount of unburnt fuel from blow-by past the pistons, reaching the atmosphere, it is directed into the airbox via a hose known as the 'crankcase breather' hose **(see illustration 2.11a)**.

There is usually a baffle chamber in the crankcase before the breather hose which traps larger oil particles and drains them back into the sump. The remaining air, which is still heavily mixed with an oil 'mist', is directed into an oil/air separator (either a separate unit before the airbox or incorporated in it), which

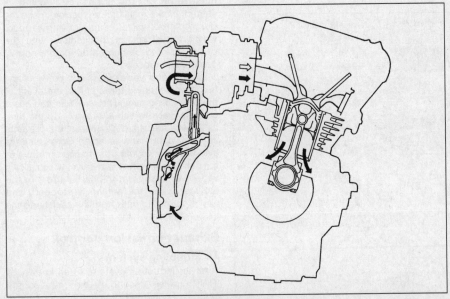

**2.11a  Typical crankcase breather system**

*Blow-by gases from the combustion process (black arrows) are swept up into the airbox where they mix with the fresh incoming air (white arrows) and pass into the carburettor to be burnt in the combustion process*

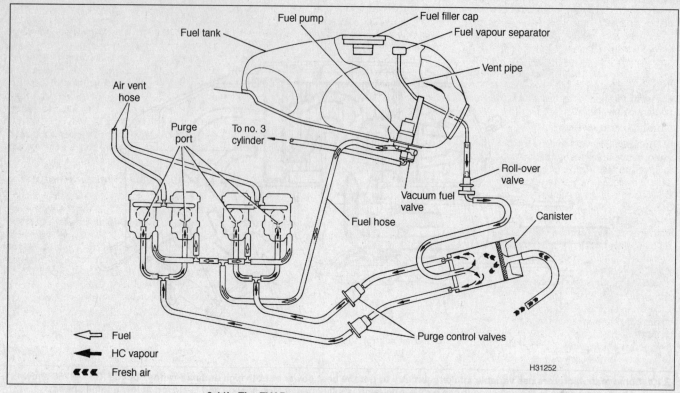

2.11b **The EVAP system used on the Suzuki GSX-R750**

separates and directs the oil into a catch tank or into a closed drain tube (which must be periodically emptied). Meanwhile the remaining air and residual 'oil mist' is re-circulated through the airbox and into the engine along with fresh air and is burnt in the combustion process.

## Evaporative emission control

This system, known as 'EVAP', prevents the escape of fuel vapour from the tank into the atmosphere by storing it in a charcoal-filled canister. The system has by law been fitted to all motorcycles in California since 1984, and is also used in Switzerland. On motorcycles without an EVAP system, the tank vents to the atmosphere via a breather in the filler cap or via a breather hose.

When the engine is stopped, fuel vapour from the tank is directed via a roll-over valve into the canister where it is absorbed and stored whilst the motorcycle is standing (**see illustration 2.11b**). When the engine is started, intake manifold depression opens the purge control valves, thus drawing vapours which are stored in the canister into the carburettors to be burned during the normal combustion process.

The roll-over valve closes and prevents any fuel from escaping through it in the event of the bike falling over. The tank filler cap has a one way valve which allows air into the tank as the volume of fuel decreases, but prevents any fuel vapour from escaping. Some systems also vent any vapour from the carburettors to the canister via a two-way valve, which allows vapour to pass from the carburettors to the canister when the engine is stopped, and allows vapour to pass from the canister to the carburettors when the engine is running.

## Exhaust emission control

### Air induction systems

An air induction system, often known as 'PAIR' (pulse secondary air) reduces the amount of unburned hydrocarbons released in the exhaust gases. It uses exhaust gas pulses to suck fresh air into the exhaust ports, where it mixes with hot combustion gases (**see illustration 2.11c**).

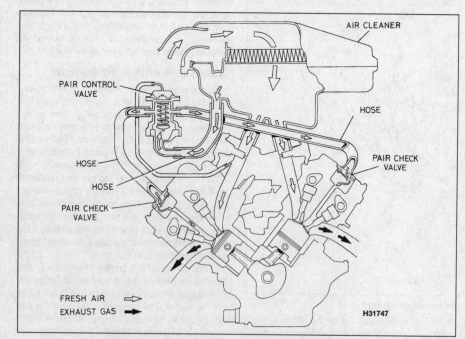

2.11c **The PAIR system used on the Honda Firestorm**

The extra oxygen promotes continued combustion, allowing unburned hydrocarbons to burn off, thereby reducing emissions. Reed valves control the flow of air into the ports, opening when there is negative pressure, and prevent exhaust gases flowing back when there is positive pressure. An air cut-off valve shuts off the flow of air during deceleration, preventing backfiring.

### Catalytic converters

The use of catalytic converters on motorcycles has been restricted due to the lack of models with fuel injection, which is almost essential if a 'cat' is being used as they only work effectively under closely defined conditions which carburettors cannot maintain. There are examples of catalytic converters being used on carburettor engined models; these systems are usually equipped with fuel cut-off valves which protect the catalytic converter from being damaged should an abnormally high level of fuel enter the combustion chambers.

A catalyst is a substance that causes a chemical reaction between other elements without being involved in the reaction itself. The bonus of this is that the catalyst does not get used up and its properties do not change, so it continues to do its job despite everything going on around it. The catalytic converter itself is maintenance-free, but is particularly fragile and can be damaged if the exhaust system is dropped; it can also be damaged by the use of leaded fuel and an incorrect fuel/air mixture.

The catalytic converter is a 'honey-combed' unit that fits into the exhaust system ahead of the silencer **(see illustration 2.11d)**. It contains catalysts, usually platinum, palladium and rhodium, which are used alone or in combination to change the noxious emissions in the exhaust gases as they pass through the exhaust.

They convert the HC, CO and $NO_x$ into harmless water vapour, carbon dioxide and oxygen. The honeycomb type construction gives a large surface area to ensure that all the noxious emissions have an excellent chance of coming into contact with the correct catalyst(s), but offers little resistance to the flow. Its position in the exhaust system is crucial as it must operate within a certain temperature range.

The 'cat' must also stay clean to do its job, which is why they only really work with unleaded fuel. Leaded fuel leaves deposits which eventually coat the catalysts, so that the noxious elements can't come into direct contact with them.

## 12 Exhaust systems

### General

The obvious purpose of the exhaust system is to direct the gases coming out of the combustion chamber clear of the machine and rider, to cool them down and to make them quieter. If the hot gases were to be expelled directly from the exhaust port, not only would the front mudguard and tyre melt, but the noise would be unbearable, and any residual fuel would burn off explosively on contact with the oxygen in the surrounding air. The exhaust system therefore directs the gases down and towards the back of the machine, allowing them to cool somewhat, negating the tendency towards unwanted external combustion.

The less obvious (but just as important) purpose of the exhaust system is to use the alternating positive and negative pulses that are created by each combustion to aid combustion chamber scavenging and filling.

Exhaust systems are made out of steel, and then either painted with heat-resistant paint or chrome-plated, though some systems use stainless steel to deter corrosion.

### Exhaust pulse scavenge effect

In simple terms, each combustion forms a high pressure wave of gas which travels down the exhaust pipe. Behind the high pressure wave is a naturally following low pressure wave. At some point in the exhaust system (determined by design), some of the high pressure wave is bounced back up the system, and as the remaining high pressure wave leaves the pipe the low pressure behind it is reflected back.

This low pressure wave is used to help suck in the fresh fuel/air mixture for the next cycle. High (positive) pressure that has bounced back is then used to stop the fresh incoming mixture from going straight out of the exhaust port as the exhaust valve is closing. The low (negative) pressure which follows is used to help suck out the exhaust gas from the chamber as the exhaust valve opens again.

The length of each pipe in the exhaust system is carefully designed so that these pressure pulses are in the right place at the right time, therefore the design of the system is quite critical. An exhaust system is designed to work best within a set rev range (along with the power characteristics of the engine), meaning that at other engine speeds there will be a compromise.

The effect of exhaust design on two-stroke engines is greater than that on four-stroke engines, but generally exhaust system contributes a surprising amount to the performance of a motorcycle.

### The silencer

Given the explosive nature of the proceedings inside the combustion chamber, it is not surprising that exhaust gases tend to be rather noisy, and to comply with noise regulations they need to be silenced. The term 'silencer' may be a little optimistic, but it is a remarkable device for all that. The object is to allow the gases to pass as freely as possible, whilst absorbing the surplus energy that manifests itself as noise.

This is often accomplished by absorption; the fast-moving gases are slowed by allowing them to expand into the body of the silencer. The pulses of noise are further fragmented by allowing them to pass through perforated baffles, or through an expanded metal mesh and into a pad of mineral wool or similar. In other words, the harsh initial vibration is

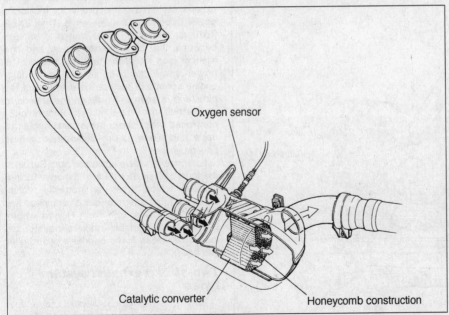

**2.11d  Typical catalytic converter**

Oxygen sensor

Catalytic converter

Honeycomb construction

*The oxygen sensor (Lambda sensor) helps the fuel injection system to maintain ideal conditions for the 'cat' to operate*

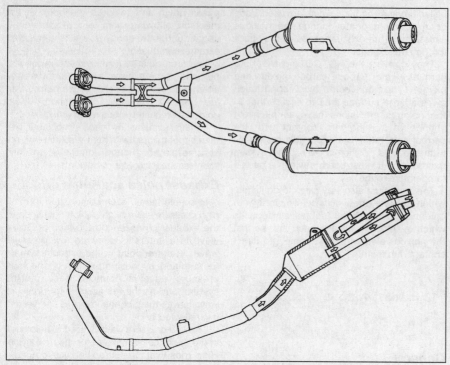

2.12a Section view of a typical four-stroke exhaust system

broken down into smaller sound waves, many of which cancel each other out. By the time the exhaust gases exit from the silencer tailpipe the noise has been subdued to an acceptable level.

Another approach to silencer construction is to split the silencer body into a number of smaller compartments, the gases being routed backwards and forwards through them in a rather tortuous path (see

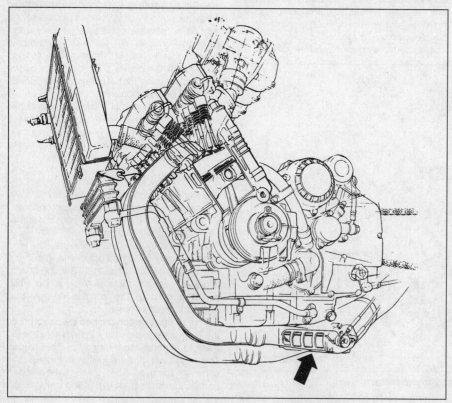

2.12b Location of the EXUP valve on the FZR1000

illustration 2.12a). The sound waves are repeatedly reflected, losing a little energy each time, until they exit at the tailpipe.

These two approaches are often combined to produce the very efficient systems in common use on most modern machines.

### Four-stroke exhaust system types

Four-stroke engines normally have one pipe coming out of each cylinder, though some large capacity single cylinder engines have two. These pipes are known as 'header pipes' or 'downpipes'. The downpipes on multi-cylinder engines quite often then merge into one silencer, but exact arrangements vary widely depending on the number of cylinders and their arrangement, the type of bike, the design brief, weight distribution and routing restrictions.

Common systems now are two-into-one, two-into-two, three-into-one, four-into-two-into-one, four-into-one, six-into-two, and so on. There are also systems that have cross-pipes linking the downpipes, or 'collector boxes' fitted between the downpipes and the silencer(s).

### EXUP, SET and H-VIX

As mentioned earlier, the exhaust pulse scavenge effect can be tuned to work best at particular engine speeds, and when this is combined with other design factors of the engine so that they all work in harmony, a good 'power-band' is produced. The downside or compromise is that when the engine is operating outside the power-band, it is running relatively inefficiently.

Yamaha was the first company to develop a system for varying the internal aperture of the exhaust system and thus producing maximum power throughout the rev range. Their EXUP (Exhaust Ultimate Power Valve) is located between the four header pipes and the silencer (see illustrations 2.12b and c). The power valve is closed at low to medium engine speeds to restrict the diameter of the pipe, and is open at higher engine speeds to de-restrict the pipe. It is electronically controlled via a servo motor and cables to open and close at pre-determined engine speeds.

Later designs have appeared from Suzuki in the form of their SET (Suzuki Exhaust Tuning) system which uses a butterfly valve, positioned just after the four downpipes have merged into one, and from Honda whose H-VIX (Honda Variable Intake/eXhaust) uses individual valves in the header pipes to alter gas flow.

### Two-stroke exhaust system types

Two-stroke engines always have one complete exhaust pipe (downpipe and silencer) per cylinder because the overall effect on engine performance of the silencer is more significant than on four-strokes. Thus to achieve

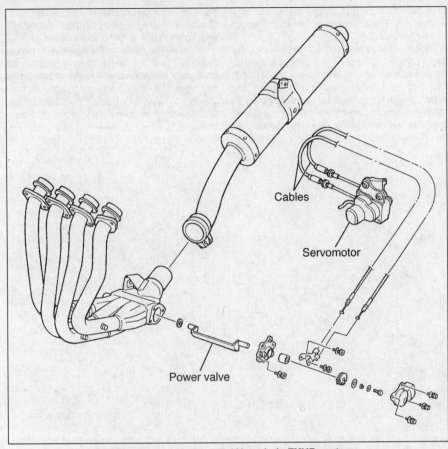

**2.12c  Component parts of Yamaha's EXUP system**

Cables

Servomotor

Power valve

the most from these effects it is necessary to have one exhaust pipe for each cylinder.

As previously mentioned, the emerging exhaust gases perform a secondary function by helping to draw the fresh mixture up into the combustion chamber through the transfer ports, and consequently the fresh charge helps to scavenge, or push out, the exhaust gases. On simple scooter or commuter bike systems the design is chosen to work as effectively as possible for the requirements of the bike. Where power is an overriding consideration, however, there is the intriguing possibility of obtaining extra 'free' power, based on the natural tendency for the exhaust pulses to resonate within the system.

This effect can be improved by careful design of the exhaust pipe and silencer as an integrated unit. The system is so constructed that the exhaust pipe gradually flares into a tapering silencer body, with a smaller reversed cone at the end, terminating in a small tailpipe. This arrangement is known as an 'expansion chamber', and is found on most high-performance road models and all racing machines. It works by controlling pressure waves within the expansion chamber to obtain better cylinder filling than would otherwise be possible.

As the exhaust port is uncovered, the gases rush out and into the exhaust system, assisted by the incoming charge emerging from the transfer ports. The exhaust gases move down the expansion chamber as a wave, gradually expanding and losing velocity **(see illustration 2.12d)**. When the wave hits

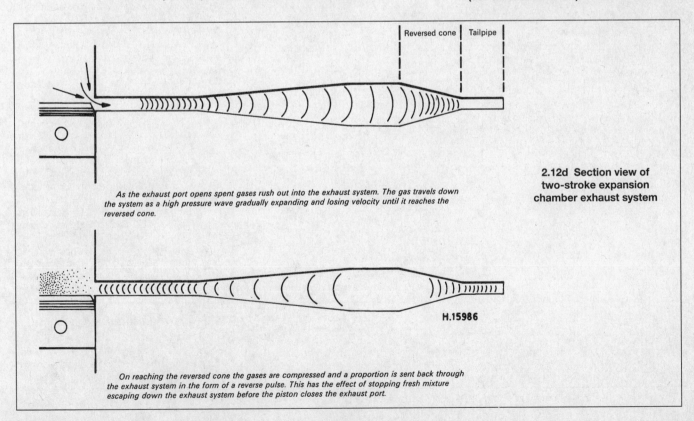

Reversed cone    Tailpipe

*As the exhaust port opens spent gases rush out into the exhaust system. The gas travels down the system as a high pressure wave gradually expanding and losing velocity until it reaches the reversed cone.*

**2.12d  Section view of two-stroke expansion chamber exhaust system**

H.15986

*On reaching the reversed cone the gases are compressed and a proportion is sent back through the exhaust system in the form of a reverse pulse. This has the effect of stopping fresh mixture escaping down the exhaust system before the piston closes the exhaust port.*

the reverse cone it is compressed and a proportion is reflected back up the system as a reverse pulse. By this time the combustion chamber is more than full, and the excess mixture is now beginning to fill the upper end of the exhaust pipe. As the piston covers and closes the transfer ports, the reverse wave reaches the port, ramming the extra mixture back into the combustion chamber where it is trapped by the rising piston. In this way there is a slight 'supercharging' effect, and the engine will produce more power than it could normally.

Unfortunately the reverse wave can only be synchronised to create this effect at a specific engine speed; above and below that speed, the engine runs as normal. To utilise the effect, the system must be carefully tuned to make maximum use of the extra power, and the kick as the engine reaches the narrow band of extra power can usually be felt quite clearly. Though of limited duration, this represents a little extra 'free' power, if at the expense of consistent power delivery. For the latter reason, expansion chambers are normally avoided on commuter machines, where an unexpected or sudden surge of power could be considered unnecessary or even dangerous in heavy traffic.

# Chapter 3
# Ignition

# Contents

## 1  Introduction

Having looked at the mechanical aspects of two-stroke and four-stroke engines, and also at the ways in which the fuel/air mixture is fed into the cylinder for combustion, we can now discuss the process of ignition. For the engine to work it is necessary to devise some method of initiating combustion at precisely the right moment in each engine cycle, and the universally popular method is to employ a

brief high-tension spark. The high tension spark is applied to an insulated electrode at the centre of a spark plug, where it is coaxed into jumping to earth (ground) across a small air gap.

The essential elements of any ignition system are as follows. Firstly, there must be some method of generating an electrical current to power the system. Even though the power is derived from a battery in many cases, it is essential that the battery is kept charged or the system would soon fail as the battery became depleted. The charge from the battery or from a separate source coil is

then applied to an ignition coil. This device converts the current from a low voltage/high current (or 'low tension') feed to the high voltage/low current ('high tension') form necessary if the plug electrodes are to be jumped – typically we are talking of converting 12 volts to around 40,000 on modern systems.

To control and vary the timing of the ignition spark, we require some sort of switch, either in the mechanical form of a contact breaker, or its electronic equivalent the pickup coil, or a crankshaft position sensor in conjunction with an electronic control unit (ECU). Also required is a method of advancing and retarding the timing of the spark, either mechanically or electronically, to optimise ignition timing at all engine speeds.

This Chapter tackles the basic theories, principles and methods involved in generating the spark and controlling its timing. The subject of ignition is covered in greater detail in the **Haynes Motorcycle Electrical Techbook**.

## 2  The power supply

The subject of generating electrical power is covered in detail in Chapter 10. Suffice to say that for ignition purposes a constant low voltage supply is required from which an ignition spark may be derived.

### Direct ignition

In its simplest form the power supply for the ignition is provided by an ignition source coil incorporated in the main generator assembly.

Its main advantage is that it offers a source of power which is unaffected by loads on the machine's electrical system. The only real drawback is that at very low engine speeds, such as those prevailing when trying to start the engine, the power output of the source coil may be insufficient to produce a strong spark. In practice, the designers will have ensured that this problem does not normally occur, though the added demands imposed by old wiring and leads and/or a fouled or badly adjusted spark plug may lead to starting difficulties.

### Battery ignition

The alternative to the above approach is to draw power from the main electrical system, and this system is common where the machine has a full electrical system with a battery to supply power when the engine isn't running or is being started.

This avoids the possible starting problems due to low output associated with direct systems, but can still be subject to wiring or spark plug problems. In addition the battery must always be fully charged to supply power to the ignition and in particular to operate the starter motor.

## 3  The ignition coil

### How it works

To create a spark, electricity has to jump across an air gap that exists between two electrodes on the spark plug. As air is a poor conductor of electricity, a very high voltage is needed to overcome the resistance offered by this gap, as well as that of the system itself

and all its components. If a system is in perfect working order this resistance is predictable, however if the wiring is old and corroded, or if the spark plug is fouled, or if the fuel/air mixture is too lean or too rich, then all these conditions will increase the overall resistance which has to be overcome.

The ignition coil transforms the low voltage supply from the battery or source coil into a high voltage (or high tension) supply. The resulting high tension circuit is of correspondingly low amperage, but is nevertheless ideal for ignition purposes. The coil achieves this by a process called electromagnetic induction: when an electrical current flows through a wire, it creates a weak electromagnetic field around it. If a second wire is passed through the electromagnetic field of the first a small current is induced in it. If the current in the first wire is switched on and off, the same effect is achieved in the second wire as the field builds up and collapses; in other words the second wire can be moved through the field, or the field can be moved past the wire to obtain the same result. With a single wire this effect is very weak, but it can be greatly increased by winding two separate coils of wire, one on top of the other.

In a working ignition coil the primary (low

tension) and secondary (high tension or 'HT') windings are built up one over the other around an iron core, which is used to concentrate the effect of the field or 'flux density'. The primary windings consist of a few hundred turns of thick copper wire, whilst the secondary windings, which feed into the thick high tension lead (and thereafter to the spark plug cap and spark plug), have many thousands of turns of thin copper wire. When power is applied to the primary windings a magnetic field is created. If the low tension feed to the primary windings is switched off, the field collapses and as it passes through the secondary windings, the high tension pulse required to create a spark is induced.

### Coil types

There are three basic types of coil in common use on motorcycles. The first is the canister type, which has a central iron core around which is the secondary winding **(see illustration 3.3a)**. The primary winding is outside this, and the whole assembly is housed in a metal canister. Sometimes the canister is filled with oil to aid the dispersal of heat generated in the coil.

Second, and more common now is the moulded coil, in which the position of the

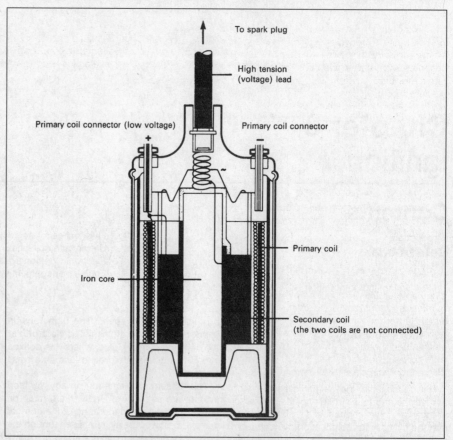

**3.3a  The canister coil**

*At the centre of the canister is an iron core. The secondary windings are wound around the core, and connect to the central high tension terminal. The primary winding are wound around the secondary windings, and are connected to the (+) and (–) primary circuit terminals.*

primary and secondary windings are reversed on the central laminated iron core **(see illustration 3.3b)**. The whole assembly is then encapsulated in resin to resist the effects of vibration commonly found on motorcycles. The moulded coil is the more popular choice because of its robust construction. On multi-cylinder machines it is common for one coil to feed two spark plugs by having two HT leads coming off the secondary windings – this is known as a 'spare or wasted spark system' **(see illustration 3.8b)**.

The third and most recent type of coil is combined with the spark plug cap **(see illustration 3.3c)** and often referred to as a 'stick coil'. Its size and weight is considerably less than that of a moulded coil and the greatest benefit is that it does away with the need for an HT lead.

## 4  The spark plug

The purpose of the spark plug is to conduct the HT pulse from the spark plug cap to the centre or positive electrode, to carry it across the air gap to the side electrode in the from of a spark, and then to send it to earth (ground). The spark plug is an expendable part of the ignition system, designed to perform its job for a period and to be thrown away when it becomes worn and eroded and be replaced with a new one.

The spark plug is remarkable for both its low cost and for the demanding role which it fulfils so reliably. In fact, the low cost of the plug is misleading as it is a precision made component, and is largely due to the vast numbers in which they are manufactured. The varying demands placed on spark plugs and the adverse and diverse conditions under which they must operate in different types of engine are such that they are produced in a bewildering array of sizes, thread reaches and heat grades.

### Construction

At the top of the plug is a round terminal to which the HT lead is connected via the spark plug cap **(see illustration 3.4a overleaf)**. The terminal is in contact with the centre electrode which is normally made of a nickel alloy to resist the effects of heat and the corrosive elements in the fuel, and often has a copper core to help conduct heat away. On some plugs, the electrode is made from more exotic alloys of silver, platinum, palladium or gold. These are designed to offer even greater resistance to erosion, and to perform well under particularly adverse conditions.

The centre electrode passes through a ceramic insulator and projects from it at the lower end. The insulator serves to protect the central electrode from electrical leakage, and to shield it from much of the engine's heat.

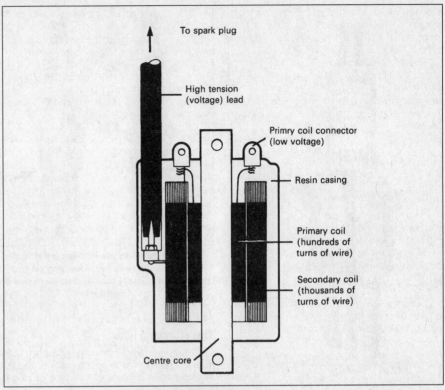

**3.3b  The moulded coil**

*The primary windings are wound around a laminated iron core, whilst the secondary windings are wound on top of the primary and are connected to the high tension terminal. The whole assembly is then encapsulated in resin to protect it from the effects of moisture and vibration.*

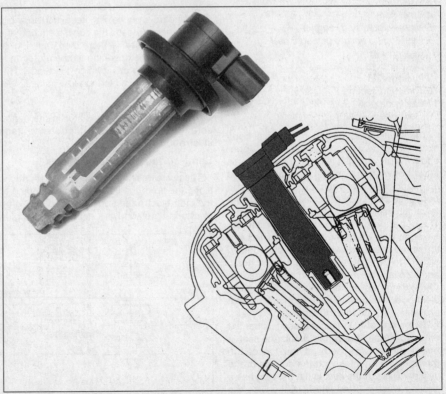

**3.3c  The combined ignition coil/spark plug cap in cross-section (left) and in situ (right)**

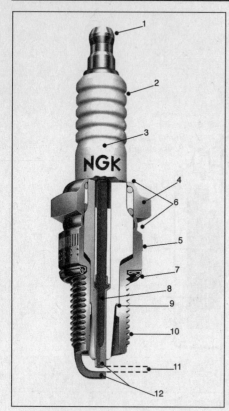

### 3.4a Spark plug construction

1 Terminal
2 Insulator ribs
3 Insulator
4 Steel body
5 Nickel-plated body surface
6 Caulking (to ensure gas-tight seal
7 Sealing washer
8 Copper core
9 Inner gasket
10 Threaded section
11 Electrode gap
12 Electrodes

The insulator is retained in the metal body of the plug by a spun-over lip at its upper edge. To prevent gas leakage there are seals fitted between the central electrode and the insulator, and between the insulator and body. The plug body is formed from steel, and is usually nickel plated to prevent corrosion. The upper part of the body incorporates the hexagon with which the plug is tightened and loosened. At its lower end it is threaded to allow it to be screwed into the cylinder head, and a collapsible metal sealing ring is fitted. At the extreme lower edge is the side or earth electrode. This is welded to the plug body and provides the path to earth for the spark.

Two types of plug seat are used, either flat or conical **(see illustration 3.4b)**. The seat is the portion of the body at the top of the threads which mates with the surface of the cylinder head. If the seat is flat the plug has a sealing washer fitted with it. Otherwise the seat is conical and requires no washer.

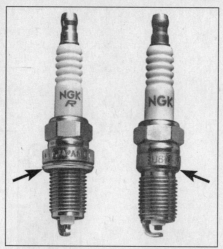

**3.4b  The plug on the left has a flat seat with a sealing washer. The plug on the right has a conical seat and doesn't use a washer**

## Types

### The standard type

The centre electrode only just protrudes from the bore of the threaded section, and the insulator nose is inside it. This type of plug is suited to older engines

### The projected nose type

The centre electrode and insulator nose both protrude from the threaded section **(see illustration 3.4a)**. The temperature of the electrodes rises more quickly from cold than the standard type, helping keep it clean, while at high engine speeds the cooling effect of the incoming mixture is increased, helping to keep it within the operating temperature range and so reducing pre-ignition tendency. This type of plug is suited to modern engines.

### Resistor plugs

These incorporate a resistor in the centre core to suppress radio interference **(see illustration 3.4c)**.

### Semi-surface discharge plugs

These are designed so that the spark tracks along the tip of the insulator when jumping to the side electrode(s) or body (depending on electrode type), and this helps keep the plug

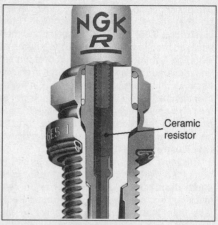

**3.4c  The ceramic resistor protects against radio interference**

Ceramic resistor

**3.4d  The semi-surface discharge type plug**

clean as the spark effectively burns off any deposits **(see illustration 3.4d)**.

Using side electrodes that do not cover the tip of the centre electrode helps expose the spark to the fuel/air mixture. Using multiple side electrodes produces multiple sparks in theory, though in practice the voltage will always take the easiest route, so if one side electrode is dirtier than another, it will use the cleaner one. The other reason for multiple side electrodes is that if the spark alternates between the electrodes, more of the plug will be kept clean.

### Thread reach

The thread reach is simply the length of the threaded section of the plug body, and this has to be matched with the depth of the thread bore in the cylinder head so that the plug electrodes are positioned in the right place in the combustion chamber **(see illustration 3.4e)**.

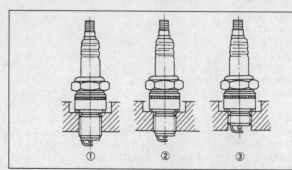

*Figure 1: Reach is too long; the earth electrode may overheat or hit the piston and carbon may accumulate around the projected thread.*
*Figure 2: Reach is correct.*
*Figure 3: Reach is too short; carbon may accumulate in the threads of the plug hole.*

**3.4e  The importance of correct plug reach**

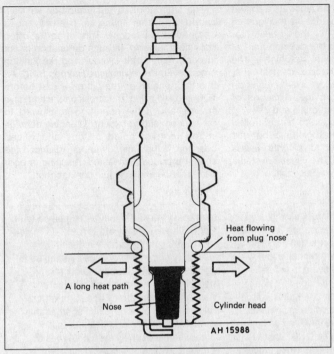

**3.4f A hot (or soft) spark plug**

*This type of plug has a long insulator nose to limit the rate of heat loss from the electrodes.*

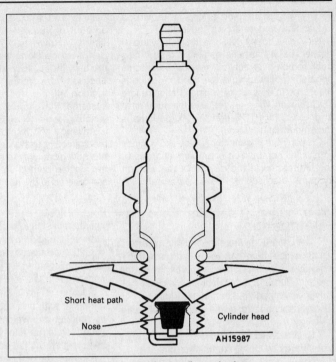

**3.4g A cold (or hard) spark plug**

*This type of plug has a short insulator nose to encourage heat loss from the electrodes.*

The diameter of the threaded section (usually 10, 12 or 14 mm) also has to match the bore in the cylinder, as does the pitch of the threads. Spark plugs in motorcycle engines seem to be getting smaller and smaller, even in large capacity performance engines.

## Heat range

The plug electrodes must be kept at the correct operating temperature, which is in the range of 400 to 800°C. If they run below 400°C they are not hot enough to burn off the carbon deposits generated by combustion, and if they run above 800°C there is increased oxide fouling and electrode burning. At 950°C the electrode is hot enough to cause pre-ignition, which is when the fuel/air mixture ignites prematurely (before the plug sparks) due to the heat of the electrode.

To allow for the different performance levels and operating temperatures of engines a range of spark plugs is necessary. To achieve this, and to ensure that whatever the temperature of the engine the plug remains within its operating range, different amounts of insulator are built into the plug, and this can be seen by the length of the insulator 'nose' which projects into the core of the threaded section of the body.

A plug with a large insulator will keep the heat in the plug, and these are termed hot or 'soft' plugs **(see illustration 3.4f)**. A plug with a small insulator will allow the heat to be conducted away and dissipated into the engine much quicker by the steel body, and

these are termed cold or 'hard' plugs **(see illustration 3.4g)**.

If an engine runs hot, it is necessary to fit a grade of plug which will dissipate heat from the electrodes rapidly. In such a case a 'cold' plug with a short insulator nose is chosen, and these are used on high speed performance engines. Conversely, if the engine runs cool, heat must be retained longer at the plug electrodes. In this case a 'hot' plug with a long insulator nose is chosen, and these are used on older or less highly tuned engines. A popular misunderstanding which seems to persist is that you should run 'hot' plugs in 'hot' engines, and 'cold' plugs in 'cold' engines, but this is definitely not the case.

## 5 Ignition timing and combustion

### Timing of the spark

The timing of the ignition of the fuel/air mixture, i.e. the point during the cycle of an engine at which the spark occurs, is extremely important. The spark must be timed so that the fuel/air mixture can burn completely and thus provide the maximum energy at exactly the right moment in relation to piston position. It would be no good if the piston was still on its up-stroke when the combustion finishes, and likewise it would be no good if the piston had completed half its down-stroke before combustion started.

The combustion of the fuel/air mix takes a short while to complete. It is not an instantaneous explosion, but controlled burning. Ideally the combustion process needs to begin just before the piston reaches TDC (i.e. in advance of TDC) so that it is at its peak and producing the most energy just after TDC as the piston commences its down-stroke. Having the peak amount of energy crammed into the combustion chamber just after it has been at its smallest volume (as it is at TDC) exerts the most pressure on the piston.

However, what is an optimum firing point at one engine speed is a bad firing point at a higher or lower speed. This is because the higher the engine speed, the less time there is for the fuel/air mixture to burn. So ideally as the speed of the engine increases, the point at which the spark occurs at the plug needs to be advanced.

### Advance and retard

In Chapter 1 the section on valve timing highlights the restrictions placed on an engine in its usability and performance across the rev range due to the fact that, for the vast majority of motorcycles, valve timing is static, i.e. it cannot be varied. This leads to a compromise in that the engine has to be set up (timed) for a particular characteristic (i.e. low down torque and pulling power at the expense of a power band high up in the rev range, and vice versa). The advantage with ignition timing, and where it has a huge advantage over valve timing, is that it can be varied relatively easily. The varying of the ignition timing is known as 'advancing' and 'retarding' the ignition.

As engine speed rises the timing 'advances' further, i.e. it happens earlier, and as it falls back to tick-over again it 'retards' back to its original amount of advance. Ignition timing is measured in degrees of engine rotation before TDC as with valve timing, and the number of degrees before TDC that the plug sparks is the amount of advance.

On early small capacity two-stroke engines with small combustion chambers, and due to the limitations in the design of the ignition systems themselves, it was acceptable to have a fixed amount of advance or a limited amount of variable advance in the ignition timing. However, with the quest for performance along with the development of multi-cylinder four-stroke machines, the necessity for more precise control over ignition timing led to improved ignition systems that would provide a means of variable advance (see Sections 6 and 7).

Advance and retard used to be controlled mechanically using centrifugal units but this has now given way to electronic control inside the ignition control unit. The various systems are covered in the next few Sections.

The amount of advance must be set very carefully. If the timing is over-advanced detonation will occur. This effect is often known as 'pinking' (though detonation is not the only cause of it – knock and pre-ignition produce similar results (see **Haynes Hint**). As this happens when the piston is just before TDC and still rising, the stress on the engine is severe, and if the condition is allowed to persist can lead to expensive engine damage in the form of holed pistons and ruined bearings. If the timing is under-advanced the energy produced is wasted, resulting in poor performance and high fuel consumption.

## Detonation

The condition where the fuel/air mixture detonates rather than burns in a controlled manner. It occurs when the flame speed (the rate of burning) is too high, and is caused by over-advanced ignition timing, a high compression ratio, or the grade of fuel being too low.

Compression ratio and octane rating, the standards by which combustion chamber pressure and fuel grade are measured, are related in that an engine with a high compression ratio needs a fuel with a high octane rating. Consequently if the fuel cannot cope with the pressure, detonation could occur.

Detonation produces a noise from the engine known as 'pinking', and if it persists could lead to extensive engine damage.

## Knock

Knock is a similar phenomenon to detonation, with similar results, but what actually happens is subtly different. It occurs when the effects of combustion pressure and heat combine to spontaneously ignite the portion of the fuel/air mix that exists in the outer extremes of the combustion chamber. This produces a flame front that burns towards the centre of the combustion chamber (see illustration 3.5a).

The knocking sound occurs as the flame front meets and collides with the gas ignited by the spark plug and vibration is produced between the two flame fronts. Pinking is the term commonly used to describe both knock and detonation.

## Pre-ignition

Pre-ignition is different to detonation and knock in that it happens before the spark plug sparks, and is basically a premature burning of the fuel/air mixture. It is caused by a 'hot-spot' in the combustion chamber, which is most often created by a piece of carbon deposit heating and remaining heated to a point of incandescence so that it spontaneously ignites the fuel/air mix as it enters the engine (see illustration 3.5b). This condition produces similar results to over-advanced ignition – a pinking noise and engine damage if it is allowed to persist.

A linked effect to pre-ignition that does not occur with detonation and knock is that of 'running-on', which is when the engine continues to run after the ignition has been switched off. As the engine turns, the red-hot carbon deposit causes the small amount of fuel/air mix that is still being drawn in to ignite, which keeps the engine running until the gradually reduced momentum due to there being very little fuel/air combined with poor timing eventually stops it.

Modern clean fuels have reduced the possibility of carbon deposits building up in engines, so its occurrence is now rare. There are also systems built into fuel injection and sometimes into carburettors which shut-off either the fuel or air as the ignition is switched off, meaning that combustion is unlikely even if there is a 'hot-spot'. This is even more important as engines become more efficient by running weaker or leaner, as weak mixtures cause higher engine temperatures.

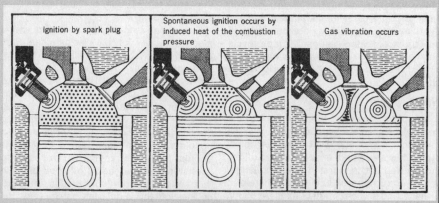

| Ignition by spark plug | Spontaneous ignition occurs by induced heat of the combustion pressure | Gas vibration occurs |

3.5a Sequence to 'knock'

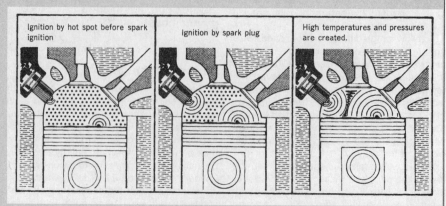

| Ignition by hot spot before spark ignition | Ignition by spark plug | High temperatures and pressures are created. |

3.5b Sequence to 'pre-ignition'

## 6 Flywheel generator (magneto) ignition systems

The flywheel generator (or flywheel magneto) ignition system is about the simplest way of obtaining an ignition spark, and as such has been popular for many years on small engines. It has the advantage of deriving its power directly from its own source coil and thus does not demand a battery for starting purposes.

The flywheel generator unit is in fact a small alternator of the rotating magnet type. It consists of a cast alloy rotor containing cast-in permanent magnets. This is attached to one end of the crankshaft and spins with it, acting as an additional flywheel. Inside the rotor, and mounted separately on a fixed circular plate called a stator, are the ignition source and lighting coils. As the rotor spins, the fields of the magnets pass repeatedly through the coil windings, and thus induce a current in exactly the same manner as that described earlier for the ignition coil **(see illustration 3.6a)**.

As its name suggests, an alternator produces alternating current (ac). This is because the polarity of the magnets in relation to the coils is constantly changing from north to south, and this in turn means that the current induced in the coils flows one way, then reverses and flows the other way. As may be expected, there is a dead point between the two extremes at which no power is produced, but since this fluctuation takes

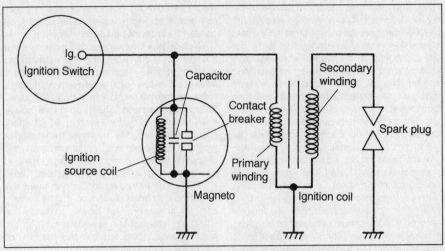

3.6a A flywheel generator (magneto) ignition system

place very rapidly it is of little importance as far as the lighting system is concerned. Those of you who own or have owned a machine with a flywheel generator will no doubt be aware of the way in which this fluctuation can be seen; flickering lights at tick-over.

### How it works

The principle of operation of this ignition circuit is known as 'energy transfer' or 'field build-up'. The ignition source coil forms a circuit with the primary windings of the ignition coil. Between the two is the contact breaker assembly, which acts as a switch, and this is connected in parallel with the coils **(see illustration 3.6b)**.

If the contacts are closed (which they are for much of the time) the current flows through them and thus to earth. The ignition coil is thus short-circuited and receives no power. The contacts are opened by a cam at the correct point for ignition to occur, and the position of the rotor is arranged so that the output from the source coil is at its maximum as the contacts separate. The current from the source coil must now flow through the ignition coil primary windings, so inducing the HT spark in the secondary windings, firing the spark plug. It is this transfer of energy to the ignition coil which gives the system its name.

There are a couple of points to note about the system. Firstly, that it is important to time

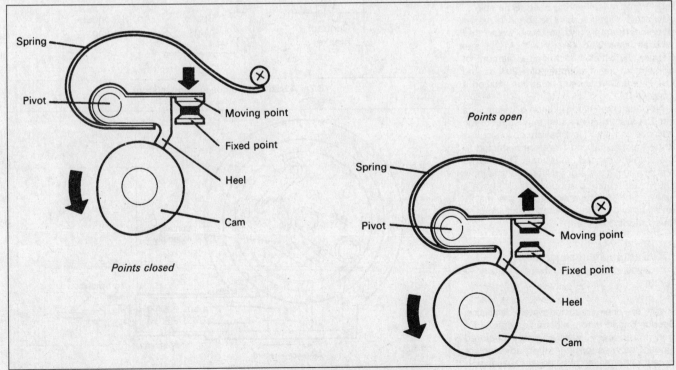

3.6b Contact breaker operation

the contact separation to make full use of the available current; if they opened at a 'dead' point in the cycle there would be no current flow, and no spark. Secondly, that there is a final component in the system which we have so far ignored. This is called a capacitor, and can be thought of as a sort of short-term battery; it can store a small charge and then discharge it again very quickly when required.

In this application its purpose is to stop the contact breaker points from acting like the spark plug. This is necessary because the contact faces move apart quite slowly by electrical standards, and when they are just moving apart they provide a more tempting path (i.e. with less resistance) to earth than the ignition coil primary windings. To prevent the charge from jumping across the contacts in the form of a spark a capacitor is connected across them, and this will store any residual current, thus preventing burning of the contact faces caused by sparking.

### Advance and retard control

The flywheel generator ignition system is a simple and inexpensive method of providing an ignition spark. In practice it works quite well, providing that full use is made of energy transfer at the correct point in the generation cycle.

It was due to the limitations imposed by this that most stators on early flywheel generator ignition systems could not be adjusted to vary the ignition timing; it was set during manufacture and could subsequently be altered by only a small amount by varying the contact breaker gap. Whilst this is sufficient on small two-stroke engines, on larger and four-stroke machines the need to be able to advance the ignition point as speed increases becomes greater, and so these were fitted with an automatic timing unit (ATU – see Section 7), which had a limited amount of adjustment (a maximum of +20° at the crankshaft, as opposed to about +40° on a normal ATU).

Nowadays the incorporation of electronics into the system means that the control of the advance and retard mechanism no longer has to be mechanical and therefore restricted to the aforementioned limitations. This means that flywheel generator ignition systems (now known as 'magneto supported CDI') have a new lease of life and are in regular use, mainly on small two-stroke off-road machines (see illustrations 3.8a and f).

### 7  Battery and coil ignition systems

With the energy transfer system detailed in Section 6 (and before electronic control of it was introduced), obtaining the required amount of variation in ignition advance for decent performance at all engine speeds was not possible. This was because the contacts

would be opening when the source coil was not at full strength, so an alternative (and constant) supply of power was required.

The new power source is derived not from a source coil, but from the main electrical system of the machine. Given the more advanced nature of the larger machines, a more substantial and stable supply is required for both ignition and lighting purposes, so we must resort to a battery system. In a battery and coil system, the flywheel generator is replaced by a more substantial alternator, the output of which is rectified (converted to direct current, or dc) and regulated (kept within certain limits) so that it can meet the changing demands placed on it. The battery acts as a reservoir of power to keep the supply constant at low speeds and when the engine has stopped, and it is the inclusion of the battery which demands a dc recharging system.

### How it works

The battery and coil ignition system works in a similar way to the flywheel generator type, but there are some important differences (see illustration 3.7a). The battery supplies power to the primary windings of the ignition coil, and the circuit is completed by the closed contact breaker points. These are connected in series (in line) with the coil rather than in parallel (across) it, as in the case of the flywheel generator version.

The magnetic field generated in the primary windings is maintained until the cam opens the contact breaker points. As this occurs, power to the primary windings is interrupted, the field collapses, and a high tension pulse is induced in the secondary windings, creating the ignition spark. A capacitor is included in the circuit and fulfils the same role as it did in the flywheel generator arrangement. The principle of operation in this system is known as 'field collapse'.

### Advance and retard control

With a constant, regulated supply to the ignition coil, we can in theory now obtain an ignition spark at any point in the engine cycle, so to turn this into practice a system for varying (advancing and retarding) the ignition timing (or firing point) is needed.

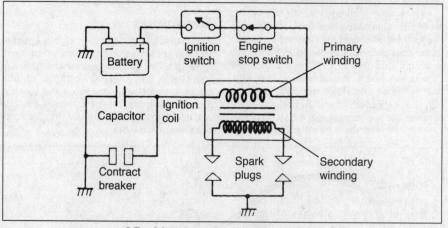

**3.7a  A battery and coil ignition system**

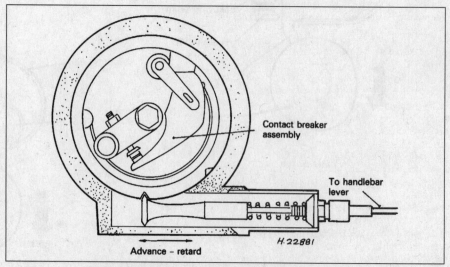

**3.7b  Manual ignition advance and retard mechanism**

The first systems were manually controlled, using a lever on the handlebar to allow the ignition to be retarded during starting and at low speeds, or advanced as required as engine speed increased (see illustration 3.7b). This worked well enough for a simple four-stroke single (provided you remembered to retard the ignition before starting to avoid being launched over the handlebars by the kickstart lever kicking back!) but on more complex multi-cylinder engines it became obvious that a constant and automatic method of adjusting the timing was needed, and so the automatic timing unit (ATU) was created.

Instead of fixing the contact breaker cam directly to the shaft that drives it, it is included as part of the ATU (see illustration 3.7c). The unit comprises a baseplate with a central support pin which carries the cam. The cam can turn on the pin, but its movement is controlled by two spring-loaded bob weights. At rest and at low speeds, the springs hold the cam in its retarded position, but as the engine speed increases the weights are flung outwards, turning the cam and thus advancing the ignition (see illustration 3.7d).

The chief drawbacks of the battery and coil system are that it is dependent on power from the battery to allow the engine to be started, and it has more moving parts. This means that wear occurs in more areas of the system, and that regular maintenance is required to keep the system working efficiently.

Not only that but improved engine design has allowed higher engine speeds and compression ratios. Higher engine speeds mean even more wear on the moving parts of the contact breaker, and inaccuracy due to centrifugal force flinging the contacts open further than they should. A higher compression ratio requires a higher voltage to produce a spark, and higher voltages lead to burning of the contract breaker surfaces. To improve precision still further it is necessary to eliminate as far as possible all of the mechanical parts of the system, and this is exactly what electronic ignition does.

## 8  Electronic ignition systems

The Achilles heel of both of the systems discussed so far is the inclusion of mechanical parts. It is difficult to manufacture components like contact breakers and ATUs with sufficient precision to ensure reliable operation, and even when this is achieved the effects of wear take an inevitable toll during normal use.

The above problems were initially solved in part by a transistor assisted coil (TAC) ignition system. This first arrangement using transistors removed much of the electrical load on the contact breakers by having the transistor act as the switch for the ignition coil

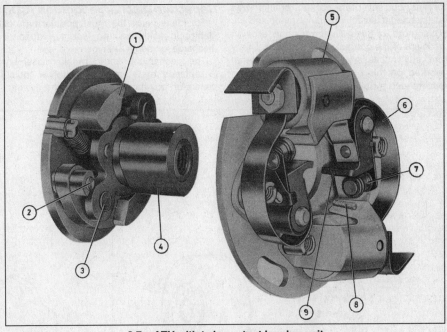

3.7c  ATU with twin contact breaker unit

| | | |
|---|---|---|
| 1  Centrifugal weights | 4  Cam | 7  Contacts |
| 2  Centrifugal weight pivot | 5  Condenser | 8  Cam lubrication pad |
| 3  Cam pivot | 6  Contact leaf spring | 9  Cam follower or heel |

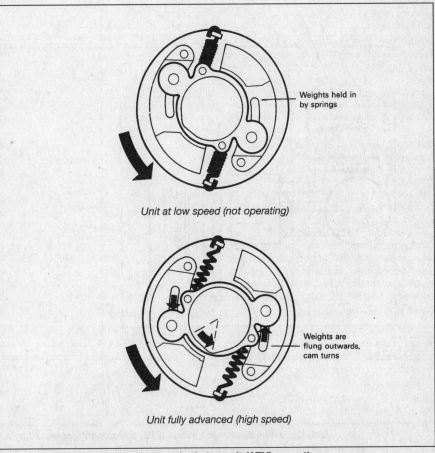

Unit at low speed (not operating)

Weights held in by springs

Weights are flung outwards, cam turns

Unit fully advanced (high speed)

3.7d  Automatic timing unit (ATU) operation

primary current, but a contact breaker was still needed to switch the transistor on and off. This more or less eliminates the erosion problem of the contacts, but means that they are still necessary. Many early systems worked on this basis, but have now been superseded by fully electronic systems.

### Capacitor Discharge Ignition (CDI)

For many years the most popular type of electronic ignition system was the capacitor discharge ignition (CDI) type.

The mechanical contact breaker assembly is replaced by a small 'pick-up' or 'pulse generator' coil mounted close to the flywheel generator or alternator rotor (sometimes as part of the stator plate assembly, sometimes mounted separately) **(see illustrations 3.8a, b and c)**.

At the firing point a small trigger magnet on the rotor sweeps past the coil thereby inducing a tiny signal current which is fed to

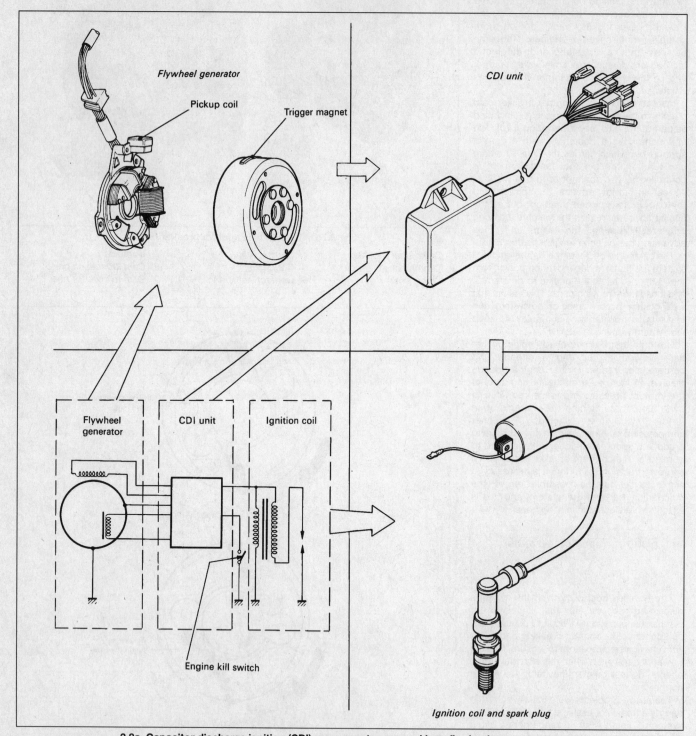

**3.8a Capacitor discharge ignition (CDI) components powered by a flywheel generator system**
*This shows the elements in a typical CDI system (Suzuki DR125 shown) together with the circuit diagram for this particular system.*

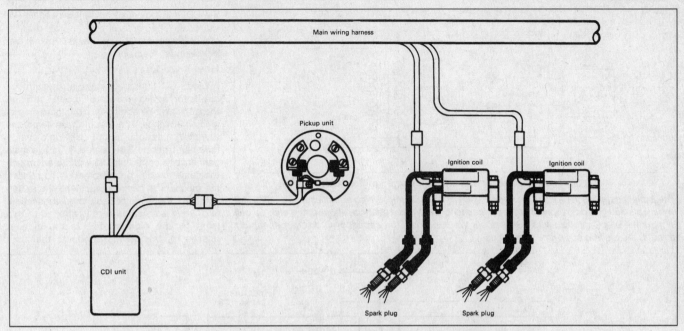

**3.8b  A typical four-cylinder type CDI system powered by battery (from alternator)**

*This shows the various ignition components. Note that two plugs are operated by a single coil and pickup. This means that each plug sparks twice per engine cycle, an arrangement known as a 'spare' or 'wasted' spark system because one of the two sparks occurs during the exhaust stroke.*

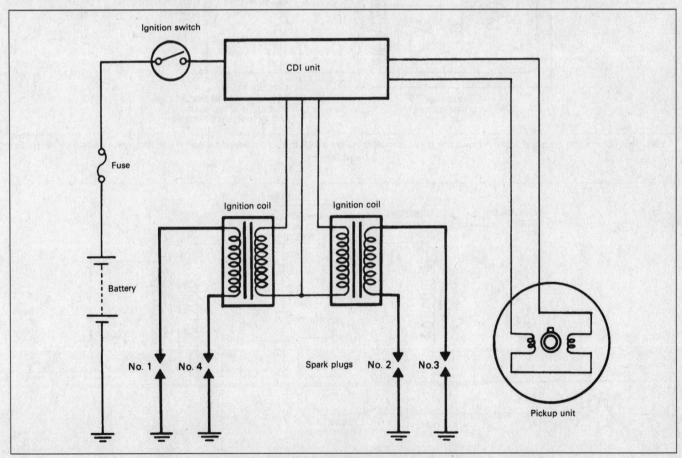

**3.8c Four-cylinder CDI system – circuit diagram**

*This is a circuit diagram of the system shown in 3.8b*

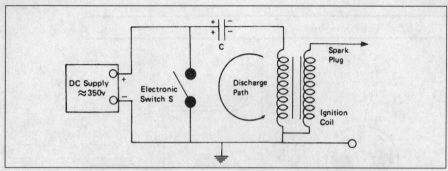

**3.8d  The principal of capacitor discharge ignition (CDI)**

*The battery supplies 12 volts to an inverter (part of the CDI unit), which amplifies it to around 350 volts. This 350 volt dc supply charges the capacitor C. When a spark is required, the pick-up coil signals the electronic to switch S to close. When it does, the capacitor C discharges rapidly through the ignition coil primary windings*

the CDI unit indicating a spark is needed. For more on the different types of pick-up coil/pulse generator and how they work, see below under 'Sensors'.

## How it works

Most CDI units contain a thyristor, a capacitor and a couple of diodes, though there will also be additional circuitry to control ignition advance. The first of these items, the thyristor, functions as the electronic switch **(see illustrations 3.8d, e and f)**. Its two main connections control the flow of current, much the same as the contact breaker. To replace the mechanical cam arrangement (the switch actuator), the thyristor has a third connection, and when a small current is applied to this (sent by the pick-up coil as the magnet passes it), the device conducts the main

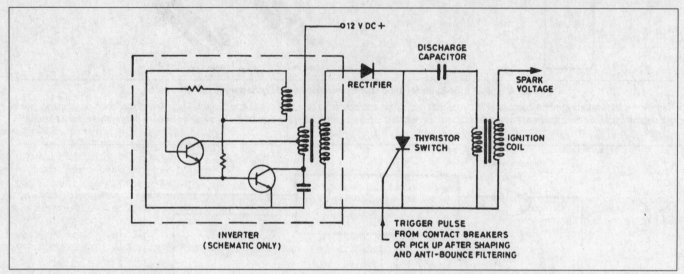

**3.8e  This schematic circuit diagram shows the basic circuitry inside a CDI that is powered by battery voltage and uses an inverter to bump it up**

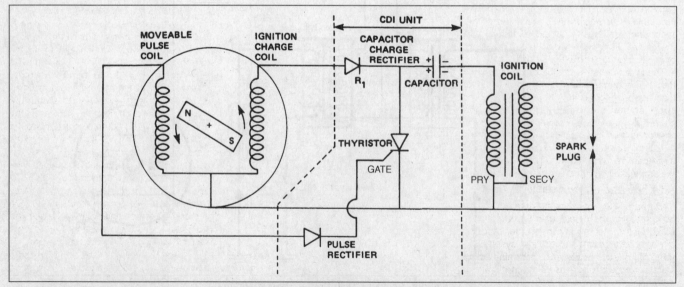

**3.8f  This circuit diagram shows the basic circuitry inside a CDI. Power in this case is supplied by a flywheel magneto, as opposed to a battery and inverter**

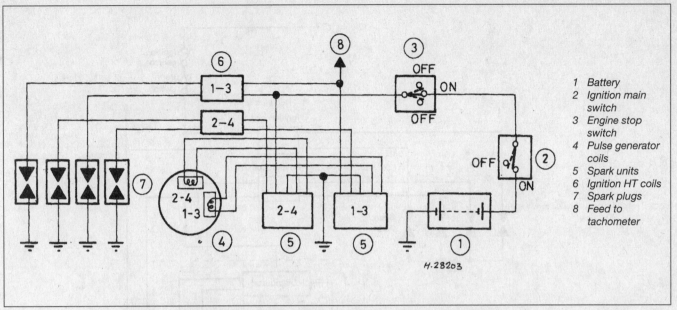

**3.8g Basic transistor ignition system for a four cylinder engine**

1 Battery
2 Ignition main switch
3 Engine stop switch
4 Pulse generator coils
5 Spark units
6 Ignition HT coils
7 Spark plugs
8 Feed to tachometer

current and will remain conductive until this falls to a low level. At this point the thyristor reverts to an 'off' state until it receives the next trigger signal from the pickup. The thyristor is also known as a silicon-controlled rectifier and often abbreviated to the initials SCR.

The next important element in the CDI black box is the capacitor, which is similar in function to the capacitor we know from the earlier systems. As before, this device stores a charge, in this case a few hundred volts, derived either from the source coil or the battery supply, according to power supply type. When the trigger current is applied to the thyristor, the capacitor discharges rapidly, sending a short pulse of energy through the ignition coil primary windings. This in turn induces a powerful HT spark from the secondary windings to ignite the mixture, and therefore works on the 'field build-up' principle mentioned earlier.

The characteristics of CDI ignition are such that the secondary voltage produced is higher than normal (around 40,000 volts) and so the spark at the plug is far more precise and powerful than in a conventional system. Ignition is thus more accurate and less prone to failure. Since there are no mechanical parts there can be no wear and once correctly set the timing will not require further adjustment.

### Advance and retard control

On early CDI systems automatic ignition advance was achieved using a secondary pickup circuit to modify the trigger point by the desired amount, and on later systems by using the effect that a change of engine speed causes in the properties of magnetism and induction (measured in voltage rise time) between the trigger magnet and the pick-up coil.

### Transistorised ignition

In many respects transistorised ignition is similar to CDI in that it has no moving parts and relies on a magnetic trigger and pick-up system to signal the control unit to produce a spark (see illustration 3.8g). One difference is that it uses the 'field collapse' principle of the battery and coil system, as opposed to the 'field build-up' principle of the CDI system.

CDI had been the preferred method of ignition control for many years, but with the development of transistors coupled with the move from analogue to digital control of the switching devices, manufacturers soon began to favour the fitting of digital transistorised ignition systems.

Circuit design began using analogue technology to keep the energy at the coil constant and to produce an ignition advance curve to suit the engine. However, and especially with the increasing use of fuel injection, the need for more and more variable parameters such as throttle position, crankshaft position, engine speed, road speed, intake air temperature and pressure, engine temperature and engine load information resulted in a change to digital control. Digital control could handle varying parameters much more quickly and efficiently and led ultimately to the development of engine management systems for control of the fuel injection and ignition systems.

### Digital ignition and engine 'mapping'

Today, the most advanced and precise ignition systems, as used on the majority of modern 'superbikes', are digital (or to be more accurate digitally controlled transistorised systems). Information on one, some or all of the variable parameters (throttle position,

crankshaft position, engine speed, road speed, intake air temperature and pressure, engine temperature and engine load) is picked up by sensors and transmitted to the electronic control unit (ECU). If the information is sent in analogue signals (as some of the sensors do) they are converted to digital form.

All the information is then processed by a computer for control of voltage and timing of the pulse that generates the spark. Not all systems use all of the sensors mentioned, and some of the earliest systems only used one sensor, the pulse generator coil/pick-up coil/crankshaft position sensor (basically the same thing), which gives information on crankshaft position and engine speed (see illustration 3.8h overleaf).

The signal receiver in the ECU receives the information from the sensor and then converts it to digital if necessary. The signal is then sent to the processor, which relays it to the read only memory (ROM). The ROM has been pre-programmed with the optimum timing characteristics for the information it is being sent, and so determines when to switch the transistor on and off, which generates the spark via the coil. When the transistor is turned on, the ignition coil's primary windings are saturated. The memory then turns the transistor off when it is time to create a spark, which is induced via the secondary windings as the field in the primary windings collapses.

The key is the pre-programmed ROM which stores all the correct ignition advance settings for all the possible variations in all the parameters used by the particular system.

When an engine is developed, it is tested over its rev range using a fixed throttle setting (so the amount of load is constant, even though the engine speed is rising). At every throttle position, the optimum ignition

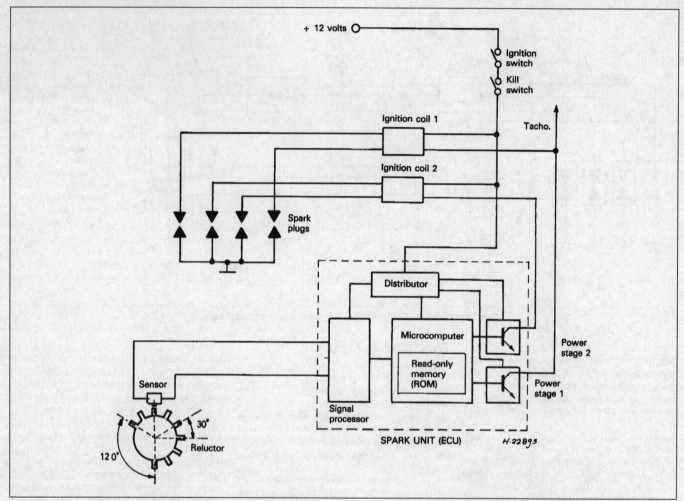

**3.8h  A digital ignition system as used by Honda – the distributor relays power to the various circuits within the ECU**

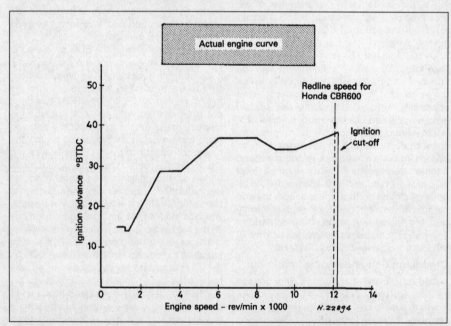

**3.8i  This single two-dimensional graph shows the ideal amount of advance at all engine speeds using a fixed throttle setting (i.e. constant load)**

advance for the actual engine speed is noted and plotted on a graph **(see illustration 3.8i)**. By amalgamating all the graphs for all the throttle positions, a three-dimensional 'map' of all the ignition settings for all engine speeds is created, and it is this map which is effectively programmed into the memory. When the map becomes three-dimensional, three values are shown, engine speed, engine load (determined by throttle opening), and ignition advance **(see illustration 3.8j)**.

The size of the ROM and the capability of the processor determines how much information can be processed by how many sensors and how many maps can be stored. On sophisticated systems many maps are created by amalgamating information from different sensors. Comparison of the shape of maps produced by a digital electronic ignition system and a mechanical contact-breaker system highlight the degree of efficiency obtained by digital control **(see illustration 3.8k)**.

## Sensors

A sensor is a conversion device which will measure or detect a quantity and produce a

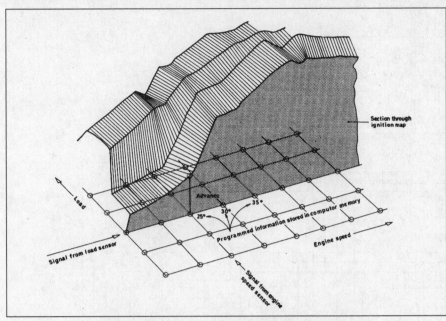

**3.8j Ignition map and stored information concept**

*When all the single two-dimensional graphs obtained from the different throttle settings are put together they become a three-dimensional 'map' giving the ideal amount of ignition advance for any engine speed and any amount of load*

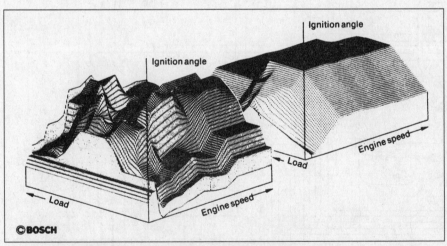

**3.8k An optimised ignition advance map (left) compared to the ignition map of a mechanical advance system**

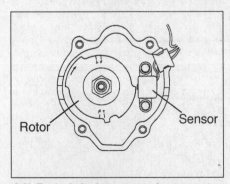

**3.8l Typical single sensor pulse generator coil and rotor**

corresponding electrical signal. Quantities usually measured on a motorcycle are speed, position, temperature, pressure, flow, level and content.

The two most important and widely used sensors in ignition systems are the crankshaft position sensor (or pulse generator/pick-up coil) and the throttle position sensor. Other sensors that are used can also relate to fuel injection and have been covered in Chapter 2.

The **crankshaft position sensor** 'assembly' consists of a rotor and one or two sensors known as, 'pulse generators' or 'pick-up coils'. The rotor has projections or cut-outs (or sometimes indentations) on it which trigger electronic pulses in the sensors as they pass

(see illustration 3.8l). By knowing which trigger is passing (by having a different sized one or a gap between them that the processor recognises as denoting a particular crankshaft position, i.e. TDC for cylinder 1) and by measuring the time lapse until the next trigger passes, the exact position of each piston in each cylinder is passed to the ECU, as is the speed at which the engine is turning. The pulses are then sent to the ECU where they are shaped (any peaks squared off for precision), amplified, converted and processed into information giving crankshaft position and engine speed that the ROM then uses to determine ignition timing.

Pulse generators/pick-up coils come in three different types: optical, Hall effect and variable reluctance, and each works slightly differently to produce a similar result.

The **throttle position sensor**, or TPS, is used to provide information regarding engine load (amount of throttle opening) and rate of change of load (how quickly the throttle is being opened or closed). Its use has been possible through having digital control over ignition timing, and it is beginning to appear regularly on top-of-the range motorcycles. On machines with digital electronic ignition but without fuel injection, it is fitted to the carburettors and the information from it enables the ignition system to provide optimum ignition timing. On machines with fuel injection, it is fitted to the throttle bodies and the information it provides is used to determine fuelling requirements, giving it a dual role.

The sensor is a small unit which acts as a variable resistor and is keyed to one end of the throttle shaft. As the throttle is turned from fully closed to fully open, the resistance of the sensor changes, which means that a voltage supplied across it will also change. The ignition control unit or engine management system constantly reads changes and rates of change in either the resistance or the voltage, and compares each reading to those before it to determine exactly how the throttle is being used, enabling it to use the information to determine engine load (along with other factors). This information is compared with the information stored in the ROM and matched to pre-programmed timing advance settings. On fuel injected motorcycles, the information is also used to vary the amount of fuel being injected.

## 9 Engine management systems

The defining parameters of engine performance and characteristics are the fuel/air mixture being in the correct proportion and volume for any given situation, and for it to be ignited at the optimum time for perfect combustion. Separate systems are unable to relate fuelling and ignition functions and

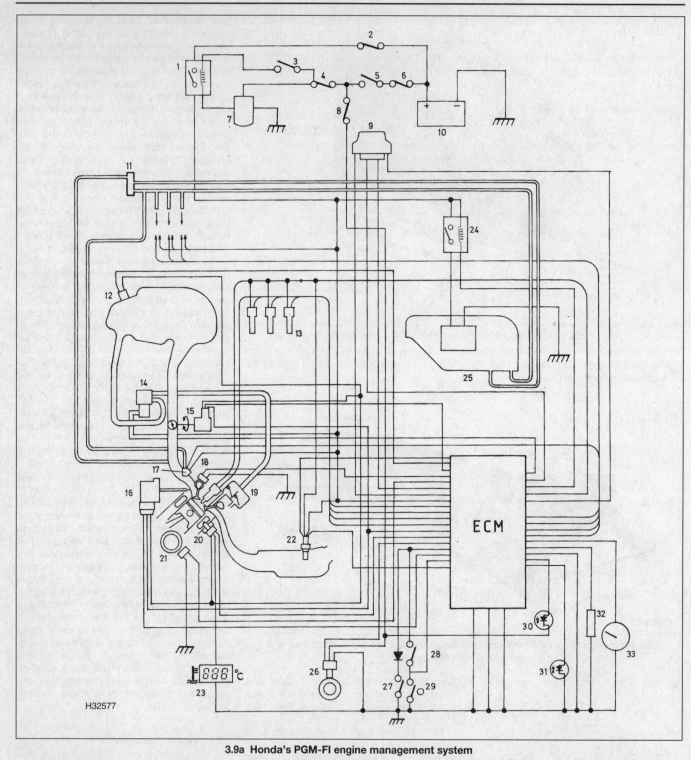

**3.9a Honda's PGM-FI engine management system**

1 Engine stop relay
2 Circuit fuse
3 Engine stop switch
4 Circuit fuse
5 Ignition switch
6 Main fuse
7 Bank angle sensor
8 Circuit fuse
9 Immobiliser unit

10 Battery
11 Fuel pressure regulator
12 Intake air temperature
   sensor
13 Combined ignition
   coil/spark plug caps
14 Pulse air injection
   solenoid valve
15 Throttle position sensor

16 Manifold absolute
   pressure sensor
17 Fuel injector
18 Cam pulse generator
   sensor
19 Pulse air injection
   check valve
20 Engine coolant
   temperature sensor

21 Crankshaft position
   (ignition pulse) sensor
22 Oxygen sensor
23 Coolant temperature
   display
24 Fuel cut-off relay
25 Fuel pump
26 Road speed sensor
27 Neutral switch

28 Clutch switch
29 Side stand switch
30 Engine management
   warning light
31 Immobiliser warning
   light
32 Diagnostic socket
33 Tachometer

H32577

despite digital control, do not provide the best means of obtaining optimum power, efficiency and exhaust emission levels.

The solution is a complete engine management system which controls the engine's fuelling and ignition requirements and has the capability to adjust its output signals automatically to suit all conditions and thus ensure optimum performance and clean running. The engine management ECU holds data in the form of maps which enable the performance to be matched to different operating conditions and in some cases permits this data to be modified.

Bosch were one of the first to realise the benefit of having combined digital control over ignition and fuel injection and their Motronic system was first seen of the BMW 16v K-series machines. Other engine management systems followed from Sagem, Denso, Marelli and Honda's PGM-FI **(see illustrations 3.9a and b)**.

### Open- or closed-loop control

Engine management systems either have open-loop or closed loop control **(see illustration 3.9c)**.

In an open-loop system there is no feedback of information on the state of the exhaust gases, and the engine thus performs in accordance with the maps pre-programmed into the ECU. This is not a problem on a new engine or on one which is well maintained, but as wear occurs in the engine and in the mechanical parts of the fuel system, the ECU is unable to compensate for this and there will be a gradual loss of performance. Additionally there is no control over maintaining the correct emission levels.

A closed-loop system overcomes this problem by measuring the state of the exhaust gases with a sensor and relaying this information to the ECU. If the content of the exhaust gases deviates from a preset figure the ECU is able to adjust fuelling and ignition timing accordingly to bring it back into line. The sensor is termed an oxygen sensor, or Lambda sensor, and is used in accordance with a catalytic converter – see Chapter 2, Section 7 for more information.

Certain systems also incorporate a knock sensor which senses any sign of detonation in the combustion chambers and relays this information to the ECU.

### ECU mapping

The ECU's data is contained in an Eprom (Erasable Programmable Read Only Memory) chip in the form of maps. Multi-dimensional maps contain base data on fuelling and ignition requirements to suit throttle opening and engine speed. This data is 'trimmed' or corrected by the information received from the ECU's input sensors, thus enabling it to provide the exact fuelling and ignition requirements for a particular situation. The ECU constantly monitors the data received enabling it to provide the optimum settings for all conditions, whether cranking, starting,

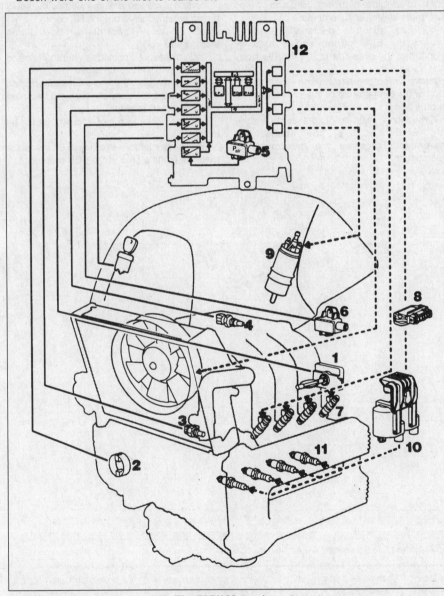

**3.9b  The BMW Motronic system**

1 Throttle position sensor
2 Crankshaft position and speed sensor
3 Engine temperature sensor
4 Air temperature sensor
5 Air pressure sensor
6 Variable resistor
7 Fuel injectors
8 Power amplifier
9 Fuel pump
10 Ignition coils
11 Spark plugs
12 Motronic control unit (ECU)

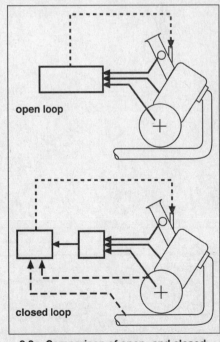

**3.9c  Comparison of open- and closed-loop control**

warming up, idling, cruising or accelerating.

In some systems the Eprom chip can be changed or re-programmed to provide new maps, thus altering the fuelling and ignition characteristics.

The ECU also has a fault diagnosis ability which is able to detect a component failure and store this information so that it can be read out in the form of fault codes; a warning light is provided in the instrument cluster to warn the rider of a fault. In the event of a fault occurring the system will usually revert to a default back-up mode to keep the engine running (albeit at reduced efficiency) until the problem is rectified. Fault codes can either be read out by monitoring instrument light flashes or digital codes, or by the use of a dedicated fault code reader, depending on the system type.

## Input sensors and output control

Input sensors provide the ECU with data or signals on the condition of the operating engine and its surroundings. Output from the ECU controls the operation of the fuel and ignition system components. Note that not all systems use all of the sensors listed.

Refer to Chapter 2, Section 7, or Section 8 of this Chapter for further information on the main sensors.

### Input sensors

*Throttle position sensor* – informs the ECU of the throttle position, and the rate of throttle opening or closing.

*Crankshaft position (ignition pulse) sensor* – provides information of piston position in the four-stroke cycle. Some systems also have a camshaft position sensor.

*Engine speed sensor* – provides the ECU with crankshaft rpm. (Often combined with the crankshaft position sensor.)

*Coolant temperature sensor* – informs the ECU of engine temperature and helps determine fuelling requirements.

*Manifold absolute pressure sensor* – informs the ECU of the engine load by monitoring the pressure in the throttle body inlet tracts.

*Intake air temperature sensor* – informs the ECU of the temperature of the air entering the throttle body.

*Atmospheric (barometric) pressure sensor* – informs the ECU of the atmospheric (barometric) pressure the motorcycle is operating in.

*Speed sensor* – measures road speed.

*Oxygen (Lambda) sensor* – measures the oxygen content of the exhaust gases.

*Battery voltage sensor* – measures battery voltage.

*Gear position sensor* – linked to the neutral switch as part of the starter interlock circuit with the sidestand switch and clutch switch.

*Bank angle (tip over) sensor* – shuts down power if the motorcycle falls over or leans beyond a certain angle.

### Output control

*Fuel injectors* – controls the opening time and duration of the injectors.

*Ignition dwell and timing* – signals the spark timing and intensity from the HT coils.

*Idle by-pass* – controls air flow during starting and idling.

*Tachometer* – provides engine speed information to the instruments.

*Coolant temperature* – provides information to the coolant temperature gauge or warning light in the instruments.

*Warning light* – warns of a fault detected by the ECU.

*Fault code memory* – facility to download or read-out faults stored in the ECU memory.

# Chapter 4
# Transmission

# Contents

## 1 Introduction

All powered two-wheelers require a means of transmitting power from the engine into drive at the rear wheel, and this is done by the 'drive train' or 'transmission' **(see illustration 4.1)**.

There are two main types of transmission, manual and automatic, the difference between them being in the level of input and control available to the rider. Manual transmission is used on all current production motorcycles, and has been used in the past on some mopeds. Automatic transmission is generally found on mopeds and scooters, although there have been examples of production motorcycles with automatic transmissions.

All transmission assemblies, manual or automatic, consist of a primary drive, a clutch, a gearbox, and a final drive, though the form

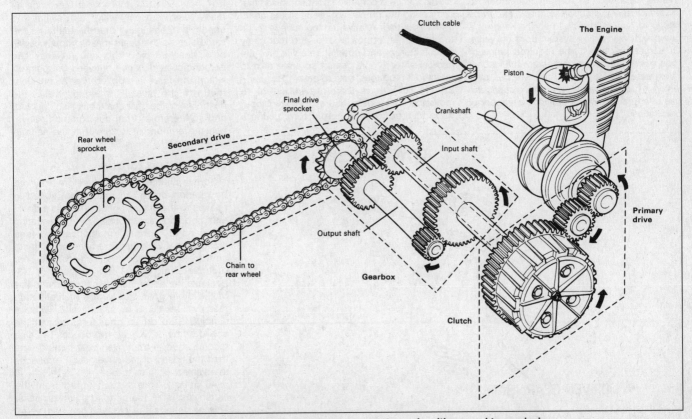

**4.1 A simplified drive train arrangement on a motorcycle with manual transmission**

that each of these takes can vary between different types of machine.

On a conventional manual transmission arrangement, the primary drive transmits power from the crankshaft to the gearbox via the clutch. The clutch is used to engage and disengage the power to and from the gearbox, thereby allowing the engine to run without the machine moving. The gearbox allows different gear ratios to be selected so that the most can be made of the speed range of the engine and its power and torque characteristics. The final drive transmits the power from the gearbox to the rear wheel.

The purpose of any transmission system is to allow the engine to operate within a narrow speed range (in terms of rpm) while giving the machine itself a relatively wide road speed range. This is because, even though all engines are capable of operating over quite a large rev range, they only operate at their most efficient within a narrow band of that range. To allow a wide road speed range over a small engine speed range, it is necessary to have different gear ratios between the engine and the rear wheel.

In its simplest form, the scooter with single-speed automatic transmission performs its job with the minimum of complexity, whilst larger machines employ far more sophisticated and complex systems. Much depends upon the role of the machine in question and the level of performance expected from it; the small capacity scooter is merely required to propel the rider at moderate speed on short journeys, and to be cheap to buy and run, and so the need for a complex transmission system does not arise. On larger machines, the required range of road speeds is far greater, as are the loads it is expected to carry and the distances over which it has to operate, and this dictates the use of a gearbox which provides a number of gear ratios.

## 2 Gearing and torque

### Gearing

Gearing is the term used to describe two linked components which turn at a different rate to each other, and the gear ratio determines the amount of difference in that rate.

The process of making a driven or output shaft turn slower than its drive or input shaft is known as gearing down, and the reverse is known as gearing up. The concept of gearing does not only apply to gears, but also to sprockets linked by a chain and to pulleys linked by a belt.

The gear ratio is defined as the number of turns a 'drive' or 'input' gear makes to turn a 'driven' or 'output' gear one full turn. For example, if you have an engine turning at 1000 rpm, and you want it to drive a wheel at 500 rpm, then you will need two gears, one with twice as many teeth on it as the other. The small gear (say with 15 teeth) needs to be the drive gear, so that by the time it has turned through one full turn, the driven gear (30 teeth) will only have turned through half a turn. So the drive gear will have to turn twice for the driven gear to turn once. This set-up is known as a 2:1 gear reduction ratio, i.e. it reduces the speed of the output gear by 1/2.

This can be a confusing concept, given that comparing the number of teeth on the gears rather than their relative turning speeds tends to produce an opposite ratio, and that many manufacturers and spec sheets will give the number of teeth on a gear or sprocket next to the ratio it produces, so it appears: 1st gear – 2:1 (15/30T). It is therefore important to remember that a gear ratio of 2:1 is two input turns to produce one output turn, giving a

reduction, and that the greater the number of teeth on the driven gear, the slower it will turn in relation to the drive gear.

### Torque

Torque can be defined as the amount of twist produced by a force acting around a pivot. Sufficient torque to drive the machine must be delivered to the rear wheel. Since petrol engines are poor producers of torque, particularly at low engine speeds, the whole transmission system needs to act as a torque multiplier.

Torque is calculated by multiplying the force (usually measured in Newtons N) by the perpendicular distance (usually measured in meters m) from the pivot that the force acts on. For example, a spanner being used to tighten a nut is applying a torque to that nut. If the spanner is 200 mm (0.2 m) long, and there is 100N of force applied at right angles to it by your hand, then the amount of torque (or twist) being applied to the nut is (100 x 0.2) = 20 Nm.

When applying this to gearbox operation it can be seen that the rotational action of a drive gear tooth on a driven gear tooth will result in the driven gear turning. If the gears are the same size, i.e. they have the same number of teeth, the speed at which they turn will be the same, and the amount of torque applied to the first gear shaft by the crankshaft will be transferred equally to the second gear shaft.

If, however, the driven gear has twice as many teeth, not only will it turn at half the speed, but, assuming that the teeth are the same size so the gears mesh properly, it will be twice as big. This means that the perpendicular distance between the point at which the force is applied (i.e. at the gear tooth) to the pivot it is acting on (i.e. the centreline of the gear shaft) has also doubled, and so therefore, from our equation above, has the amount of torque that the second gear produces.

### Gearing and torque

Torque multiplication is therefore achieved by gearing down the rear wheel speed in relation to the engine speed. There is a direct and proportional relationship between gearing ratios and torque multiplication **(see illustration 4.2)**: if the drive gear has 10 teeth and the driven gear has 30 teeth, the gear reduction ratio is 3:1, or by a factor of 1/3. Because the driven gear has thrice the radius of the drive gear, the torque multiplication ration will be 1:3, or by a factor of 3. To put it simply, if the driven gear turns at half the speed of the drive gear, it produces twice as much torque. If the driven gear turns at one third the speed of the drive gear, it produces three times as much torque.

All parts of the system, apart from the clutch, assist in the gearing down process. This is despite the highest gears in some gearboxes actually providing a direct drive (no

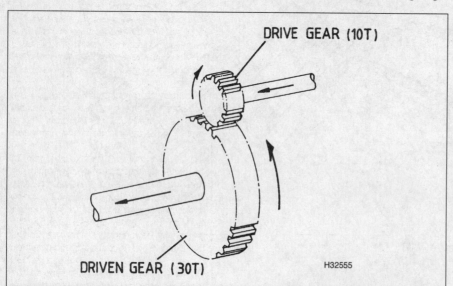

DRIVE GEAR (10T)

DRIVEN GEAR (30T)

H32555

**4.2 Showing the relationship between gear reduction and torque multiplication**

gearing difference) or an overdrive (gearing up) between the gearbox shafts, although this does not mean an overall gearing up between the crankshaft and the rear wheel.

## 3 Primary drive

### *Manual transmission*

The primary drive is the first stage in transmitting the power from the crankshaft to the rear wheel **(see illustration 4.1)**. It also acts as the first stage of gear reduction and torque multiplication. Typically a primary drive system will give a gear reduction of 3:1 and so a torque multiplication factor of 3.

A gear arrangement is normally used for primary drive. A chain and sprocket arrangement can also be used, and was the usual fitting on pre-unit engines, where the gearbox and clutch are remote from the engine unit.

Three types of gears can be used in the primary drive, straight-cut, split or offset straight-cut, and helical (angled) **(see illustration 4.3)**.

Straight-cut gears are the cheapest to manufacture but are not as strong. Due to a certain amount of clearance or 'backlash' being necessary between the teeth for the gears to run freely, they are also relatively noisy.

Helical gears require a specific lubricating oil than straight-cut gears, and also cause axial thrust on the crankshaft bearings, but there is no backlash noise as there is always more than one tooth engaged.

Using split or offset straight cut-gears is a direct compromise, but quite rare. It necessitates having two straight-cut gears on each shaft but with their teeth out of alignment. This means, as with helical gears, there is more than one tooth engaged, and backlash noise is minimised.

On early pre-unit engines a simple roller chain was sufficient to transfer power from the crankshaft to the clutch, but as engines developed duplex and even triplex chains were needed to handle the power extra power they produced. More recent primary drive chains have been of the Hy-Vo type, which is much stronger and quieter, and creates less friction than a conventional roller chain; additionally its rate of wear and stretch is considerably less.

The gear reduction provided by primary drive is beneficial in many aspects of design, one of them being that it allows the gearbox to be more compact. If there wasn't a primary reduction, then that amount of reduction would still have to be built into other components so that the overall reduction remained the same. This would probably have to be taken up in the gearbox, as having too small a final drive front sprocket increases chain wear, and too large a rear sprocket gets in the way and increases the amount of chain needed. It would also necessitate an increase in the size of the driven gears on the output shaft, resulting in a less compact engine/transmission unit.

One other design aspect is that the primary driven gear serves as an excellent mounting for the clutch. With the clutch positioned after the gear reduction its rotational speed will be reduced and it will run cooler.

Not all motorcycles use the same engine/clutch/gearbox design. The K-series BMW's do have a helical gear primary drive but it has no gearing reduction, and the gear link is between the crankshaft and engine output/balancer shaft. On BMW Boxer engines and many Moto Guzzi engines the clutch is mounted directly to the end of the crankshaft, and so there is no primary drive as such; there is however a primary reduction through gears in the first stage of the gearbox.

### *Automatic transmission*

Automatic transmissions work on a completely different basis of gearing and reduction and there are no rules regarding a primary drive. On the majority of scooters the drive pulley is mounted on the end of the crankshaft and incorporates a speed governor (more of which later), which acts as a variable reduction, but is not a primary drive as such.

On the few motorcycles using an hydraulic automatic transmission which operates on the same basis as a car, the torque converter acts as a variable gear reduction, torque multiplier and clutch all at the same time.

## 4 Clutches

An essential feature on any motorcycle is the ability to disconnect the drive to the rear wheel so that the engine can be run without the machine moving. On very early machines this was not always the case, and many employed a form of direct drive, using a belt running between pulleys on the crankshaft and the rear wheel, that could not be disconnected. This form of power transmission worked up to a point, but it did mean that to stop at a junction it was necessary to stop the engine as well. It follows that the engine could not be started with the machine stationary, so it was necessary to push-start it on each occasion – hardly a convenient arrangement.

Separation of the running engine from the drive to the rear wheel is achieved by having an assembly known as a 'clutch' situated somewhere between the two. It allows the drive to be disconnected, and has the incidental advantage of allowing a different gear ratio to be selected on machines that have a choice of ratios, or in other words, a gearbox.

The clutch works using friction, and the simplest form of clutch consists of a circular plate on the end of a crankshaft and a corresponding circular plate facing very close to it which is connected via a drive mechanism of some sort (belt, chain, gear) to the rear wheel. When there is a small gap between the two plates, the engine runs with the other plate remaining stationary. If we now move the plates into contact with other, the rotation of the plate on the end of the crankshaft is transferred by friction to the second plate, which because it is connected to the rear wheel, results in the rear wheel turning. And so the power from the engine can be applied to or disconnected from the rear wheel at will.

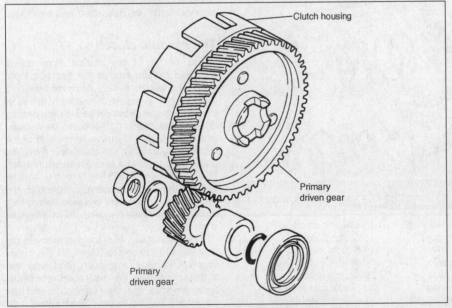

Clutch housing

Primary driven gear

Primary driven gear

**4.3 A helical gear primary drive arrangement**

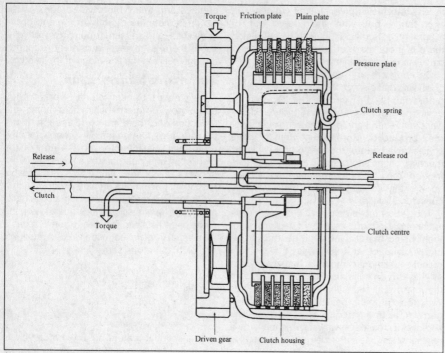

4.4a Cross-section view of a multi-plate clutch with coil springs

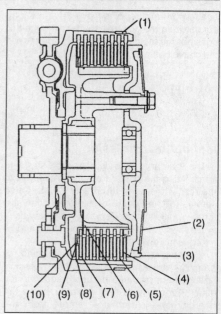

4.4b Cross-section view of a multi-plate clutch with a diaphragm spring and anti-judder spring (Yamaha YZF-R1)

1 Strengthening ring
2 Diaphragm spring
3 Pressure plate
4 Plain plates
5 Friction plates
6 Wire retaining ring
7 Inner plain plate
8 Inner friction plate (with larger inside diameter)
9 Anti-judder spring
10 Anti-judder spring seat

Motorcycle clutches are usually manually-operated from a handlebar lever, but scooters use a simple automatic centrifugal clutch that works according to engine speed. The various arrangements are described and illustrated below.

### The manual clutch

The whole of the clutch assembly is mounted on the end of the gearbox input shaft. The clutch housing (or drum) runs on a bearing and is free to turn independently of the shaft, but is directly linked via the primary drive to the crankshaft (except on designs where the clutch is bolted to the end of the crankshaft), so when the crankshaft turns, the clutch housing turns **(see illustration 4.4a)**. The clutch centre (or hub), which is smaller and fits inside the housing, is bolted to the gearbox input shaft end and is locked onto it by splines, so when the centre turns, the input shaft turns.

The clutch plates fit in the gap between the housing and the centre. There are two types of plate, friction and plain, and they are layered alternately, the exact number of plates depending on the type of clutch and the machine it is fitted to **(see illustrations 4.4b and c)**. The friction plates have tabs on their

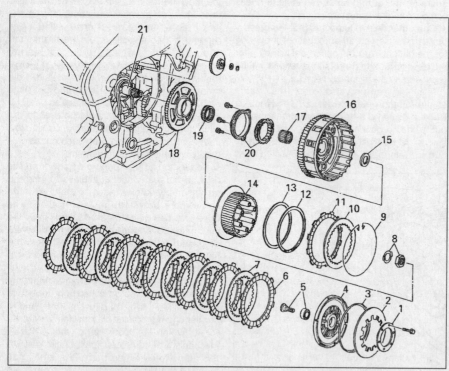

4.4c Exploded view of the Yamaha YZF-R1 clutch

1 Diaphragm spring retainer
2 Diaphragm spring
3 Diaphragm spring seat
4 Pressure plate
5 Pullrod and bearing
6 Friction plates – 7 off
7 Plain plates – 6 off
8 Clutch centre retaining nut and lockwasher
9 Wire retaining ring
10 Inner plain plate
11 Inner friction plate
12 Anti-judder spring
13 Anti-judder spring seat
14 Clutch centre
15 Thrust washer
16 Clutch housing
17 Needle bearing
18 Starter clutch gear
19 Needle bearing
20 Starter clutch sprag
21 Gearbox input shaft

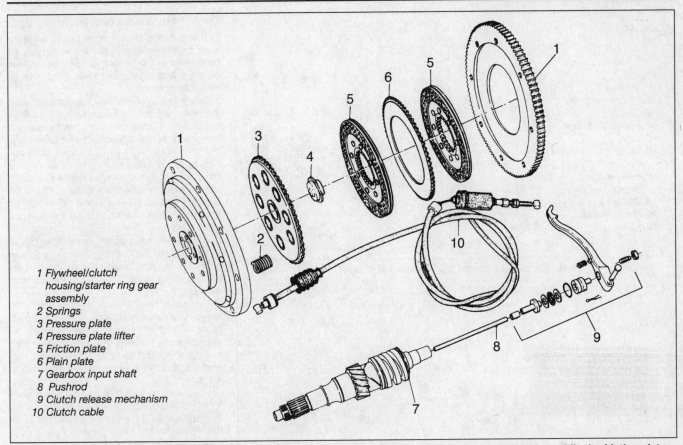

1 Flywheel/clutch
   housing/starter ring gear
   assembly
2 Springs
3 Pressure plate
4 Pressure plate lifter
5 Friction plate
6 Plain plate
7 Gearbox input shaft
8 Pushrod
9 Clutch release mechanism
10 Clutch cable

**4.4d The double plate clutch used by Moto Guzzi. On this clutch the plain plate turns with the clutch housing, while the friction plates are splined to the gearbox input shaft - there is no clutch centre as such**

outer rim which locate into slots in the housing. The plain plates have teeth cut into their inner rim which locate into grooves in the clutch centre.

In normal use (when the motorcycle is being ridden) the friction and plain plates are held pressed together by the force of springs acting on a plate, known as the pressure plate, and so when the crankshaft turns, the clutch housing turns and, because of the friction between the plates, the clutch centre and hence the gearbox input shaft also turns.

When the clutch lever is pulled in, a cable or hydraulic mechanism lifts the pressure plate off the friction and plain plate assembly, against the pressure of the springs, and so the plates are no longer being pressed together. As there is now no hard contact between the plates there is very little friction, enabling the clutch housing to turn independently of the clutch centre. As the clutch lever is let out, the plates again begin to press against each other, and so the movement of the clutch housing is gradually transferred to the clutch centre by friction, allowing the torque to be transferred gradually to the gearbox and rear wheel, and so preventing stalling or 'kangarooing'.

The ability of a clutch to transfer torque is dependent on several factors: the number of plates, the diameter of the plates, the spring force holding them together, and the coefficient of friction between the plates. On a small machine fewer plates are needed than on a larger more powerful model, assuming the other dependants are the same. Similarly, for the same amount of torque, if the diameter of the plates is increased, you do not need so many. The friction plates carry the friction material, while plain plates are made of steel.

### Single or multi-plate clutch?

Most modern motorcycles use a clutch of the 'wet multi-plate' type. The wet or dry aspect is dealt with in the next sub-section.

Multi-plate clutches use more than one set of friction and plain plates, and commonly there are seven or eight, and sometimes nine friction plates. There is always one less plain plate than friction plates as the friction plates are fitted innermost and outermost so that the plain plates are always sandwiched by them.

The majority of unit engines with a transverse crankshaft use a multi-plate clutch, the reason being that the clutch can be kept small in diameter. Multi-plate clutches are also a lot lighter than single plate ones, while still offering greater friction area and strength.

Single or double plate clutches are used where the crankshaft runs in line with the frame and the clutch bolts onto the rear end of it, having its own housing between the engine and gearbox (see illustration 4.4d). Because of its location, it does not have to be compact, and so with a large diameter only one or two plates are needed. In this application the clutch housing allows the use of a large flywheel.

### Wet or dry clutch?

Wet clutches run in oil, and dry clutches don't. To run something in oil that uses friction as its working principle may seen illogical, but the reasons are good, and of course the friction material used is designed to run in oil. The oil acts as a coolant to prevent the clutch burning out, and also as a lubricant for the bushes or bearings that the clutch housing runs on, and for the tabs and teeth on the plates to slide on. It also means that the primary drive can be kept lubricated without having to seal off the clutch in its own chamber.

Not surprisingly a wet clutch does not produce as much friction between the plates as a dry clutch, so they need to be larger in diameter or have more plates (or both) and so are not as compact. This is one reason why dry clutches are often used on racing motorcycles, plus the other benefit of less oil being needed which therefore reduces overall weight.

Single or double plate clutches with a large diameter are invariably run dry.

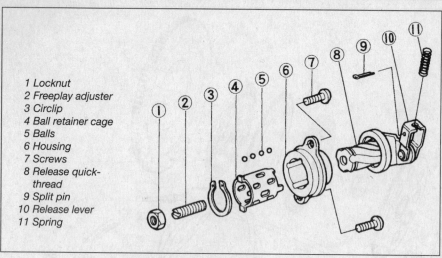

1 Locknut
2 Freeplay adjuster
3 Circlip
4 Ball retainer cage
5 Balls
6 Housing
7 Screws
8 Release quick-
   thread
9 Split pin
10 Release lever
11 Spring

**4.4e  Spiral quick-thread type release mechanism**

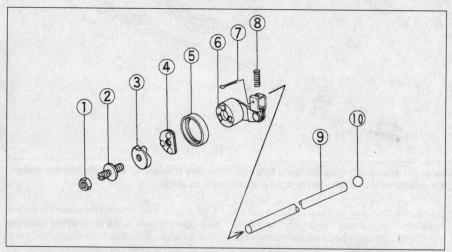

**4.4f  Ball and ramp type release mechanism**

| 1 Locknut | 4 Ball assembly | 6 Release lever | 9 Pushrod |
| 2 Freeplay adjuster | 5 Grease seal | 7 Split pin | 10 Ball |
| 3 Ball ramp plate | | 8 Spring | |

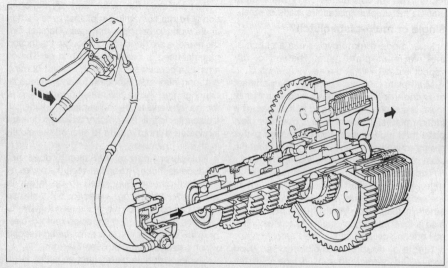

**4.4g  Hydraulic clutch operation**

## Cable or hydraulic operation?

The clutch is always operated by pulling a lever on the handlebar, but the action can be transferred to the release (or lifter) mechanism on the clutch itself using either a cable or an hydraulic system.

Cable is by far the most commonly used method, principally because of it relative cheapness. Cables do stretch and wear, and they need regular adjustment and lubrication, but they are simple to maintain and renew. The cable connects to the clutch either by a release mechanism situated inside the clutch cover, or by a release mechanism on the opposite side of the crankcase which acts on a long pushrod located through the gearbox input shaft.

The release mechanism varies from model to model, but can be a sprial quick-thread type, ball and ramp type, rack and pinion type or cam and plunger type **(see illustrations 4.4e and f)**.

Hydraulic clutches are used primarily on top-of the range machines. They cost a lot more and still require a fair amount of maintenance, which can be tricky, but their major benefit comes in that they give a very smooth and light action **(see illustration 4.4g)**.

They work on exactly the same principal as a front brake system: when the lever is pulled in the pushrod in the master cylinder acts on the hydraulic fluid and pushes it down the hose. The fluid then pushes the piston in the release or 'slave' cylinder out, and this acts on a pushrod inside the input shaft.

With the exception of regular fluid level checks the hydraulic system is virtually maintenance free, although the fluid and seals do require periodic renewal to ensure system efficiency. Also the nature any hydraulic system does means that the fluid is capable of absorbing water and becoming aerated.

An advantage of the hydraulic system, particularly on high powered motorcycles which use heavy duty clutch springs, is that the clutch lever action can be kept fairly light compared with a cable system. Refer to Chapter 6 for the principles of hydraulic leverage multiplication.

## Coil or diaphragm spring?

The majority of motorcycle clutches use between four and six coil springs, though some single plate designs use eight or so due to the extra diameter of the clutch. The alternative is a diaphragm spring, which is a common fitment on cars and has appeared on a number of multi-plate motorcycle clutches plus BMW's single plate clutch. A diaphragm spring is a circular conical disc with a hole in its centre, and made of spring steel.

Coil springs are cheaper to manufacture, but any unevenness in their tension can result in clutch drag, chatter, slipping and vibration. To cure the problem all springs must be

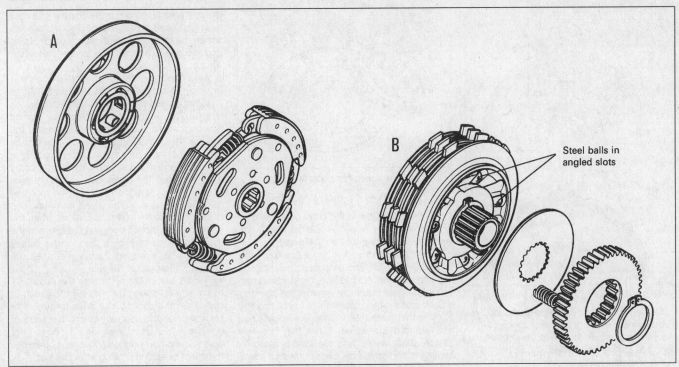

**4.4h Centrifugal clutches**

**A** *The shoe-type centrifugal clutch is the most commonly used arrangement. The shoes are flung out against return spring pressure until they begin to turn the clutch drum.*

**B** *Plate-type centrifugal clutches are operated by a number of steel balls running in inclined slots. As the clutch spins, the balls fly outwards, pressing the pressure plate onto the clutch plates and therefore engaging drive.*

Steel balls in angled slots

replaced as a set. The other characteristic of coil springs is that the pressure they exert increases the more they are compressed, which means that the clutch lever becomes progressively stiffer as you pull it in. The beauty of a diaphragm clutch is that once you have overcome the initial compression and deformation of the spring, it starts to move easier, and is therefore 'lighter' to keep held in – a feel similar to an hydraulically operated clutch.

Most clutches are also fitted with an 'anti-judder' spring, which is a diaphragm type spring that helps eliminate judder felt when releasing and engaging the clutch. The anti-judder spring separates the friction plates from the clutch centre when the clutch lever is pulled in, thus preventing any of the plates sticking.

### The 'automatic' or centrifugal clutch

This type of clutch is commonly used on mopeds and scooters, where its automatic operation reduces the number of controls the rider has to concentrate on. This means that, with the exception of the throttle twistgrip, the machine can be as easy to operate as a bicycle (if not easier!).

#### Shoe-type

This type of centrifugal clutch consists of a clutch centre, around the edge of which are two or more friction shoes, very similar to drum brake shoes **(see illustration 4.4h, part A)**. These are pivoted at one end, and are held against the centre by springs. Outside the centre and running close to the friction surface of the shoes is a drum.

At low engine speeds the clutch centre spins and the drum remains stationary. As engine speed rises, centrifugal force acting on the pivoting shoes throws them outwards and into contact with the drum surface. In this way the drum begins to revolve and the machine moves off. When engine speed drops again the shoes are drawn away from the drum by the return springs and drive is disconnected.

#### Ball and ramp type

The ball and ramp automatic clutch is similar to the manual multi-plate clutch in that it uses friction and plain plates located between the housing and centre **(see illustration 4.4h, part B)**. The difference is that it has balls which run in angled ramps acting on a pressure plate.

As engine speed rises and the clutch housing turns faster, the balls move outwards up the ramps under centrifugal force, pressing against the pressure plate. The pressure plate presses the friction and plain plates together, transferring drive to the clutch centre. When engine speed drops again the balls return down the ramps and the pressure is taken off the plates.

This arrangement is ideal in moped and scooter designs where simplicity of operation is an important requirement, but it has the disadvantage that it is not easy to incorporate a gearchange. This is because it is necessary to de-clutch during the change, for which a manual control is normally required.

One way to overcome this problem is to arrange a method whereby the clutch is disconnected as the gearchange control is operated, and this system does work, though not with such control or smoothness as is found in manual systems. Another possibility is to employ a fully automatic transmission using two or three ratios as on cars, or a variable ratio belt drive system (see Section 7).

### The one-way clutch

A one way clutch allows drive through it in one direction of rotation only, and in the other direction it runs freely. It's main use is in providing drive from the starter motor to the crankshaft when starting the engine, and in this role it is called a starter clutch. The one-way clutch prevents drive from the engine being transmitted back to the starter motor.

The clutch body is engaged on a shaft (on the crankshaft itself, or mounted on the alternator rotor, or incorporated in the main clutch housing on the gearbox input shaft, or on an auxiliary shaft linked by gear or chain to the crankshaft) so that it can transmit drive to the crankshaft.

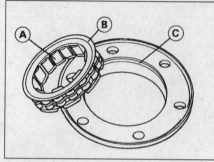

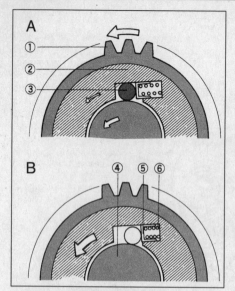

A

① ② ③

B

④ ⑤ ⑥

**4.4i Starter clutch operation (roller type)**

*In diagram A the rotation of the starter clutch gear causes the rollers to lock in their channels and transmit drive to the crankshaft. Once the engine has started, the starter clutch disengages (B).*

| | | | |
|---|---|---|---|
| *1* | *Starter clutch gear* | *4* | *Crankshaft* |
| *2* | *Starter clutch body* | *5* | *Spring caps* |
| *3* | *Rollers* | *6* | *Springs* |

The starter driven gear has an integral hub which locates inside the body of the clutch. The body contains either sprung rollers or pivoting 'sprags' which are so positioned and shaped that when the driven gear turns in one direction they lock against the gear hub, but

**4.4j The sprag type starter clutch**

*A Sprags    B Cage    C Holder*

when the gear turns in the other direction they are turned away from the hub so that it can turn freely **(see illustration 4.4i and j)**.

When the starter button is pressed, the motor turns an idle and reduction gear (both on the same shaft), which turns the starter driven gear. The gear hub locks against the one-way clutch and so the clutch shaft turns, thereby turning the crankshaft. When the engine has started, the crankshaft turns the one-way clutch shaft faster than the starter motor is turning it, and so the direction of rotation inside the clutch is effectively reversed, and the clutch therefore disengages from the driven gear hub. While the engine is running the one-way clutch is therefore spinning, but the starter driven gear, the idle/reduction gear and the starter motor are all stationary.

### The 'slipper' clutch

The slipper clutch limits what is known as 'back-torque', which occurs under engine braking from a high speed or when dropping

down through the gearbox. Slipper clutches are often used on large-capacity sports bikes which have high speed high compression engines and produce large amounts of back-torque.

When the throttle is open the engine is driving the rear wheel, via the clutch. When the throttle is closed and the motorcycle is on overrun, the rear wheel is effectively turning the engine via the clutch, but because the engine is providing a lot of resistance (because of its compression, and especially at high revs and in a low gear), there may come a point where the resistance or back torque from the engine is too much for the rear tyre to cope with, and so the wheel locks up. This is especially likely in wet conditions when the coefficient of friction between the tyre and the road is much reduced, and under heavy braking where weight transfer reduces the amount of traction at the rear.

The slipper clutch eliminates the possibility of the wheel locking by allowing the clutch to slip when the direction of drive through it is reversed, and in this way is another form of one-way clutch. However, it does not disengage drive completely because otherwise the effect of engine braking would be lost.

One type of slipper clutch, as used by Kawasaki, has the clutch centre engaged on ramps and cams **(see illustration 4.4k)**. When the direction of drive is reversed the centre slides up on the ramps and releases pressure on the plates. Another type, as used by Aprilia, works by using a vacuum operated servo to move the clutch centre, with the vacuum sourced from the inlet ducts to the engine. When the throttle is closed the increase in manifold depression

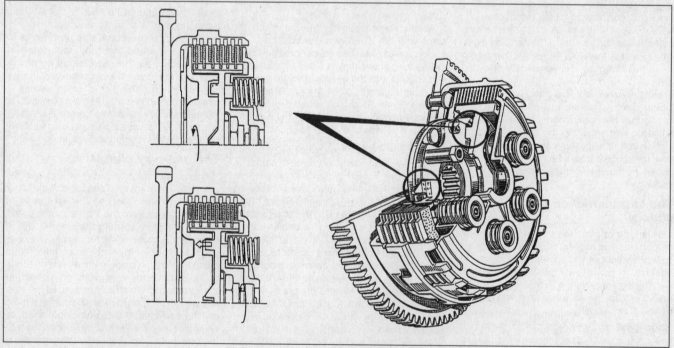

**4.4k The slipper clutch (Kawasaki ZXR750)**

creates a vacuum in the airline to the servo, which then pushes the clutch centre out to release pressure on the plates. There is an added advantage of both systems – when drive is in the normal direction through the clutch, the slipper mechanism works in the opposite way to actually increase pressure on the clutch plates, reducing the possibility of clutch slip.

Some clutches incorporate a one-way sprag clutch to act as a slipper, with the sprags designed to allow slip just before the wheel locks, rather than acting as an on-off drive as with the starter clutch. This type does not give any extra pressure when the drive is in the normal direction.

## 5  Why are gears needed?

The principle of gearing is fairly simple; it can be used to alter the speed of a rotating shaft to the desired rate for a specific purpose. If for example a shaft is turning at 2000 rpm and we wish to halve that rate, then we must fit to the shaft a drive gear, and connect this to a driven gear on another adjacent shaft. If the drive gear has half the number of teeth of the driven gear, for every two rotations of the drive gear, the driven gear will turn once, and so the shaft to which it is attached will turn at half the speed of the shaft that is driving it.

When we apply this to a motorcycle transmission, there is another factor to be considered; not only does the gearing change the engine speed to a rate which translates to the desired road speed, it also determines the number of power strokes applied during each revolution of the rear wheel. Thus in bottom (1st) gear, there will be more power strokes, and thus more power, during each revolution than in successively higher gears. This is necessary to enable the machine to overcome inertia when moving off from rest, as can be demonstrated by trying to pull away in top gear.

As we have seen, the requirement for gearing is a direct result of the characteristics of the internal combustion engine. Taking an imaginary engine, useful power may only be produced in a relatively narrow band between about 2000 rpm and 8000 rpm. First of all it is necessary to reduce this rate of revolution to something that, at the rear wheel, represents a reasonable road speed. This is dependent on the outside diameter of the wheel, itself an element in the gearing, and the power output of the engine.

In the case of a single-speed scooter, for example, we may find an overall reduction of around 15.00:1. This means that for every 15 revolutions of the engine, the rear wheel will revolve once. This ratio will have been chosen after the wheel size has been decided, and will make best use of the available power. If the gearing were too high, the machine would be incapable of moving off from a standstill. If it were excessively low, however, the machine would accelerate rapidly, but its top speed would be limited by the maximum speed of the engine.

With an engine of greater capacity and power, a much higher gearing could be used to attain a higher top speed, but there remains the problem of moving away from rest. Even though the engine is more powerful, it is still limited by its power band, and so it becomes necessary to add intermediate gears to build up to the final gear ratio. These must be spaced so that as high revs are reached in one gear, selection of the next gear will drop the engine speed to the lower end of the power band.

We need a selection of fixed ratios which change the gearing in steps. On the majority of machines four, five or six gears are used, this being about the best compromise between the ideal spacing of the ratios and the problems that using more would introduce; imagine how tedious changing up through ten gears would become. More importantly, the time taken at each change, where the machine is not accelerating, would probably make it slower overall than a similar model with fewer gears.

The number of gears is also related to the use of the motorcycle. For instance on racing two-stroke engines, where the power band is extremely narrow (within 2000 rpm), and outside the band there is no useful power, it is important to keep the engine within the power band to make use of the power. To do this and achieve the highest possible speed, it is necessary to have more gears.

## 6  Manual gearbox operation and layout

### *How a gearbox works*

A gearbox is made up of a number of gear pairs, each pair forming a ratio, and the number of pairs corresponds to the number of gears the machine has. One gear from each pair is on the input shaft (sometimes called mainshaft) and the other gear is on the output shaft (sometimes called layshaft or countershaft). All motorcycle gearboxes are of the 'constant mesh' type, which means all the pairs are constantly meshed together, irrespective of whether they are actually selected to provide the drive **(see illustration 4.6a)**.

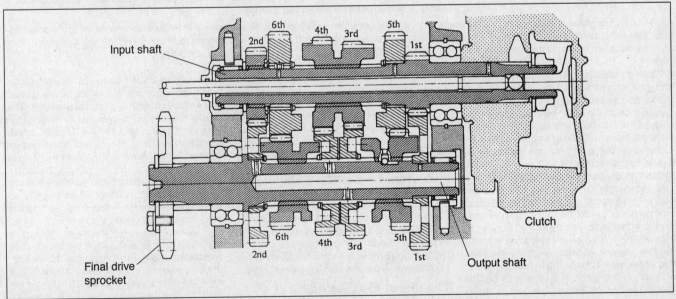

**4.6a  A typical six speed gearbox showing the gear pairs**

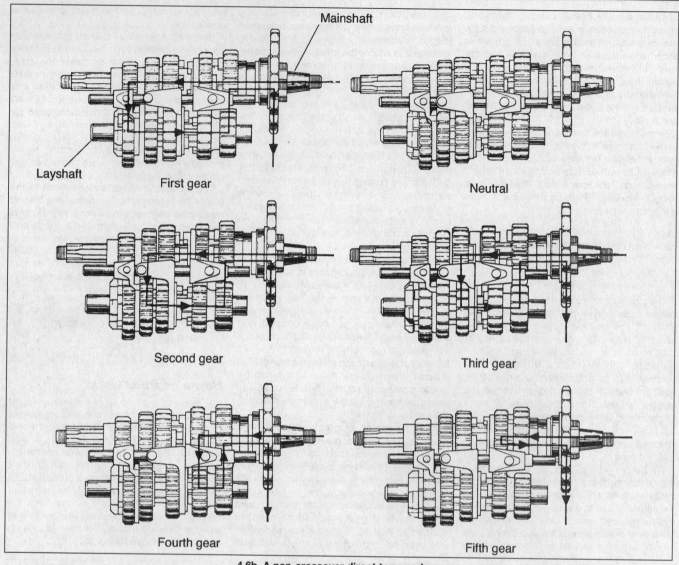

Mainshaft

Layshaft

First gear

Neutral

Second gear

Third gear

Fourth gear

Fifth gear

**4.6b  A non-crossover direct top gearbox**

*As the output sprocket is attached to the top gear pinion, all ratios drive through top gear. Power comes in through the mainshaft to the selected gear, then crosses to its pair on the layshaft. The top (fifth) gear pinion, locked to the layshaft and so turning at the speed the selected gear dictates, transfers power to the top gear pinion and output sprocket.*

When a particular gear position is selected, that pair of gears become locked to their shafts, and so provides the drive through the gearbox. Of all the other pairs, one gear from each pair is unlocked and so rotates freely on the shaft, therefore having no influence.

Some of the gears on are permanently locked to their shaft and so turn with it, while others run on plain bushes on the shaft and turn independently of it. For one of these gears to become locked to the shaft to provide drive, it must mesh with another gear next to it that is constantly locked. For this to happen the locked gear must slide towards the free one and engage with it via dogs and dog holes, whilst remaining in constant mesh with its mating gear. A dog is a projection sticking out of the side of the gear, and this fits into the dog hole in the free gear.

The gears are moved on their shafts by the action of the selector mechanism. When this is done, the gear selector drum rotates, and moves the selector fork, which has one end located in a track in the drum and the other end located in a groove in the gear, thereby moving the gear (see below for more on gearchange mechanisms). Typically there are three selector forks, two fitting into mid-outer gears on one shaft, the other fitting into a central gear on the other shaft.

There are two basic types of gearbox that have been used on motorcycles over the years, the 'direct top' gearbox and the 'all-indirect' gearbox, and each one can be either a 'crossover' type or a 'non-crossover' type.

### The direct top gearbox

The majority of vintage and classic motorcycles have direct top gearboxes, in which the input and output shafts are termed the mainshaft and layshaft respectively. The name 'direct top' comes from the fact that when top gear is selected the gearbox output sprocket, which is integral with the top gear pinion and normally free to rotate independently of the mainshaft, becomes locked to the mainshaft and therefore turns at the same speed; in other words there is no gearing down or up in top gear, and so the drive through the gearbox is direct.

Power is fed in at the clutch which is mounted on one end of the mainshaft **(see illustration 4.6b)**. From here, it is fed through the pair of gears (one on the mainshaft, one on the layshaft) selected using the gearchange mechanism, and are therefore locked to their shafts. Then, irrespective of which other pair of gears has been selected, power is fed through the top gear pinion on the layshaft, which is always locked to the shaft, to the top gear/output sprocket on the clutch end of the mainshaft (the sprocket sits behind the clutch assembly). As the top gear pinion on the mainshaft is free to rotate on its shaft, the ratio is determined by the pair of gears that has been selected. In this way, power through the gearbox starts and finishes at more or less the same point, and hence the term non-crossover. None of the other gear pairs have any influence until they are selected, and so until then one gear out of every ratio pair rotates independently of the shaft.

This arrangement is ideally suited to the pre-unit engines of that era, with their separate engine, primary drive and gearbox assemblies. The drawback with this type of gearbox is that because in every gear except top the power is fed through two pairs of gears (the selected pair and the top gear pair), there is considerable frictional drag. The exception being in top gear, when there is very little frictional drag as only the top gear on the mainshaft is locked.

There are, inevitably, variations on the above layout. In some applications, the top gear/output sprocket assembly is fitted at the opposite end of the mainshaft to the clutch, and thus the drive crosses over from one side of the machine to the other, and hence the term crossover. The second shaft in this type of gearbox, the layshaft, is blind at both ends (in other words it has nothing attached to it and so does not exit the crankcase), and thus serves only to provide the means of routing the power through the selected gear to provide the required ratio.

### The all-indirect gearbox

All modern motorcycles with manual transmission use the all-indirect gearbox. This differs from the direct top type in that the power is fed in on one shaft (the input shaft) and out on the other (the output shaft) **(see illustration 4.6a)**. In most designs the gearbox is of the crossover type; power being fed in via the clutch at the right-hand end of the input shaft and emerging at the output sprocket on the left-hand end of the output shaft.

Power is fed in at the clutch which is mounted on the right-hand end of the input shaft. From here, it is fed through the pair of gears (one on the input shaft, one on the output shaft) that have been selected using the gearchange mechanism, to emerge at the output sprocket on the left-hand end of the output shaft **(see illustration 4.6c)**. The ratio is determined by the pair of gears selected. None of the other gear pairs have any influence until they are selected, and one gear of every pair is able to rotate independently of the shafts.

This arrangement is better suited to unit construction engines, as it gives a more even

weight distribution and a narrower width than the non-crossover type, and also access to the output sprocket is easy. As power is fed through one pair of gears only in every gear, frictional drag is the same in every gear, which is an improvement on the direct top layout, even though there is a drag disadvantage in top gear.

### The 'cassette' gearbox

The cassette gearbox is an all-direct gearbox that has been developed to enable easy changing of the gearshafts. Its purpose is to enable works race teams to easily switch between different gearboxes to suit particular race circuits.

The complete gearbox assembly (input shaft, output shaft and gear selector

mechanism) slots in and out of the crankcase – much like a cassette slots in and out of a hi-fi unit – so that it can be changed without having to remove the engine from the frame and separate the crankcase halves. Although not a necessary feature for production motorcycles, the system is beginning to filter down to production motorcycles, particularly where models have been homologated for racing.

### Gearchange mechanisms

Gearchanging on very early gearboxes was achieved by sliding rotating pinions in and out of mesh with each other, and these were known as 'crash' gearboxes, due to the 'hit and miss' nature of smooth gearchanges, and the horrendous noise created by a missed

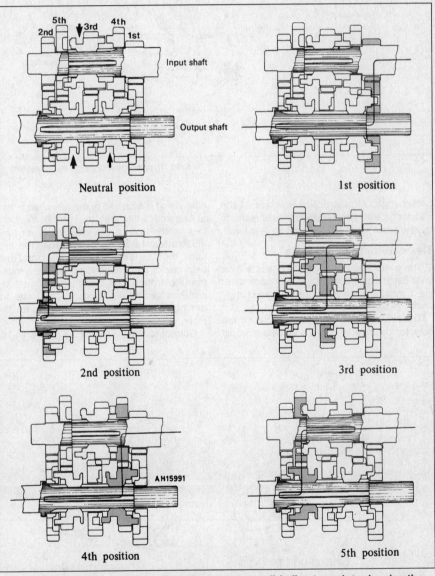

**4.6c Cross-sections of a typical 5-speed crossover all-indirect gearbox showing the power route through the shafts in all gears – selected gears are indicated by shading. Note how the positions of the sliding gears change with each gearchange, and how they interlock with their adjacent gears**

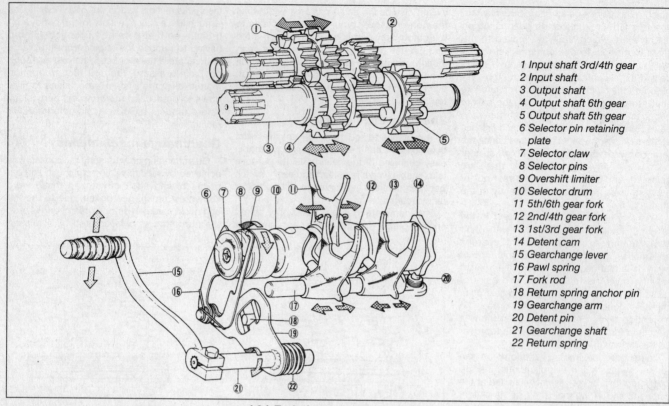

1 Input shaft 3rd/4th gear
2 Input shaft
3 Output shaft
4 Output shaft 6th gear
5 Output shaft 5th gear
6 Selector pin retaining
   plate
7 Selector claw
8 Selector pins
9 Overshift limiter
10 Selector drum
11 5th/6th gear fork
12 2nd/4th gear fork
13 1st/3rd gear fork
14 Detent cam
15 Gearchange lever
16 Pawl spring
17 Fork rod
18 Return spring anchor pin
19 Gearchange arm
20 Detent pin
21 Gearchange shaft
22 Return spring

**4.6d  Typical gearchange mechanism**

gearchange. All gearboxes now are of the constant mesh type, negating the necessity to try and smoothly mesh the rotating gear teeth.

### The 'external' components

The gearchange process starts at the gear lever itself, which is clamped, either directly or via a linkage mechanism, to the gearchange shaft.

The most common method of rotating the selector drum is by using a clawed selector arm, which is attached to the gearchange arm at one end, while the other end hooks onto pins in the end of the selector drum **(see illustration 4.6d)**. As the gearchange arm turns, the claw is moved up or down, and then onto one of the pins moving the drum round **(see illustration 4.6e, f and g)**. Each selector arm has two hooks on each claw, one for turning the drum one way, and one for the other.

Correct rotation and precise positioning of the selector drum by the gearchange shaft is achieved using two or more of many methods, known varyingly as 'overshift limiters', 'indexing systems', 'positive stop' or 'stopper' mechanisms, and centralising or return mechanisms. All ensure that full movement of the gearchange lever only turns the selector drum just enough to position the selector forks, and therefore the gears, in the correct position for the next gear up or down.

An 'overshift limiter', may be either an

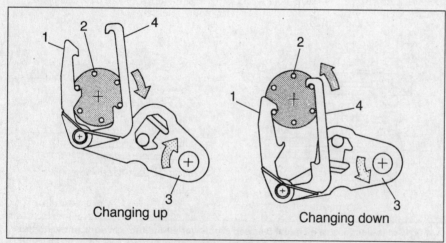

**4.6e  Gear selector claw operation**

1 Selector claw    2 Selector drum pins    3 Gearchange arm    4 Overshift limiter

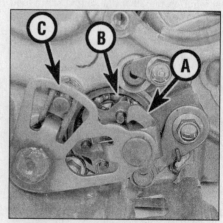

**4.6f  This mechanism uses a clawed selector arm (A) to hook onto pins (B). Note the centralising mechanism and movement limiter (C)**

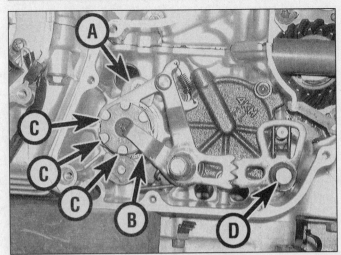

4.6g  On this mechanism the selector arm (A) is again of the claw type, while the overshift limiter is an arm (B) which movers with the selector arm and butts against stops (C) to prevent excess rotation. Imagine the whole assembly moving from the gearchange shaft (D) to see how it works

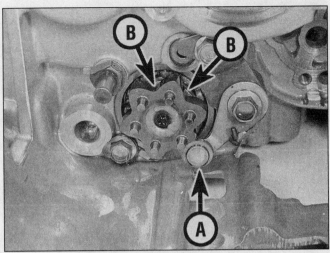

4.6h  With the selector mechanism removed, note how the stopper arm roller (A) locates in the detents (B) to ensure positive changes

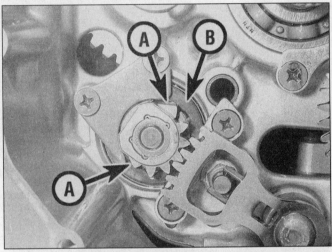

4.6i  As the cam is turned by the toothed selector arm, sprung pawls (A) locate into cutouts in the drum end (B) and so push the drum round

4.6j  This is a planetary gearchange mechanism. Note the overshift limiter (arrowed)

opposed claw or an arm that catches onto one of the pins or butts onto a stop as it goes past, preventing further rotation of the drum than is necessary to achieve the next gearchange.

All gearchange shafts have a centralising mechanism (a centralising spring around a stopper pin) and a movement limiter (a cutout in the arm which hits the same stopper pin). Many gearchange mechanisms have a rolling disc on the end of a 'stopper' arm which is held onto a star-shaped cam by a spring and moves in and out of detents in the cam, the number of detents corresponding to the number of gears, plus an extra smaller detent for neutral **(see illustration 4.6h)**. This assists positive movement into each gear.

Another much used mechanism has a toothed arm which locks into a toothed cam that translates the movement of the shaft to the drum by locking sprung pawls into cutouts, thereby pushing the drum round **(see illustration 4.6i)**.

The mechanism which differs most from the above, but which effectively produces the same end result of turning the selector drum, is the planetary gear type **(see illustration 4.6j)**. This relies on three planetary gears which are meshed with a sun gear on the end of the selector drum. When the gearchange lever actuates the shaft, movement is translated to a plate on which the planetary gears sit. Around the gears is a toothed plate which is bolted to the crankcase. As the gear

plate moves, the planetary gears turn as they move in the toothed plate, and so turn the sun gear, which rotates the drum.

There are of course many variations which use slightly different components and arrangements of selector and stopper mechanisms, but the principal remains the same whatever the design.

### The 'internal' components

The selector drum has tracks cut into it which act as guides for the selector fork pins. The forked end of each selector fork fits into a groove which runs around a particular gear. The forks usually slide on a shaft or rod, although there are designs of fork which fit around and slide on the selector drum itself.

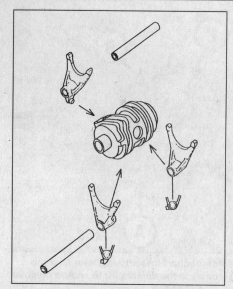

**4.6k Selector drum tracks and fork guide pins**

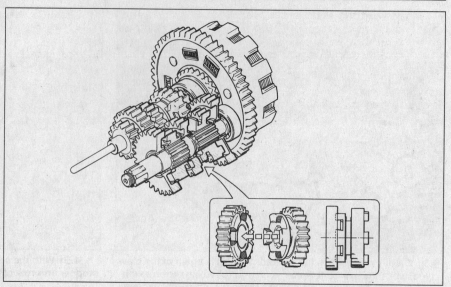

**4.6l Gear engagement**

As the selector drum turns, the position of the fork is guided by the pin running in its track **(see illustration 4.6k)**. The fork is moved to the left or right in accordance with the track profile.

Each of the gears to which the selector forks are attached is permanently keyed to its shaft splines and so always turns at the same rate as the shaft. The gear also has projections, known as dogs, and these are round or square-shaped projections which fit into holes or slots machined into the adjacent gears **(see illustration 4.4l)**. These adjacent gears run freely and independently of the shaft on a plain bush.

When the drum rotates and the gear is moved sideways by the fork, its dogs mesh with those of the free gear, locking them together. When this happens, the free-running gear becomes locked to the shaft, and as its pair mate is also locked to the shaft, that pair becomes the ratio that determines the speed of the output shaft. At the same time as one gear pair is selected, another selector fork will have moved in its track and unlocked the previous gear pair of the previous ratio selected, so drive is transferred from one ratio to another.

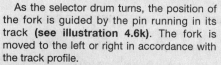

## 7 Automatic transmissions

The most common automatic transmission system used on modern scooters is the 'V-belt' (or variable ratio belt drive) which varies the gear ratio according to engine load and road speed. Previous systems used centrifugal clutches to provide automatic systems of two or more gears.

The few motorcycles which have been produced with automatic transmission have used an hydraulic torque converter similar to those used in a car automatic transmission system.

### Variable ratio belt drive transmission

The variable ratio belt drive transmission (often known as CVT – Constantly Variable Transmission) utilises a dual pulley system linked by a V-belt, a centrifugal clutch to engage the drive to the rear wheel as the throttle twistgrip is opened, and a single speed gearbox to provide a final reduction **(see illustration 4.7a)**. The drive (front) pulley is attached to the end of the crankshaft; it acts as the speed governor and works using centrifugal force. The driven (rear) pulley runs on a bearing on the gearbox input shaft. The

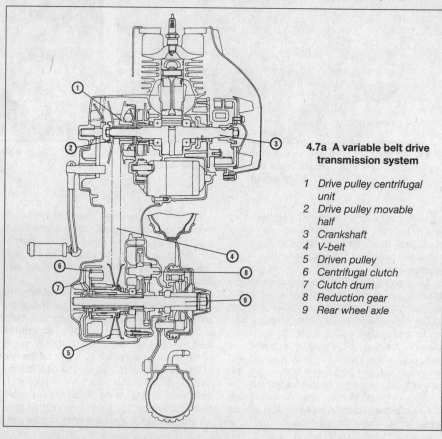

**4.7a A variable belt drive transmission system**

1 *Drive pulley centrifugal unit*
2 *Drive pulley movable half*
3 *Crankshaft*
4 *V-belt*
5 *Driven pulley*
6 *Centrifugal clutch*
7 *Clutch drum*
8 *Reduction gear*
9 *Rear wheel axle*

centrifugal clutch centre is attached to the driven pulley and so spins with it, and the drum is splined onto the input shaft and so turns the shaft when drive is taken up by the clutch.

The drive and driven pulleys are both formed in two halves, with one half fixed and the other half able to slide axially towards or away from it along a shaft. At rest the gap between the drive pulley halves is greatest and the gap between the driven pulley halves is at its minimum.

The movement of the front pulley is controlled by the wedging action of rollers, and functions in the same way as the pressure plate on a multi-plate centrifugal clutch: as engine speed rises, the rollers are thrown outwards and up 'ramps', and this pushes the moveable half of the pulley towards the other half, therefore closing the gap between them. As the gap closes the belt is forced outwards, and so is running on a larger diameter. As the belt cannot stretch, its movement outwards on the front pulley means it must run on a smaller diameter on the driven pulley to compensate **(see illustration 4.7b)**.

The force of the drive pulley halves pushing the belt out is greater than the pressure of the spring holding the driven pulley halves together, and so the driven pulley halves are forced apart and the belt drops towards the middle, and so is running on a smaller diameter. As engine speed falls again, the drive pulley rollers slide back down their ramps allowing the pulley halves to open up; simultaneously the spring pressure on the driven pulley halves closes them up forcing the belt to run on a larger diameter at the rear and therefore smaller at the front.

The movement of the pulley halves towards and away from each other effectively alters the diameter of each pulley on which the belt is running, and is therefore acting to continually vary the gearing ratio between the pulleys.

In this way the gear ratio is gradually altered as the machine gathers speed, with no need for control from the rider. As the machine slows on steep hills or when slowing in traffic, the sequence is reversed. The lower ratio is then available to allow the hill to be climbed or to provide better acceleration in traffic.

### Multiple clutch systems

Another way to achieve similar results is to fit more than one centrifugal clutch **(see illustration 4.7c)**. In its simplest form, there is a centrifugal clutch on the crankshaft end, and this takes up the initial drive. Driven by a gear running off the first clutch is a second clutch which has stronger springs and so remains inoperative up to a certain speed. When the second clutch comes into operation, drive is transmitted by it at a higher ratio, and drive from the first clutch is bypassed.

There are many variations of the above system, and much depends on the way in

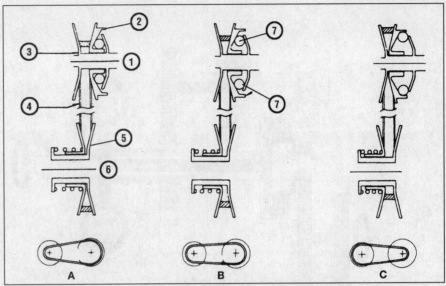

**4.7b  Belt pulley operation and V-belt position**

*Diagram A – At rest or starting off, the front pulley halves are open and the gear ratio is high (about the same as 1st gear in a manual gearbox)*

*Diagram B – At medium speeds, the front pulley halves are partially closed by the centrifugal action of the rollers. The belt moves outward on the front pulley and inwards on the rear pulley, decreasing the gear ratio.*

*Diagram C – At high speed, the rollers in the front pulley are thrown fully outwards, closing the pulley halves and moving the belt fully outwards. The belt moves fully inwards on the rear pulley reducing the gear ratio still further.*

| | | |
|---|---|---|
| 1  Crankshaft axis | 3  Drive pulley movable half | 6  Rear wheel axle axis |
| 2  Drive pulley centrifugal unit | 4  V-belt | 7  Rollers |
| | 5  Driven pulley | |

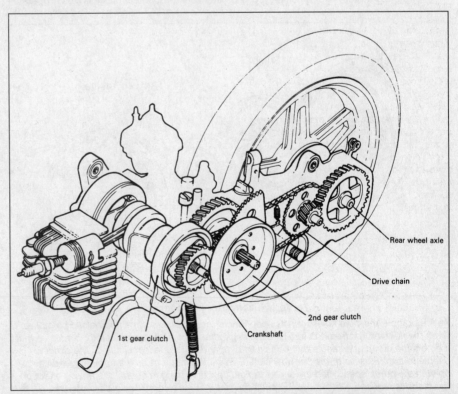

**4.7c  A typical 2-speed 'multiple clutch' automatic transmission**

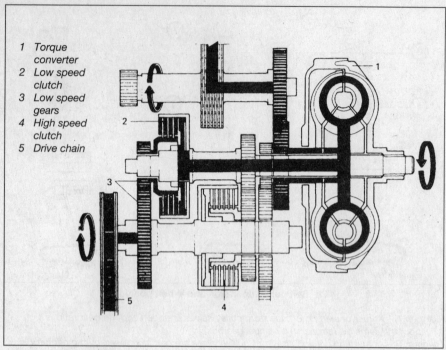

1 Torque converter
2 Low speed clutch
3 Low speed gears
4 High speed clutch
5 Drive chain

**4.7d Automatic transmission of the Honda CB750A, shown in low gear**

which the transmission is laid out. In the case of small-capacity scooters or mopeds, the second speed clutch is often located at the rear of the transmission casing, near to the stub axle which carries the rear wheel.

An improved system is often employed on larger-capacity scooters which have more than two speeds. A typical example would have shoe-type centrifugal clutches for the 1st and 2nd gears, with a multi-plate centrifugal clutch for third gear. The crankshaft-mounted 1st gear clutch operates

in the normal way, transmitting drive to the stub axle. As engine speed rises, the second gear clutch engages and the drive from the 1st gear is interrupted by a one-way clutch (covered briefly in Section 4, and in Chapter 10 under starter systems). When the 3rd gear clutch engages, the drive from 2nd gear is disconnected in a similar manner. The transmission is designed so that the change between 2nd and 3rd gears occurs at a point determined by the amount of load on the engine. In this way the transmission will remain in 2nd longer if accelerating or climbing a hill than it would if under a light load.

### Hydraulic torque converters

The torque converter takes the place of a clutch, and because it also acts as a torque multiplier it can also take the place of a gearbox. However as the torque multiplication of a simple single-stage converter is limited to about 2:1, it is used in conjunction with a manually operated gearbox (on motorcycles) offering high and low ratios **(see illustration 4.7d)**. Multi-stage torque converters, as used in car automatic transmission systems, offer far more multiplication and do not require a gearbox.

The torque converter has three basic components: a pump (or impeller) rotated by the engine, a turbine connected to the gearbox input shaft, and a 'stator' (or reactor) that is mounted on a one-way clutch and so is able to turn in one direction only (the same direction as the pump and turbine) **(see illustration 4.7e)**.

As the pump is rotated by the engine, hydraulic fluid flows from the periphery of the pump vanes to the periphery of the turbine vanes, making it turn and so providing drive to the gearbox; the fluid then returns to the pump via the stator vanes. The curvature of the different vanes is designed so that when there is a difference in speed between the pump and the turbine, the angle of flow of the fluid returning from the turbine to the pump is changed by the stator vanes in such a way that it assists in driving the pump, and this is where the torque multiplication occurs.

The stator is prevented from turning by the one-way clutch, otherwise the angle of the fluid would try to turn the stator in the opposite direction to the pump and turbine. As the turbine catches the pump up, the flow angle of the returning fluid changes and its assistance in driving the pump (the multiplication effect) reduces. At a certain speed difference (when the turbine speed is around 80% of the pump speed) the 'coupling point' is reached, and the angle of fluid flow starts to turn the stator in the same direction as the pump and turbine, and from there on there is no multiplication effect.

The system is essentially the same as that employed in cars with automatic transmission, and the same drawbacks apply: there is power loss through the torque

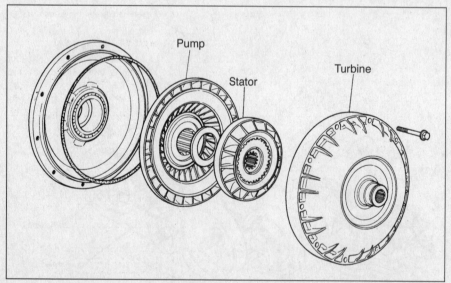

Pump
Stator
Turbine

**4.7e Torque converter components**

*As the pump turns, fluid flows from its periphery to the periphery of the turbine and so makes it turn. The fluid returns from the turbine at an angle that deflects it from the stator blades so that it enters the pump at an angle that helps it to turn, and so torque is multiplied. The stator is unable to turn because of the one-way clutch. This effect reduces as the turbine speed catches up with the pump speed, and the angles of fluid flow are changed so that the driving effect on the pump is reduced. At the coupling point the stator starts to turn, being driven by the changed angle of fluid flow. At this point there is no torque multiplication.*

converter which reduces performance and gives poor fuel economy when compared with a manually operated equivalent. A secondary problem is that of transmission 'creep' at road junctions. For most people, automatic transmission can be regarded as not having characteristics suited to motorcycles, and this is why automatics of the torque converter variety have never been welcomed. Honda have used the system on their CB750A and CB400A Hondamatic models, and Moto Guzzi on their Hydro-Convert model.

## 8  Final drive arrangements

The final drive is the last stage in transferring power from the engine to the rear wheel. It also acts as the last stage of gear reduction and torque multiplication. Typically a final drive system will give a gear reduction of between 2.5 and 3 to 1, depending on the arrangement and the motorcycle's characteristics.

Final drive systems on motorcycles are treated as a separate part of the overall transmission system, whereas scooters do not really have a final drive as such – they usually have a final gear reduction via one pair of gears, but this is considered to be an extension of the 'gearbox' and not a drive arrangement in its own right. For that reason, this Section concentrates on motorcycle applications.

Final drive can be achieved using chain and sprockets, belt and pulleys, or a shaft drive system. Chain and sprockets is the most common form of final drive, with shaft drive being used for touring models and certain cruisers or customs; only a few machines have belt final drive.

### Chain drive

To the motorcycle designer, chain drive is an obvious choice, being compact and relatively easy to arrange on most conventional designs (see illustration 4.8a).

As a transmission medium, a well lubricated and properly adjusted chain is the most efficient method of power transmission. It has low unsprung weight compared to a shaft drive system, and is relatively cheap to manufacture. A chain and sprocket system also provides an easy means of altering the final drive gear ratio by changing the sprocket sizes.

The only drawbacks to the chain and sprocket system are that they operates in a hostile environment where road dirt and water can reduce the chain's efficiency if lubrication and cleaning are neglected. Also the chain will stretch with wear and the sprocket teeth will become hooked, the rate of wear varying with riding style. The chain requires frequent lubrication and freeplay adjustment. Chain life can be extended by chain enclosure cases or

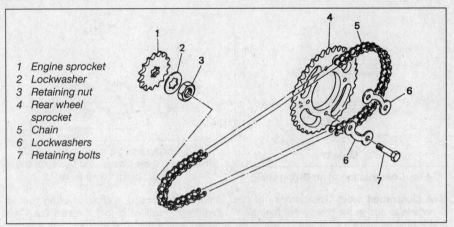

1  Engine sprocket
2  Lockwasher
3  Retaining nut
4  Rear wheel sprocket
5  Chain
6  Lockwashers
7  Retaining bolts

**4.8a  Typical chain drive components**

by the fitting of an automatic chain oiler system.

The development of sealed link chains (O-ring or X-ring) have solved some of the problems inherent in standard roller chains by keeping the dirt out of the rollers and the lubricant in. Also, development of chain materials has enabled lighter, yet stronger, chains, thus helping in the reduction of unsprung weight.

All chains run on sprockets, which are cheap and easy to manufacture, but wear just as badly as chains. The constant action of the chain rollers pulling against the teeth soon wears them out, and they eventually require renewing as a set along with the chain. The front or gearbox sprocket is secured to the exposed end of the gearbox output shaft (except on direct top gearboxes where it is on the input shaft). The rear sprocket is normally fitted onto a carrier that fits into the rear wheel, or onto a hub assembly on machines with single-sided swingarms.

### The standard roller chain

A standard roller chain is made up of roller links and pin links (see illustration 4.8b). A roller link consists of two sideplates, two hollow bushes which are pressed into holes in the sideplates, and two rollers which fit over the bushes. A pin link is made up of two sideplates and two pins which are pressed into holes in the sideplates. The pin links join the roller links by fitting into the hollow bushes. The rollers are free to turn on the bushes, and the bushes can turn on the pins.

The standard roller chain is the cheapest type and is usually used on small and some medium sized 'commuter' motorcycles.

In a solid impregnated roller chain, the roller and bush are combined into one non-rotating drum that is pressed into the holes in the sideplates. The pins on the pin links pass through them and the gap between the pin and the drum wall acts as a reservoir for lubricant.

### O-ring and X-ring roller chains

The construction of an O-ring roller chain is basically the same as a standard roller, with the exception that it has O-ring seals fitted between the roller link and pin link sideplates

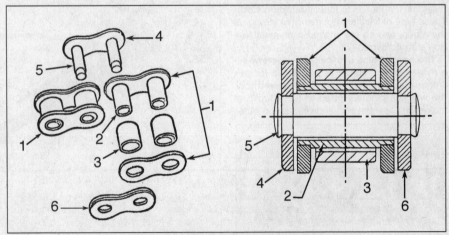

**4.8b  Construction of a standard roller chain**

| | | |
|---|---|---|
| 1  Roller link | 3  Roller | 5  Pin |
| 2  Bush | 4  Pin link | 6  Sideplate |

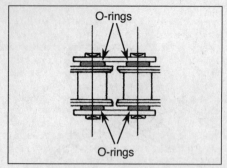

4.8c Construction of an O-ring chain

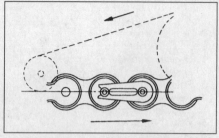

4.8d Spring link clips must always be fitted with their closed end facing in the direction of chain travel

4.8e Chain size is stamped on sideplate

(see illustration 4.8c). The purpose of the O-rings is to seal in the grease that the rollers and bushes are lubricated with on construction, and to keep out dirt and moisture during use. X-ring chains work on the same principle, but the cross section of the sealing ring is X-shaped as opposed to circular; this improves the sealing qualities and reduces the frictional drag of the ring on the sideplates.

Sealed chains are more expensive, and often heavier and bulkier as well, but these disadvantages are outweighed by the extended service life offered. Weight and bulk do not necessarily mean a stronger chain however, as ultimately it is the material that the chain is made of and the method of construction (mainly how the pins are attached to the sideplates) that determines its strength. Racing chains are actually thin and light, and some have hollow pins or cutouts in the sideplates to further reduce weight – they are also unsealed.

### Joining methods

There are three types of chain, two of which use a removable joining link that means the chain can be separated, and one which is manufactured in a loop to a required size and has no joining link, and is in effect endless.

The first type of joining link is known as a split or master link. This has a spring clip securing a removable side plate that enables the pin link to be slid out sideways from the roller link it attaches to (see illustration 4.8d). These type of links are not nearly as strong as the others and so are only used on small low power motorcycles.

The second type of joining link is known as a riveted or soft link. It is similar to a master link in that a sideplate can be removed, but the way the pins are fitted to the sideplates makes the link almost as strong as the other

links in the chain. A chain riveting tool is required to split and join the soft link. The advantage of this type of chain is that it can be removed without having to remove the swingarm for access.

Endless chains are the strongest as all the links are identical, and are used as standard on the majority of performance machines with a standard or single-sided swingarm. Replacement of the chain does mean having to remove the swingarm, though.

### Chain sizing

Chains are sized using a three digit number, for example 525 (see illustration 4.8e).

The first digit (5 in the example) represents the 'pitch' of the chain (the distance between the centre of one pin and the centre of an adjacent pin), and is expressed in eighths of an inch (see illustration 4.8f). So 5 denotes a 5/8 inch pitch, 4 denotes are 4/8 or1/2 inch pitch, and 6 denotes a 6/8 or 3/4 inch pitch.

The second two digits (25 in the example) represents the width of the rollers, and is expressed in eightieths of an inch. So 25 denotes a 25/80 or 5/16 inch width, 30 denotes are 30/80 or 3/8 inch width, and 20 denotes a 20/80 or 1/4 inch width.

But of course there are exceptions to the rules, and some manufacturers alter the last digit to represent a stronger version of the chain, whereby the pitch and width are the same but the sideplates are thicker.

### Shaft drive

Motorcycles have been using shaft drive for many years, though it has never looked like taking over from the chain as the popular choice (see illustration 4.8g). It is arguable that shaft drive is the best final drive system – it is robust, clean and the only routine maintenance is changing the gear oil in the bevel casing. However it is expensive to manufacture, heavy (giving high unsprung weight), and it absorbs a lot of power.

To use shaft drive effectively it helps if the crankshaft runs in line with the drive shaft. Consider the arrangements employed on BMW's R and K series models, the Moto Guzzi range and Honda's CX/GL500 and 650, Pan European and Goldwing, and you can see the advantages quite clearly. If the crankshaft runs across the frame, as in an in-line four, it is necessary to turn the drive through right-angles using a pair of bevel gears before it can connect to the shaft. This might seem complicated, but a look at Yamaha's shaft-

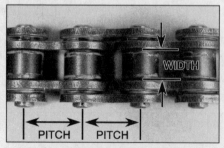

4.8f Chain pitch and width dimensions

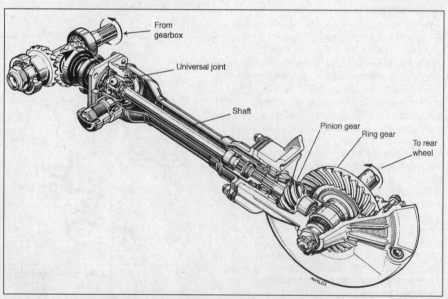

4.8g Cutaway showing the workings of shaft drive assembly

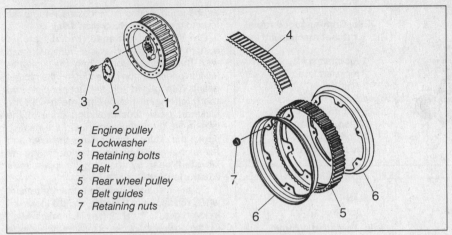

1 Engine pulley
2 Lockwasher
3 Retaining bolts
4 Belt
5 Rear wheel pulley
6 Belt guides
7 Retaining nuts

**4.8h Typical belt drive system**

obviously overcomes any tendency to slip and gives the same effectiveness as a chain. The pulleys need to be larger than the sprockets on a chain final drive to reduce the amount of bend in the wrapping and unwrapping process, and this also ensures that the drive is spread over as many teeth as possible.

The toothed belt is slightly less efficient than a new, clean chain, but in use this difference is soon negated. The belt system is lighter and quieter than a chain, does not require lubrication or adjustment, lasts longer and provides a much smoother drive.

To date, there has been little sign of a general swing to toothed belt in place of chains, though Kawasaki and Harley-Davidson have each released models using the system.

## 9 Kickstart mechanisms

The kickstart mechanism provides the means of turning the engine over to enable it to start. A lever on the outside of the engine is indirectly connected to the crankshaft via a gear train that produces the desired overall ratio between the lever and the crankshaft. An engagement mechanism allows the mechanism to engage when the engine is stationary, and disengage automatically when the engine starts.

### Engagement mechanisms

There are four types of engagement mechanism used: the ratchet and pawl, the cam-engaged radial ratchet, the threaded spindle and the toothed quadrant.

On the **ratchet and pawl** mechanism a spring-loaded pawl locks the kickstart drive gear to the kickstart shaft. On the downward stroke of the lever they lock together and the shaft turns, tensioning the return spring as it does. On the release stroke the pawls ride over the teeth

equipped XS and XJ range, Kawasaki's GT models and Honda's NTV600/650 show that it can be fairly neatly done.

To allow for movement in the shaft assembly for the rear suspension, a universal joint (UJ) or constant velocity (CV) joint is used at the front end of the shaft. The shaft itself (driveshaft) runs inside the swingarm and the final drive housing bolts onto the end of the arm (see Chapter 8 for more information and illustrations).

There are a couple of side-effects, or characteristics, of shaft drive, which were perhaps more evident on earlier designs. The first of these is harshness in the transmission, which the 'give' in a chain helps smooth out, although this is reduced by the fitting of a damper system in the gearbox. The second is the inclination of some shaft driven machines to rise at the back end under acceleration. This is a reaction transferred up the swingarm pivot and realised in the suspension, and is caused by torque as the shaft tries to climb up or down the bevel gear under load. BMW have overcome this torque reaction with their 'Paralever' rear suspension, which incorporates pivots in the swingarm (one behind the main pivot with the frame and one between the final drive housing and the swingarm) and two universal joints in the shaft to offset and counteract the rising effect in the rear suspension (see Chapter 8 for illustration).

Final gear reduction and torque multiplication occurs in the final drive housing, through having a small pinion gear and a large ring gear (see illustration 4.8g).

### Toothed belt drive

The earliest motorcycles used a belt drive to the rear wheel, and this worked satisfactorily as the engines' power output was low. The leather or rubber and canvas drive belts ran quietly and were good at absorbing transmission shocks, but they did have a tendency to slip when wet and stretch. Belt drive soon gave way to chain as increasingly powerful engines were developed and it wasn't until much later that belt technology enabled belt drive systems which were capable of carrying the high loads imposed by modern motorcycles (see illustration 4.8h).

The belt is constructed of internal cords of man-made fibre (kevlar) set into rubber with teeth moulded into the inner face to run on correspondingly toothed pulleys (see illustration 4.8i). The use of teeth

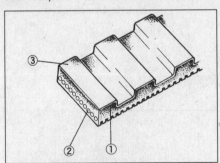

**4.8i Belt construction**

1 Polyurethane compound
2 Kevlar tensile cord
3 Nylon fabric facing

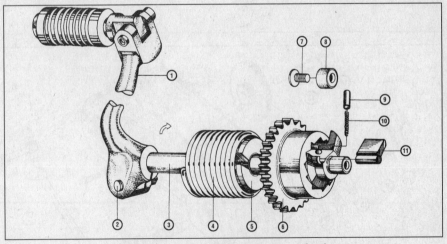

**4.9a Ratchet and pawl engagement mechanism**

| | | |
|---|---|---|
| 1 Kickstart lever | 5 Spring guide | 9 Pawl spring cap |
| 2 Pinch bolt | 6 Kickstart gear | 10 Pawl spring |
| 3 Kickstart shaft | 7 Screw | 11 Pawl |
| 4 Spring | 8 Stop | |

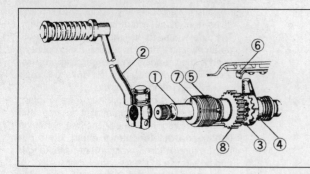

**4.9b Cam-engaged radial ratchet mechanism**

1 Kickstart shaft
2 Kickstart lever
3 Ratchet
4 Spring
5 Return spring
6 Stopper plate
7 Spring guide
8 Kickstart gear

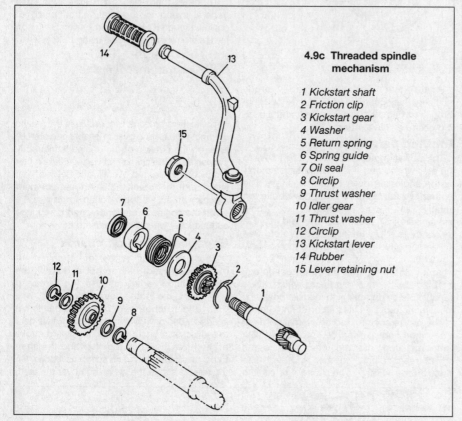

**4.9c Threaded spindle mechanism**

1 Kickstart shaft
2 Friction clip
3 Kickstart gear
4 Washer
5 Return spring
6 Spring guide
7 Oil seal
8 Circlip
9 Thrust washer
10 Idler gear
11 Thrust washer
12 Circlip
13 Kickstart lever
14 Rubber
15 Lever retaining nut

as the return spring unwinds and returns the lever to the top (see illustration 4.9a).

On the **cam-engaged radial ratchet** system the kickstart gear is in constant mesh with the transmission. When the kickstart lever is operated, the projection on the ratchet gear is disengaged from the stopper plate and the ratchet gear moves into mesh with the kickstart gear, thus providing drive to the engine via the transmission. On the release stroke the return spring returns the lever and the ratchet gear is drawn out of mesh with the kickstart gear by the stopper plate (see illustration 4.9b).

On the **threaded spindle** system a ratchet wheel running on a threaded spindle locks the kickstart gear to the shaft (see illustration 4.9c). On the downward stroke of the lever the spindle turns and so the ratchet locks into engagement with the gear and turns the shaft, tensioning the return spring. On the release stroke the spindle turns the other way and so the ratchet is threaded out of engagement. The toothed quadrant mechanism, used on many scooters, is a variation of the threaded spindle type of kickstarter (see illustration 4.9d).

## Kickstart arrangements

There are two ways of arranging the drive train to the crankshaft: the primary kickstart and the non-primary or direct drive kickstart.

On the **primary kickstart** system, the kickstart driven gear freewheels on the input shaft, and its engagement mechanism locks it into the primary driven gear on the clutch housing. This turns the crankshaft via the primary drive gear. This system allows the engine to be in gear when it is kicked, but the clutch must be disengaged. This system is used mainly in off-road motorcycles.

On the **non-primary kickstart** system, the kickstart driven gear is locked to the input shaft which therefore turns with it. Drive to the crankshaft is therefore via the clutch, which must be engaged. This means the engine must be in neutral when it is kicked.

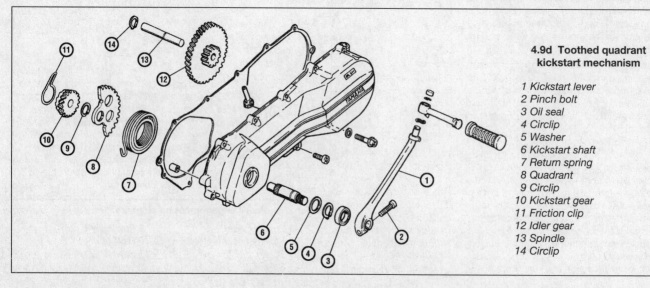

**4.9d Toothed quadrant kickstart mechanism**

1 Kickstart lever
2 Pinch bolt
3 Oil seal
4 Circlip
5 Washer
6 Kickstart shaft
7 Return spring
8 Quadrant
9 Circlip
10 Kickstart gear
11 Friction clip
12 Idler gear
13 Spindle
14 Circlip

# Chapter 5
## Engine lubrication and cooling

# Contents

## 1 Introduction

### Lubrication

The internal moving parts of the engine are machined to fine tolerances and to a smooth finish to minimise wear. When viewed under a microscope, however, apparently smooth surfaces are actually quite rough, and to minimise the friction and heat which would occur if the surfaces were in contact it is necessary to introduce a film of lubricant to separate them.

By maintaining a film or coating of oil on the internal surfaces of the engine, the lubrication system effectively cushions the various parts and holds them apart from each other. If the lubrication system fails at any point, there will be a rapid and localised build-up of heat. In extreme cases this may cause the affected areas to seize by becoming welded together.

In addition to its main role of lubrication, the oil performs a number of secondary tasks. The oil film effectively coats all the internal parts, thereby excluding air and acidic deposits which could otherwise cause corrosion. On four-stroke engines, where the oil is constantly recirculated, it carries away any contaminants, which then become trapped in the oil filter, and thus cleans the engine.

The oil is also used to improve sealing between the piston and rings and between the reed or disc valves and the crankcase on two strokes. Finally, it helps to disperse heat from areas subject to very high local temperatures such as the piston, rings and cylinder bore surface.

### Cooling

Despite the high efficiency of modern engines, fuels and oils, there remains the problem of heat. Ideally, an engine would convert all of the energy in the fuel into power, and would be mechanically frictionless, and thus would remain cold. In practice there is a considerable amount of unwanted heat generated in all engines, and this must be kept to a reasonable level to prevent damage.

This can be done directly, by radiating heat into the surrounding air (air-cooling), or indirectly, by conducting the heat away with a liquid coolant which is itself cooled in a radiator (liquid-cooling).

## 2 Four-stroke lubrication and lubricants

### Types of lubrication

There are three types of lubrication, 'boundary', 'thin film' and 'hydrodynamic'. The difference between them is in the amount of lubricant between two bearing surfaces and the way this affects lubrication. All three can be found between the same components under different conditions of speed and load.

The quality of lubrication depends on the viscosity of the lubricant, the smoothness (or roughness) of the bearing surfaces, and the ability of the lubricant to stick its molecules to the bearing surfaces and stay there (known as its 'film strength').

### Boundary lubrication

Boundary lubrication is when two bearing surfaces are coated with a thin film of oil (see

**illustration 5.2a)**. There is only enough oil for a few molecules to stick to and cover the high spots between the two surfaces.

If there is high pressure or load between these two surfaces, the oil will break down in these places and rapid wear follows. Boundary lubrication is the least effective form and can only tolerate low bearing loads.

### Thin film lubrication

Here the oil has a thickness that is about the same as the roughness depth of the bearing surfaces **(see illustration 5.2b)**. While there is some support given by the oil film, there is little 'laminar flow' of the oil, and the film is likely to be ruptured by increasing loads, whereupon boundary lubrication takes over.

### Hydrodynamic lubrication

If the oil film can be made thicker than the roughness depth of the bearing surfaces, metal-to-metal contact is avoided altogether **(see illustration 5.2c)**. This ideal form of lubrication depends on the viscosity of the oil, sufficient oil pressure, and the rotation of a shaft in a plain bearing.

As the shaft rotates it pulls the oil around, and the viscous drag causes it to form a wedge of high pressure oil at the point where the shaft rests in the bearing. This pressure wedge pushes the shaft up from the surface of the bearing, enabling it to turn on a cushion of oil.

## *Types of lubricant*

### Animal and vegetable oils

Animal oils and fats used to be used for greasing cart axles (horse and cart, that is, not go-cart), but are unsuitable for engines as they oxidise (burn) at low temperatures to form a clogging gum and varnish. The same is true of all vegetable oils except one, castor oil.

Caster oil has excellent lubricating properties under heavy load, which helps boundary lubrication, but it still suffers from easy oxidation, often requiring frequent engine strips to remove deposits. It was used quite widely in racing applications years ago, and still is in certain applications. You can always tell an engine using castor oil because of its distinctive smell.

### Mineral oils

These are the most widely used oils and are derived by fractional distillation from crude oil, which comes out of the ground. Petrol is obtained from the same source using the same method.

Mineral oils are able to withstand higher temperatures and are less prone to oxidation, making it much more suited to conditions inside an engine.

### Synthetic oils

Synthetic oils are a chemically manufactured alternative to mineral oils. Although they are a lot more expensive, they do not suffer from oxidation and have even better lubricating

qualities, making them more suited to the high power high speed engines of today.

Both semi- and fully-synthetic oils are available, semi-synthetic being a good compromise on performance and expense for many engines which do not actually need fully-synthetic oil.

## *Oil classification*

The 'American Petroleum Institute' (API) and 'Society of Automotive Engineers' (SAE) are the organisations responsible for testing and classifying oils, and all oils in the UK are now classified in terms of use (API grade) and viscosity (SAE grade).

### Application

A double letter code classifies oils for specific uses. The first letter defines the type of engine an oil can be used in. All oils used in petrol engines are classified 'S' for spark ignition engines, whereas oils for diesel engines are classified 'C' for compression ignition engines.

The second letter defines the quality of the oil. Ratings start with the letter A, and currently run to the letter J, which is the highest quality. As oils develop consecutive letters of the alphabet will be used, and earlier grades will become obsolete. Motorcycle manufacturers specify a minimum grade of oil for a particular engine, e.g. SE, SF or SG grades.

To confuse the issue a different system is used by the Association of European Automobile Constructors (ACEA). They use a G to signify gasoline and D for diesel, with a number after the letter to denote the grade.

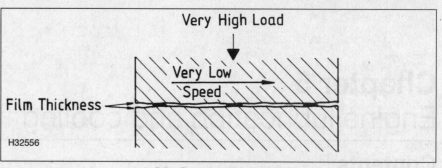

**5.2a Boundary lubrication**

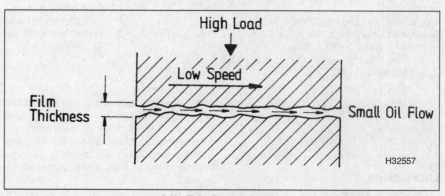

**5.2b Thin film lubrication**

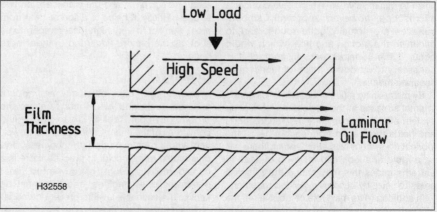

**5.2c Hydrodynamic lubrication**

The equivalent of SE is G1, SF is G2, and SG is G4 and 5.

## Viscosity

Before the 1920's oils were graded light, medium or heavy according to their thickness, or 'viscosity'. But as time went on it became necessary to develop a much more precise system; the SAE therefore produced standardised oil grades which were achieved by conducting viscosity tests at 0°F and 200°F.

The grades standardised at the higher temperature for 'summer oils' were SAE 20, 30, 40 and 50. The grades standardised at the lower temperature for 'winter oils' were SAE 5W, 10W, 15W, and 20W. The higher the number, the thicker the oil, and therefore the higher the temperature it can operate under whilst maintaining its viscosity. All oils were thereafter classified with one number according to viscosity.

The problem with single grade (or mono-grade) oils is that they can only operate efficiently over a small temperature range – a thin oil is good in the winter or for cold starting, but becomes too thin for effective lubrication as temperatures rise. Conversely a thick oil works well in hot conditions and once engines are hot, but is too thick to circulate quickly and provide lubrication when starting from cold, and causes drag. Years ago it was necessary to change oil according to the season, not to mileage!

In the 1960's, the use of long chain polymers as viscosity index improvers led to the creation of multi-grade engine oils, which is what we all use now. The most widely used is probably a 10W40, which operates as a thin 10W weight oil at 0°F, and as a 40 weight oil at 200°F.

Gear oils, which are mono-grade, have their own range of SAE viscosity grades which do not correspond with those of multi-grade engine oils. Gear oils are used where the machine has a separate gearbox and SAE80 and 90 grades are common. As a rough guide an SAE90 gear oil will be of the same viscosity as an SAE 50 engine oil. Gear oils used for certain applications are prefixed 'EP', for extreme pressure.

## Oil additives

Various oil additives are blended during the manufacturing process to improve the performance of oils:

**Detergents** improve the cleanliness of the engine, particularly in hot areas, by holding the by-products of oxidation in suspension, and so preventing coagulation of deposit-forming gums and varnishes. One reason oil becomes dirty quickly is because the detergents are doing their job.

**Dispersants** control cold-sludging and carry finely divided combustion products in suspension.

**Oxidation and corrosion inhibitors** reduce the rate of oil oxidation and control any corrosion due to acids and water vapour.

**Anti-wear agents** protect rubbing components against wear by improving film strength. This is especially good for valve train components where there is usually only boundary lubrication.

**Oiliness agents** reduce friction of heavily loaded rotating and reciprocating components.

**Anti-foaming agents** reduce foaming, which is caused by the air in the crankcase mixing with oil under turbulence, by breaking the surface tension of the bubbles. Foaming reduces the oil's ability to lubricate and cool, and increases oxidation.

**Pour depressants** lower the solidification temperatures of oils so they do not thicken so easily when cold.

**Viscosity-index improvers** help to reduce thinning when hot and thickening when cold, and so control oil consumption and improve cold starting. They enable the oil to flow like a thin oil and lubricate like a thick oil at all times.

## 3  Four-stroke lubrication systems

### Circulation

All modern four-stroke engines use a recirculating oil system (**see illustration 5.3a**).

An engine-driven pump forces the oil through a filter and then into passages in the engine castings, or through external pipes, to the main areas of stress in the engine. The

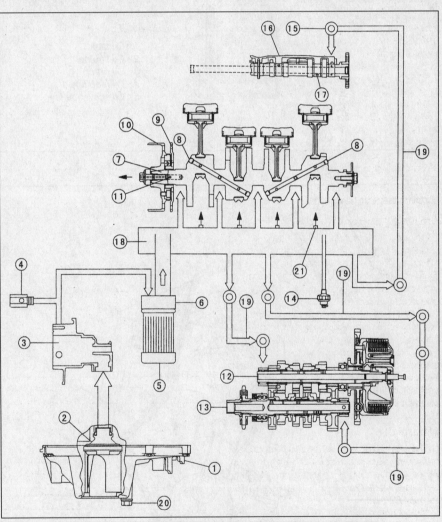

**5.3a  A typical recirculating lubrication system (Kawasaki ZX-6R)**

| | | |
|---|---|---|
| 1  Sump (oil pan) | 8  Oil feed to con-rod journals | 15  Oil feed to cylinder head |
| 2  Oil strainer | 9  Starter clutch gear | 16  Camshaft caps |
| 3  Oil pump | 10  Alternator rotor | 17  Camshaft |
| 4  Pressure relief valve | 11  Oil feed to starter clutch | 18  Oil gallery |
| 5  Oil filter | 12  Gearbox input shaft | 19  Oil pipes |
| 6  Oil cooler (coolant type) | 13  Gearbox output shaft | 20  Oil drain plug |
| 7  Crankshaft | 14  Oil pressure switch | 21  Oil jets (nozzles) |

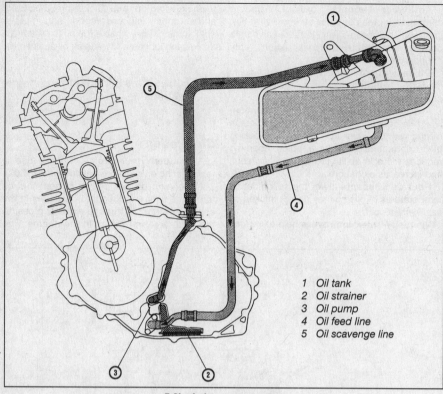

1  Oil tank
2  Oil strainer
3  Oil pump
4  Oil feed line
5  Oil scavenge line

**5.3b  A dry sump system**

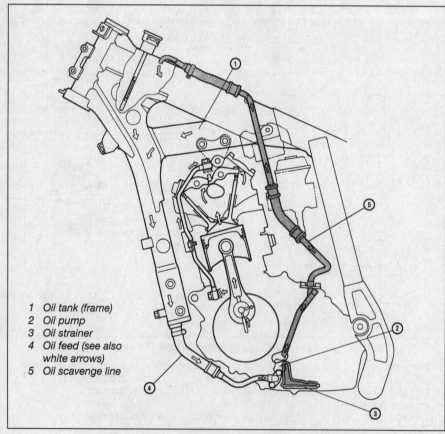

1  Oil tank (frame)
2  Oil pump
3  Oil strainer
4  Oil feed (see also white arrows)
5  Oil scavenge line

**5.3c  A dry sump system which utilises the frame**

main feed directs a high pressure supply to the big-end and main bearings on the crankshaft. A second feed, at a lower pressure, takes oil to the top of the engine where it lubricates the valve train components before draining back down to the crankcase.

On some engines, a drilling in the connecting rod splashes oil on the piston and cylinder walls to lubricate and cool them. Others use a similar principle with passages in the crankcase leading to oil nozzles which spray oil onto these areas. Otherwise they rely on the oil vapour present in the crankcase and on 'splash' lubrication (the action of the crankshaft webs hitting the oil in the sump as the crankshaft rotates) to protect them.

On the majority of engines (unit construction) the oil is also fed to and through the transmission shafts where it lubricates the bushes the gears run on via holes in the shaft. This oil and oil from the sump also lubricates the meshing teeth of the individual gear pinions by the splash method.

### Storage

There are two basic recirculating systems employed on four-stroke engines, and these differ in the way the oil is stored on the machine.

In a 'dry-sump' system, the oil drains down into the bottom of the crankcase where it is picked up through a strainer by the scavenge side of the oil pump and transferred to an external oil tank for storage (see illustration 5.3b). Several dry sump systems use the motorcycle's frame as the oil tank (see illustration 5.3c).

The 'wet sump' system is the most common form of lubrication. The oil is contained in an extension of the crankcase, known as a sump (or oil pan) (see illustrations 5.3d and e). This eliminates the return side of the system and is thus simpler in operation, and also eliminates the need to find somewhere to put the oil tank, though the engine does tend to be taller because of the need to accommodate the sump.

### Cleaning

Before it enters the pump, the oil is drawn through a fine mesh gauze strainer, located either in the sump or the oil tank according to the system. This strainer picks up any large particles of swarf, carbon, gasket or sealant before they can enter the pump or any of the passages.

After the oil has passed through the pump, it is fed either directly or indirectly to a filter, which then cleans the oil of all remaining fine particles. Filters can either be of the centrifugal type or the pleated paper element type.

### Centrifugal filters

Oil is passed through a drum or 'slinger' attached to the end of the crankshaft (see

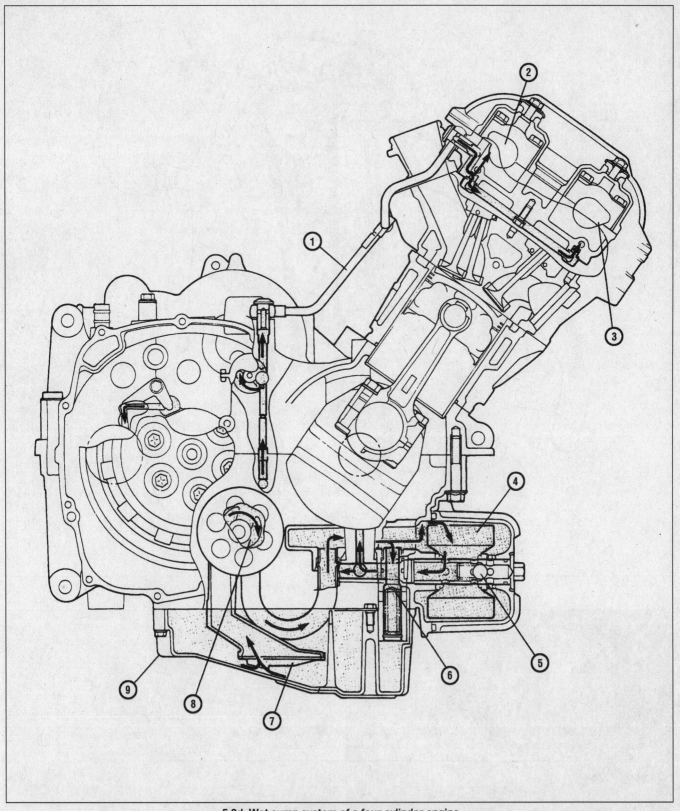

**5.3d  Wet sump system of a four cylinder engine**

| 1 | Oil delivery pipe to cylinder head | 4 | Oil filter | 7 | Oil strainer |
|---|---|---|---|---|---|
| 2 | Inlet camshaft | 5 | Bypass valve | 8 | Oil pump |
| 3 | Exhaust camshaft | 6 | Pressure relief valve | 9 | Sump (oil pan) |

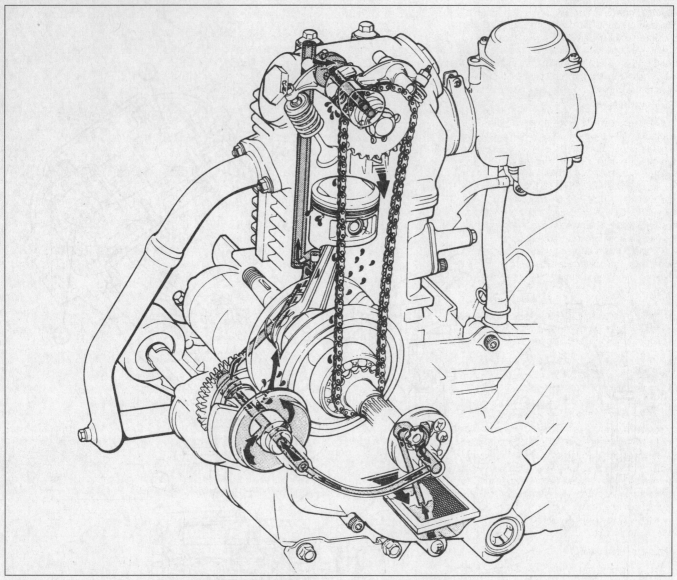

5.3e  Wet sump system of a single cylinder engine

5.3f  A centrifugal oil filter (arrow) attached to the end of the crankshaft

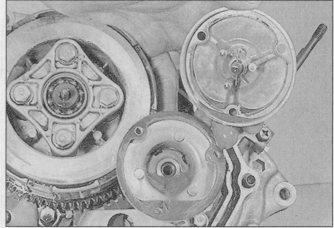

5.3g  Removal of the cover allows any foreign particles in the oil to be wiped from the inside of the drum

**illustrations 5.3f and g)**. The drum spins at the same speed as the crankshaft, so any foreign particles that are heavier than the oil are flung outwards by centrifugal force and stick to the wall of the drum, leaving cleaned oil to pass through the centre of the drum and on into the engine.

### Element filters

There are two different types of filter: the replacement element type, whereby the pleated paper element is housed in a casting which is a part of the engine **(see illustration 5.3d)**, or the replacement unit type whereby the element and its housing are one disposable unit which threads onto a projection on the crankcase **(see illustrations 5.3h)**. The replacement type (or spin-on filter) is now common fitment.

Oil from the pump enters the filter via an aperture in the crankcase. The oil then passes through the pleated paper element where it is cleaned, and then returns to the crankcase for distribution around the engine. The filter unit normally incorporates a by-pass valve which allows oil to by-pass the filter element should it become clogged (see Section 4).

### 4 Four-stroke systems – oil pumps

In the recirculating lubrication system of a four-stroke engine the oil has to be forced under pressure through the oil passages and pipes in the engine, and this is done using a pump, driven by the engine. There are three basic types of pump: the plunger pump, the gear pump and the eccentric rotor or trochoid pump. Of the three the trochoid pump is the most common.

### *Plunger pump*

The plunger pump is most usually found on older machines with dry sump systems, and thus it has feed (delivery) and return (scavenge) plungers **(see illustration 5.4a)**.

The pump body is mounted near the end of the camshaft, and the pump plungers are operated from an offset pin in the camshaft end. The pin drives a sliding block which in turn raises and lowers the plungers. The feed plunger is of smaller diameter than the return plunger, and this ensures that the amount of oil ultimately finding its way to the crankcase is less than the return side of the pump can cope with. This means that the crankcase is kept clear of residual oil which would otherwise cause drag on the flywheels. At the bottom of each pump chamber is a one-way valve which controls the flow of oil to the engine and oil tank.

The plunger pump can deliver oil at a high pressure, but only in a small volume.

### *Gear pump*

The gear pump has a pair of meshed gears

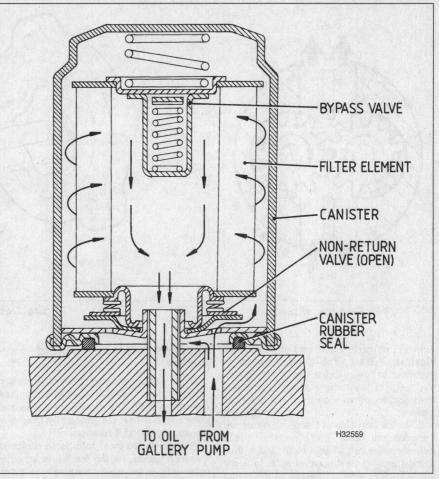

BYPASS VALVE

FILTER ELEMENT

CANISTER

NON-RETURN VALVE (OPEN)

CANISTER RUBBER SEAL

TO OIL GALLERY    FROM PUMP

H32559

**5.3h  The replacement unit (spin-on) type filter**

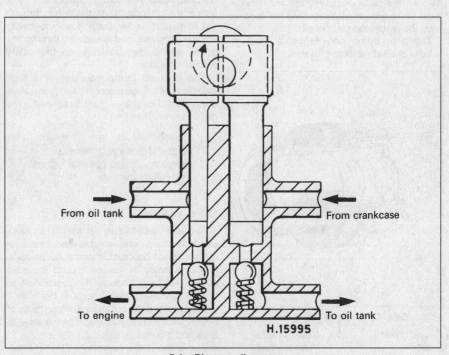

From oil tank

From crankcase

To engine

To oil tank

H.15995

**5.4a  Plunger oil pump**

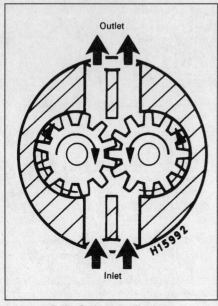

5.4b  Gear-type oil pump

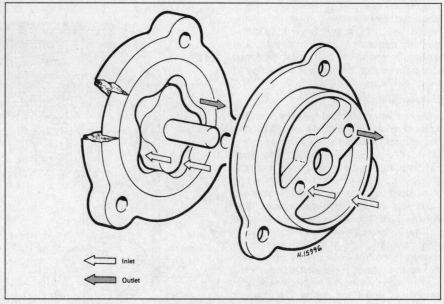

5.4c  Trochoid oil pump

running in a closely confined chamber **(see illustration 5.4b)**. The pump chamber is machined to fit very closely around the gears, the teeth of the latter running only a few thousandths of an inch from the chamber walls.

Oil at the inlet side of the pump is trapped between the pump body and the space between each pair of gear teeth, and is thus carried around to the outlet side. In a dry sump engine, a second stage of the pump provides the return or scavenge to the tank. As with the plunger pump, the return side must be of greater capacity than the feed to keep the crankcase clear of oil.

The gear pump can deliver a medium volume of oil at medium pressure.

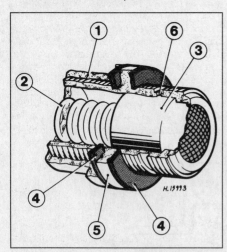

5.5a  Oil pressure relief valve

| 1 | End cover | 4 | Sealing washer |
| 2 | Spring | 5 | Valve housing |
| 3 | Valve | 6 | Outlet hole |

### Eccentric rotor or trochoid pumps

The trochoid pump has a pair of concentric rotors inside a circular pump body **(see illustration 5.4c)**. The shapes of the inner and outer rotors is best understood by looking at the accompanying illustration.

The four-lobed inner rotor is so designed that as it rotates, turning the five-lobed outer rotor with it, the cavity between the lobes becomes alternately larger and then smaller. By positioning inlet and outlet ports on one face of the pump body, oil is drawn in through the inlet port under suction as the cavity volume increases, and is expelled through the outlet port under pressure as the cavity volume decreases.

The trochoid pump can deliver a high volume of oil at high pressure, and is therefore the preferred choice of manufacturers for the majority of engines.

### 5  Four-stroke systems – oil pressure, pressure relief valves and bypass valves

### Oil pressure

For the lubrication system to work effectively the oil circulating around it must be at the correct pressure in particular areas. A higher pressure is needed around the main and big-end bearings in the crankshaft to ensure hydrodynamic lubrication. However if it was at the same pressure in other parts of the engine that pressure could cause seals to blow and gaskets to leak.

The pump is the component that creates the initial pressure in the system, and

thereafter it is regulated by the size of the passages and pipes, and by 'restrictor valves' (which restrict the flow of oil in a passage by acting as a partial block). A restrictor valve helps maintain pressure in the main oil gallery to the crankshaft and reduces the pressure of the oil to the valve train components.

The majority of motorcycles are fitted with an oil pressure switch **(see illustration 5.3a, item 14)** and warning light, which illuminates when there is insufficient or no pressure, and extinguishes when pressure is built up. Others, and particularly Yamahas, have an oil level sensor and warning light. The operation of oil pressure switches and level sensors is covered in Chapter 10.

Manufacturers usually specify an oil pressure check figure which enables the pressure of the lubrication system to be checked if a fault is suspected. The check is made with an oil pressure gauge, usually at the main oil gallery, and is measured at a specific engine speed and temperature.

### Pressure relief valve

A pressure relief valve is fitted to limit the overall pressure in the system. The valve, in the form of either a steel ball or a small piston, is held closed against oil pressure by a spring **(see illustration 5.5a)**.

As oil pressure rises with engine and therefore pump speed, it eventually reaches a point where it forces the relief valve open and allows excess oil to drain back to the crankcase. The relief valve is necessary to prevent the engine oil seals and gaskets from being burst under excess pressure when the engine is running at high speed, and therefore allows a high enough pressure to be maintained at low speeds.

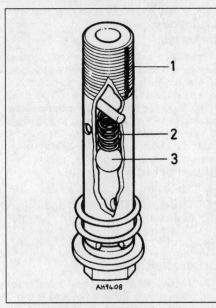

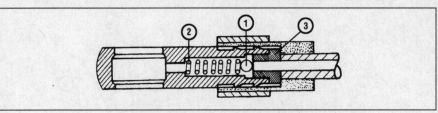

**5.5c Non-return or 'check' valve**

*1 Steel ball    2 Spring    3 Valve seat*

**5.5b Filter housing bolt type bypass valve**

*1 Valve housing    2 Spring    3 Steel ball*

### Bypass valve

The bypass valve is a type of pressure relief valve, fitted in the oil passage from the filter to the engine, inside the oil filter itself (replacement unit type), or in the oil filter housing bolt **(see illustration 5.5b)**.

It is designed to open when internal resistance in the oil filter is such that the flow of oil to the engine is likely to be seriously reduced, i.e. if filter has become clogged. In normal circumstances the valve should never open, but if regular oil and filter changes are ignored, the filter element will eventually become badly blocked by accumulated debris.

The bypass valve, as its name suggests, bypasses the filter and allows the oil to continue to circulate. The oil is now unfiltered, however, so the contaminants in it are carried round the engine and will cause accelerated wear.

### Non-return or 'check' valve

Non-return valves or check valves ensure that oil flows in the correct direction round the system **(see illustration 5.5c)**. The valve is held closed by a spring until oil starts to flow, whereupon the valve opens, allowing flow in one direction only. If the flow stops, the valve closes, preventing any oil draining back in the reverse direction.

## 6   Four-stroke systems –
### oil coolers

### Usage

The circulating oil performs a valuable job in transferring heat away from localised high temperature areas of the engine. To prevent the oil overheating, it must be cooled before it returns to these hot-spots. Hot oil combined with oxygen oxidises and forms carbon and varnish.

In a dry sump system the oil tank radiates a good deal of the accumulated heat and this is aided by the cooling effect of the air flowing around it. Similarly in the case of wet sump engines, the sump extension of the crankcase is often finned to present the maximum surface area to the air. On high performance engines, however, this natural dispersal of heat may not be sufficient when the machine is ridden hard or in hot climates, or where the air flow is restricted due to fairing panels. To improve heat dissipation an oil cooler is fitted.

### Cooler types

There are two types of oil cooler, one in the form of a radiator which uses air as its cooling medium, and one in the form of a jacket which uses engine coolant as its medium.

### Radiator type

These can be used on air- and liquid-cooled machines. A small radiator is mounted at the front of the machine in the airstream, and the oil circulates through passages in the radiator **(see illustration 5.6a)**. These passages have fins designed to maximise

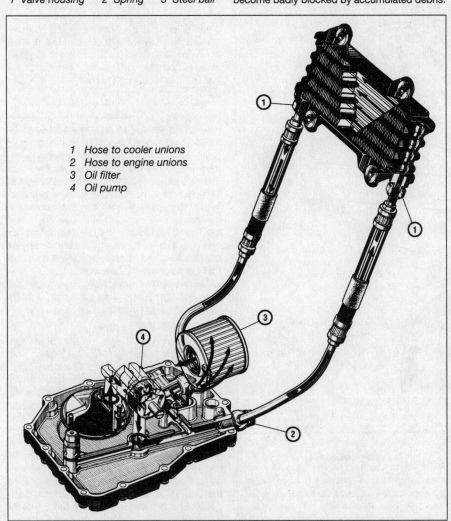

1  Hose to cooler unions
2  Hose to engine unions
3  Oil filter
4  Oil pump

**5.6a A typical radiator type oil cooler system**

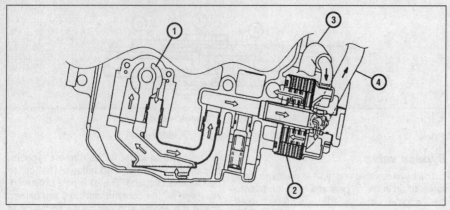

**5.6b  Oil cooler jacket**

1  Oil pump     2  Oil cooler     3  Coolant inlet     4  Coolant outlet

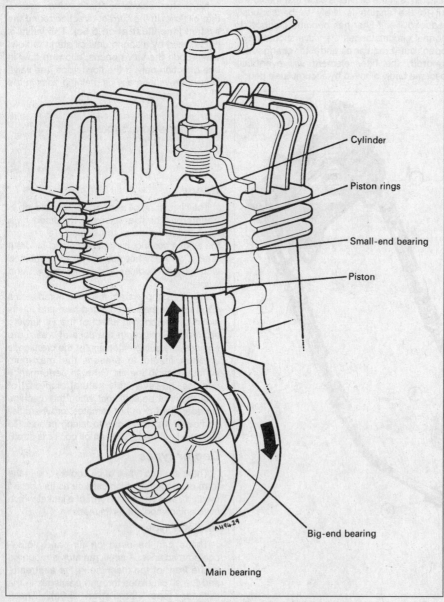

Cylinder

Piston rings

Small-end bearing

Piston

Big-end bearing

Main bearing

**5.7a  Areas needing lubrication on a two-stroke engine**

surface area, and the air flows over these fins and dissipates the heat.

### Jacket type

These can only be used on liquid-cooled machines. A housing is mounted on the front of the engine and is often used as the mounting base for the oil filter. Oil from the pump is routed through the centre of the housing (or jacket) before being routed to the oil filter **(see illustration 5.6b)**. The housing contains coolant passages which allow coolant to flow through the housing and dissipate the heat from the hot oil.

## 7  Two-stroke lubrication and lubricants

### Lubrication

All two-stroke engines use a total-loss lubrication system. It is not possible to use a recirculating oil system because the crankcase's secondary function as a pumping chamber would send excessive amounts of oil through the transfer ports and into the combustion chamber with the fuel/air mixture. Instead, two stroke engines employ a system in which the oil used for lubrication is supplied in small quantities, and is then burnt with the fuel/air mix and expelled with the exhaust gases, hence the term total-loss.

The problem with lubricating the engine components is that the oil is constantly washed off by the fuel **(see illustration 5.7a)**. This is why main, big-end and small-end bearings are all of the caged roller type as they require less lubrication than the shell and plain bearings used in four-stroke engines. The gearbox is housed and lubricated separately using gear oil. On certain engine designs the outer main bearings are lubricated externally by oil fed from the gearbox, and inner bearings are drip-fed by oil drained from the transfer port via a passage that opens above the bearing.

There are two ways of supplying the oil, either by pre-mixing it with the petrol, or by injecting it using a pump.

### Pre-mix systems

A small amount of oil is mixed with the fuel in the fuel tank in a pre-determined ratio.

When the fuel/oil/air mixture is drawn into the crankcase and compressed, some of the oil condenses on the engine parts to lubricate them, whilst the residual oil is transferred to the combustion chamber to lubricate the cylinder wall and piston rings, and is then burnt and expelled with the exhaust gases **(see illustration 5.7b)**. This approach is known as premix, the fuel often being known as 'petroil' due to its oil content. The ratio of fuel to oil is usually about 20:1 to 50:1 depending on the engine and the oil used (synthetic and concentrated oils allow ratios of up to 60:1).

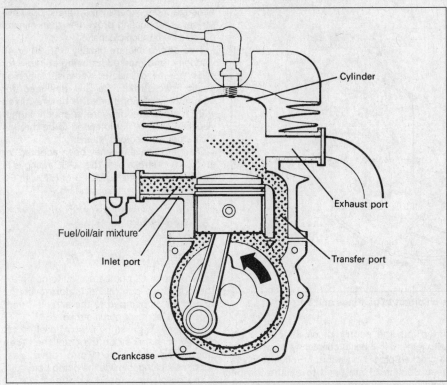

**5.7b Two-stroke engine lubrication by pre-mixed oil and fuel (petroil)**

Labels: Cylinder, Exhaust port, Transfer port, Crankcase, Inlet port, Fuel/oil/air mixture

Despite the small quantity of oil used it is impossible to do anything other than provide the amount needed by the engine at full load. Inevitably, this means that at lower speeds there is an excess of oil which results in oily exhaust smoke and rapid build-up of carbon in the engine and exhaust. Other problems are oil starvation when coasting with high engine revs and no throttle, and of the fuel and oil in the tank not mixing fully.

### Oil pump systems

Pump-fed arrangements overcoming the problem of excess oil at low speeds by metering the oil delivery to suit the throttle opening. By connecting the throttle twistgrip to the pump using a cable splitter it can be regulated by altering the effective stroke of the pump as required. The ratio of fuel to oil is usually about 100:1 at idle and 20:1 at full throttle, though actual ratios depend on the engine itself and the oil recommended by the manufacturer. The oil is carried in a separate tank and is gravity-fed to the pump.

There are two ways in which an oil pump can be used. On some machines it injects the oil into the fuel/air inlet manifold so that it mixes with the fuel and air (**see illustration 5.7c**). Thereafter the fuel/oil/air mixture acts in the same way as on a pre-mix system. Alternatively it is fed via pipes and nozzles to

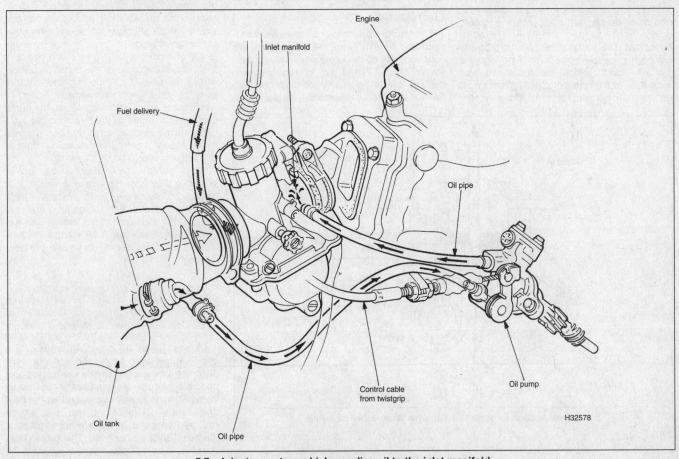

Labels: Engine, Inlet manifold, Fuel delivery, Oil pipe, Oil pump, Control cable from twistgrip, Oil pipe, Oil tank, H32578

**5.7c  Injector system which supplies oil to the inlet manifold**

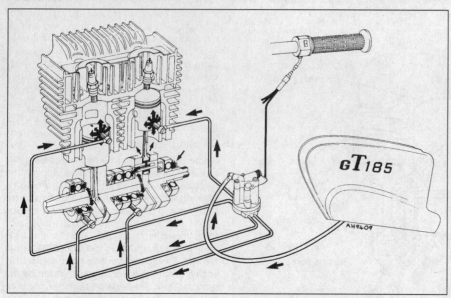

**5.7d Injector system which supplies oil direct to bearings and bores**

Although more expensive, synthetic oils have far better lubricating properties than mineral oils and burn much cleaner.

Two-stroke oils are usually SAE 30 or 40 viscosity, and marked as being suitable for either pre-mix or injector systems. Many high quality two-stroke oils are designed for competition use and need to be pre-mixed with fuel; these oils are a much higher viscosity and are not intended to go through the pumps of injector systems.

Standards have recently been adopted for grading two-stroke oils. This JASO rating is in the form of two letters, FA, FB or FC, with FC representing the highest standard.

## 8 Two-stroke systems – oil pumps

Two-stroke oil pumps are quite complex. There are two controlling factors over the amount of oil pumped to the engine, pump speed and length of pump stroke.

The pump is driven by a worm gear, either directly or indirectly off the crankshaft **(see illustration 5.8)**. The worm drive gear operates a plunger inside the pump body.

The oil pump's speed, or output rate, is controlled partially by the speed of the plunger, which is driven by the worm drive gear; in this respect the output of the pump is proportionate to crankshaft speed. The other factor governing the pump's output is the length of its stroke – the greater the stroke of the plunger the more oil the pump displaces. Stroke is altered by moving the plunger position via a cam arrangement, linked to which is the pump operating cable. The pump cable is connected to the throttle cable via a cable splitter mechanism so that pump stroke is increased at rate proportional to throttle twistgrip opening.

Most pumps incorporate a method of checking their opening setting to ensure that the pump delivers the correct amount of oil. If the pump stroke is insufficient there is a danger of oil starvation to the engine, whereas too great a stroke would deliver too much oil leading to excessive exhaust smoke and poor running.

be sprayed directly onto the relevant areas in the engine **(see illustration 5.7d)**. In this way, the bearings do at least receive some neat oil, even though it is later washed off by the fuel and transferred to the combustion chamber. Some engines use both methods of injection.

The pump lubrication system is now almost universal on all but competition engines, where lightness and simplicity are more important. The pump must be kept properly adjusted to ensure correct metering, and the system must remain sealed (with the exception of the oil tank) to ensure that no air enters the pipes or pump. Air in the system interrupts the supply of oil, or cuts it off altogether if it is being constantly drawn in via a cracked pipe. Non-return or 'check' valves (see Section 5) are used to ensure the oil flows correctly and is not simply pumped back and forth without actually flowing.

### Lubricants

Two-stroke oils can be mineral, semi-synthetic or synthetic. All two-stroke oils contain many of the same additives as four-stroke oils, with the aim of reducing ash content, smoke emissions and oxidation. See Section 2 for more information on lubricants.

## 9 Air cooling

As heat builds up in certain areas of the engine it needs to be dispersed to prevent distortion of the components concerned and possible seizure. Heat naturally dissipates from hot areas to cold areas, and so the heat that builds up in the piston and valves naturally dissipates to the external surfaces of the barrel and cylinder head. The excess heat then has to be dissipated from these surfaces to the air (remember that not all the heat

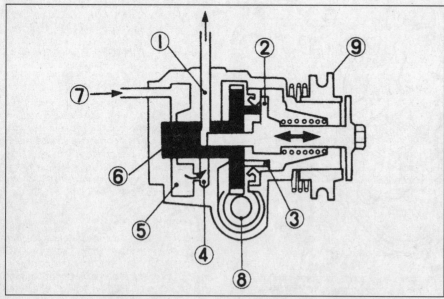

**5.8 Cross-section through the Yamaha 'Auto-lube' oil pump**

| 1 | Oil outlet | 4 | Oil inlet | 7 | Oil supply from | 9 | Operating cable |
| 2 | Guide pin | 5 | Oil chamber | | tank | | pulley |
| 3 | Cam | 6 | Plunger | 8 | Worm drive gear | | |

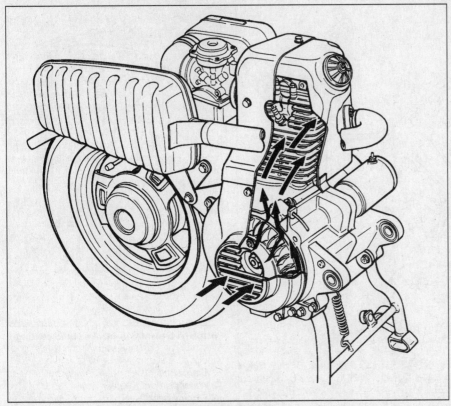

**5.9 Forced air-cooling**

*Fan powered air cooling systems of this type are often found on scooter engines. The ducting directs the air past the relevant engine components.*

wants to be lost, as the engine has to be maintained at its optimum working temperature).

The best method of dissipating heat is to optimise the surface area of the external parts so that the required amount of heat can be lost to the air, and this is done by incorporating cooling fins in the hot areas. If you look at any air-cooled engine you will notice immediately that the main area of heavy finning is around the cylinder head and barrel. The crankcase area is not in immediate contact with the heat from combustion and so needs little or no finning. The exception to this generalisation is in the case of wet sump four-strokes, where finning is used to help cool the oil.

The principles of air cooling were established along with the first motorcycles, and little has changed in the intervening years. The designer must calculate the fin area to suit the rate at which heat must be dispersed, and this is why finning may vary from one engine to another. In the case of a road machine, for example, the cooling effect is aided by the machine's passage through the surrounding air. This is less true of a competition bike, because it is often working hard whilst moving only slowly. This is why many off-road engines have heavy finning. It is also why road machines become excessively hot when caught in traffic. There

is also a noticeable difference in the amount of finning between a two-stroke engine and a four-stroke – two-strokes have twice as many power strokes and so require more cooling.

Another way to employ air cooling, and one which is used where the engine is not directly in the air flow (i.e. on scooters), is to fit ducting over the finned areas and then cool them by blowing air from a fan through the duct **(see illustration 5.9)**. Although power is lost in turning the fan, this method gears the rate of cooling to the engine speed, rather than the road speed, and thus is more closely related to the engine's cooling requirements.

The main disadvantage of air cooling is the wide range of air temperatures under which the engine must function. As the temperature varies, so does the efficiency of cooling (rate of heat transfer varies with the amount of difference in temperature – the greater the difference, the faster the rate).

The problem of varying rates of expansion and contraction of the various engine components means that manufacturing tolerances have to be quite low, and the rate of heat production of a large or highly tuned engine can sometimes prove difficult for air cooling to cope with. Forced air cooling using an engine-driven fan goes some way towards improving the situation, but fan cooling a large engine leads to extra bulk.

## 10 Liquid cooling

Liquid cooling resolves many of the problems associated with air cooling, at the expense of extra cost, weight and complexity. The major advantage of a liquid cooled engine is that it maintains a more consistent operating temperature than an air cooled engine. This permits higher manufacturing tolerances between moving parts.

Liquid cooling also conceals much of the engine noise, and this is a major factor for the engine designer in achieving low noise limits.

### The principle

Liquid cooling works on the principle of thermosyphonic action. The hot areas of the engine, the cylinder head and barrel, incorporate a 'water jacket' or a system of passages. The jacket is connected to the radiator by a pipe running from the top of the jacket to the top of the radiator. A second pipe runs from the bottom of the radiator to the bottom of the jacket.

The liquid in the jacket absorbs the heat from the engine and becomes less dense than the cooler liquid in the radiator. This heavier liquid runs in through the bottom hose, displacing the heated liquid upwards and into the top of the radiator. The liquid loses heat as it passes down through the radiator (which has air flowing over its fins) until it eventually becomes quite cool as it nears the bottom. In this way the liquid automatically circulates without mechanical assistance, albeit rather slowly.

In reality thermosyphonic action does not provide a fast enough rate of flow unless large bore passages and a large radiator are used, and on motorcycles this is impractical. Therefore all systems use a water pump to assist the flow.

### The system components

A typical liquid cooling system consists of a radiator (usually with an electric fan), a pressure cap, an expansion tank or reservoir, a pump, a thermostat, and the various hoses and pipes that connect them **(see illustrations 5.10a and b overleaf)**. There is normally also a temperature gauge and/or a coolant temperature warning light (see Chapter 10).

### The coolant

Cooling systems can be run on plain tap water, but there are inherent problems with this, mainly involving freezing and corrosion. An ethylene glycol anti-freeze is usually added to prevent the coolant freezing when the machine is parked in cold weather. If an antifreeze solution is omitted expanding ice will usually destroy the radiator and may warp or crack the cylinder head or barrel. A 50/50 mixture of distilled water and ethylene glycol

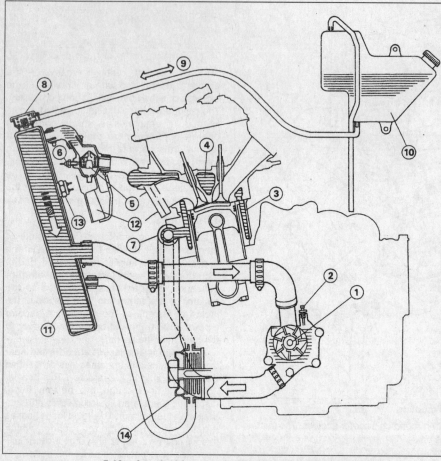

5.10a A typical four-stroke liquid cooling system

| | | |
|---|---|---|
| 1 Water pump (driven off | 5 Thermostat | 10 Expansion tank |
| oil pump shaft) | 6 Water temperature sensor | 11 Radiator |
| 2 Air bleed bolt | 7 Coolant union | 12 Cooling fan |
| 3 Cylinder jacket | 8 Pressure cap | 13 Fan switch |
| 4 Cylinder head jacket | 9 Overflow hose | 14 Oil cooler jacket |

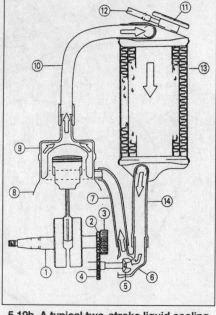

5.10b A typical two-stroke liquid cooling system

1 Crankshaft
2 Water pump drive gear
3 Primary gear
4 Water pump driven gear
5 Water pump
6 Pump cover
7 Hose to engine
8 Cylinder
9 Cylinder head jacket
10 Radiator top hose
11 Pressure cap
12 Overflow hose to expansion tank
13 Radiator
14 Radiator bottom hose

anti-freeze is the normal recommended coolant for motorcycles.

The other advantage of using an anti-freeze is that it contains corrosion inhibitors. If plain tap water were used, the impurities in it would speed up the rate of electrolytic action between the various metals in contact with the liquid causing it to become acidic, leading to corrosion. Also the minerals in tap water, especially hard water, form scale which blocks the passages. This can be avoided by using only distilled water, but in practice most manufacturers add inhibiting chemicals to prevent the problem altogether.

### The radiator

The radiator consists of a number of narrow tubes contained within a housing and linked by numerous metal fins. The coolant enters the radiator at the top, flows through all the tubes, and leaves the radiator at the bottom. Heat from the coolant dissipates to the fins around the tubes, and is then dissipated to the air as it flows over the fins (see illustration 5.10c). As air is involved, the efficiency of the cooling system still varies with air temperature, but to a lesser degree than with pure air cooling.

A temperature controlled electric fan is normally mounted behind the radiator, and is designed to provide extra air flow, particularly when the machine is a standstill. At a pre-determined temperature, the fan switch (mounted in the radiator or thermostat housing) closes and the fan motor operates the fan, which in turn draws air through the radiator.

### The pressure cap

Because water boils at temperatures regularly exceeded by the engine, the cooling system is sealed, and so becomes pressurised as the coolant heats up. As the pressure increases, the boiling point of the liquid rises. Thus, by pressurising the system the boiling point becomes higher than the normal temperature range of the engine. Using ethylene glycol anti-freeze raises the boiling point of the coolant further as it has a higher boiling point than water.

The system is sealed by a pressure cap with a spring loaded valve designed to withstand a pre-set pressure (usually around 1.0 to 1.5 bar). Above this pressure the valve in the cap opens and vents excess coolant through a small pipe to the expansion tank or

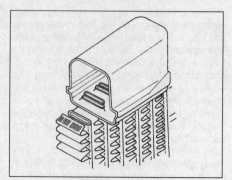

5.10c Radiator construction

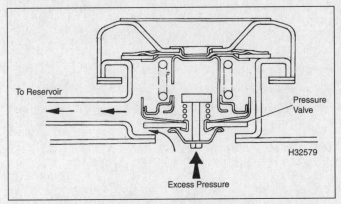

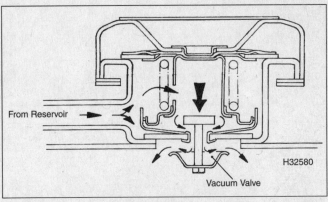

5.10d **Pressure cap operation – when the pressure in the system is high, the pressure valve opens**

5.10e **Pressure cap operation – when the pressure in the system drops, the vacuum valve opens**

reservoir **(see illustration 5.10d)**. When the temperature and pressure drop again a vacuum is created in the cooling system. At this point a vacuum valve in the cap opens and coolant is drawn back from the reservoir and through the cap to replenish the system **(see illustration 5.10e)**. The reservoir itself is not sealed, and has an overflow hose out of its top.

The cap incorporates a pressure release system that opens when the cap is turned anti-clockwise to its first stop, and allows any pressure to be released with the cap still in place. This is a safety feature designed to prevent scalding if removing the cap when the system is hot – if the coolant is hot enough it can actually boil as the pressure is released.

### The pump

The pump is a fairly simple device consisting of an impeller in a housing with inlet and outlet pipes or hoses. On a four-stroke engine the shaft usually interlocks with the oil pump shaft and is driven by it. Because of this the pump shaft has two seals, a mechanical seal and a normal lipped seal. The seals prevent coolant and oil mixing. If one of the seals fails, the chamber between the seals has a drain hole.

On a two-stroke the pump is usually driven off the crankshaft.

### The thermostat

Most liquid cooling systems are controlled by a device called a thermostat. This is a temperature-sensitive valve which closes off circulation to the radiator when the engine is cold, only allowing restricted coolant flow through its air bleed hole. When the engine reaches the correct temperature the valve opens **(see illustrations 5.10f and g)**. The purpose of the thermostat is to allow the engine to warm up more rapidly, and so minimises the higher wear rates present when an engine is running below its correct temperature.

The valve is operated by a wax filled chamber. As the wax heats up it expands, opening the valve, allowing the coolant to flow. The spring closes the valve when the wax contracts. The strength of the spring determines the opening and closing temperatures of the valve.

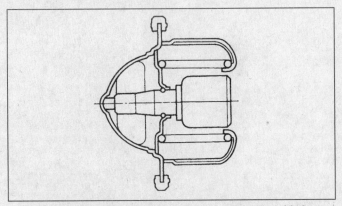

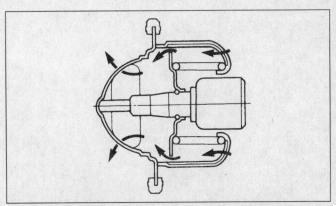

5.10f **Thermostat operation – when the engine is cold, the thermostat is closed and no coolant flows**

5.10g **Thermostat operation – when the engine heats up, the thermostat opens to allow the coolant to flow to the radiator**

# Chapter 6
# Wheels, tyres and brakes

## Contents

## 1 Introduction

The job of the wheel is to support the motorcycle, provide an accurate and reliable mounting for the tyre, and cope with the loads imposed on it by braking, acceleration and road surface irregularities. In addition, the wheel must be as light as possible. Out of necessity the wheel has developed over the years to match the increasing demands placed on it by successively more powerful engines.

Tyres are far more complicated than you might think, and again have developed with the motorcycle into the sophisticated items we now take for granted. Tyres have to provide safe, reliable performance under a wide range of loads, speeds, temperatures and weather conditions. They are fundamental to the rider's safety, but have to be kept down to a reasonable price as they are a disposable item.

The brakes must be able to disperse the stored-up energy of a large, fast moving motorcycle and its rider in a matter of seconds. It converts this energy into heat and radiates the heat rapidly – a fact which rarely crosses our mind when riding.

Taken together, the three areas discussed in this Chapter are perhaps the three most important safety-related items. Each is fulfilling a complex job in a most inconspicuous manner.

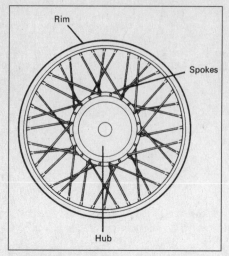

**6.2a Wire spoked wheel construction**

## 2 Wheel construction – wire spoked wheels

The wire spoked wheel, which almost everyone is familiar with in one way or another, is really quite a remarkable device. It has three main elements; the hub, the rim, and the spokes which connect the two **(see illustration 6.2a)**.

### The hub

The hub is the centre component of the wheel **(see illustration 6.2b)**. It may take the form of a straightforward spool type, or may be enlarged to incorporate a drum brake or the rear sprocket carrier and cush drive assembly. If it doesn't incorporate a drum brake then it has mountings for a brake disc.

The wheel axle passes through bearings housed in the hub, allowing the wheel to rotate freely on the axle. The bearings have an internal spacer between them to prevent side loadings when the axle nut or bolt is tightened. The hub anchors the domed heads of the spokes which fit into a countersunk

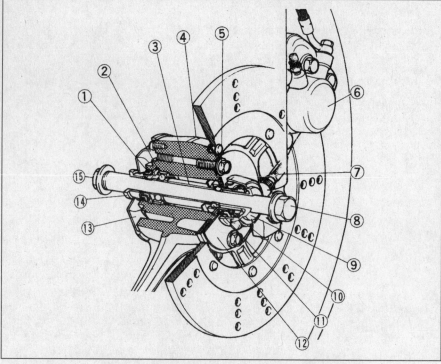

**6.2b Exploded and sectional view of a typical hub**

| | | |
|---|---|---|
| 1 Grease seal | 6 Brake caliper | 11 Bearing |
| 2 Bearing | 7 Speedometer cable | 12 Retaining plate |
| 3 Spacer | 8 Axle | 13 Hub cover |
| 4 Hub casting | 9 Speedometer drive unit | 14 Collar |
| 5 Brake disc bolt | 10 Speedometer drive gear | 15 Axle nut |

hole in the hub flange **(see illustration 6.2c)**. The spoke is often angled through 90°, though on some wheels a straight spoke is chosen for additional strength.

### The rim

The rim is a shaped band of metal which carries the tyre, and provides the anchor point for the outer end of the spokes. The rim is made from chromium-plated steel or aluminium alloy and has a number of different shaped levels when looked at in cross-section. These are chosen to suit a particular application or tyre size.

The spokes are secured at the rim by thin sleeve nuts called nipples. These thread onto the spoke end to allow the wheel to be trued initially and to permit subsequent tensioning. The ends of the spokes are ground off flush with the head of the nipple and then covered by a rim tape to prevent chafing of the tyre inner tube.

### The spokes

It is the spokes themselves which are the most remarkable part of this type of wheel. If you look at a spoked wheel on a parked motorcycle you may wonder how the spoke nearest the ground can support all that weight. After all, if you take a spoke and push the ends together it will bend and collapse quite easily. Spokes have little compression strength, but a great deal of tensile (pulling) strength. A motorcycle with spoked wheels is literally hanging from the spokes uppermost in the wheel; the remaining spokes are only locating the hub in the centre of the rim and preventing the rim from bowing outwards under the weight of the machine.

Another consideration is the loading imposed under braking and acceleration; in each case the rim and hub are under pressure to twist in relation to one another, and so the spokes must be so arranged to cope with these forces. The spokes are fitted in a tangential pattern, rather than in a radial

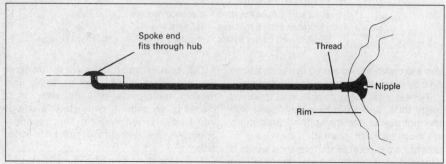

**6.2c How spokes are fitted on a conventional spoked wheel for tubed tyres**

*The spoke has a domed head which fits through a hole at the hub end. The spoke passes through holes in the rim and is secured by a threaded nipple. This can be used to set up the rim alignment when the wheel is first built and allows subsequent adjustment.*

pattern, to accomplish this **(see illustration 6.2d)**.

If the wheel is viewed edge on, it can be seen that each alternate spoke runs from the rim to opposite sides of the hub. This results in a triangulated structure which will resist any tendency for the rim to move sideways in relation to the hub. On a motorcycle these thrust loadings are not very great because the machine banks through corners, so the forces tend to be felt as downward pressure on the centreline of the wheel. This is not the case where a sidecar is fitted, and many sidecar enthusiasts have their wheels rebuilt to provide greater strength in this direction.

### The tyre

On the majority of spoked wheels the necessity for a hole in the rim to take the spoke means that an inner tube must be fitted, otherwise the air would leak out. The fact that the majority of road-going motorcycles don't use spoked wheels any more means that the choice of tubed tyres is somewhat limited. Off-road motorcycles often use spoked wheels and so there is still a reasonable selection of off-road tyres.

Moto Guzzi and BMW have both developed a double rim spoked wheel that can take tubeless tyres, giving the double benefit of having attractive wheels and tubeless tyres.

### 3  Wheel construction – cast alloy wheels

Cast wheels also consist of a hub, a rim and spokes, but the difference is that they are manufactured in one piece from the same material. The 'spokes' are vastly different in that there can be as few as three and rarely more than six, and they can extend radially from the hub, though often don't for cosmetic effect **(see illustration 6.3)**.

Cast wheels first appeared on racing machines in the interests of weight saving (thereby reducing rotational inertia and gyroscopic effect) and greater precision. They had an incidental advantage in that the width at the hub could be much less than a wire spoked type, and this simplified the fitting of disc brakes.

The original racing wheels were made from magnesium alloy and were significantly lighter than an equivalent spoked wheel. However magnesium is very expensive and has a limited life, being prone to corrosion and cracking over long periods of use. Cast wheels fitted to the majority of road-going production machines are made from aluminium alloy, which is cheaper, more durable and equally stiff, but heavier than magnesium alloy wheels.

The wheel is cast in one piece and is then machined at the rim, spoke edges and hub, to produce a wheel that is perfectly true. Once

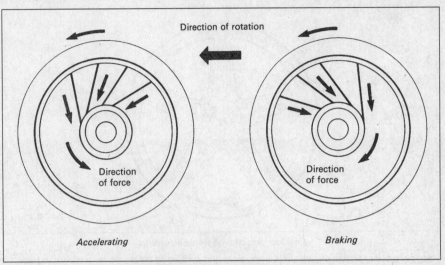

**6.2d  Spoke loadings in a wire wheel**

*The spokes are not arranged radially from the centre line of the hub; the angled arrangement is used to brace the wheel against the torque of the engine (rear wheel) and that of braking (both wheels). These illustrations show a wheel with only one set of spokes in position. Note how the two sets of spokes are designed to absorb loadings in different directions.*

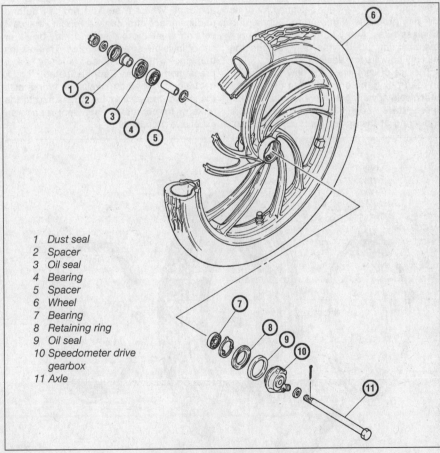

1 Dust seal
2 Spacer
3 Oil seal
4 Bearing
5 Spacer
6 Wheel
7 Bearing
8 Retaining ring
9 Oil seal
10 Speedometer drive gearbox
11 Axle

**6.3  Cast wheel construction**

*This exploded and cross-section view of a cast wheel shows its one-piece construction. In this example (Yamaha RD125 LC) the spokes have a spiral pattern for cosmetic reasons only. Note that on this example a tubed tyre is fitted; most wheels have a rim designed to be used with tubeless tyres.*

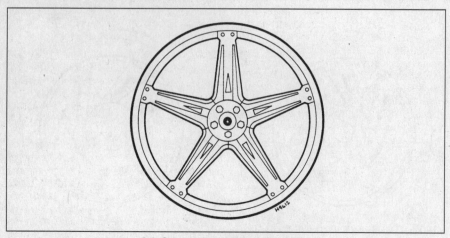

**6.4 Composite wheel construction**

*Composite construction allows various rim sizes and profiles to be built onto a common hub unit. The pressed steel or aluminium spokes are attached by bolts or rivets at the hub and rim.*

finished, the wheel needs no truing or adjustment, and maintenance is confined to ensuring that the surface finish of the wheel is kept in good condition.

Cast wheels allow tubeless tyres to be fitted, but only if they are designed for it, as the rim profile is different for tubed and tubeless tyres. Many early cast wheels are designed for tubed tyres only, though the majority now are for tubeless.

The use of cast wheels is now widespread on road-going motorcycles, but despite the undeniable advantages, there are drawbacks. There have been instances of cracks appearing at the spoke roots as a result of prolonged impact stresses. Although a complete fracture is rare, it is often sudden and always dramatic, and so the wheel must be renewed to prevent the possibility. The same problem applies in the event of an accident. Whilst a spoked rim will deform under impact and can be rebuilt, the cast version is far more rigid and may break or suffer invisible stress fractures. This means that the wheel must be renewed as a precaution unless sophisticated crack detection facilities are available. Worse still, the impact forces may be transmitted to the forks or frame, making accident repairs an expensive proposition.

## 4  Wheel construction – composite wheels

The composite wheel is a hybrid between the wire spoked and cast alloy types, intended to combine the advantages of both **(see illustration 6.4)**. From a manufacturing viewpoint, various rim profiles can be built onto a basic hub/spoke combination, and this reduces costs appreciably.

The rim is an extruded alloy section, similar to the alloy rims used on wire spoked wheels, but without the spoke holes, thus enabling the use of tubeless tyres. A flange on the inner face of the rim provides an attachment point for the spokes. These are made from pressed steel or alloy, and can be riveted or bolted to the rim and hub.

In use, the composite wheel is much the same as a cast wheel, but can be designed to deform in a controlled manner during a crash. This avoids transmitting the impact forces to the frame or suspension. The best known example of composite wheel construction is probably Honda's Comstar wheel. This, like a cast wheel, must be renewed if it becomes bent or buckled, though there are others, which can be rebuilt in the event of accident damage.

## 5  Wheel construction – specialist wheels

### Split rim wheels

This type of wheel is uncommon in the motorcycle world, but can be found on certain scooters and on most All Terrain Vehicles (ATV's). The wheel is formed from steel pressings and is in two halves **(see illustration 6.5)**. The rim halves bolt together at the centreline, and thus can be separated to permit easy tyre changes.

This type of construction is ideal where a wheel of small diameter is needed because it avoids the problems of working the bead over the rim which would otherwise make tyre fitting a nightmare. In the case of scooter wheels an inner tube is fitted, but a tubeless tyre is fitted to some ATV's, requiring an O-ring seal to be fitted between the two rim halves.

### Magnesium alloy and carbon fibre wheels

Magnesium alloy wheels first appeared in the racing world, but are now starting to be fitted as standard on some cutting edge production sports bikes. They are very much lighter than aluminium alloy wheels, and so dramatically reduce rotational inertia and gyroscopic effects, but are generally not as robust, and are more expensive.

Carbon fibre is also now being used to

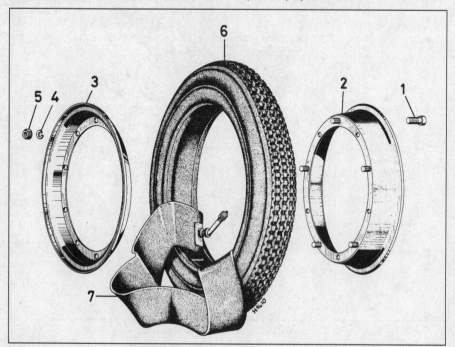

**6.5 Split rim wheel construction**

| 1 Bolt | 3 Rim half | 5 Nut | 7 Inner tube |
|--------|------------|-------|--------------|
| 2 Rim half | 4 Spring washer | 6 Tyre | |

make wheels, and has the benefits of being lighter than magnesium and stronger than aluminium; they are however very expensive. Some racing teams use them, and they are starting to appear as accessories for some sports bikes.

## 6  Tyres – construction

Though the tyre is a consumable item like oil and fuel, it is a very complicated device. Every tyre built is labour, material and technology intensive, a factor which is reflected in its price. Amongst all road vehicles the motorcycle asks more of its tyres than any other. Not only must the tyre perform faultlessly if disaster is to be avoided, it must do so under conditions far more severe than those imposed by cars and trucks.

The foundations of a tyre are the plies that makes up its carcass; plies are layers of rubberised synthetic fibre cords laid one on top of another and bonded together in the finished tyre. The plies are covered by a layer of soft rubber to which the tread layer is bonded. At the inner edges of the tyre is the bead, a carefully shaped and reinforced area which holds the tyre against the rim edge. Where the tyre is designed for tubeless operation the bead is more heavily reinforced and the inside of the tyre is covered with an airtight layer of rubber, known as an airseal liner. To understand the function of each part of the tyre, let us look at each one in turn.

### The carcass plies

The carcass plies forms the strength and control the shape of the tyre, both at low speeds and at high speed where the centrifugal forces are trying to distort it. The plies must be stiff enough to prevent the adverse effects of this distortion, and to prevent the tread from rippling under hard acceleration and braking. In contrast to the above, the plies must allow the tyre to flex in a controlled manner where it contacts the road to spread the rubber and so provide a larger contact patch, and to absorb surface irregularities and thus keep the tread in constant contact with the road. Many motorcycle tyres have four plies (sometimes denoted on the tyre sidewall as 4PR, or four ply rating). Where a stiffer carcass is needed, the tyre may use six plies.

Plies are made up of cords, made from either rayon, nylon, polyester or Kevlar, and set in rubber. The plies wrap around the bead wires on the edge of the tyre.

There are two basic types of carcass, cross-ply and radial.

### Cross-ply

For years all motorcycle tyres were of cross-ply construction. This refers to the way alternate layers of plies are laid in an X pattern to provide stiffness in the sidewall **(see illustration 6.6a)**. It goes without saying that to have the sidewall deforming along the machine's centreline would be very unpleasant – the bike would squirm from side to side in much the same way as it does on a deflated tyre. It would be impossible to control properly and this is why cross-ply construction has always been necessary on two-wheeled vehicles.

However cross-ply tyres expand at high speeds due to centrifugal force, becoming taller and narrower, leading to overheating and adverse handling effects. Bias-belted cross-ply tyres went a long way to solving this, using a 'belt' around the plies to prevent distortion from centrifugal forces.

### Radial ply

On a radial tyre the carcass plies run across the tyre from bead to bead, and there are one or two belts around the carcass as on a bias-belted tyre **(see illustration 6.6b)**. The drawback with this arrangement is that the sidewalls are not as strong as on cross-ply tyres, and this prevented their use on motorcycles until tyre, wheel and motorcycle manufacturers all got together and designed bikes with wider wheels capable of taking low profile tyres without any loss of contact patch area, but with a vast improvement in sidewall strength. Cars use radial tyres without a problem because it is actually a bonus for them to have sidewalls that deform – if they didn't, under hard cornering the inner side of the tyre would tend to lift off the road, reducing grip.

Radial tyres can be made lighter than cross-ply, providing better performance and wear characteristics. They tend to run cooler meaning that a softer compound rubber can be used without increasing wear too much.

A recent development of the radial tyre is the monospiral radial design, which uses no pre shaped belts, replacing them with a single length of material or steel, applied as you would wind cotton onto a bobbin. These lighter tyre constructions have increased straight line stability at high speeds. This has lead to the term 'Zero degree' tyre, denoting that there is a zero degree difference between the angle in which the belts runs, and the rotation of the tyre. As such there is no ply steer effect, where the inherent angles used in pre-shaped belts would contribute to poor handling at higher speeds.

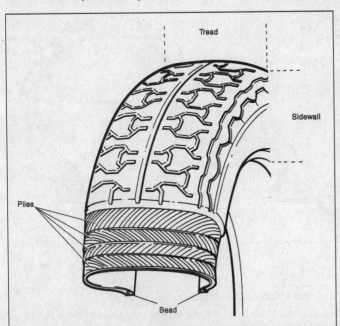

6.6a  Cross-ply tyre construction

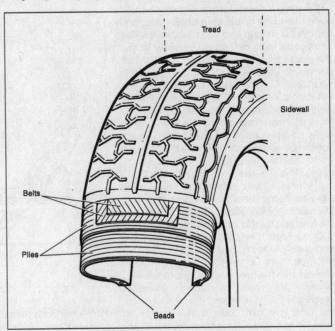

6.6b  Radial ply tyre construction

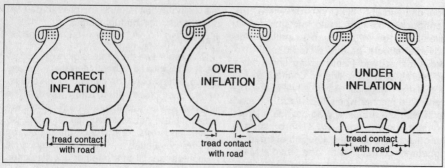

CORRECT INFLATION | OVER INFLATION | UNDER INFLATION

**6.6c Tyre tread contact patterns**

## The beads

The inner edges of the tyre are moulded into a reinforced bead which locates the tyre on the rim. The bead consists of continuous strands of high tensile steel set in rubber. The bead profile is designed to fit correctly on a variety of the rim sections normally used on motorcycle wheels, and most tyres can therefore be used on most manufacturer's rims. Occasionally a specialised rim type will be used requiring a particular type of tyre to be used.

With tubed tyres, the bead is designed to be fairly flexible so that it can be stretched over the rim edge during fitting. Where a tubeless tyre is fitted, its beads are stiffer and a much closer fit on the rim. This is to ensure an airtight seal between the bead and the rim, and may cause some difficulty during fitting. This is why the repair and fitting of tubeless types is best carried out by a specialist who will have the necessary equipment to carry out the work without damage to the tyre or rim.

## The tread

The tread is the visible part of the tyre and is composed of a synthetic rubber compound chosen for its grip and wear properties. The compound must be chosen carefully to suit the application of a particular tyre; a soft compound gives excellent grip but has a high wear rate. A harder compound has less grip but lasts a lot longer. The compound used is always a compromise between the two, and must be chosen according to use and riding style. Some manufacturers offer dual-compound tyres which have a hard compound in the centre and a soft compound on the edges. This provides good grip in corners with a generally lower wear rate, and most significantly prevents the tyre squaring off in the middle, which affects the overall shape of the tyre, and therefore its performance.

Under ideal riding conditions a tyre with a completely smooth tread would ensure that the maximum amount of rubber was in contact with the road surface, and this is why 'slicks' are used in racing whenever conditions permit. For road use, it is essential that the tyre can cope with all types of weather and road surface conditions. If a slick were to be used on a wet road, a film of water

would be trapped between the tread and the road surface, and the tyre would slip. The network of grooves or 'sipes' moulded into the tread allows the surface water to escape to the sides of the tyre, and the slight flexing of the tread is used to pump the water film clear. The tyre's ability to cope with water reduces as the tread wears down, which is why most manufacturers recommend that a tyre should be renewed when worn down to about 2 mm.

In the case of off-road machines, a different tread pattern is used to cope with the muddy or dusty surfaces. The heavy block tread of the motocross knobbly is designed to bite into a loose surface which would clog a road tyre in seconds. The tread blocks are shaped to throw off any mud trapped between them. The trials type tyres used on both trials and trail bikes are a compromise between road and motocross treads; the blocks are less heavy (and thus do not destroy the surface so readily) and can also cope with road use to some extent.

One of the most important and overlooked variables that affects the performance of a

tyre is the pressure of the air in it. Manufacturers always recommend a certain pressure for each tyre, and a variance either side of this affects handling and wear **(see illustration 6.6c)**. Too high a pressure and the ride will be harsh, but more significantly the contact patch with the road will be smaller. Too low a pressure and the contact patch will be larger, but the tyre will deform more easily, causing excessive heat build-up, rapid wear and strange handling. Individual preferences for feel can be catered for by varying the pressure either side of the manufacturers recommendation, but anything more than a 4 psi variance will be detrimental.

Many people are under the misconception that fitting a wider than recommended tyre will improve handling. This is not necessarily the case. While a one-size wider tyre will fit on the original rim, by squashing it in slightly to make it fit the shape is being altered, and this could have adverse affects on handling. Fitting a tyre with a lower aspect ratio (profile) is one way of getting the extra width without altering the overall diameter, and therefore the gearing. But motorcycle manufacturers spend a surprising amount of time testing tyres and wheels for their machines, and you can be pretty sure that the wheel and tyre size are chosen because they are the best for that machine. Even if you fit a wider rim to accept the wider tyre, this could still upset the overall handling characteristics of the machine, especially as the rear wheel and tyre work in conjunction with the front wheel and tyre.

## Tubed and tubeless tyres

The tube is simply a thin rubber ring with a one-way valve that fits inside the tyre and is inflated with air to the specified pressure **(see illustration 6.6d)**. Tubes have a number of

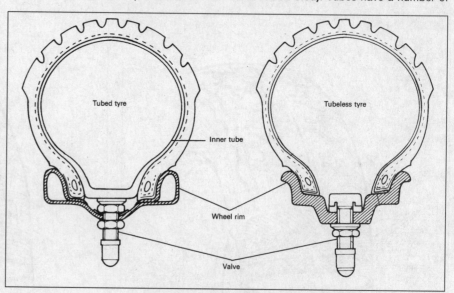

Tubed tyre | Tubeless tyre | Inner tube | Wheel rim | Valve

**6.6d Tubeless and tubed tyres**

*With tubed tyres the valve is attached to the tube; the seal between the tyre and rim is not so important and the rim need not be airtight around the valve. With tubeless tyres, the seal is formed between the wheel rim and the tyre bead, and the rim must be airtight around the valve.*

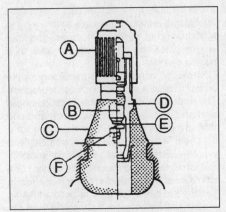

**6.6e  Section through a rubber bodied tyre valve**

A  Valve cap       D  Stem
B  Core            E  Seat
C  Seal (rubber body)  F  Open position

disadvantages. If punctured, the tube will tear quite readily, and this can result in a sudden deflation or blowout. It is also possible for some degree of movement between the tyre and rim under acceleration or braking. This can drag the tube round the rim tearing out the valve. The other drawback is a tendency for heat build-up especially when used at constant high speeds. This affects the rate of wear of the tyre and also indirectly requires a slightly harder compound to be used to combat this problem.

Instead of an inner tube the inside of a tubeless tyre is coated with a thin airseal liner, and the tyre bead and wheel rim are designed so that a tight seal is made between them. The air valve is fitted and sealed into the rim **(see illustration 6.6e)**. The tubeless tyre reduces or avoids most of the problems with tubed tyres. In particular, the airseal liner is designed to grip around anything that punctures it so that blowouts are avoided and deflation is slowed, making them generally safer.

## 7  Tyres – ratings and markings

The sidewall of most motorcycle tyres contains information concerning its construction, dimensions and intended application **(see illustration 6.7)**.

The size marking is of obvious importance and thus a good place to start.

For years the section (width) and the diameter of the tyre have were given in inches, for example 4.10H 18. This means it is 4.1 inches wide, fits on an 18 inch rim and has an 'H' speed rating (described in more detail below). Now most tyres are sized in a metric format, for example 100/90H 18. This means it is 100 mm wide, has an aspect ratio of 90 (the height of the tyre from bead to tread centre expressed as a percentage of its width – in this example, given the 100 mm width, the height is therefore 90 mm), fits on an 18 inch rim (oddly enough rim size is still normally imperial), and has an 'H' speed rating. The two tyre sizes shown above are roughly equivalent.

Since the adoption of ECE Regulation 75,

tyre codings now have to show speed and load details in the following manner 180/55 ZR17 (73W). Split into its component parts it signifies the following; 180 is the width in millimetres, 55 the aspect ratio as before, Z denotes that it is capable of service over 240 kmh, R means radial, 17 is the wheel diameter the tyre must be fitted to (in inches), 73 is the load index number, referring to a figure in a table – in this case it relates to an axle load of 365 kg, and W means that it is capable of use at 270 kmh. However, in this case, because the load and speed rating are enclosed in brackets, this signifies that the tyre is capable of speeds in excess of 270 kmh. Additionally a manufacturer may also add a final top speed after this to denote the final speed rating of the tyre, such as V280 (280 kmh or 174 mph).

As a general rule the tyre size and rating should not be varied from that recommended as standard by the manufacturer. There are exceptions to this where one tyre manufacturer may have found a fitment of slightly higher rating works better on a particular machine. It is never advisable to use a tyre of a lower rating than standard, and to do so may mean that you are breaking warranty terms, and the law in the UK and some other countries.

### Tyre type

Cross-ply tyres do not usually carry a marking to denote them as such, whereas a bias-belted tyre will normally have the letter 'B' (normally after the speed rating letter, e.g. VB), and radial tyres will normally have the letter 'R' (normally after the speed rating, e.g. ZR).

### Aspect ratio

This marking follows the section (width) marking and is separated from it by an oblique stroke; /. Where the tyre height is the same as its width it has a 100% aspect ratio. This is considered as being a standard figure, and so is not included on the sidewall. Where the tyre has an aspect ratio of less than 100% it is termed low profile, and the aspect ratio is shown on the tyre wall.

The low profile radial tyres which are now commonplace allow a wider tread area without increasing the height of the tyre sidewall. This in turn means a stiffer tyre with less risk of instability at higher speeds. In some applications it allows updating to a wider section without altering the overall diameter of the tyre and thus the gearing of the machine. A 50% aspect ratio is now common on sports bike applications.

### Speed rating

The speed rating (or index) letter indicates the maximum sustained speed possible on the class of machine for which the tyre is intended. It assumes that the tyre is at the correct pressure, is in good condition, is operating within its load rating, and is fitted to the correct rim. The most common speed

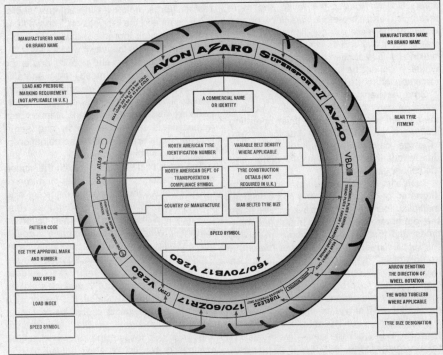

**6.7  Common tyre sidewall markings**

rating letters and corresponding speeds are shown below:

| Speed rating | Max. speed (mph) |
|---|---|
| P | 95 mph (153 kmh) |
| R | 105 mph (169 kmh) |
| S | 113 mph (182 kmh) |
| H | 130 mph (209 kmh) |
| V/VB | 149 mph (240 kmh) |
| ZR | 150 mph (241 kmh) and above (the upper limit may be given after the letter) |
| W | 168 mph (270 kmh) |
| Y | 187 mph (301 kmh) |

## Load rating

The load rating (or index) numbers, which appear after the size markings indicates the maximum load that a tyre can carry. It assumes that the tyre is at the correct pressure, is in good condition, is operating within its speed rating, and is fitted to the correct rim. Some load rating letters and corresponding loads are shown below, but the range actually extends sequentially from 0 to 99:

| Load rating | Max. load (kg) |
|---|---|
| 40 | 140 |
| 50 | 190 |
| 60 | 250 |
| 65 | 290 |
| 75 | 387 |
| 88 | 560 |

## Diameter

This denotes the rim size for which the tyre is intended and is the diameter of the rim measured at the point where the tyre bead seats on the flat section inside the raised rim. The diameter is normally given in inches, but may be marked in millimetres as well on some tyres.

## Other markings

The sidewall may carry further sets of letters and numbers and also direction arrows. Arrows are used to indicate the correct direction of rotation for a particular tyre. For example the plies in a front tyre may be arranged to give it particular strength under braking. If the tyre is reversed on the rim this extra reinforcement will not be used to advantage and the tyre may wear very quickly. Where a tyre is suited to front or rear fitment it needs to be braced against acceleration when on a rear wheel and braking if fitted at the front, so two opposing arrows may be found marked FRONT and REAR.

A maximum pressure figure may be found and this indicates only the maximum safe pressure that the tyre is capable of withstanding. It is NOT an operating pressure, which will be much lower. Finally all recent tyres are marked either TUBED TYPE or TUBELESS for reasons which should be self-evident.

## 8 Brakes

The purpose of any brake system is to slow down a moving part by using friction to convert the kinetic energy of the moving part into heat. Motorcycle brakes create the necessary friction by forcing a component lined with a special friction material against another component that is part of or is attached to the wheel.

There are two types of brake used on motorcycles, 'drum' brakes and 'disc' brakes, and there are two ways of actuating the brakes, either mechanically or hydraulically.

The drum brake was the standard method of braking for many years and its simplicity and cheapness still make it a popular choice on small capacity machines. However disc brakes are far more efficient in terms of energy conversion because of their ability to disperse the heat that is generated, and they can therefore be made more powerful.

### Brake power and leverage

The power of a brake is determined by leverage, and the amount of leverage is determined generally by the amount of force applied through the system and the distances from the pivot points at which that force is applied.

For example, the point on the front brake lever at which the rider's fingers rest has a marked effect when braking. If you apply X amount of force at a point mid-way up the lever, you will not brake as hard as you would if the same force was applied at the end of the lever. So the longer the lever, the more leverage, and therefore braking power. However there are obvious limitations to the size of lever that can be used. Similarly, if the braking force is applied near the centre of the wheel, it will not be as effective as the same force applied to the rim of the wheel.

On a mechanically operated brake system, leverage can be multiplied at every point in the system where there is a lever operating around a pivot. On a hydraulic system, leverage can also be multiplied through differences in size of the master piston and the caliper (slave) piston.

Basically, if the slave piston is twice the diameter of the master, the force will be multiplied four times. If the slave is three times the diameter, the force is multiplied nine times, and four times the diameter multiplies the force sixteen times. However there is a compromise, and therefore a limit. An hydraulic system depends on fluid displacement to provide movement. If the master and slave pistons are the same size, a movement of 10 mm in the master will provide a displacement of 10 mm in the slave. However the bigger the slave gets in relation to the master, the less it will displace in relation to the movement of the master, and

this is because the actual amount of hydraulic fluid that is moved is the same all through the system, and so in a wider cylinder, the fluid will displace the piston less far than in a narrow cylinder.

In reality, achieving the necessary brake power to stop a motorcycle is not a problem. The important design factor is producing a system that is as light as possible, and one that gives the best feel and response for a practical amount of lever movement and pressure. Front and brake power compatibility is another factor. Additionally, the system as a whole must be matched to the one controlling factor – the tyres. It is easy to build a braking system that will stop any motorcycle from any speed very quickly, but there is no point in doing this if every time you pull the lever in the front wheel locks up.

### Friction materials

Friction is the main factor involved in braking, and so the components that rub against each other must be made of materials that will not only create a large amount of friction, but can withstand that friction by not rubbing away and withstand the heat generated by not distorting or melting.

Friction material is composed of many different elements which are bound together under conditions of extreme temperature and/or pressure and then attached to a backing material. There are numerous combinations of materials which result in there being many types of brake pad available, each having its own particular application. There are combinations of copper, brass, lead, graphite, carbon, Kevlar, resins, fibres, unknown ingredients, secret ingredients and the list goes on. The type and amount of each ingredient that goes into a compound affects the way it works.

The most common and popular pad is the sintered type, made mostly from metallic particles but mixed other materials. There are also organic and semi-metallic pads. Organic pads are made from Kevlar and aramid fibres (asbestos is no longer used), and semi-metallic pads are basically a combination of organic and sintered materials.

The drum or disc, against which the friction material bears, is normally either cast iron or stainless steel, though carbon discs are also being used in racing applications. Heat retention and dissipation properties, distortion factors, weight, manufacturing costs, compatibility with friction materials, anti-corrosion and wear resistance properties are all taken into account when the designer selects disc material, but in general stainless steel is the preferred choice. It is better than cast iron in all respects except for cost, heat dissipation and wet weather performance (though in this respect the difference can be eliminated by using a particular friction material).

## 9 Drum brakes

A typical drum brake has a cylindrical drum that is formed in the wheel hub and lined with iron or steel (see illustration 6.9a and b). The drum is enclosed by the brake backplate on which the brake shoes and operating cam(s) are mounted. Drum brakes on motorcycles are always mechanically operated (on cars they are normally hydraulically actuated).

On the front brake the cam is actuated by a cable which is connected to the front brake lever. On the back brake the cam is actuated either by a cable or steel rod which is connected to the rear brake pedal. The other end of the cable or rod is attached to an arm which fits over a shaft on the outside of the backplate, and this shaft has the cam on its inner end.

At rest the friction material on the shoe is held slightly clear of the drum by the return springs. When the brake lever or pedal is operated the cam forces the shoes outwards against the drum surface, creating the friction required to slow the machine.

In its simplest form the brake has a single cam acting on one end of each shoe, and the other end of each shoe locates on a pivot pin. When the cam turns one end of each shoe is pushed outwards to contact the drum. When the wheel is rotating, one shoe moves outwards in the same direction as the wheel is turning, and this is known as the leading shoe (see illustration 6.9c). The other shoe moves in the opposite direction to the wheel, and this is known as the trailing shoe. When the leading shoe contacts the drum, the frictional force tends to drag the shoe harder into the

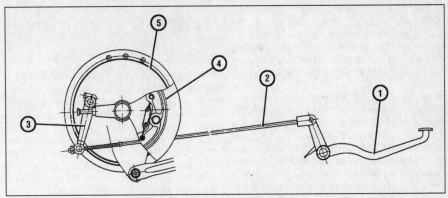

**6.9a Drum rear brake operation**

*1 Brake pedal   2 Operating rod   3 Brake lever   4 Brake shoe   5 Drum*

1 Brake shoes
2 Return springs
3 Backplate
4 Operating cam
5 Washer
6 Seal
7 Operating lever
8 Pinch bolt

**6.9b Drum rear brake components**

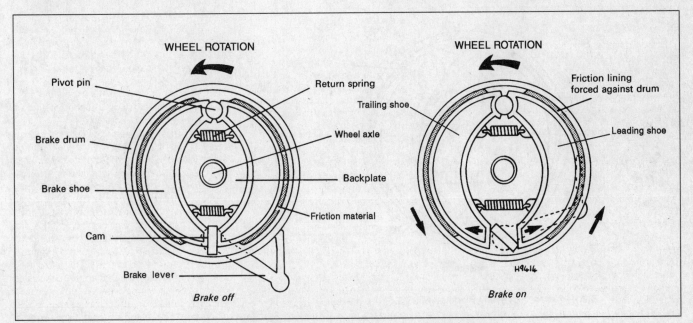

**6.9c Operation of a simple single leading shoe (SLS) drum brake**

drum, creating a self-servo action that increases braking power. Conversely, the trailing shoe is effectively pushed away from the drum. The above arrangement utilising one leading and one trailing shoe is generally known as a single leading shoe brake, or SLS for short.

To obtain extra braking power without increasing the size of the drum, each shoe can have its own cam at the leading end and its own pivot at the trailing end (see illustration 6.9d). The two cams are synchronised via an adjustable linkage between the arms, which are connected to the same cable or rod. This arrangement is known as a twin leading shoe, or TLS, brake. To extract yet more effort from the brake it can be made double sided, with a TLS brake fitted on each side of the wheel. This arrangement is by no means common but was used primarily in racing applications before the introduction of the disc brake.

The drum brake system is simple and requires no complicated mechanisms or systems to be effective. The real problem with the drum brake is heat retention. A brake works by converting movement into heat, so it is not heat generation that is the problem, but getting rid of it. As heat builds up in the linings the coefficient of friction between the shoe and the drum reduces and the friction material becomes glazed which reduces the braking force, a condition known as fade.

The heat can be dispersed better if the drum is ventilated and many TLS brakes have air scoops to direct air past the shoes to cool them. Unfortunately the air scoop also worked well as a rain scoop and the water reduced efficiency. The problem is resolved by using an exposed disc rather than an enclosed drum.

## 10 Disc brakes

The disc brake first appeared on aircraft in response to the problem of coping with the heat generated in a drum brake. As aircraft became heavier and faster the drum brake soon proved woefully inadequate when attempting to stop it. The same problem was experienced with motorcycles as they became faster and more powerful. The solution is simple enough: replace the enclosed drum with an exposed disc.

The disc is mounted on the wheel and so turns with it. A 'caliper' containing one or more pistons and two brake pads is mounted adjacent to the disc and fits over one section of it (see illustration 6.10a). When the brake lever or pedal is applied, the piston moves out and presses the brake pad friction material against the rotating disc, creating friction.

The disc, being open to the air, disperses the heat much more readily than a drum, and so the fade problem is reduced. Since disc brakes do not benefit from any self-servo action like drum brakes, the force required to operate a disc brake is much greater, and this is why they are operated hydraulically (there were a few cable-operated disc designs in the 1970s).

The first mass produced production version appeared in 1969 on Honda's CB750. Since then the disc system has been used almost exclusively on all medium to large displacement machines, and is becoming more widely used on small machines and scooters. The systems used have developed somewhat since 1969, but the basic principle remains unchanged.

It is now common to fit a twin disc arrangement on the front wheel. Rear disc brakes are also used, though they do not need to be so powerful because of the effects of weight transfer during braking. It is common for 75% of the machine's weight to be concentrated on the front wheel during braking, and this in turn means that most of the available tyre traction is also at the front. In these circumstances it is a disadvantage to have excessive braking power at the rear wheel, so a rear disc unit will be comparatively weak.

### Disc development

One way of making a disc brake more effective is to use a disc with a larger diameter. The 'leverage around a pivot' principal works here. As the distance from the pivot increases, so the force generated by the lever increases. Similarly the force required to stop an object already moving (i.e. the disc rotating about the axle) is less; alternatively the same force will stop it quicker. Using many small pistons in a brake caliper as opposed to one large one actually creates the effect of having a larger disc (see Section 13).

Another approach, not yet really established but still to be found, is to fit a large diameter disc to the wheel rim, rather than the hub. This means that the disc is passing through the caliper at higher speed, but that less pressure is needed to stop it due to the greater surface area of the disc. The caliper is inverted, operating from the inner edge of the disc, but the system is in most other respects conventional.

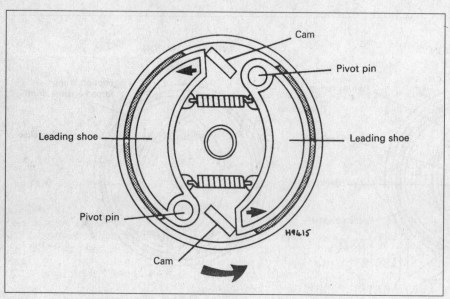

**6.9d Operation of a twin leading shoe (TLS) drum brake**

*Note that each shoe has its own pivot and operating cam, allowing much greater braking effect than is possible with a single leading shoe unit.*

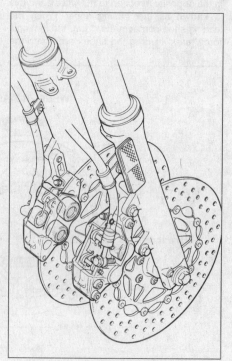

**6.10a The caliper attaches to the fork slider and fits over the disc**

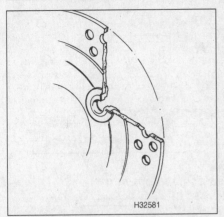

6.10b Floating disc construction

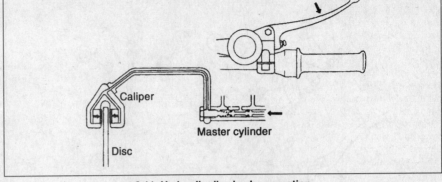

6.11 Hydraulic disc brake operation

## Floating discs

When discs first appeared the friction surface of the disc was solidly fixed to the carrier that bolts to the wheel. There are two fundamental problems with this: firstly, the slightest misalignment between the disc and the pads will drastically reduce braking performance and increase pad wear. Secondly, rapid heat build-up can produce distortion which will create misalignment because the disc is solidly mounted.

By separating the disc itself from the carrier and allowing it some free movement both problems are eliminated, and this is termed a 'floating disc'. The inner rim of the disc and the outer rim of the carrier have semi-circles cut into them. When they are aligned, circles or holes are formed. By fitting a large but loose fitting rivet into each hole, the disc becomes captured by the carrier, but is still free to move and to expand and contract on the carrier **(see illustration 6.10b)**.

## Wet weather performance

In the past, disc brakes were notorious for poor wet weather performance. This is due to the water film which builds up on the disc and must be swept clear before braking can commence. The problem can be worsened by using an inappropriate friction material. The slightly porous structure of cast iron makes this an ideal disc material for wet weather, but it tends to rust at the first hint of moisture.

Drilled or grooved discs are believed by many to improve the rate at which water is removed, but they can actually reduce braking performance as water tends to collect at the outer edges of the holes instead of being spun off. The biggest benefit of drilled discs is in weight reduction, which reduces rotational inertia and gyroscopic effects.

By far the most effective innovation for wet weather braking has been the introduction of sintered metal pads. These have a limited quantity of metal particles embedded in them, and as a result tend to wear unevenly. Their rippled surface allows the high spots to bite through the water film much more quickly than conventional pads.

## 11 Hydraulic brake operation

Hydraulics are used to operate brake systems because it is easy to achieve the high pressure/low movement action required at the caliper using only relatively low pressure over a larger movement at the lever or pedal (principles of hydraulic leverage – see Section 8). All hydraulic brake systems on motorcycles are of the disc type as opposed to drum.

A master cylinder is used to create the braking force by using a piston to push against the hydraulic fluid. The force is transferred by the fluid to a caliper, which contains one or more pistons **(see illustration 6.11)**. These pistons move out in response to the force from the master cylinder piston pushing the fluid. The caliper pistons press against the brake pads, which are then forced against the disc to create the required friction. The master cylinder and caliper are covered in detail in Sections 12 and 13.

### Brake fluid

Because a liquid cannot be compressed, it is used to transfer the force and movement in hydraulic systems.

Brake fluid for motorcycles is currently available in four basic varieties, DOT 3, DOT 4, DOT 5 and DOT 5.1. DOT is an American Department of Transport classification system which grades brake fluids according to dry and wet boiling points and viscosity. DOT 3 and DOT 4 fluids are mineral oils based on polyglycols. DOT 5 is a silicone-based fluid, and cannot be mixed with polyglycols. DOT 5.1 is similar to and compatible with DOT 3 and 4, but is not silicone-based. It has a lower viscosity and was designed for use in anti-lock brake systems.

DOT 3, 4 and 5.1 fluids are hygroscopic, which means they absorb moisture from the air. The presence of moisture in the fluid lowers its boiling point, and the temperature of a working brake disc and pad usually exceeds this. This is why both dry and wet boiling points are given. The wet boiling point is measured when the moisture content is 3.5%. This hygroscopicity is the reason why brake fluid should be changed at least every two years. The friction material on the brake pad serves to insulate the caliper from the heat generated in the disc, and this is a very good reason for renewing pads well before they are worn right down.

DOT 5 is not hygroscopic and does not mix with water, and if water does enter the system it sinks to the bottom, placing it close to the hottest area of the system. This means it will boil very easily and quickly, resulting in a pocket of gas which is easily compressible, which then gives the brakes a spongy feel. The other problem with DOT 5 is that the fluid itself becomes compressible as it nears its boiling point, and so will give a spongy feel if the brakes are used hard and often.

### Brake hoses

The master cylinder and caliper(s) are connected by specially reinforced hydraulic hoses which allow unrestricted suspension movement. Some systems also use rigid metal pipes where there is no movement.

Standard hoses are made from a rubber which is compatible with brake fluid. However the rubber deteriorates over time and can crack, which means that the hose will expand under pressure and absorb braking power. This is why rubber brake hoses should be renewed at least every four years. Some hoses have nylon threads embedded along the hose in the rubber to make them stiffer.

Most racers and many road riders fit after-market hoses that are made from Teflon and covered in a steel braid. The Teflon is less prone to expansion than rubber and also offers less resistance to the movement of fluid along it. The steel braid minimises expansion even further. But the requirements of a racer and your average road rider are completely different, and some hoses can be too stiff for road use, unless in the hands of a very experienced rider. Under hard or 'panic' braking on the road a little bit of expansion is generally perceived as being a good thing.

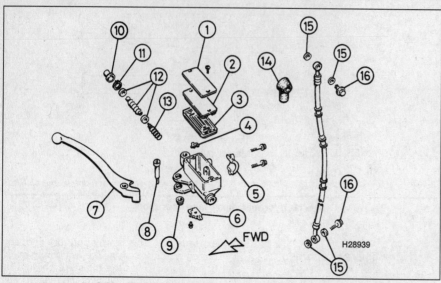

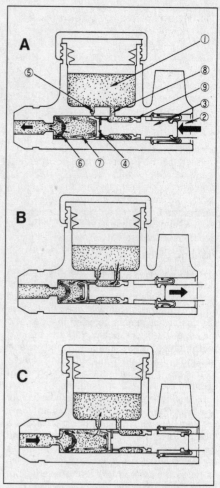

**6.12a Typical front brake master cylinder assembly**

1 Reservoir cover
2 Diaphragm plate
3 Rubber diaphragm
4 Protector
5 Clamp
6 Brake light switch

7 Brake lever
8 Lever pivot bolt
9 Pivot bolt locknut
10 Dust boot
11 Circlip

12 Piston assembly (primary
   cup, piston and seal)
13 Spring
14 Rubber boot
15 Sealing washer
16 Banjo bolt

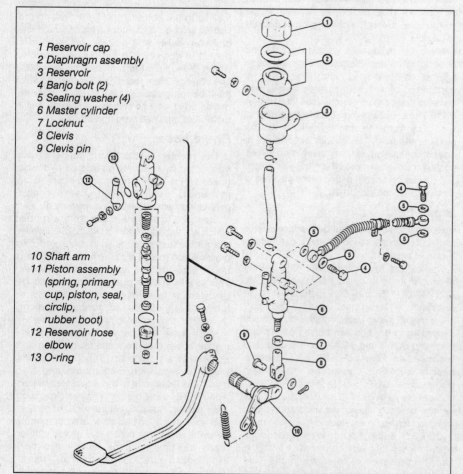

1 Reservoir cap
2 Diaphragm assembly
3 Reservoir
4 Banjo bolt (2)
5 Sealing washer (4)
6 Master cylinder
7 Locknut
8 Clevis
9 Clevis pin

10 Shaft arm
11 Piston assembly
   (spring, primary
   cup, piston, seal,
   circlip,
   rubber boot)
12 Reservoir hose
   elbow
13 O-ring

**6.12b Typical rear brake master cylinder components**

**6.12c Front brake master cylinder operation**

**A** Applying the brake. The end of the brake lever (2) pushes the master cylinder piston (3) along its bore. Once the return port (5) has been passed by the primary cup (4) fluid is forced past the check valve (6) and along the brake hose to the caliper.

**B** Releasing the brake. Once lever pressure is released the spring (7) pushes the piston assembly back up the bore. Until the pressure in the brake line is significantly higher than that of the master cylinder body, the check valve remains closed and fluid is drawn past the primary cup via small bleed holes in the piston. Once the check valve opens, fluid flows back from the caliper until pressure is equalised.

**C** Completion of return stroke. With the piston at rest, fluid continues to flow past the check valve and back to the reservoir (1). When the check valve is closed by the pressure of the return spring, the fluid continues to flow via a small notch in the end of the body until the pressure in the system is equalised. The secondary cup or seal (9) fits around the piston.

## 12 Hydraulic brake systems – master cylinders

The master cylinder consists of a cylinder and piston assembly, either incorporating a fluid reservoir or linked by hose to a remote reservoir **(see illustrations 6.12a and b)**. A return spring fits between the inner end of the piston and the cylinder, and the piston is retained by a circlip.

When the brake lever or pedal is operated, the piston is pushed along the cylinder, displacing fluid from its outlet via a check valve and along the hydraulic hose **(see illustration 6.12c)**. When the lever is released the fluid and piston move back to their original positions. The reservoir is connected to the cylinder via a port which is open when the piston is at rest. This allows the system to be constantly topped up. When the piston begins to move, the port is covered, preventing pressure in the system from forcing fluid back into the reservoir.

The master cylinder piston is sealed by specially designed synthetic rubber seals, often known as cups, which prevent pressure and fluid loss from the system and the ingress of air and water. The inner seal, known as the primary cup (and is actually cup shaped), fits on the inner end of the piston and effectively acts as a scoop to push the fluid along. The outer seal, known as the secondary cup, fits around the piston and seals it to the cylinder wall.

## 13 Hydraulic brake systems – calipers

At the lower end of the hydraulic line is the caliper, consisting of one or more pistons and cylinders, depending on the type used. When the brake lever or pedal is operated, the piston is pushed outwards in the cylinder, forcing the brake pad against the disc. Unlike the master cylinder, the piston is of large diameter, and it is this difference in size which makes use of the hydraulic multiplier effect.

The caliper pistons are sealed by specially designed synthetic rubber seals which prevent pressure and fluid loss from the system and the ingress of air. Typically two seals are used for each piston. The inner seal is known as the piston seal and prevents fluid getting out. The outer seal is a dust seal preventing dirt getting in.

The piston seal performs a very important second function. It is specially shaped so that it twists slightly as the piston moves out, and this is sufficient to pull the piston back into the caliper when the brake is released, returning fluid back up the hose to the master cylinder and drawing the friction material off the disc **(see illustration 6.13a)**. The range of movement at the pads is actually very small,

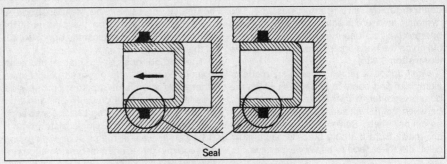

**6.13a  Piston seal operation**

*The piston seal is designed to distort slightly as the brake is applied so that it draws the piston back again when the lever is released. As the pads wear, the piston is pushed through the seal to compensate, but will always be returned by a standard amount. This means that the caliper automatically adjusts for pad wear.*

just sufficient to ensure that the pads are clear of the disc when the lever is at rest. As the friction material of the pads wears away, the caliper piston needs to move further to bring them into contact with the disc surface. The piston distorts the seal as before, but beyond a certain point it moves through the seal and into a new position. In this way the system is self-adjusting, and can compensate automatically for pad wear.

There are two types of caliper, 'opposed piston' and 'sliding'. The quality of a caliper comes in its rigidity, or its ability to resist flex under extreme braking pressure. Obviously any distortion in the caliper takes away braking power.

### Opposed piston calipers

In an opposed piston caliper, the caliper body is mounted rigidly on the fork leg or swinging arm. There are an equal number of pistons and cylinders on each side (either one, two or three) opposing each other **(see illustrations 6.13b)**. The cylinders are

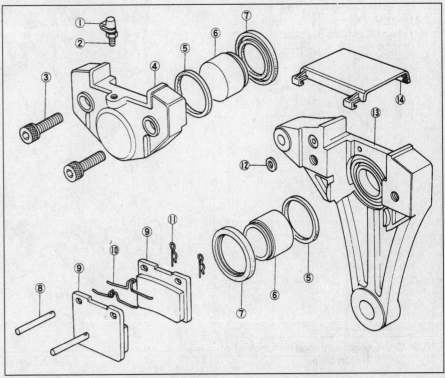

**6.13b  A typical single opposed piston rear brake caliper**

| | | |
|---|---|---|
| 1 Dust cap | 6 Piston | 11 R-clip |
| 2 Bleed nipple | 7 Dust seal | 12 O-ring |
| 3 Allen bolt | 8 Pin | 13 Caliper half/mounting |
| 4 Caliper half | 9 Brake pad | bracket |
| 5 Piston seal | 10 Anti-rattle spring | 14 Pad cover |

connected by an internal passage, so
hydraulic pressure is equal. When the brake is
operated, all pistons move towards the disc,
clamping the pads against each side of it **(see
illustration 6.13c)**.

Most opposed piston calipers are made of
aluminium and come in two halves which are
bolted together, with the hydraulic passages
between the halves sealed by O-rings known
as caliper seals. Some aftermarket calipers
are made from a single piece of aluminium
billet, but these tend to be very expensive.

### Sliding or floating calipers

The sliding caliper consists of the caliper
body and a caliper bracket **(see illustration
6.13d)**. The bracket is rigidly mounted and
has pins which the caliper slides on, allowing
it an amount of sideways movement. The
caliper body has one or more pistons in
cylinders in one side of the caliper only, and
these apply pressure to a pad. An extension
of the caliper body cradles the opposite pad
on the other side of the disc. When the brake
is operated, the piston pushes the pad against
the disc surface **(see illustration 6.13e)**. With

continued pressure, the caliper body is
pushed away, sliding on the pins until the
other pad is pressed against the opposite side
of the disc.

The sliding design eliminates problems
sometimes found with opposed-piston units,
where corrosion jams a piston on one side.
This leads to unequal pressure being exerted
on the two pads, reducing braking efficiency.
The drawback with the single piston type is
corrosion or wear in the pivot or sliding pins.
This too can cause unequal braking effort and
can also allow chattering between the bracket
and caliper. But due to the fact that there are
half as many pistons and cylinders, the sliding
caliper is cheaper and easier to manufacture,

making it an excellent choice in many
applications.

### Caliper development

The two basic types described above cover
the majority of applications found in the
motorcycle world. There are variations and
developments of these, however, and these
are concerned with obtaining better braking
performance.

### Using multiple pistons

A larger number of small pistons can be
used to reduce the overall weight of the disc
and caliper without reducing braking
efficiency. One large piston means having a
large disc, which makes it heavy **(see**

**6.13c  Cross section through an opposed
piston caliper**

| 1 Pad cover | half/mounting |
|---|---|
| 2 R-clip | bracket |
| 3 Anti-rattle spring | 8 Dust cap |
| 4 Pin | 9 Bleed nipple |
| 5 Brake pad | 10 Caliper half |
| 6 Piston | 11 Piston seal |
| 7 Caliper | 12 Dust seal |

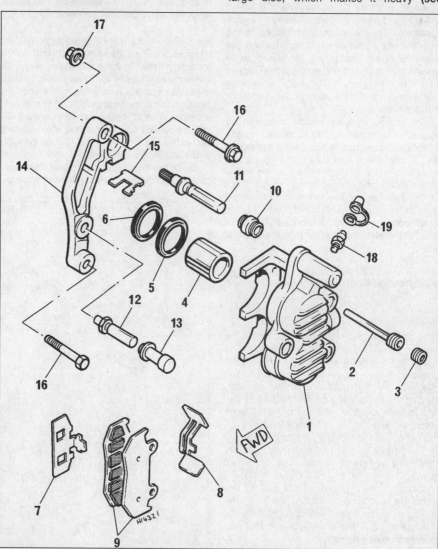

**6.13d  A twin piston sliding caliper**

| 1 Caliper body | 8 Anti-rattle spring | 15 Pad guide |
|---|---|---|
| 2 Brake pad retaining pin | 9 Brake pads | 16 Caliper bracket mounting |
| 3 Plug | 10 Rubber boot | bolt |
| 4 Piston (2) | 11 Slider pin | 17 Nut |
| 5 Piston seal (2) | 12 Slider pin | 18 Bleed nipple |
| 6 Dust seal (2) | 13 Rubber boot | 19 Cap |
| 7 Anti-squeal shim | 14 Caliper bracket | |

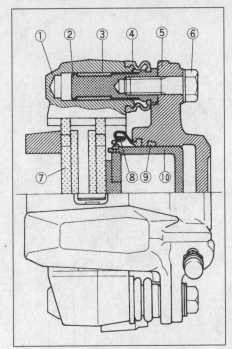

**6.13e  Cross section through a sliding caliper**

| | |
|---|---|
| 1 Mounting bracket | 6 Slider pin bolt |
| 2 Slider pin | 7 Brake pad |
| 3 Sleeve | 8 Dust seal |
| 4 Dust boot | 9 Piston seal |
| 5 Caliper body | 10 Piston |

**illustration 6.13f)**. Having two or three small pistons in a row gives the same overall pad area, but reduces the size of the disc. Not only that but the effective disc diameter is increased, which increases the torque effect and braking power.

### Varying piston size

Many manufacturers are now using two or three different sizes of piston in one caliper, and this makes braking more progressive. In Section 8 the effect of a difference in size of slave piston in relation to the master piston was shown. From that it can be seen that using different size slave pistons will produce different amounts of movement for the same amount of lever travel. This means that a narrower diameter piston will move further and therefore contact the brake pad before the wider piston. As more pressure is applied through the lever, the second piston comes into effect and increases braking force.

### Using multiple pads

Normally one pad is used on each side of the disc, with the pad spanning all the pistons on its side. Some aftermarket and racing calipers have one pad per piston, meaning six separate pads in a six 'pot' caliper. These work particularly well in any caliper using pistons of different sizes as the different rates of piston movement are applied without cocking the pad sideways.

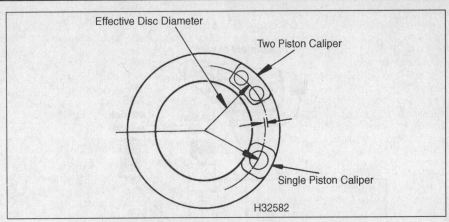

**6.13f  The benefits of using a larger number of smaller pistons**

---

### 14 Specialised brake systems –
anti-lock brakes and linked brakes

#### Anti-lock brakes

An anti-lock braking system (ABS) prevents the wheels from locking up under excessively hard braking or on very uneven road surfaces.

The system is managed by a highly complex system of electronics and hydraulics.

Sensors pick up wheel speed information from toothed rings mounted on the wheel hubs and send this information in the form of a voltage to the ABS control unit **(see illustration 6.14a)**. The control unit compares the front and rear wheel rotational speeds and if they differ by more than a fixed amount (usually 30%), which would indicate the onset

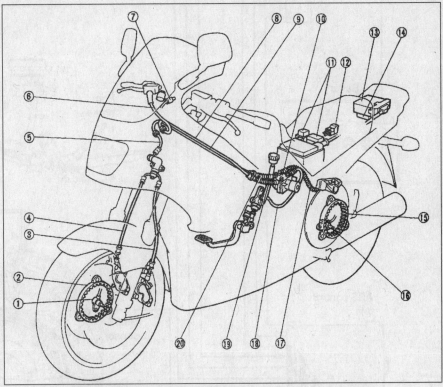

**6.14a  Location of ABS components on the Yamaha FJ1200A**

| | | |
|---|---|---|
| 1 Speed sensor (front) | 8 Metal brake line | 15 Toothed rotor (rear) |
| 2 Toothed rotor (front) | 9 Metal brake line | 16 Speed sensor (rear) |
| 3 Brake hose | 10 Hydraulic unit | 17 Brake hose to rear |
| 4 Brake hose | 11 Fuses |   caliper |
| 5 Brake hose | 12 ABS diagnostic connector | 18 Brake hose |
| 6 Brake hose | 13 ABS control unit | 19 Brake hose |
| 7 ABS warning light | 14 Fail-safe relay | 20 Brake hose |

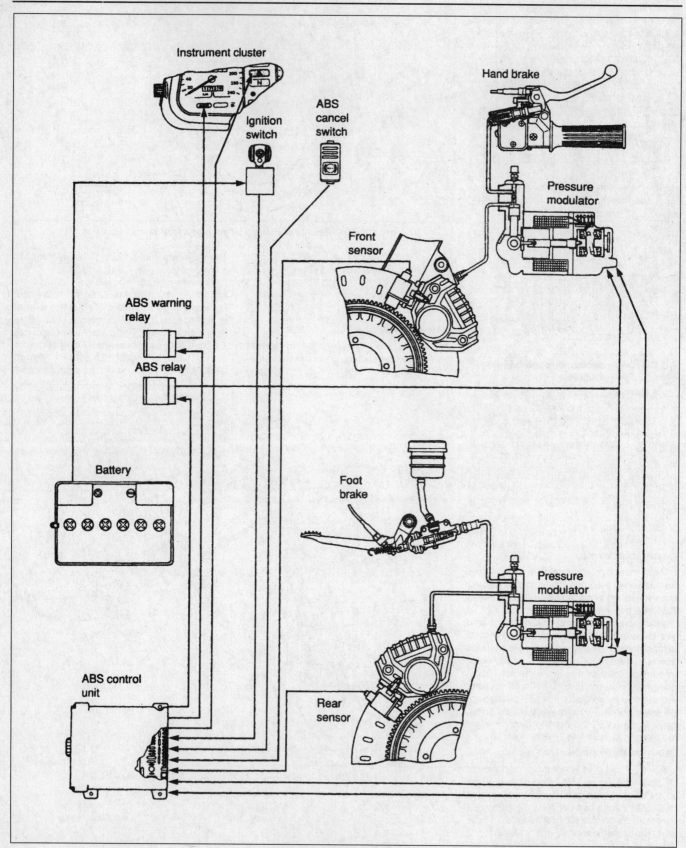

**6.14b  BMW's ABS system**

*ABS system I is shown. The mark II system uses a combined pressure modulator for front and rear brakes.*

of skidding, a signal is sent to the hydraulic unit (pressure modulator) to momentarily reduce pressure in the braking system **(see illustration 6.14b)**. The alternating reduction and increase in hydraulic pressure may be felt as a pulsating sensation at the brake lever or pedal in certain systems, on others the fitting of a valve prevents reflow. The hydraulic unit continues reducing the braking pressure until there is no further sign of wheel locking.

In the event that the rider applies even pressure to both brakes causing them to lock-up simultaneously, the control unit is able to sense the sudden decrease in wheel speed and brings ABS into operation on both wheels.

Almost all control units have a self checking function, which monitors the operation of the system components and voltage, and a warning light in the instruments to inform the rider if ABS is inoperative. On certain systems, ABS can be manually switched off by the rider.

### Linked brakes

Certain manufacturers, notably Honda and Moto Guzzi, have developed linked braking systems.

The Moto Guzzi system is the simpler of the two and has been in operating for many years. Operating the handlebar brake lever actuates the right-hand front brake caliper only. Operating the brake pedal actuates both the left-hand front caliper and the rear caliper at the same time. A proportional control valve decides how much front and rear brake should be used according to how hard the brakes are applied. The harder the brake pedal is applied, the greater is the proportion of braking directed to the front caliper to take advantage of the weight transfer, thus giving more grip through the front tyre than the rear.

The Honda system applies both front and rear brakes even if only either the front brake lever or rear brake pedal is applied. Operating the front brake lever activates some or all pistons in each front brake caliper (depending on the model it is fitted to) and a proportion of the rear caliper, the amount depending upon how hard the front brake lever is applied **(see illustration 6.14c)**.

The left front caliper is hinged and linked to the rear caliper via a secondary master cylinder and a proportional control valve. When the braking force is sufficient, the left caliper operates the secondary master cylinder and the rear brake is applied.

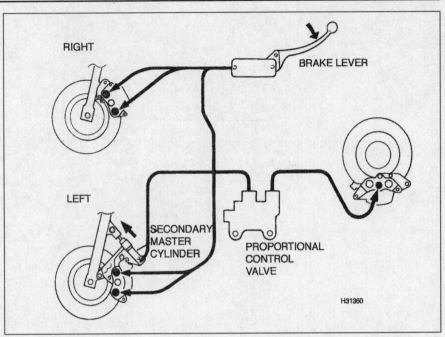

**6.14c Honda's dual combined braking system front brake operation (VFR800)**

Operating the rear brake pedal activates either the whole or a proportion of the rear brake caliper (depending on the models it is fitted to) and a proportion of each front caliper equally. A delay valve in the rear pedal system provides progressive braking, enhancing control on rough or slippery surfaces **(see illustration 6.14d)**.

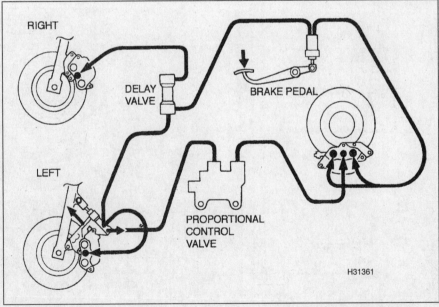

**6.14d Honda's dual combined braking system rear brake operation (VFR800)**

# Chapter 7
# Front suspension and steering

## Contents

## 1 Introduction

The purpose of any suspension system is to absorb bumps in the road while keeping the wheels on the ground, and to isolate the motorcycle and rider from the effects of the bumps. To do this a component that compresses and extends is needed, and the ideal component for the job is a spring. However a spring has a tendency to oscillate around its natural position as a result of compressing it and letting it go, and this would result in a very bouncy ride. To control the oscillation a method of damping is required, and the best medium for this job is oil.

Over the years manufacturers have tried using rubber, either blocks in torsion or bands in tension, instead of springs, and bands are still used on leading link set-ups on some grass-track outfits. However rubber deteriorates very easily. Gas has also been used, and is still used in conjunction with springs on some machines. It has the benefit of being easily adjustable (an increase in pressure makes the suspension harder and vice versa), and of providing a natural 'rising rate' (i.e. the more it is compressed, the harder it becomes). The problem with gas is keeping it contained, and the fact that variations in temperature through atmospheric changes and through use lead to the pressure changing, which alters the 'spring rate'.

So the combination of springs and hydraulics is the most popular in the majority of applications, the question is how to arrange this in conjunction with the steering. Again over the years there have been many variations in design, falling into four major categories: the telescopic fork, leading and trailing link, wishbone and parallelogram. The girder fork may appear to be the only omission, but this is a type of parallelogram arrangement.

The steering arrangement commonly used on most powered two-wheelers is derived in principle from that of the bicycle, namely a tube that pivots in relation to the frame that is connected to the front wheel to permit steering. Variations in design occur with different suspension set-ups, but there are few of these and in any case the principal remains the same.

## 2 Unsprung weight – what is it and why is it important?

### What is unsprung weight?

The weight of the components supported by the suspension is classed as sprung weight, whereas the weight of those components not supported by the suspension is 'unsprung weight'. Note that the tyres absorb a certain amount of shock, and in this context it could be said that the entire weight of the motorcycle is sprung.

To understand unsprung weight imagine a motorcycle held upright, off its stand. A person sits on the motorcycle, and the springs compress as the rider's weight is taken. All the components on the motorcycle that move when the rider sits down and the springs compress have sprung weight – they move with the suspension (fuel tank, seat, frame, engine etc.). All the components that do not move have unsprung weight (wheels, tyres, brakes etc.).

Which begs the questions: what about the swingarm, the shock absorber and the forks –

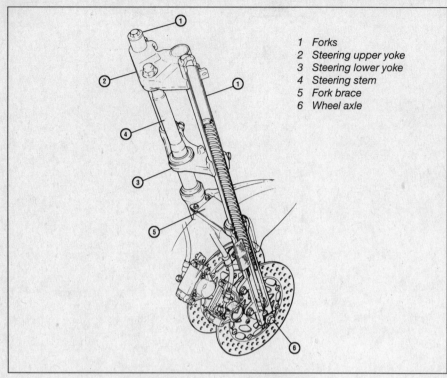

1 Forks
2 Steering upper yoke
3 Steering lower yoke
4 Steering stem
5 Fork brace
6 Wheel axle

**7.3a A typical telescopic fork arrangement**

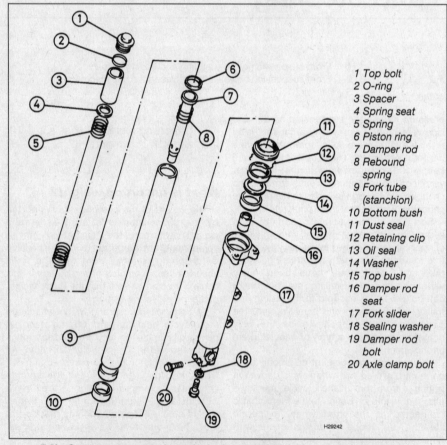

1 Top bolt
2 O-ring
3 Spacer
4 Spring seat
5 Spring
6 Piston ring
7 Damper rod
8 Rebound spring
9 Fork tube (stanchion)
10 Bottom bush
11 Dust seal
12 Retaining clip
13 Oil seal
14 Washer
15 Top bush
16 Damper rod seat
17 Fork slider
18 Sealing washer
19 Damper rod bolt
20 Axle clamp bolt

H29242

**7.3b Component parts of a typical telescopic fork with conventional damper (Suzuki GSF600)**

are they sprung or unsprung? For sake of argument, it is accepted that any part of the swingarm that is to the rear of the shock absorber mounting is unsprung, and the part that is ahead of the mounting, i.e. between the mounting point and the swingarm pivot, is sprung; the bottom half of the shock absorber is unsprung, and the top half is sprung; the fork lower leg or slider is unsprung, the inner tube or stanchion is sprung.

### Why is low unsprung weight important?

When a bike hits a bump, the unsprung components gain momentum as they start to move – the higher the unsprung weight, the greater the momentum. The momentum developed by the unsprung components increases the loading on the suspension and harder suspension springs are needed to cope with it. Also more force is transmitted up the springs to the sprung parts of the bike, affecting their operation. A similar situation occurs when the unsprung components drop into a pothole.

To allow the suspension to do its job perfectly there would need to be no unsprung weight, but of course this is impossible. The idea is to keep the unsprung weight as low as possible in relation to the sprung weight, and it is this ratio which is actually more important than the amount of unsprung weight itself.

On a bike like a Honda Goldwing, the ratio is good because there is a huge amount of sprung weight, more so than most bikes, whereas the unsprung weight is about the same as it would be on another large bike. However on a sports bike the sprung weight is kept to a minimum, so it is difficult to keep the ratio good by using conventional wheels and other unsprung components. The only way to get around the problem is to use exotic and expensive lightweight materials such as magnesium or carbon fibre for the wheels.

### 3 Front suspension types – the telescopic fork

Telescopic fork suspension is by far and away the most widely used method of front suspension. It consists of two 'forks' which are clamped into the steering yokes, the yokes being part of the steering assembly (more of which later) **(see illustration 7.3a)**. The wheel axle passes through the bottom of each fork and the wheel fits between them.

### Fork construction

A standard fork leg consists of an upper tube (or stanchion) which is clamped in the yokes **(see illustration 7.3b)**. Fitting closely over the stanchion, is the slider (or leg), often a light alloy casting. There are often renewable bushes between the stanchion and the slider. Inside each leg is a coil spring, allowing the slider to slide up the stanchion in

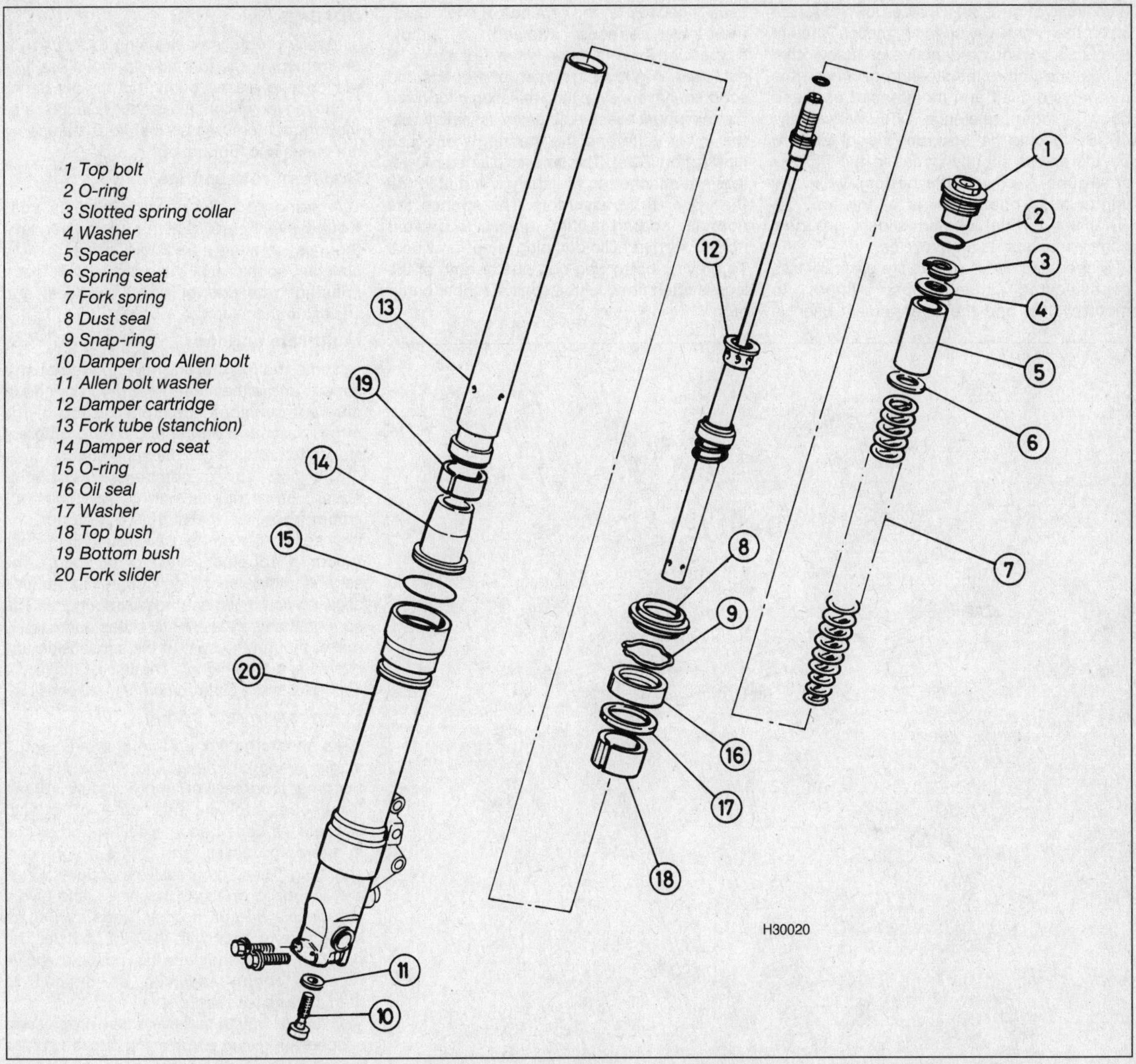

1 Top bolt
2 O-ring
3 Slotted spring collar
4 Washer
5 Spacer
6 Spring seat
7 Fork spring
8 Dust seal
9 Snap-ring
10 Damper rod Allen bolt
11 Allen bolt washer
12 Damper cartridge
13 Fork tube (stanchion)
14 Damper rod seat
15 O-ring
16 Oil seal
17 Washer
18 Top bush
19 Bottom bush
20 Fork slider

H30020

**7.3c Component parts of a typical telescopic front fork with cartridge damper (Honda CBR900RR)**

a telescoping effect. To prevent the fork from bouncing uncontrollably, some form of damping is normally incorporated.

As a method of suspension, telescopic forks work very well. They provide a good amount of travel, not too much unsprung weight or rotational inertia, and in theory allow an unlimited steering lock that is only restricted in practice by other factors, mainly handlebars. The real drawback is in a lack of stiffness – a fork has a fair amount of flex in it, and while a little is not a bad thing, too much is undesirable. A fork 'brace', a metal bracket fitted between the tops of the fork sliders, is often used to reduce this.

One of the biggest influences on how well telescopic forks function is the friction between the two tubes. Most forks now have renewable low-friction bushes containing PTFE (Teflon) between the two tubes to minimise friction, and more importantly 'stiction' (the initial resistance between the two components before they start moving). The bushes are made of a special material not dissimilar to main and big-end shell bearings, and of course they run in oil. One bush fits into the top of the outer tube (or the bottom in upside-down (USD) forks) and the inner tube slides through it. The other bush fits over the

bottom of the inner tube (top on USD forks) and slides up and down with it inside the outer tube.

The majority of forks are similar in construction, differing only in their damping arrangement **(see illustration 7.3c)** and adjustment facility (see below).

The upside-down (USD) fork is a departure from the standard fork. It is basically a standard fork that has been turned upside down so that the wider outer tube, previously the slider, now becomes the stanchion that is clamped in the yokes, and the inner tube, previously the stanchion is now at the bottom, attached to the wheel, and acts as the slider (see illustration 7.3d). Upside-down forks are stiffer than right-way up forks, though whether this is an advantage depends on many other things, the frame, the steering geometry, the motorcycle itself and its intended use, and above all rider preference. One disadvantage of USD forks is that unsprung weight tends to be increased slightly because the heavier steel tube is now at the bottom, while the lighter alloy outer tube is at the top. Tin (Titanium nitride) coated sliders are now common on sports motorcycles.

Moped and scooter forks are generally less sophisticated than those fitted to motorcycles, and the arrangement used is usually chosen on the grounds of cost. Given the lower speeds attained, a simple suspension system, often without damping, is sufficient. A good proportion of mopeds and scooters have a simplified telescopic fork with the two upper tubes built as an assembly with the lower yoke and the steering stem (see illustration 7.3e). The smaller diameter lower legs are attached to the springs and fit inside the upper tube assembly. The springs are normally coated in thick grease to prevent noise, but hydraulic damping is not provided. To prevent bottoming out, one or both of the legs is often fitted with a conical rubber bump stop.

## Springs

Ideally progressive or rising rate action is desirable; i.e. the fork should move easily in response to a small bump, but the resistance to the movement should gradually increase as the fork compresses so that large bumps do not cause it to 'bottom out'.

### Constant rate springs

A standard coil spring has all its coils wound evenly, so that the space between them is constant, and this gives them a constant spring rate. The advantage is that a constant rate spring is the cheapest and easiest to manufacture.

### Multi-rate springs

Some manufacturers have looked at this aspect and either combined two springs of different constant rates, one on top of the other, or wound one spring in two different stages to produce two different rates.

The first spring compresses easily to absorb small ripples and bumps, giving a smooth ride. As the bumps get bigger, the first spring becomes 'coil bound', its coils touching together making it solid. The second, stiffer, spring now comes into effect, allowing continued and heavier springing. The springs themselves are still cheap and easy to make, though the cost of the suspension unit overall is a little higher. The use of multi-rate springs is more common on rear suspension.

### Progressive rate springs

As an alternative, and an improvement, a single spring can be wound so that its coils become progressively more widely spread from one end. In this type of spring, successive coils become coil bound as the spring compresses, giving true progressive springing. These progressively wound springs are now used on many machines, and give a responsive ride on normal roads as well as being able to cope with the odd pothole. The problem is that they are the most expensive type of spring and can be difficult to manufacture with accuracy.

The best way to achieve a fully progressive suspension giving a true rising rate is to use a standard single rate spring connected to the wheel by a linkage that alters the leverage on the spring as the suspension compresses. This type is widely used on rear suspension set-ups (see Chapter 8), but has yet to find its place on the front.

## Damping

When a motorcycle hits a bump, energy is used to compress the springs. The natural tendency is for the spring to unload this energy immediately into the sprung weight of the machine. Controlling the rate at which the springs respond is called 'damping'. An undamped suspension would result in the motorcycle bouncing uncontrollably when ridden over a series of bumps.

Friction damping was used on early machines, and is still used on some scooters.

**7.3d Component parts of a typical upside-down (USD) telescopic front fork with cartridge damper (Yamaha YZF750R)**

1 Top bolt assembly
2 O-ring
3 Locknut
4 Spacer
5 Spring
6 Felt washer
7 Slide washer
8 Fork tube (stanchion)
9 Bottom bush
10 Washer
11 Oil seal
12 Retaining clip
13 Dust seal
14 Damper cartridge
15 Top bush
16 Fork slider
17 Damper cartridge bolt and sealing washer

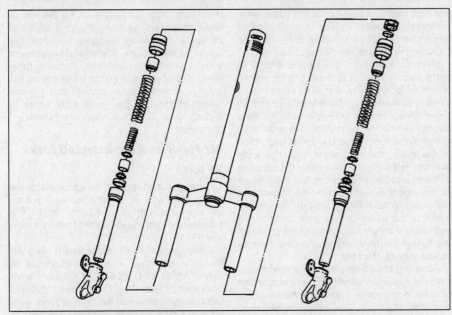

**7.3e  Component parts of a typical scooter telescopic front fork – Piaggio Typhoon**

The problem with friction is that it produces its greatest resistive force before it starts moving, and the amount of damping decreases as the speed of movement increases. The rubbing parts also wear very quickly. Simple scooter dampers consist of a piston and ring running in the fork tube, but with enough resistance to create the required friction.

The principle of the standard oil damping arrangement is to fit a valve or drill a specific sized hole in the base of the fork tube, and then to fill the slider with oil. As the slider is deflected upwards, the oil is trapped and must flow up through the valve or drilling and into the tube. This imposes a resistance on the movement of the suspension, which is repeated on the downstroke. As a result, any tendency towards bouncing is prevented.

In practice, there needs to be little damping effect on the upstroke – for the sake of rider comfort it is better if the wheel can move easily in response to bumps. On the downstroke, however, the damping effect needs be stronger for the sake of handling. There also needs to be different rates of damping depending on the speed of compression or extension of the fork. To provide this, there are different valves and holes used for compression and rebound, and extra valves for when the pressure of the oil reaches a certain level due to a high speed compression or extension from a large bump or hole.

Damping is achieved using either a damper rod or a cartridge damper **(see illustrations 7.3b, c and d)**. Both bolt to the base of the fork slider and fit into a seat or 'oil lock' piece, itself part of the damping arrangement.

### The damper rod

The damper rod is a tube with holes in it that sits in the oil **(see illustration 7.3f)**. At its

**Compression stroke**

**Extension stroke**

**7.3f  Fork operation showing flow of damping oil**

| | |
|---|---|
| 1  *Main spring* | 8  *Damper valve seat* |
| 2  *Oil seal* | |
| 3  *Dust seal* | 9  *Spring* |
| 4  *Piston ring* | 10  *Valve* |
| 5  *Fork tube (stanchion)* | 11  *Valve body* |
| | 12  *Fork slider* |
| 6  *Damper rod assembly* | 13  *Damper rod seat (oil lock piece)* |
| 7  *Rebound spring* | |

*During **compression**, oil trapped in the bottom of the slider (below the fork tube) is flows through compression damping holes and the valve in the bottom of the tube. The fork is prevented from bottoming out when the tube covers the lower holes, forming an oil lock.*

*During **extension** or rebound, oil in the fork flows through rebound damping holes, but the valve in the bottom of the tube closes. The fork is prevented from topping out when the tube covers the lower holes, forming an oil lock, and by the rebound spring on the damper rod.*

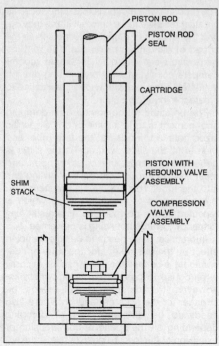

**7.3g The cartridge damper**

top is a wider section (effectively a piston) with a sealing ring that bears against the inner wall of the fork tube. As the slider moves up and down in the tube, so the damper rod moves up and down in the oil, which is forced to flow through its various holes.

There is a one-way or 'check' valve in the bottom of the fork tube that allows oil to flow through it on compression but closes on extension to prevent flow. This provides the damping characteristics required for comfort on compression and handling on rebound.

### The cartridge damper

The cartridge damper works on the same principle of moving oil through restrictive valves, but is different in that it has a piston with a number of holes in it on the end of a rod **(see illustration 7.3g)**. The rod extends from the top of the cartridge and is attached to the top of the fork so that when the fork compresses and extends the piston moves up and down in the cartridge. The compression damping valves are in the bottom of the cartridge. The rebound damping valves are on the piston. When the fork compresses, the one-way rebound valves close and so the piston pushes the oil through the compression valves. When the fork extends, the rebound valves open and the oil is drawn through them.

The valves consist of low speed and high speed oilways (speed of compression/ extension, not road speed of machine). The low speed oilway is either fixed, therefore offering one-rate damping, or it is adjustable (see below) so that the rate can be changed to a higher or lower one. It is designed to cope with mild undulations in the road. The medium

and high speed oilways come into effect when the pressure build-up due to the speed of movement so determines, and is designed to cope with bumps rather than undulations.

Medium and high speed movement is controlled by what is termed a 'shim stack', which is basically a number of shims of varying diameter and thickness stacked on top of one another and covering the hole through which the oil passes. On a medium speed movement caused by a mild undulation in the road, the thin shim with the wide diameter will deflect easily under the pressure of the oil and allow oil to pass, but the amount of movement is restricted by the thicker and narrower shims. A high speed movement, for example riding up over a kerb or hitting a pothole, will create extra pressure and deflect the thicker narrower shims, allowing more oil to flow through the hole.

Achieving the correct set-up for a particular machine requires the correct number and size of holes in the piston and the correct number and size of shims. This is much easier to achieve on a race bike that will only perform on a relatively smooth surface, than on a road bike which has to operate on various road surfaces and with widely varying loads.

The damping principles used in the cartridge damper have really been adapted from methods used for years in rear shock absorbers.

### Rod versus cartridge – the pros and cons

There is no doubt that that the cartridge damper offers better damping properties than the damper rod, not least from the aspect of adjustability, but also because the actions of compression and rebound are separated using different valves. Another advantage with a cartridge damper is that it doesn't suffer from the effects of aeration of the oil as the forks compress and extend. Conventional damper rods often come close to the surface of the oil where turbulence causes aeration, and the tiny bubbles of air mix with the oil and get drawn through the damper before they have the chance to surface and dispel. If air gets into the oil the damping characteristics of the fork are drastically altered.

One drawback with the cartridge fork is that of wear. The internal surface of the aluminium outer tube is hard anodised to prevent wear from the bush on the inner tube as it slides up and down. But the anodised surface is crystalline and so not perfectly smooth, and this wears out the bush, scraping off particles of PTFE (Teflon) which then mix with the oil and contaminate it.

The problem of wear is not a new one, but the difference with cartridge forks is that the rate of flow of the oil is very much faster than with a conventional damper rod, and so the effectiveness of the damping is more susceptible to changes in the oil's properties. Its ability to transmit loads is reduced and so the damping is affected. As the oil becomes

more and more contaminated, so the rate of wear increases, as does the probability of particles becoming trapped between the shims in the stacks. Material development should solve this problem. Yamaha have taken a different route on the R1 by having the bush fixed in the outer tube so that it is the chromed steel of the inner tube which is sliding over it rather than the anodised aluminium.

### Air forks and air-assisted forks

#### Air forks

Instead of a coil spring, the space inside the fork is filled with air under pressure. Air is an excellent springing medium, giving a progressive rate ideally suited to suspension use.

Although air forks have been used on motorcycles, their main drawback is in achieving an air-tight seal to ensure proper operation. With the seal and material technology available at the time air forks were not a practical application for motorcycles.

#### Air-assisted forks

In air-assisted forks the initial springing is provided by conventional constant rate coil springs. The forks are also fitted with air valves (usually incorporated in the top bolt) and are often linked by a hose to ensure equal pressure in each leg **(see illustrations 7.3h)**. This combination of springing benefits from the advantages of air springing, but because the air pressure is much lower than in an air fork, seal failure is less likely. If the seal does fail, the fork can still operate using spring pressure only.

There is a commonly-held belief that air forks provide adjustable damping. Though the air pressure in the fork does affect the damping to a small degree, air itself is a very bad damping medium. This is because it is easily compressed and is why it is such a good springing medium. The damping effect is still provided by forcing oil through a restriction, and thus damping can only be adjusted by altering the size of the restriction.

### Adjustable spring pre-load and damping

Many fork types are adjustable, giving the facility to set up the fork for almost any conceivable use or condition. The need for adjustment serves to underline the fact that the fork can only work at its best under fine limits of loading and surface type.

#### Spring pre-load

Spring pre-load is the amount of compression already in the spring when the fork is assembled and before the fork telescopes under the effects of bumps. Spring pre-load adjustment enables the rider to change the effective length of the spring by compressing it within the fork to suit different loads, road surfaces or riding styles. The mechanism usually consists of an adjuster

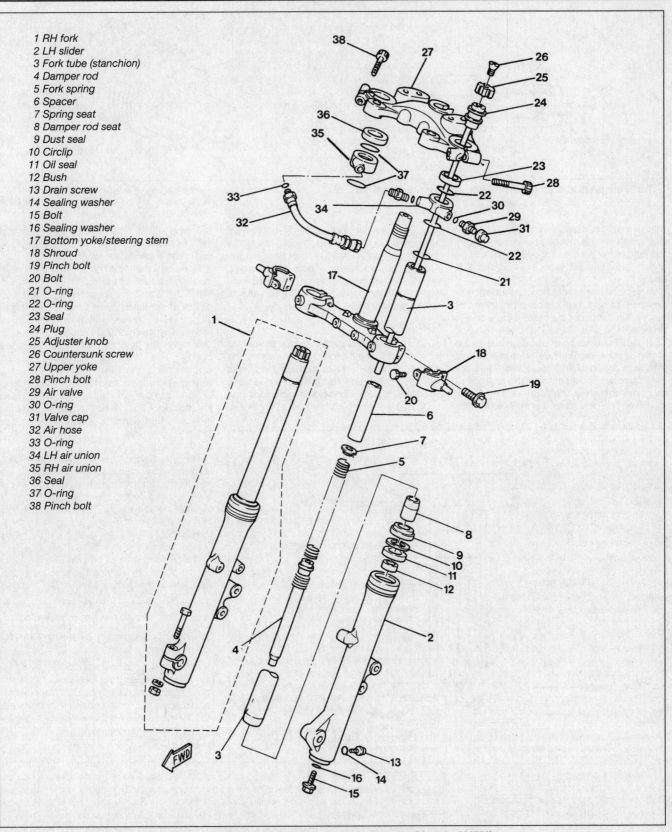

1 RH fork
2 LH slider
3 Fork tube (stanchion)
4 Damper rod
5 Fork spring
6 Spacer
7 Spring seat
8 Damper rod seat
9 Dust seal
10 Circlip
11 Oil seal
12 Bush
13 Drain screw
14 Sealing washer
15 Bolt
16 Sealing washer
17 Bottom yoke/steering stem
18 Shroud
19 Pinch bolt
20 Bolt
21 O-ring
22 O-ring
23 Seal
24 Plug
25 Adjuster knob
26 Countersunk screw
27 Upper yoke
28 Pinch bolt
29 Air valve
30 O-ring
31 Valve cap
32 Air hose
33 O-ring
34 LH air union
35 RH air union
36 Seal
37 O-ring
38 Pinch bolt

**7.3h Air-assisted forks with adjustable damping (Yamaha XJ750)**

*Note in particular the air connecting hose (32) which links the fork legs to ensure equal pressure. Damping rate is controlled by knurled knobs (25) at the top of each leg.*

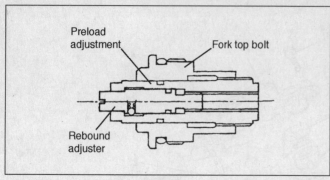

**7.3i  Fork preload adjuster which is in direct contact with the spring**

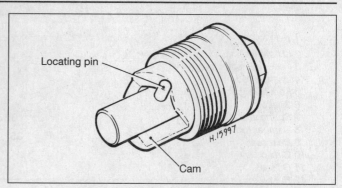

**7.3j  Cam type fork spring preload adjuster**

that is in direct contact with the top of the spring and can be moved in or out of the fork top bolt, either via conventional threads or on a cam arrangement **(see illustrations 7.3i and j)**.

A popular misconception is that altering pre-load makes the suspension softer or harder, but this is not the case. If you increase pre-load, the bike will sag less when you sit on it, but the amount of compression in the spring when it sags will be the same as that with less pre-load and more sag. Thus the only thing which changes is the amount of sag, and therefore the 'ride height' of the machine. The best thing way to illustrate this is to increase the pre-load on a motorcycle while on its stand, and notice the forks extend, which is raising the ride height. Altering the ride height affects many things, including steering geometry (rake and trail) and the centre of gravity. This in turn affects handling and traction respectively.

**Damping**

Adjusting the damping changes the rate at which the oil is able to move by varying the size of the holes it moves through. Only forks with cartridge-type damping have built-in adjusters, though standard damper rods can be 'tuned' by enlarging the size of the holes.

Damping adjustment can be varied in one or both of two ways, when the fork compresses and when it extends or rebounds.

Rebound damping is usually controlled from an adjuster at the top of each fork leg. When this is turned it either moves a needle in or out of an oilway, or it turns a cylinder to align a different size orifice with the oilway **(see illustration 7.3k)**. Both increase or decrease the flow rate of oil through the oilway and so the damping effect. Compression damping is controlled in a similar way, but the adjuster is normally found at the bottom of the fork slider **(see illustration 7.3l)**. Certain fork arrangements have rebound damping adjustment on one fork and compression damping adjustment on the other fork.

The three adjustments (spring pre-load, rebound and compression damping) are frequently found together in the most sophisticated forks, giving a wide range of possible combinations. Other forks may only provide adjustment on one or two of the three possibilities, usually depending on the needs of the machine and its intended use.

The performance of non-adjustable forks can be altered by varying the amount and/or viscosity of the damping oil, fitting a spring

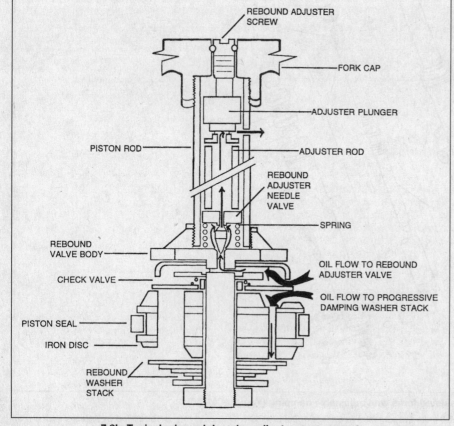

**7.3k  Typical rebound damping adjuster arrangement**

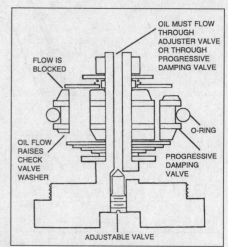

**7.3l  Typical compression damping adjuster arrangement**

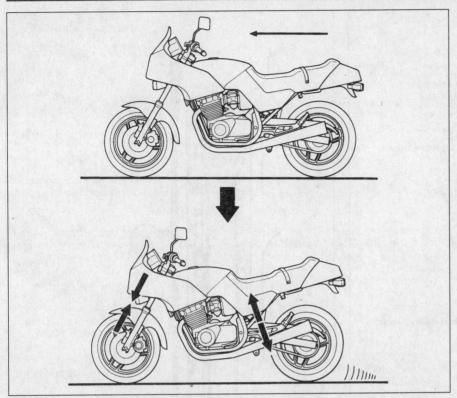

**7.3m  Weight transfer during braking**

*When the brakes are applied, forward momentum shifts the machine's centre of mass forward. This compresses the front suspension and causes the rear to lift. Much of the available suspension movement is lost.*

with a different rate, fitting a spacer above the spring, or altering the damping characteristics by enlarging the oil flow holes or varying shim stacks.

## Anti-dive systems

Anti-dive forks offer some measure of control over one of the less desirable characteristics of all telescopic forks – the front suspension dives due to the effect of weight transfer under braking **(see illustration 7.3m)**. Because much of the suspension movement is taken up by the diving effect, the front suspension is virtually inoperative until the brake is released. The problem of dive can be completely offset by using an alternative suspension arrangement, such as leading link or Telelever, but in the case of the telescopic fork there is nothing you can do.

Anti-dive systems provide a form of automatic damping adjustment controlled by the front brake **(see illustration 7.3n)**. The exact method of operation varies from one manufacturer to another, but the main elements of most systems are as follows.

When the machine is being ridden normally, the movement of damping oil through the anti-dive unit is relatively unrestricted. As soon as the front brake is applied, the restriction in the valve inside the anti-dive unit is increased, either hydraulically from the

braking system, mechanically by a torque link from the caliper, or electrically by a solenoid that is triggered by the brake light circuit **(see illustration 7.3o overleaf)**. There have also been solely mechanical systems that restrict the amount of compression in the forks, and an hydraulic system using a link to a slave piston that compresses the spring in the fork.

The damping effect is increased dramatically, and the fork can only compress very slowly. If a large bump is encountered, a small diaphragm valve will be opened momentarily to allow normal movement, and so the suspension is not 'locked' by the system **(see illustration 7.3p overleaf)**. Most systems provide an adjuster so that the effect of the anti-dive unit can be set as required.

All anti-dive systems restrict and control front-end dive under braking, but do not remove it. This is not a bad thing as the weight transfer means more grip from the front tyre as it is effectively pressed into the ground. The use of an anti-dive system does allow the use of a much lighter and more responsive initial spring and damper rate.

Anti-dive systems really came about because of inefficient damping in telescopic forks. Marked improvements in fork design have now done away with the need for anti-dive systems.

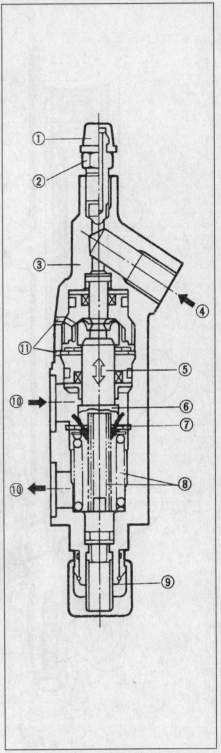

**7.3n  Cross-section of anti-dive unit (Yamaha FJ1100)**

| | |
|---|---|
| 1 Cap | 6 Valve |
| 2 Bleed valve | 7 Valve seat |
| 3 Body | 8 Spring |
| 4 Brake fluid | 9 Adjuster |
|    passage | 10 Fork oil passages |
| 5 Plunger | 11 Pilot holes |

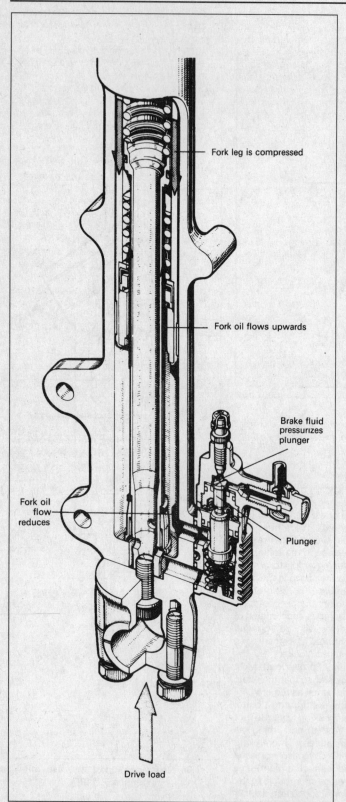

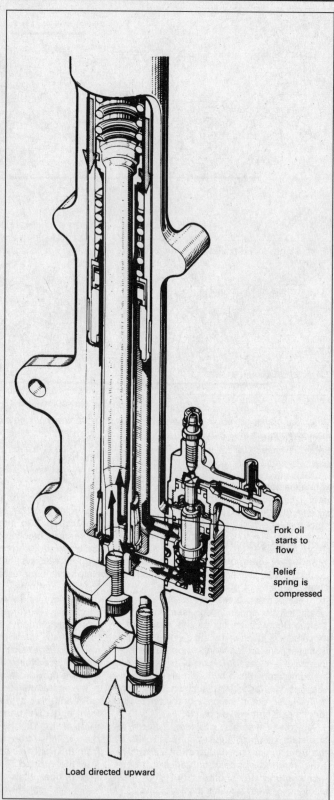

**7.3o Anti-dive unit operation during braking (Suzuki GSX550)**

*When the front brake is applied, hydraulic pressure pushes down the plunger. This in turn restricts the flow of damping oil, stiffening the fork to resist the normal pitching motion.*

**7.3p Anti-dive unit relief valve operation (Suzuki GSX550)**

*If the machine encounters a bump while the anti-dive unit is in operation it is necessary to allow normal fork action to occur. This is achieved by fitting a relief valve which will open under sudden pressure to bypass the restricted anti-dive damping.*

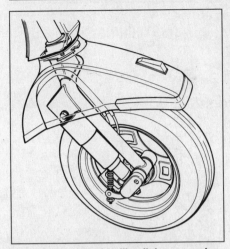

**7.4a  Single-sided trailing link suspension**

## 4  Front suspension types – leading and trailing links

One approach to building a lightweight and low cost front suspension system is to choose a leading or trailing link type **(see illustration 7.4a)**. With this arrangement the fork tubes extend to within a few inches of the wheel spindle, and a fabricated link arm pivots on the bottom of the fork and projects forwards or backwards from the pivot. The end of the link holds the wheel axle, and a mount between the pivot and axle carries the bottom end of the shock absorber, with the other end attached to the fork, either internally or externally. A leading link has the axle in front of the pivot **(see illustration 7.4b)**. A trailing link has the axle behind the pivot.

The spring and damping arrangement is kept simple, with either a spring extending up inside the fork, or an external shock absorber unit similar to those used on the rear. Where

the application is for a scooter damping is not really considered, but better quality rear-type shock absorbers with hydraulic damping can be used for custom or heavier applications.

Where a trailing link design is chosen (with the link pivot in front of the wheel spindle) the fork behaves in much the same way as a telescopic type; when a bump is encountered or the brake is applied the wheel deflects upwards, moving through a small arc. With leading link types, however, the behaviour under braking is different; the front of the machine does not tend to dive and in some cases rises in response to brake pressure. Given the lack of damping this can be used to good effect if the angle of the links is chosen with care.

Both arrangements can be made cheaply and simply and so are ideal for scooters. They give low unsprung weight and fair rotational inertia.

One notable example of the leading link arrangement is the Earles fork. These differ in that the pivoting link is much longer and the pivot is behind the back of the wheel **(see illustration 7.4b)**. This gives very good steering stiffness but high rotational inertia, which makes it not so good for motorcycles, but excellent for sidecar outfits and trikes. A good quality rear shock absorber (usually a monoshock type) is used in conjunction with the Earles set-up on modern sidecar kits and well-built trikes.

## 5  Front suspension types – alternatives to the telescopic fork

### The problems with telescopic forks

Despite their widespread use there are many problems with telescopic forks:
a) *None of the different forces acting on*

*them (braking, suspension, steering) are separated. All the forces pass through all the components on the front end, meaning that they have to be built stronger and therefore heavier than if the forces were separated.*
b) *The steering geometry (rake and trail) changes when the forks compress, due to the fact that the wheelbase changes.*
c) *The distance between the axle and the steering pivot is huge, which makes the forks flex when under force. To compensate, extra stiffness has to be built into the forks and steering head, making them heavy.*
d) *The load path is long and indirect, meaning the frame has to be bigger and heavier than it would be if the load path were directly between the two axles.*

Alternative designs have two main aims. First, to separate the braking, suspension and steering forces, and second to create a more direct load path, which would mean a smaller and lighter frame, or for the same weight a much stiffer frame. Reducing unsprung mass and rotational inertia should come about naturally from achieving these aims.

### The alternatives

The leading and trailing link designs covered in Section 4 are only really suitable for small lightweight and undemanding applications. Larger heavier versions for motorcycles would create as many (if not more) problems than would be resolved, not that this bothered Harley-Davidson when they combined a girder fork style with and a leading link arrangement.

#### Girder forks

The girder fork was used on most early motorcycles. It falls into the category of 'parallelogram' suspension, because of the parallel arrangement and movement of the two linking arms.

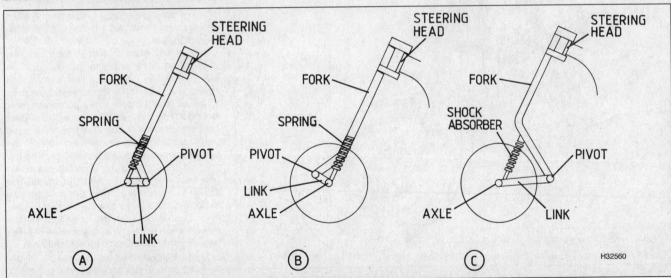

**7.4b  Leading-link front suspension (A), trailing-link front suspension (B), Earles type leading link (C)**

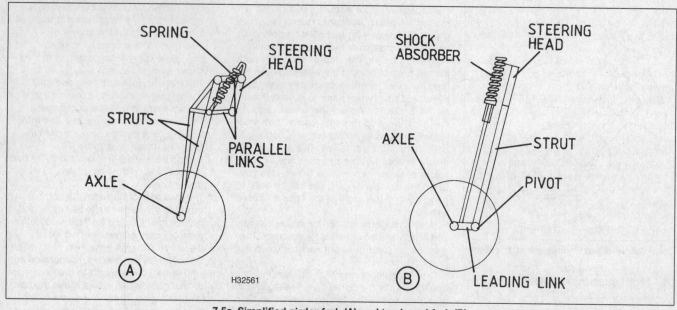

SPRING

STEERING HEAD

STRUTS

PARALLEL LINKS

AXLE

(A)

H32561

SHOCK ABSORBER

STEERING HEAD

AXLE

STRUT

PIVOT

(B)

LEADING LINK

**7.5a Simplified girder fork (A) and 'springer' fork (B)**

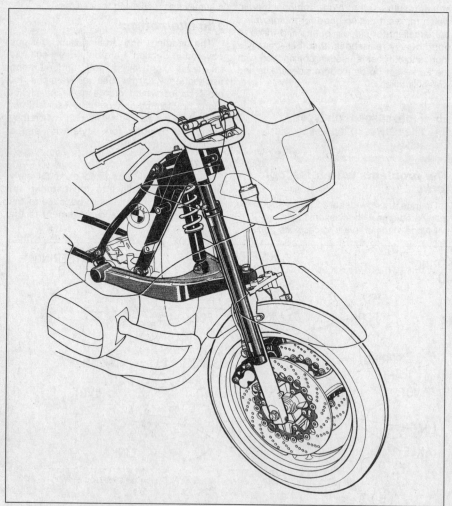

**7.5b BMW's Telelever system, which uses telescopic forks for steering and a single wishbone with rear-style shock absorber for suspension**

Two solid struts or 'girders', normally strengthened by two additional triangulating struts, are attached to the steering head by two pivoting parallel links, and between these is a shock absorbing unit (normally consisting of a spring and separate friction damper) attached to a bridge between the girders and to the steering head **(see illustration 7.5a)**. Harley-Davidson combine the girder fork style with a leading link arrangement for their 'springer' fork. Custom builders favour it because of its looks.

The main drawbacks with girder forks are high unsprung weight and high rotational inertia, but on the positive side they reduce dive under braking and have reasonable steering stiffness.

### Wishbone suspension

A wishbone arrangement is commonly used on cars, but BMW has adapted the principle for motorcycles.

The BMW Telelever system looks slightly strange at first because of the pair of conventional looking telescopic forks which clamp in a yoke at the top and hold the front wheel at the bottom, and compress and extend to ride the bumps as you would expect **(see illustration 7.5b)**. But the forks have nothing to do with the suspension of the motorcycle – they purely serve to provide the method of steering, pivoting on two ball joints, one between the yoke and the frame, the other between the fork brace and the wishbone. The forks are oil filled and have nylon bushes between the tubes to minimise friction and stiction. There is a large overlap between the fork tubes to provide stiffness.

A wishbone (similar to a swingarm) pivots on each side of the engine, and the front of the bone is mounted on a bracket, acting like a bottom yoke or fork brace, between the forks. The bottom of the suspension unit mounts on the top of the wishbone, and the top of the suspension unit mounts on the underside of the 'frame' behind the steering head. The suspension unit itself functions in the same way as a rear shock absorber in terms of both springing and damping.

Steering, suspension and braking forces are all nicely separated on this system, and there is good steering stiffness. Rotational inertia is also reduced due to the lack of fork internals, and unsprung weight is reduced slightly. One of the main differences in feel when riding the bike is in the lack of dive under braking, which has the benefit of maintaining a near-constant steering geometry.

### Single-sided swingarm suspension

A single-sided swingarm arrangement is a form of leading link, but goes further in separating forces and reducing rotational inertia by using hub-centre steering. The suspension arrangement is similar to a single-sided rear swingarm. Various arrangements have appeared, one of the most popular being the Di Fazio arrangement. Production bike versions have been the Bimota Tesi and the Yamaha GTS1000, which will be used as an example **(see illustration 7.5c)**.

The swingarm pivots on the side of the 'Omega' frame (so called because of its shape), and the wheel connects to its front end. A shock absorber mounts between the swingarm and the frame.

An upper arm that is linked to the swingarm by the 'knuckle arm' and also mounts on the frame forms a 'parallelogram' arrangement, which gives excellent steering stiffness. The knuckle arm transmits the steering forces from the handlebars via a telescoping tube which rides with the suspension movement. The knuckle arm pivots on the swingarm and upper arm and carries the wheel axle. When the handlebars are turned, the knuckle arm turns, bringing the wheel with it, but the swingarm and upper arm remain parallel to the frame. This means that the steering lock is restricted by the offset in the swingarm, which has to kept to a minimum for the sake of width, weight and weight distribution.

The load path on this arrangement is excellent, and better than the wishbone system, but the wishbone is not restricted in its steering. The geometry of both arrangements can be varied easily by using a different size swingarm or wishbone, and rear-style rising rate suspension linkages could easily be incorporated if required.

### 6 Steering

Irrespective of the front suspension set-up, steering always begins with a pair of handlebars which pivot in or on part of the

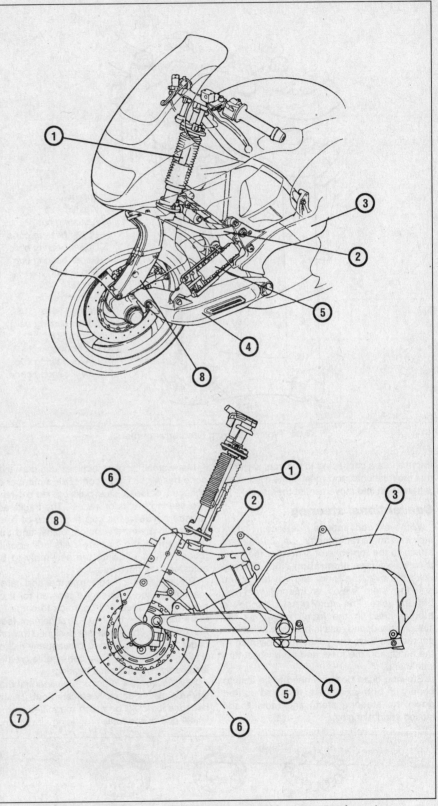

**7.5c Single-sided swingarm suspension and hub centre steering setup (Yamaha GTS1000)**

| | | |
|---|---|---|
| 1 Steering tube | 3 Frame | 5 Shock absorber | 7 Wheel axle |
| 2 Upper arm | 4 Swingarm | 6 Ball joint | 8 Knuckle arm |

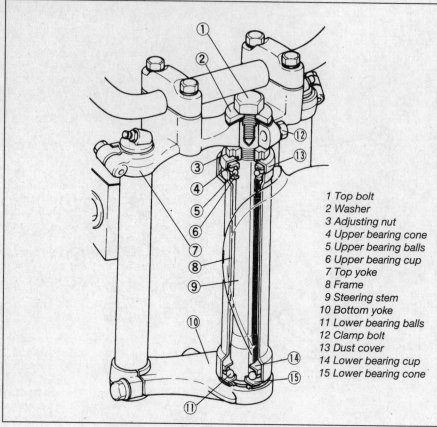

1 Top bolt
2 Washer
3 Adjusting nut
4 Upper bearing cone
5 Upper bearing balls
6 Upper bearing cup
7 Top yoke
8 Frame
9 Steering stem
10 Bottom yoke
11 Lower bearing balls
12 Clamp bolt
13 Dust cover
14 Lower bearing cup
15 Lower bearing cone

**7.6a  Typical steering head arrangement**

frame and are connected to the front wheel so that the rotational movement of the handlebars is translated into movement of the wheel.

### Conventional steering

With a conventional telescopic fork suspension arrangement the handlebars attach to the top yoke or slide over the forks themselves **(see illustration 7.6a)**. The top yoke fits over the forks and the top of the steering stem which is integral with the bottom yoke. The stem passes through a tubular head in the frame known as the steering head, and runs in bearings. When the handlebars turn, the yokes turn, pivoting in the head, and the forks and front wheel turn with them.

Steering head bearings need to be able to cope with both axial loads (directed up and down the steering stem) and radial loads (acting at right angles).

Many small or old machines use cup-and-cone bearings. These comprise a number of uncaged, or loose, steel balls carried between two bearing tracks or 'races'. The tracks are formed between the cup and cone of each bearing in a slightly conical plane, and this ensures that the bearing balls are equally loaded whilst allowing the assembly to be adjusted to remove free play.

The majority of performance and large machines use either caged tapered roller or bearings or caged ball bearings to ensure a more robust steering head arrangement **(see illustration 7.6b)**. These are designed to work under a slight pre-load to prevent any risk of unwanted free play. They can handle greater loads than cup-and cone bearings.

Whichever type is used it is essential that any free play is carefully adjusted out. This is because it would be much magnified at the wheel end of the fork, producing sloppy and imprecise steering and strange handling.

### Alternative steering

On BMW's Telelever system the handlebars attach to a single yoke which pivots on a ball joint on the frame **(see illustration 7.5b)**. There is no bottom yoke and steering stem or head as such. Otherwise the system is the same in that rotational movement of the handlebars turns the forks and front wheel.

The Yamaha GTS has what is known as 'hub centre steering', which is basically what cars have. Hub centre steering is when the hub itself pivots in relation to the suspension arm, while the suspension arm remains in line with is up-and-down movement **(see illustration 7.5c)**. Alternative hub-centre steering designs use a double-sided suspension arm and the wheel pivots on a ball in the middle of the hub.

### Steering geometry

#### Rake, trail and offset

The steering line is set at an angle, known as the 'rake', so that the forks extend forward of the steering head, rather than vertically downwards **(see illustration 7.6c)**. The rake angle partly determines an important feature of the steering geometry, the trail. Trail is also determined by the amount of fork offset and axle offset.

Trail is important because it is responsible for the self-centring, or 'castor' action of the steering. When the front wheel is displaced from the centreline by hitting a bump, the contact patch of the tyre moves away from the centreline. The friction between the road and the tyre turns the wheel back to the straight-ahead position.

When you sit on a motorcycle and turn the handlebars from one side to the other, the steering head rises and falls. Consequently it

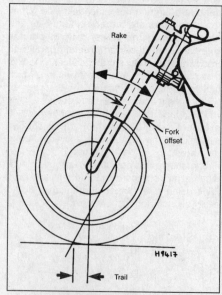

**7.6c  Rake, trail and offset of a typical steering head arrangement**

Uncaged ball    Caged ball    Tapered roller

**7.6b  Steering head bearing types**

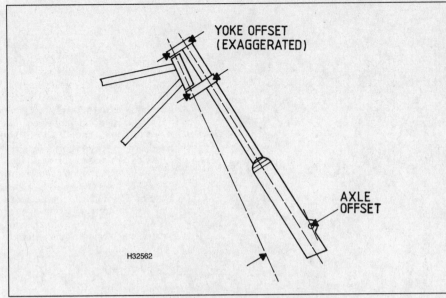

YOKE OFFSET
(EXAGGERATED)

AXLE
OFFSET

H32562

**7.6d  Axle offset and yoke offset**

Rake – The angle of the steering axis from the vertical, typically 23° to 30° **(see illustration 7.6c)**.
Trail – The distance between the point where a vertical line through the wheel axle touches the ground, and the point where a line through the steering axis touches the ground – typically 60 to 100 mm.
**Fork offset** – the perpendicular distance between a line drawn through the centre of the fork and a line drawn through the steering axis.
**Wheel axle offset** – the perpendicular distance between the front wheel axle and a line drawn through the steering axis, and can be different from fork offset if the axle is held either in front of or behind the centreline of the fork **(see illustration 7.6d)**.
**Yoke offset** – when the fork offset is different at the top and bottom yoke, creating an angle between the forks and the steering axis.

is easier to turn the handlebars from centre than bring them back to centre. This steering head drop is caused by rake, and increases with it, and reduces the castor effect. However as rake increases, so does the castor effect, and so in a way they work together to determine the feel of the steering through the handlebars when cornering. But offset can be used to increase or reduce the amount of trail while the rake angle stays the same. Similarly the wheelbase can be shortened by reducing the rake angle, but to maintain the same amount of trail part of the wheelbase reduction can be achieved by reducing the fork offset or increasing wheel axle offset to the rear. Adjustable yokes (for either fork or yoke offset) have been used in racing for a while, and are beginning to appear on some production sports bikes. Adjustment is either via an eccentric mount around the steering stem, or by varying the

size of spacer between the halves of a split yoke.

So you can see that the effects of rake, trail and offset are all inter-linked and the permutations are endless, and in some way each is a compromise. When you consider that under the compression and extension of the telescopic fork the effective rake and trail are constantly changing (not to mention the wheelbase), it is clear that achieving perfect handling for all situations is impossible.

Ultimately the intended purpose of the bike determines the rough amounts of rake, offset and trail, and these are then fine tuned to fit in with overall weight, weight distribution, and desired handling characteristics, along with rear suspension geometry, to achieve the best possible compromise.

**Wheelbase**

The wheelbase is the distance between the two wheel axles. The combination of front and

rear suspension and steering geometry determines the wheelbase (and vice versa), and this on its own has a major effect on steering and handling.

A long wheelbase gives a motorcycle excellent stability in a straight line but makes it slower to turn into corners. A short wheelbase gives very nimble turning capabilities but reduces straight line stability. Typically touring bikes have a long wheelbase and sports bikes a short one. Hitting a bump at high speed on a sports bike with a short wheelbase results in a far bigger twitch than on a touring bike with a long wheelbase.

Under the action of the front suspension the wheelbase is constantly changing. When the forks compress, their inclination means the front wheel is actually getting closer to the rear wheel. At the same time the rake angle tends towards the vertical, and so the trail changes.

# Chapter 8
## Rear suspension

## Contents

### 1  Introduction

**Note:** *Refer to the general principles involved with suspension in Chapter 7, particularly the importance of unsprung weight, why damping is needed and how it is achieved, spring rates and how to vary them, rising rate suspension, the use of air etc.*

Rear suspension first appeared relatively late on in the motorcycle's history. Whilst the need for front suspension became very evident early on, it was far less crucial at the rear until speeds increased. For decades, girder forks at the front were teamed with a solidly mounted rear wheel (affectionately known by many as a 'hardtail'), the worst of the bumps being tamed by the fitting of a well-sprung single saddle. Any pillion passenger was obliged to endure a rudimentary pad lodged above the rear mudguard, and with it the majority of the bumps and vibration transmitted up through the rear wheel.

After the second World War the lack of rear suspension soon became a problem on racing machines; as speeds increased, so did the amount of time the rear wheel spent off the road surface. This meant that the absence of springing was beginning to impose a limitation on the overall performance of the machines.

The earliest version of rear springing was the plunger unit. This was little more than a pair of two-way vertical spring units set at the rear of the frame between two fork ends on each side and with the axle running between them and held between the upper and lower springs. Though undamped, the plunger

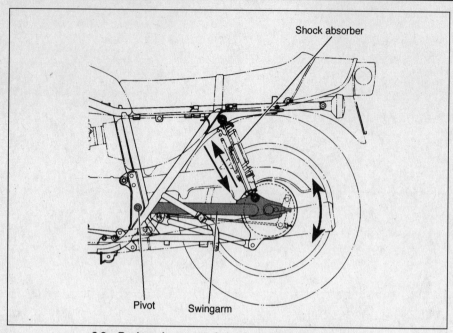

**8.2a  Basic swingarm and shock absorber arrangement**

The introduction of Triumph's spring hub in the 1950s represented a further development of rear suspension. The springing mechanism was contained inside the rear hub and enabled the rear wheel axle to be spring loaded, thus providing a limited amount of suspension to an otherwise rigid frame.

The real breakthrough in rear suspension came with the pivoted rear fork, or swinging arm (shortened generally to 'swingarm'). Its use soon became universal, and still is today, though many variations on the original have developed through design and material innovation, and improvement in the shock absorbing units they are used with.

One of the most important features of any rear suspension set-up is the ability to maintain wheel alignment and to keep the axle at right angles to the steering axis. This depends on the strength and stiffness of the set-up, and the ability of the pivot points to withstand high axial and radial loads.

## 2  The swinging arm

### The principle

The swingarm is a variation on a car wishbone theme. In its basic form it consists of a lateral pivot at the front that fits between the side members of the frame or onto the rear of the crankcase, enabling it to move up and down in an arc (see illustration 8.2a). Two arms extend from the pivot and the rear wheel sits between these arms, located on an axle that is attached between the ends of the arms.

One or two suspension units, known as shock absorbers or 'shocks', connect between the swingarm and the frame to provide springing and damping. They vary considerably in complexity depending on the machine, but normally feature a coil spring fitted around an oil filled damper unit (see Section 3). The mounting at each end of the unit allows the shock to pivot in reaction to movement of the swingarm.

The traditional set-up was to have two shock absorbers, one on each side and mounted on the arm just ahead of the axle, and inclined forwards slightly to mount on the rear sub-frame. With the exception of a few traditionally designed models, motorcycles now use a single shock absorber or 'monoshock' mounted centrally on the swingarm ahead of the wheel, with a three-way linkage between the swingarm, shock absorber and frame.

### Swingarm construction

For many years tubular or pressed steel was used for making swingarms, with strengthening in the form of gussets around the joints between the arms and the pivots (see illustration 8.2b). Steel has a good

frames did allow a measure of comfort and rear wheel control, and they were soon widely used on road models. The main drawbacks were wear (and therefore the tendency for the wheel to twist in relation to the frame because of the lack of interconnection between each fork end), and lack of travel (which was restricted because the chain tightens as the wheel moves vertically either side of the central position – this also meant the chain was at its slackest in its central equilibrium position).

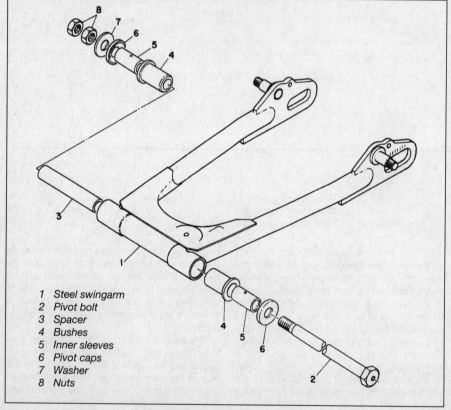

1  Steel swingarm
2  Pivot bolt
3  Spacer
4  Bushes
5  Inner sleeves
6  Pivot caps
7  Washer
8  Nuts

**8.2b  A typical tubular steel swingarm**

strength-to-weight ratio, but to obtain the stiffness that is required for a good swingarm in a performance application, the size of section required in steel made the swingarm heavy.

Aluminium alloy is the best alternative to steel **(see illustration 8.2c)**. It has roughly one third the strength and one third the weight of steel, so you would assume that three times as much would be needed to make as good a swingarm as steel. But stiffness comes with area of material, and an aluminium swingarm that is as strong and heavy as a steel one is in fact much stiffer. So stiffness is increased without extra weight, or alternatively you can achieve the same stiffness as steel for a reduced weight. Some swingarms, notably Honda's 'Gull-Arm' are curved to increase stiffness.

Another way of achieving extra stiffness without having to make the arms too bulky is to triangulate the swingarm, e.g. Honda's Tri-Arm **(see illustration 8.2d)**. This is also done to incorporate a mounting for the shock absorber in the case of a cantilever set-up **(see illustration 8.4b)**.

Where large area sections of aluminium are used, the aluminium is laminated or extruded to create internal walls that give a triangulated or boxed cross-section, which greatly increases stiffness. It also means that the outer walls of the arm can be thinner.

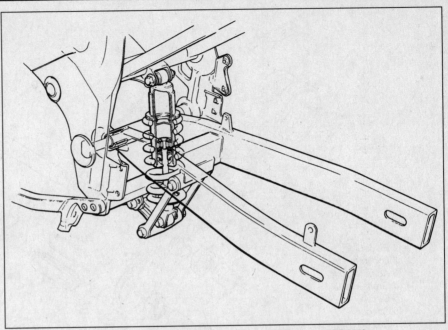

**8.2c  Aluminium alloy swingarm design (Yamaha FZR600)**

Magnesium alloys and carbon fibre now provide the best combination of stiffness and weight, but they are still considered exotic materials and are very expensive. Composite materials such as carbon fibre combined with an aluminium honeycomb can provide immense stiffness in particular directions of stress.

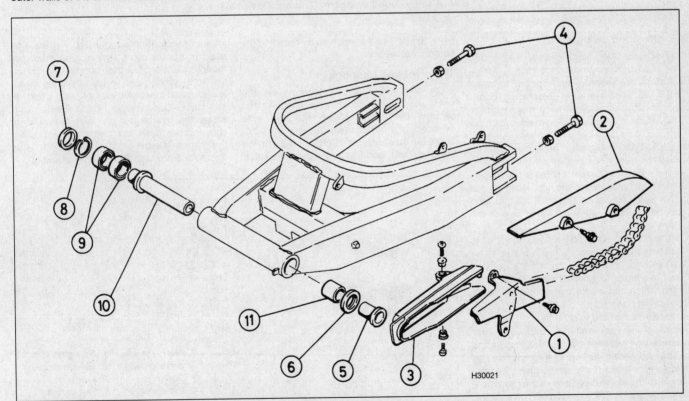

**8.2d  A triangulated aluminium swingarm (Honda CBR900RR)**

1  Front chain guard
2  Rear chain guard
3  Drive chain slider
4  Drive chain adjusting bolt
5  Collar
6  Dust seal
7  Dust seal
8  Snap-ring
9  Ball bearings
10  Centre spacer
11  Needle roller bearing

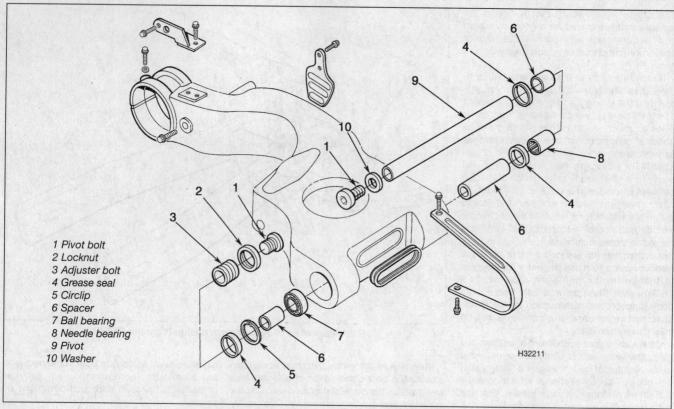

1 Pivot bolt
2 Locknut
3 Adjuster bolt
4 Grease seal
5 Circlip
6 Spacer
7 Ball bearing
8 Needle bearing
9 Pivot
10 Washer

H32211

**8.2e A single-sided swingarm (Triumph Daytona)**

## Single-sided swingarms

The use of single-sided swingarms occurred through endurance racing, where pit-stops are essential and needed to be as quick as possible **(see illustration 8.2e)**. Single-sided arms allow for a much quicker rear wheel change, as the wheel is located onto a hub unit which carries the rear sprocket and brake disc, meaning the chain does not have to be slipped off the sprocket, and the disc can remain located in the caliper. The wheel is secured to the hub, locating onto drive pins that are integral with the hub, and can be drawn off sideways rather than to the rear.

The problem with single-sided swingarms is that they have to be made much bulkier to be stiff enough, as a single arm flexes a lot more than two arms. They also have a tendency to twist which can create gyroscopic moments that upset handling.

However flex and twist in the arm can be a good thing as well as bad, and the comparison between double and single arms under cornering forces is interesting. The single arm twists more easily, giving a wider angle to the longitudinal axis of the machine – in other words the wheel turns towards the direction of the corner being taken. This is potentially negative as it changes the radius of the curve, making the machine turn wider. However, this self-steering effect actually

helps to stabilise the machine by reducing the tendency to weave.

## The pivot and bearings

On the majority of motorcycles the swingarm pivots on a through-bolt that secures the arm between the two side members of the frame **(see illustration 8.2f)**. There are also designs that pivot the arm on the crankcase, and this is usually done either

where longitudinally mounted V-twins are used in sports bikes (the engine must be mounted further back than normal to allow for the front cylinder, and would otherwise mean an excessive wheelbase or too short a swingarm – Ducati range, Honda Firestorm) or where the overall design dispenses with a conventional frame, and everything (including the front suspension) bolts onto the engine/gearbox unit (BMW 4-valve Boxers).

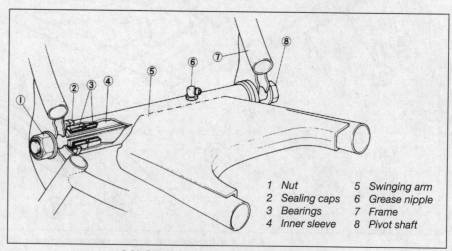

1 Nut
2 Sealing caps
3 Bearings
4 Inner sleeve
5 Swinging arm
6 Grease nipple
7 Frame
8 Pivot shaft

**8.2f Section through a swinging arm pivot**

*In this example, needle roller bearings are used. Many other models use plain bushes, whilst some machines use taper roller bearings.*

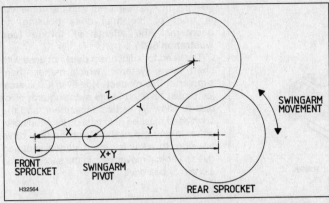

**8.2g Comparison of sprocket centre distances at different swingarm positions**

When the swingarm pivot and sprocket centres are aligned, the total distance between the sprocket centres is the distance between the front sprocket and the swingarm pivot (X) plus that between the swingarm pivot and the rear sprocket (Y), i.e. X + Y.

When the swingarm moves up or down, the distance (Z) between the sprocket centres becomes less than the distance X + Y, and thus the chain becomes slack.

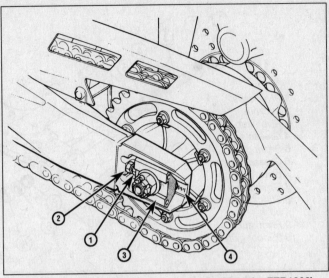

**8.2h Chain freeplay adjuster mechanism (Yamaha FZR1000)**

| | | | |
|---|---|---|---|
| 1 | Adjuster bolt | 3 | Adjuster block |
| 2 | Locknut | 4 | Wheel alignment marks |

On shaft driven machines it is not possible to use a through-bolt for the pivot as the shaft runs inside the arm. Instead stub pivots are used **(see illustration 8.2i and j)**. The bearings on arms that incorporate shaft drive need to be more robust to cope with the extra weight.

Most types of bearing are used across the range of motorcycles, the choice depending on the machine itself and its intended use. Plain bearings are used in small machines where performance is not an issue but cost is. Needle roller bearings are the most widely used bearing, though sometimes in conjunction with caged ball bearings. The combination is good for coping with both axial and radial loads that they are subjected to.

Taper roller bearings are sometimes used, as these cope with all loads very well, but as they are designed to operate under a certain amount of pre-load, the tightness of the pivot must be just right. Often the choice depends on the way the swingarm is actually fitted in the frame and how this affects the loads on it.

One recent adoption which is becoming common is to use an adjuster bolt that sets the fit of the swingarm, which is then secured in the frame by a locknut. This eliminates tightening the frame itself onto the swingarm and is used mainly in conjunction with alloy frames.

### Incorporating the final drive

The swingarm pivot needs to be as close to the gearbox output shaft as possible to ensure that the distance between the output shaft and the rear axle is kept constant. When the pivot is located behind the output shaft, the effective distance between the shaft and the axle varies as the swingarm moves up and down, and so chain and belt tension or shaft length is constantly varying **(see illustration 8.2g)**. To keep the distance constant the shaft and pivot need to be in the same axis, but this is impractical. Therefore any final drive system must allow for this variable and accept its drawbacks.

### Chain and belt drive

On chain and belt drive machines the swingarm pivot is to the rear of but close to the front sprocket or pulley.

Where chain drive is used it is necessary to provide some sort of adjustment in the distance between the front and rear sprockets to allow for the fact that the chain will stretch in use. This is accomplished by moving the rear wheel axle forwards or backwards in relation to the output shaft **(see illustration 8.2h)**.

Normally, this is done by having slotted fork ends, though some manufacturers prefer to mount the swinging arm pivot eccentrically in a rotating adjuster (necessary on single-sided swingarms), making it easier to maintain rear wheel alignment. The only minor drawback with an eccentric adjuster is that the height of the axle varies slightly with adjustment as well as the distance.

### Shaft drive

The driveshaft runs inside one of the arms across the axis of the pivot, meaning that a normal through-pivot cannot be used, so instead stub pivots are used **(see illustration 8.2i)**. The final drive housing bolts onto the

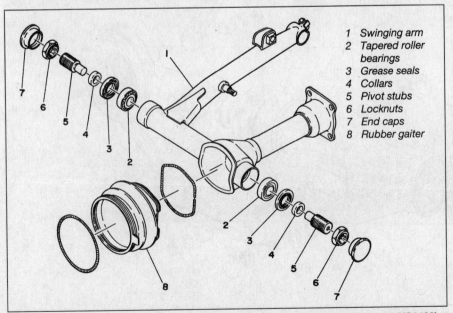

| | |
|---|---|
| 1 | Swinging arm |
| 2 | Tapered roller bearings |
| 3 | Grease seals |
| 4 | Collars |
| 5 | Pivot stubs |
| 6 | Locknuts |
| 7 | End caps |
| 8 | Rubber gaiter |

**8.2i A conventional swingarm, with one side housing the driveshaft (Yamaha XS1100)**

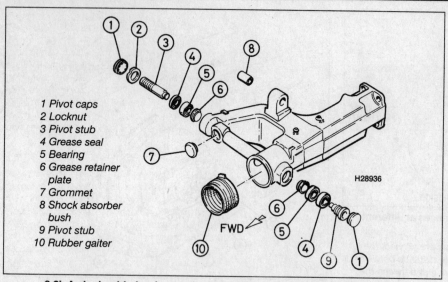

1 Pivot caps
2 Locknut
3 Pivot stub
4 Grease seal
5 Bearing
6 Grease retainer plate
7 Grommet
8 Shock absorber bush
9 Pivot stub
10 Rubber gaiter

FWD

H28936

**8.2j  A single-sided swingarm incorporating shaft final drive (Honda NTV)**

end of the arm. Honda and BMW have both incorporated shaft drive into a single-sided swingarm, Honda on their NTV range and BMW on their 4-valve Boxer range **(see illustration 8.2j)**. BMW's 'Paralever' arm is jointed and pivots at the front and back

(just behind the main pivot with the frame and in front of the final drive housing) to counteract the effects of torque **(see illustration 8.2k)**.

The need for adjustment does not arise with shaft drive systems, which makes them simpler in this respect. However a universal joint must be fitted at the swinging arm pivot axis to allow for vertical movement, and the shaft itself must be able to slide longitudinally, either in and out of the UJ or the final drive housing, to allow for the distance variation due to vertical movement, in the same way as a chain or belt drive.

## 3  The shock absorber

### Shock absorber construction

The vast majority of shock absorbers consist of a damper unit with a coil spring fitted around it **(see**

1 Bevel drive housing
2 Pivot stub
3 Pivot bearing
4 Pivot shaft
5 Locknut
6 Plastic cap
7 Clamp
8 Gaiter
9 Clamp
10 Torque arm
11 Bolt
12 Bush
13 Washer
14 Nut
15 Circlip
16 Washer
17 Front torque arm mounting bolt/brake pedal pivot
18 Bush
19 Washer
20 Nut
21 Rear suspension unit
22 Bolt
23 Washer
24 Bush
25 Nut
26 Washer
27 Bush
28 Swinging arm
29 Plastic cap
30 Locknut
31 Pivot shaft
32 Pivot bearing
33 Grease retainer - where fitted
34 Clamp
35 Gaiter
36 Clamp

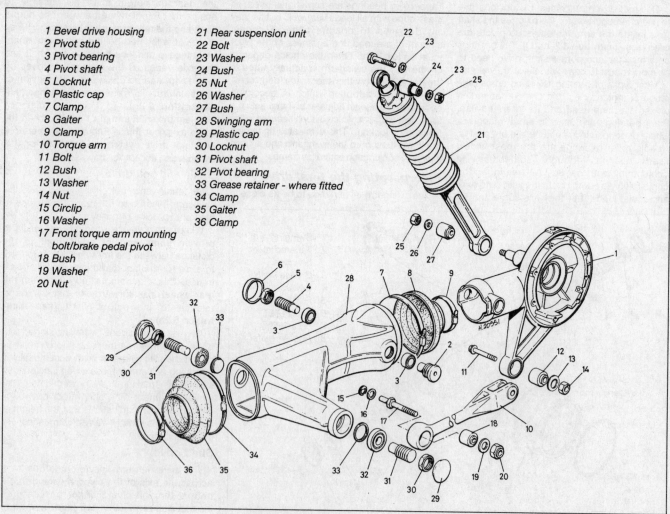

H20551

**8.2k  BMW's Paralever swingarm and final drive**

illustration 8.3a). However there are many variations on this theme, especially where damping is concerned.

The level of sophistication of the shock absorber reflects the type of machine it is fitted on. On a simple scooter, for example, the units often consist of a concentric pair of tubes with mounting lugs at each end, around (or inside) which the spring is fitted. Like the front suspension on machines of this type, no damping is provided. On larger machines more is required of the suspension system, so some form of damping must be incorporated.

Springing and damping requirements are much the same as for front suspension. For the springs a rising rate effect is desirable, and for damping different rates are required for compression and rebound and for low and high speed movement of the shock. A rising spring rate can be created to a greater or lesser degree in a number of ways, as will be shown. Damping needs are met using multi or variable rate springs or arranging different valves and shim stacks which all perform according to the speed of movement or pressure of the oil in the damper.

## Springs and springing

### Multiple and progressively-wound springs

Some degree of rising rate effect can be obtained by fitting more than one spring to the damper body. These are normally fitted one above the other, each spring being of a different rate. During the initial suspension movement, the softer of the two springs compresses quite easily, allowing the wheel to follow small irregularities in the road surface. When a larger bump is encountered, the soft spring soon becomes coil-bound, and subsequent movement is then controlled by the stiffer spring. This arrangement gives only a limited rising rate effect, and is divided into two distinct stages. Despite this, it offers a finer degree of wheel control than is possible with a single rate spring.

Progressively-wound springs, like those used in some telescopic fork legs, are designed to become coil-bound in a progressive manner from one end (see illustration 8.3b). As successive coils come into contact, the effective rate of the spring increases. Like the multiple spring units, this means that the springing becomes harder as wheel travel increases, but the effect is more progressive than would be the case with two separate springs.

### Air-assisted and air suspension units

With the simplest versions of this type of unit, the standard coil spring is supplemented by internal air pressure to give a rising spring rate. The spring provides a basic (relatively soft) spring rate, but as deflection increases the rising air pressure comes into play. The units normally have a valve through which air pressure can be set using a pump or air line. The volume of air in the units is small, so to maintain equal pressure in twin units, the two are often linked by a pressure hose (see illustration 8.3c).

The logical extension of the above is to dispense with the coil spring entirely, leaving air pressure as the sole springing medium

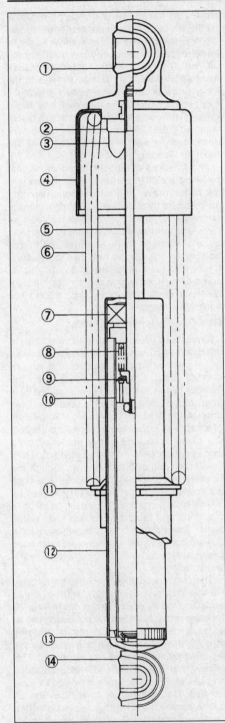

**8.3a Component parts of a basic oil damped shock absorber**

1 Upper mounting eye
2 Nut
3 Rubber stop
4 Shroud (decorative only)
5 Damper rod
6 Spring
7 Oil seal
8 Inner spring
9 Damper valve
10 Damper piston
11 Spring seat
12 Damper body
13 Compression valve
14 Lower mounting eye

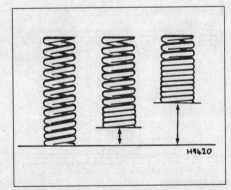

**8.3b Rising rate effect from multi rate springs**

*Note how the spring coils become progressively bound as the spring is compressed.*

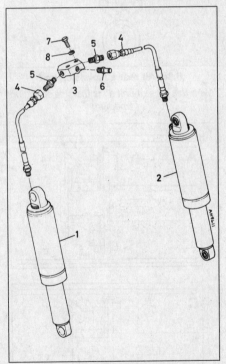

**8.3c Linked air-assisted rear suspension units**

*Where twin units are fitted, they are usually linked by a pressure hose to ensure equal pressure in the two.*

1 Left-hand suspension unit
2 Right-hand suspension unit
3 Air valve union
4 Air hoses
5 Connector
6 Air valve
7 Mounting bolt
8 Spring washer

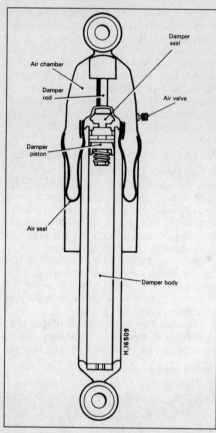

**8.3d Air rear suspension unit**

*With this type of unit air is the sole springing medium*

**(see illustration 8.3d).** Until recently units of this type were available only as rather expensive after-market items, but some of the larger Japanese tourers now fit full air suspension as standard. In its most developed form, the machine carries an on-board compressor which allows the spring rate to be raised or lowered while riding. This type of unit works very well indeed, its only real drawback being the initial expense and complexity of a full compressor-based installation.

## Damping

### Oil-damped coil-spring suspension units

The damper body takes the form of a tube in which the damper rod and piston move through a light oil. As with the front suspension, the damping effect is minimal during compression, and this allows the wheel to deflect readily when it encounters a bump in the road surface. During the extension or rebound stroke the effect is much higher, and this prevents the wheel from pattering over surface irregularities.

In its simplest form, damping is achieved by forcing oil through a small hole in the piston, but this means that the damping effect is similar in both directions. The damping rate can be made different in each direction by incorporating a simple one-way valve so that extra bleed holes are uncovered during the compression stroke only to allow relatively easy movement.

A typical valve arrangement has one or more thin flexible washers supported in a particular way at their inner and outer edges. During compression, the washer distorts under hydraulic pressure from the damping oil, which flows past the outer edge **(see illustration 8.3e).** On the rebound stroke, the inner edge of the washer opens offering a more restricted passage for the oil and thus a greater damping effect. Where two valve washers are fitted, one is used for compression damping and the other for rebound damping.

The functions of rebound and compression damping are often partially separated, so that the piston mainly controls rebound damping as it moves through the oil (though there is some damping effect on compression as well), and compression damping is controlled by a stationary valve arrangement in the bottom of the shock that has oil moving through it **(see illustration 8.3a).** This is common on double-tube shocks which have a reservoir contained in the wall around the body of the damper

### Gas-filled suspension units

Under hard use, the problem of cavitation in the damping oil can cause the damping effect to be diminished by turning the oil into an aerated foam. Cavitation occurs when the damper piston is moving faster than the oil is able to cope with. The oil is unable to flow through the valve quickly enough, so cavities of air appear in the stream of oil. The effect is the same as can be easily observed on a motorboat propeller – when it starts to turn it creates a whirl of bubbles, even though the propeller is completely under water and does not break the surface. The air is generated by the difference in pressure between one side of the blade and the other. As has been noted earlier, gas makes a poor damping medium; it can be compressed or decompressed quite easily, so the damper will 'fade' and allow the unit to bounce.

The obvious solution would seem to be to fill the damper completely with oil, thus excluding the air which causes cavitation. The problem is that dampers get hot during use as a result of the friction of the oil passing through the valves at high pressure and the repeated compression of any air present. This means that the oil expands and contracts, and so there must be some provision to allow for this. One solution is to replace the air space above the oil with a sealed bladder, usually containing nitrogen as an inert gas. Expansion can still take place, but the cavitation problem is avoided because there is no direct contact between the oil and gas.

The 'De Carbon' shock absorber (originally pioneered for cars) contains nitrogen or air under pressure above or below the oil, but separated and sealed from it by a floating piston **(see illustration 8.3f).**

### Remote reservoir units

To avoid the problem of heat build-up (which thins the damping oil, so increasing its

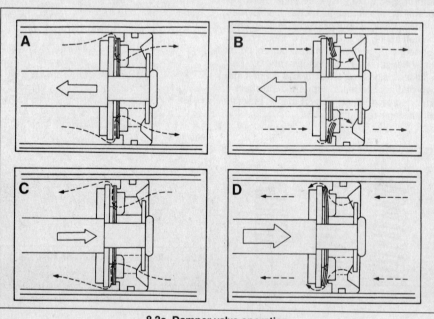

**8.3e Damper valve operation**

*In this unit a variable damping rate is obtained by using a thin spring steel washer which can deform under pressure. In drawing (A) the damping oil flows through a conventional fixed orifice to give compression damping. If the rate of compression increases, the washer will deform as shown in (B). A similar pattern occurs during rebound damping: in (C) the oil flows through the fixed orifice, whilst in (D) the washer has deformed to allow faster response.*

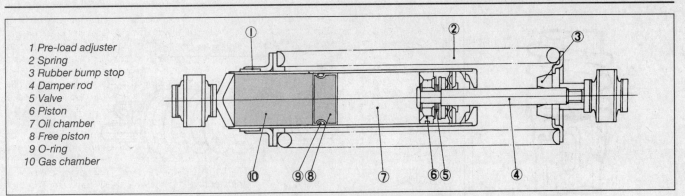

1 Pre-load adjuster
2 Spring
3 Rubber bump stop
4 Damper rod
5 Valve
6 Piston
7 Oil chamber
8 Free piston
9 O-ring
10 Gas chamber

**8.3f  De Carbon type gas-filled damper unit**

*Gas under pressure is contained at one end of the unit, separated from the damping oil by a floating piston (8).*

flow rate and thereby reducing the effectiveness of the damping), remote reservoir designs have been developed. There is a reservoir of oil attached to the shock absorber and connected to it rigidly by a passage or flexible hose **(see illustration 8.3g)**. A floating piston or bladder in the reservoir allows the unit to be pressurised as above. The damper itself contains only oil, so the heat build-up is greatly reduced. Any expansion of the oil is catered for by the reservoir.

Many of these units have an external air valve to allow the reservoir to be pressurised. This should not be confused with air-sprung or air-assisted suspension units; the air in a remote reservoir type serves only to prevent the cavitation of the damping oil.

### Rotary damping

Suzuki introduced a rotary damper system (similar to that used by the Williams F1 team) on their TL1000S V-twin and then further developed the design on the TL1000R model **(see illustration 8.3h)**.

The design separates the springing and damping functions of the traditional shock absorber to two different units. The spring unit is visibly the same as a shock absorber but with the damping function removed and transferred via a separate linkage to an oil filled cylinder containing a 'paddle' with one-way valves in it. Movement of the swingarm is translated into rotary movement of the paddle in the oil, which provides resistance regulated by the valves through which the oil must pass.

### *Adjustable spring pre-load and damping*

Many of the more sophisticated shock absorbers are adjustable, giving the facility to set up the unit for almost any conceivable use or condition. The need for adjustment really serves to underline the fact that the shock absorber can only work at its best under fine limits of loading and surface type, but the provision of adjustment does at least go some way towards compensating for its weaknesses.

### Spring pre-load

All but the simplest types of suspension

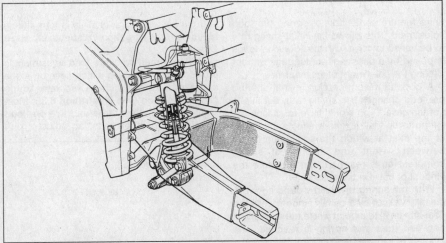

**8.3g  Shock with separate gas/oil reservoir (Yamaha FZR1000)**

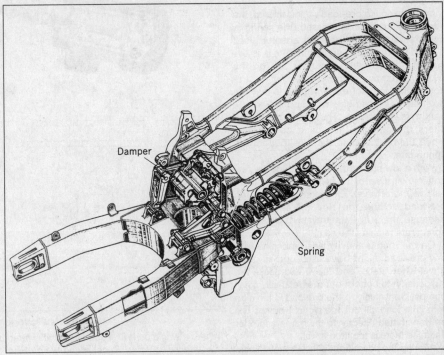

Damper

Spring

**8.3h  Rotary damper system (Suzuki TL1000S)**

**8.3i Spring pre-load adjuster**

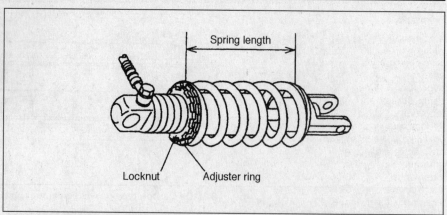

**8.3j A thread type adjuster and locknut gives linear as opposed to staged adjustment**

units feature some sort of spring pre-load adjustment. This allows the initial spring rate to be varied to cope with the additional loads imposed by a passenger or luggage without altering the ride height of the machine.

A popular misconception is that altering pre-load changes the spring rate, but this is not the case – you would have to change the spring to do that. It merely affects the height of the seat at which the equilibrium point between weight and amount of spring compression is reached, and therefore the amount of travel in the suspension.

With the spring pre-load wound right off, the bike will sag by a certain amount when the rider sits on it; to a point where the equilibrium between rider and spring is reached. The amount of sag will be significant because the spring is very 'soft' to start with, and will compress by a large amount.

With the spring pre-load wound fully up, the spring is already compressed (the spring is compressed, but not the shock absorber itself – the distance between its mountings is the same), and so when the rider sits on the bike it hardly compresses before the equilibrium is reached. This means that the bike hasn't sagged so much, and so the ride height is increased. Thus spring pre-load alters the amount the spring compresses when the rider sits on the bike, but not the spring rate.

With a low pre-load setting the ride will feel softer over a series of bumps because there will be more travel. Conversely with a high pre-load setting the ride will feel harder because there is less travel; however the spring rate remains the same.

On the road a heavily laden machine with low pre-load might have used up half of its travel when static, and this would cause the suspension to bottom out over relatively small bumps. Conversely, if the pre-load is too high with little load, all but the biggest bumps will be transmitted directly to the frame and rider because there is too little travel.

Altering the ride height affects many things, including steering geometry (rake and trail)

and the centre of gravity. This in turn affects handling and traction respectively (see Chapter 8).

The usual method of pre-load adjustment is provided by a cam ring which rides on stops and can be turned with a C-spanner to the desired position **(see illustration 8.3i)**. Most units have between three and five pre-load positions. On other units, an adjuster ring

threads onto the damper body against the upper or lower spring seat, and thus can be screwed up or down to the desired setting **(see illustration 8.3j)**. A locknut ensures the adjuster cannot come loose. Remote hydraulic adjusters are also used where access to the shock absorber itself is restricted by its position or by bodywork **(see illustration 8.3k)**.

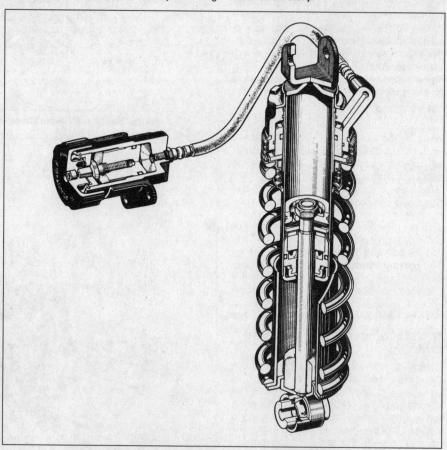

**8.3k Hydraulic spring pre-load adjustment**

*Where a single central suspension unit is fitted it can be impossible to reach a conventional mechanical adjuster. To get round the problem the pre-load is set by a remote hydraulic control linked to the unit by a hose.*

## Damping

Adjusting the damping varies the rate at which the oil is able to move by varying the size of the orifices it moves through. Damping adjustment can be varied in one or both of two ways, when the shock absorber compresses and when it extends or rebounds.

Damping is usually controlled from an adjuster that either moves a needle in or out of an oilway, or it turns a cylinder to align a different size orifice with the oilway (see illustration 8.3l). Both increase or decrease the flow rate of oil through the oilway. Alternatively, the adjuster may increase or decrease the amount of pre-load on a coil spring which sits on the shim stack or on one thick shim covering an oil passage, making the shim(s) easier or more difficult to deflect or lift.

On certain designs needle adjusters are incorporated into a heat sensitive capsule that contains a wax or liquid that expands with heat. As the shock absorber heats up and the damping oil thins (reducing viscosity and so increasing flow), the wax or liquid expands and pushes the needle further into the oilway to inhibit the flow and so restore the damping to its original rate. The needle lifts again when the temperature drops.

The three adjustments (spring pre-load, rebound and compression damping) are frequently found together in the most sophisticated shocks, giving a wide range of possible combinations. Other shocks may only provide adjustment on one or two of the three possibilities, usually depending on the needs of the machine and its intended use.

The performance of non-adjustable shocks can be altered by varying the amount and/or viscosity of the damping oil, fitting a spring with a different rate, or altering the damping characteristics by enlarging the oil flow holes or varying shim stacks.

## 4  Rear suspension arrangements

### *Rising rate suspension*

Just as the front forks benefit from some arrangement whereby the spring rate can be progressively increased as the suspension is compressed, so too does the rear suspension. To some extent this can be achieved in much the same way, by fitting multi-rate or progressively-wound springs, or by including air or some other gas as a supplementary springing medium.

### Inclined suspension units

With a normal twin-shock arrangement, a single rising rate effect can be obtained by inclining the units in relation to the swinging arm (see illustration 8.4a).

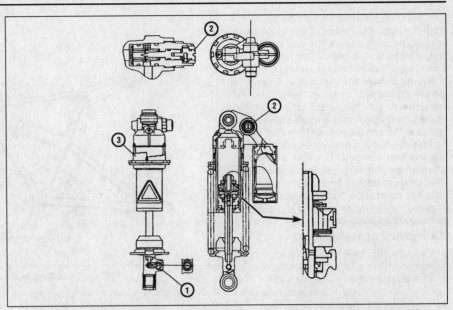

**8.3l  Rebound damping (1), compression damping (2) and pre-load adjuster (3)**

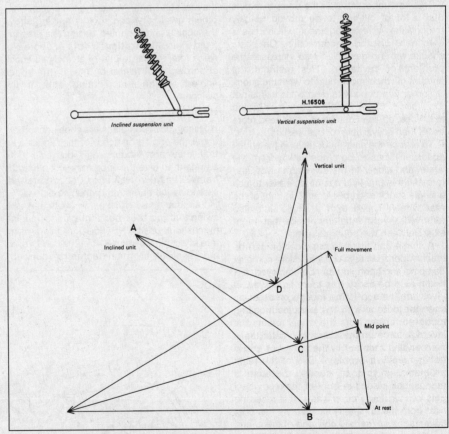

**8.4a  Rising rate effect from inclined suspension units**

*When the swinging arm is at rest the suspension unit length (A to B) is exactly the same for the inclined and vertical unit. As the swinging arm moves upwards and consequently the suspension unit becomes compressed the amount of compression of the vertical unit is greater than that of the inclined unit (A to C). At full swinging arm movement (A to D) the amount of compression of the vertical unit is progressively greater than that of the inclined unit.*

*In each case the distance from the 'at rest' to mid point positions of the swinging arm is exactly the same as the mid point to full movement positions.*

If the units are fitted at right angles to the swinging arm, the amount of rear wheel travel is roughly proportional to the amount of suspension unit travel. If the front upper mounting is moved forward, leaving the unit at a steeper angle to the swinging arm, the initial wheel movement takes up very little unit movement, but this relationship becomes more proportional as the angle between the unit and the arm increases. The result of this is that the initial wheel movement is softly sprung and damped, but that it becomes increasingly stiff as the deflection continues. This principle offers a limited rising rate effect and has been used for many years, but to improve the overall range more sophisticated techniques are required.

### Twin shock or monoshock?

Because of the general layout of a motorcycle, twin shock absorbers have to be positioned quite close to the back of the bike, usually with the lower shock mounting close to the line of the wheel axle. This means that the shock absorber travel is roughly the same as wheel travel when going over a bump.

This amount of travel in the damper means that a lot of oil has to be moved quickly through the valve arrangement, which causes it to heat up and become thin. On basic shocks with no gas cell it also increases the problem of cavitation. This restricts the amount of wheel movement to what the shock absorber can cope with, and while this is not too much of a problem on road-going machines, off-road machines often need more travel than is available for best results.

To reduce the amount of travel in the shock absorber it has to be placed away from the wheel and closer to the swingarm pivot, and to make this practical it is much easier to use a single shock absorber located in front of the rear wheel. The use of a single unit also removes any potential imbalance that might exist between two separate units.

A single unit fitted in this position can be much wider than twin units, so more complex damping and springing can be employed, but it can also be shorter as there is less travel involved. The sub-frame mounting has to be stronger to cope with the extra loads (being mounted further from the wheel means the leverage force on the shock is greater, as is the bending moment in the arm), but this is not generally a problem. One of the main problems is that of cooling because a monoshock placed in front of the rear wheel gets less air-flow around it as well as receiving heat from the engine. A monoshock has cost advantages as there is only one of them, and weight advantages, both in overall weight and unsprung weight.

### Cantilever suspension

The first monoshock arrangements used a triangulated swingarm, with the shock absorber mounted between the triangular section and part of the frame, and this was known as 'cantilever suspension'. Some

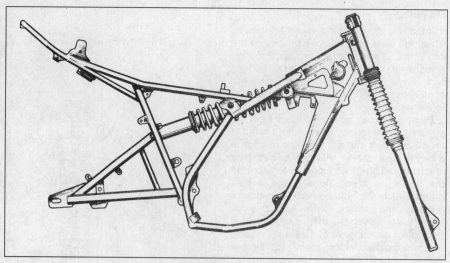

**8.4b  Cantilever suspension**

*In its simplest form, cantilever suspension uses a triangulated swinging arm with a single suspension unit located below the seat and fuel tank.*

models used short shocks that mounted on the rear sub-frame (Vincent in the fifties), while others used very long shocks running above the engine and mounted behind the steering head **(see illustration 8.4b)**. A degree of rising rate, similar to that of an inclined shock absorber, is obtained by having the shock angled to the triangulating arm of the swingarm.

### Horizontal shocks

Harley-Davidson place the shock absorbers under the engine on some of their models so that they are hidden, and disguise their swingarm to give the appearance of a hardtail frame. They use twin shock absorbers that extend over a bump rather than compress.

Yamaha used a linkage between the swingarm and their horizontal under-engine monoshock on the RD500LC to give a rising rate effect **(illustration 8.4c)**. Buell and Voxon are two other manufacturers currently

positioning the shock horizontally under the engine, and Suzuki did so (though not quite under the engine) on their TL1000S as the rotary damper was located where the shock would normally have been.

### *Rising rate linkages*

Rising rate monoshock rear suspension systems are now common-place, and by using a three-way linkage represent the mechanical answer (if a rather complicated one) to the problem of obtaining a rising rate system with sufficient range to cover all possible operating conditions. This is particularly true of off-road machines, but it also applies to road models. The linkage means that the spring can be a simple single-rate one.

The various systems currently in use differ widely in appearance, but do the same job in practice. In each case the effect described

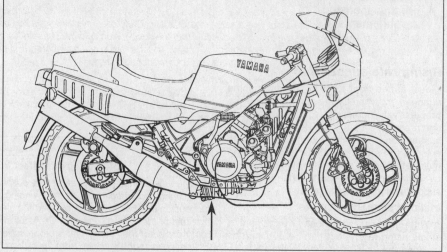

**8.4c  Shock absorber position on the Yamaha RD500LC**

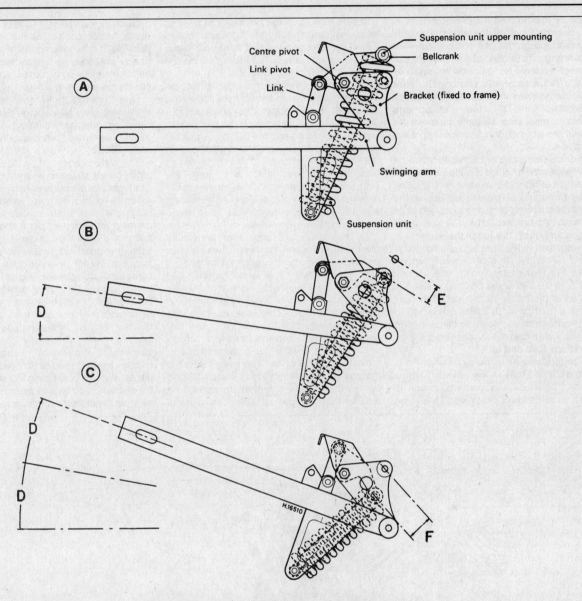

**8.4d  Rising-rate rear suspension system operation**

The accompanying sequence of line drawings shows the operation of a rising-rate suspension system in three stages; at rest, at half travel and at full travel. The arrangement shown is Suzuki's Full Floater system, so called because the suspension unit is not attached to the frame at any point, but is allowed to "float" within the suspension linkage. The relative movement of the linkage components has been exaggerated somewhat in the interests of clarity, and it should be remembered that the rising rate effect operates progressively throughout the range of wheel travel: there are no clearly-defined stages.

**A** Here we see the major components of the "Full Floater" rear suspension system. The single most important item is the bellcrank, shown in dotted lines where it would otherwise be masked by other components. It will be noted that the bellcrank has three pivot points, the link pivot and centre pivot being closer together than are the centre pivot and suspension unit upper mounting. It is the changing relationship between these three pivot points which creates the rising rate effect at the suspension unit in response to linear movement of the swinging arm.

**B** If the swinging arm is moved through a fixed distance (D), movement is transmitted through the link to the link pivot of the bellcrank. The centre pivot of the bellcrank is fixed in relation to the frame, so the bellcrank pivots at this point, pushing the top of the suspension unit downwards by a small amount (E).

**C** If we move the swinging arm further, but through the same distance (D) as shown above, the bellcrank again turns about the centre pivot, pushing the top of the suspension unit downwards. In this position, however, the altered geometry of the bellcrank causes the suspension unit to be compressed further than it was in the previous stage – compare (E) and (F). It will be seen that as the swinging arm deflects further it must compress the suspension unit by a proportionally greater amount. In practice this means that the initial travel of the rear wheel is softly sprung and damped, allowing it to follow closely any surface irregularities. Over more drastic bumps the system offers progressively greater resistance and is thus able to cope with a wide variety of surfaces.

previously for inclined suspension units is used, but the range of the effect is greatly increased through the use of a bell crank or similar linkage. To understand the workings of a typical system, let us look in detail at Suzuki's Full Floater suspension. The term 'full floater' comes from the fact the shock compresses from the top and bottom, whereas on most other systems the top of the shock is mounted on the frame and so does not move.

The Suzuki arrangement is based around a single, vertically mounted suspension unit located just in front of the rear wheel. The unit passes through a U-shaped cut-out at the front of the swinging arm, and is located at its lower end to a bracket just to the rear of the swinging arm pivot. The top of the suspension unit is attached to the front end of a specially-shaped bell crank via a pivot arrangement. Just to the rear of this point, and slightly below it, is the bell crank pivot by which it is attached to the frame. At the rear of the bell crank is a third pivot, this time connected to the tie-rods which run down to the swingarm at a point just behind the suspension unit **(see illustrations 8.4d and e)**.

To understand how the system works it should be noted that as the swinging arm is deflected upwards, the suspension unit is pushed up at the lower mounting. At the same

time, the rods force the bell crank to pivot at its frame mounting, so the front end moves down, compressing the unit from both ends. The rising rate effect is introduced by the shape of the bell crank and the relative positions of its three pivot points. At rest, the angle formed between the tie-rods, the tie rod pivots and the bell crank frame pivot is about 90°, whilst the angle between the suspension unit, its top mount and the bell crank pivot is roughly half this. This means in practice that the maximum amount of leverage exists between the swinging arm and the suspension unit, so the initial movement is relatively easy; the suspension unit deflecting a small amount in response to a large movement at the rear wheel.

As the swinging arm approaches its maximum deflection, however, these angles are changed quite drastically. The original right-angle between the tie-rods and the bell crank has become much more acute, whilst the suspension unit to bell crank angle is approaching 90°. This means that the leverage exerted by the swinging arm has become far less, and the movement of the unit must be greater for a corresponding movement at the wheel. The overall effect is that the spring rate increases steadily as the swinging arm moves further upwards, and with it the damping effect. This is more useful

than changing the spring rate alone, giving much better control at the rear wheel. If possible, it is suggested that the effect of this or any similar rising rate system is observed on a motorcycle so that the changing leverage can be more easily studied.

Every manufacturer now has their own three-way rising rate linkage design, some of which are marginally different in arrangement to that described, but basically all have the same effect.

The advantages of a full rising rate arrangement are clear when compared to the fixed rate of a simple twin-unit arrangement or a cantilever mono-shock arrangement. Full rising rate systems are now a common fitment on most motorcycles, but it should be noted that they are not without disadvantages. Apart from the practical problems of siting the suspension unit where it does not obstruct some other component, and where it can still be cooled by the airflow past the machine, there is the question of wear. With three or more extra pivot points in the suspension, the build-up of play in the various bushes and bearings will eventually cause sloppy suspension movement. Another problem involves keeping road dirt and water out of the pivots which will ultimately increase friction in the pivots and so reduce performance; not an easy job given their vulnerable location.

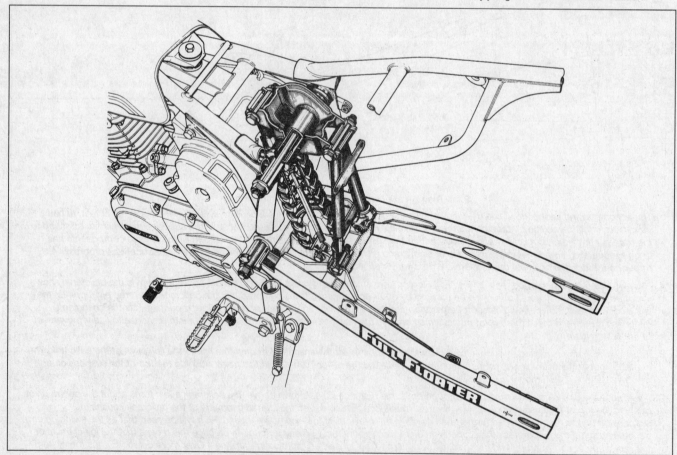

**8.4e  Suzuki 'Full Floater' suspension (DR125)**

# Chapter 9
# Frames and handling

## Contents

### 1 Introduction

#### The purpose of the frame

The frame has several purposes which come under the headings of 'structural' and 'geometrical'.

From a structural point of view, the frame must locate and support the engine, transmission, suspension and all ancillaries. To do this effectively it must be rigid and strong, and preferably light.

From a geometrical point of view, the frame must provide the desired steering and suspension geometry, wheelbase, and centre of gravity. Furthermore, and very important, the frame must hold the wheels in line, and be rigid enough be able to keep them in line under the forces of cornering, acceleration and braking without affecting steering and suspension. The key factors here are the steering head and the swingarm pivot – the frame has to hold the steering head in a vertical plane and the swingarm pivot in a lateral horizontal plane, and maintain their perpendicularity at all times.

It is these factors which have governed frame designs since the very first motorcycles appeared. Without adequate strength and rigidity in the frame, the resulting flexing between the front and rear wheels can be anything from mildly disconcerting to downright dangerous. Not only can a poor frame make the machine difficult or unpleasant to ride, it can detract from the benefits of the engine, enforcing a wary riding style which would leave the model outclassed by more sophisticated rivals. There have been countless examples of this in racing over the years where machines with superior frames but poor engines have triumphed over rivals with superior engines and dubious chassis.

In the commercial world of road-going machines there are other factors which govern the type of frame eventually chosen for a particular model, and in this context cost and fashion have almost as much significance as the frame's actual performance. What is undeniable is the fact that a well-engineered frame can transform almost any machine. The attention to detail that is possible only with small production runs (and the resulting high costs) explains why after-market frame kits continue in popularity. It is in the rather rarefied specialist areas occupied by the racing frame manufacturers, and the road frame equivalents like Bimota and Harris, that the blend of instinct, science and craftsmanship are most evident.

## 2 Weight distribution and the centre of gravity

The distribution of the weight of all the components on a motorcycle determines the centre of gravity of the machine as a whole. Motorcycle design does not leave much scope for altering the general position of major components such as the engine, the front and rear suspension and the fuel tank, and fortunately the layout of these components is fairly convenient for the overall weight distribution. But even so, minor alterations in the centre of gravity can have a marked effect on the handling of a machine.

There are two main areas of importance that the centre of gravity influences, firstly acceleration and braking, and secondly cornering. But it will probably surprise you that its importance in cornering has less influence on its position for designers than in acceleration and braking.

The centre of gravity determines the amount of weight transfer under acceleration and braking forces, and therefore has a pronounced effect on the amount of traction in the tyres.

If the centre of gravity were in the ideal position, under acceleration the rear wheel would start to spin just as the front wheel leaves the ground, and under braking the front wheel would start to lock just as the rear wheel leaves the ground. If the centre of gravity is high, 'wheelies' and 'stoppies' are easy without losing traction. If the centre of gravity is low the tyre will always spin or lock before a wheelie or stoppie is achieved.

Weight transfer is greater with a high centre of gravity, and this tends to improve traction. Under acceleration it is desirable to have as much traction as possible through the rear tyre and under braking you want as much traction as possible through the front tyre, and

the centre of gravity on a racing bike is set so that this is obtained, which is why they spend so much time on one wheel! The length of the wheelbase is also influential on traction – if you extend the wheelbase while maintaining the height of the centre of the gravity, you will in fact lose traction because of the relative angles between the wheels.

When cornering equal grip through both tyres is desirable, meaning a centre of gravity that is central in the wheelbase. The height, however, is a compromise. A high centre of gravity will give more traction which allows greater acceleration (or braking if you get it all wrong) through the corner. A high centre of gravity also means a smaller lean angle for a given radius of turn. However a low centre of gravity means less inertia about the roll axis, which makes it more responsive to steering input. On the road this makes it feel less top heavy and more flickable, and easier to control at low speeds or in a slide.

So once again a major design aspect is a total compromise situation – you change the centre of gravity and it has some positive effects and some negative. As with all other aspects of design, it is the intended use and purpose of the machine that determine the required characteristics – there is no best way to cover all situations.

## 3 Frame construction and materials

### Construction

Originally sections of steel tube were held together at various points by lugs which formed the steering head and swingarm mounting points. Before welding was commonly used, the tubes passed through the lugs and were braised. The increase in the use of welding meant that the tubes merely

had to be butted against the lugs to form the joint, and welding remains the most universal joining method for the most commonly used materials, steel and aluminium (see illustration 9.3a).

The use of composite materials in frame construction brings with it different methods of fabrication, and the use of the engine as a 'stressed member' has resulted in frames becoming ever smaller and lighter, and in some cases almost obsolete.

### Triangulation

The traditional approach to frame design is based on triangulation, and this is well illustrated in the standard bicycle frame and the modern trellis frame (see illustration 9.3b). The bicycle frame is commonly known as a diamond frame by virtue of its shape. The diamond shape is divided into two triangles by a tube running between the saddle and the pedal crank area. This gives the diamond great strength and rigidity, each tube being effectively braced against bending. The same approach is employed in most old and many current motorcycle frame designs.

Frames that appear poorly triangulated are often making use of the engine as a 'stressed member' by having it mounted in three places between open sections of frame. This works very well as the engine itself is very stiff, and saves weight overall by having less frame. This gives a good strength-to-weight ratio. Frames such as a trellis frame are however expensive to build as there are lots of welded joints, and can reduce access to certain areas for servicing.

### Strengthening stressed areas

Strengthening around areas of stress is achieved using braces, gussets and sleeving around the joints and between the sections of tube (see illustrations 9.4a and 9.4b). However anything like this that stiffens sections of frame, and indeed even the addition of brackets that hold various

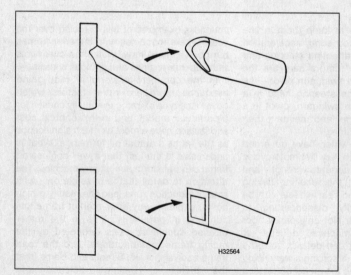

9.3a  Methods of joining tubes

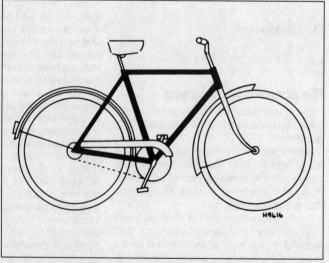

9.3b  The bicycle frame showing simple triangulation

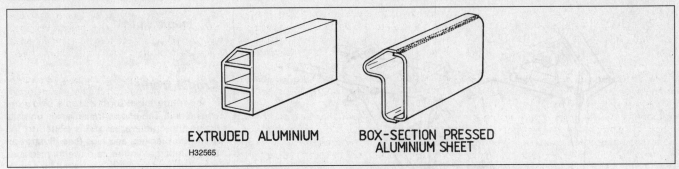

EXTRUDED ALUMINIUM
H32565

BOX-SECTION PRESSED
ALUMINIUM SHEET

**9.3c Cross-sections showing different methods of constructing an aluminium beam frame**

components, can increase the resonant frequency of the frame which can cause fatigue and cracking.

### Avoiding stress raisers

At points where a frame uses gussets or sleeves for strengthening, or where a frame tube is joined to a heavier and stiffer component, there is a possibility of actually increasing stress at the joint by making the strengthener too stiff in comparison to the frame tube itself.

This is avoided by curving gussets gently into the frame or by tapering frame lugs. Sleeving tubes have their ends cut at an angle or in a fishtail shape.

### Design

Modern design techniques allow a prototype frame to be 'built' on the computer screen, and then subjected to various loading and vibration simulations. As a result, the frame geometry can be developed well in advance of the physical prototype stage. From the initial use of these techniques it soon became evident that most of the tubes in the frame needed to be much stronger in one plane than the other. Round tubing has the same strength in all directions, whereas a square or rectangle has greater strength in one direction to another. As a result, square or rectangular section tubing can be used to provide added rigidity where needed, and to reduce unnecessary weight where loadings are light.

Where the frame uses the engine as a stressed member, the mounting points on the engine itself must be designed to cope with the extra forces imparted on it, and so ultimately need to be stronger than the same engine in a cradle frame. It is interesting to note that using the engine as a stressed member is nothing new, as Vincent did so very successfully in the fifties.

Ultimately the design of the bike itself and its intended use determine the material used and the shape of a frame.

## Materials

### Steel

Steel has been the most widely used material since motorcycles were first thought of. Its low cost and strength make it an obvious choice, and the fact that it can be easily shaped and welded, not to mention repaired, still makes it the first choice in many applications. Its only problem is that of weight where performance applications demand extreme strength and stiffness for as little weight as possible. To provide the required strength the frame would simply be too heavy.

Pressed steel is also used in many scooter applications as it is cheaper than tube steel. But one of the main problems is corrosion on the inside of the frame caused by trapped water, which can go unnoticed and is very difficult to repair.

### Aluminium

Aluminium alloy has become the best alternative. It has roughly one third the strength and one third the weight of steel, so you would assume that three times as much would be needed to make as good a frame as steel. But stiffness comes with area of material, and an aluminium frame that is as strong and heavy as a steel one is in fact much stiffer. So stiffness is increased without extra weight, or alternatively you could get the same stiffness as steel for a reduced weight.

Where large area sections of aluminium are used, the aluminium is extruded through a mould in a semi-molten state to create a triangulated or boxed cross-section, which greatly increases stiffness **(see illustration 9.3c)**. It also means that the outer walls can be thinner. Aluminium can also be cast, forged and laminated quite easily, and so can be shaped to give optimum weight and stiffness for any particular application. The problem is that compared to steel it is relatively expensive, and more difficult to repair.

### Magnesium

Magnesium is a very light material and therefore an obvious choice, if it weren't for several drawbacks. It has very poor resistance to oxidation unless it is treated with expensive coatings. It is not as strong as aluminium and so bulk would be needed, but the weight factor would not make this a problem. However it is very difficult to weld, which makes it a poor choice for frames, and it is very expensive. In applications where pieces do not need to be joined, such as wheels and engine covers, it is a good choice.

### Titanium

With titanium now being more affordable it is used in certain racing applications for sub-frames, but not for main frames. Future applications of titanium depend on its cost and competition with composite materials. Titanium has similar properties to steel but is very much lighter and does not corrode.

### Composites

Composite materials such as carbon or Kevlar combined with a resinous matrix and sometimes an aluminium honeycomb can provide immense stiffness in particular directions of stress when structured in a certain way. This makes the manufacturing process very costly.

With further research, however, the manufacture of composites will provide the designer with materials which are extremely effective for particular situations while remaining very light. They are definitely the materials of the future.

| A comparison of relevant material properties | | | | | |
|---|---|---|---|---|---|
| | Breaking strength (N/sq.mm) | Shear modulus (N/sq.mm) | Specific weight (N/cu.mm) | Specific strength (mm) | Specific rigidity (mm) |
| Steel | 1250 | 210 | 78.6 | 15.9 | 2672 |
| Aluminium alloy | 420 | 72 | 27 | 15.6 | 2667 |
| Magnesium | 260 | 45 | 18 | 14.4 | 2500 |
| Titanium | 800 | 112 | 45 | 17.8 | 2533 |
| High shear modulus carbon | 1300 | 200 | 16 | 81.3 | 12500 |
| Kevlar | 1200 | 85 | 14 | 85.7 | 6071 |

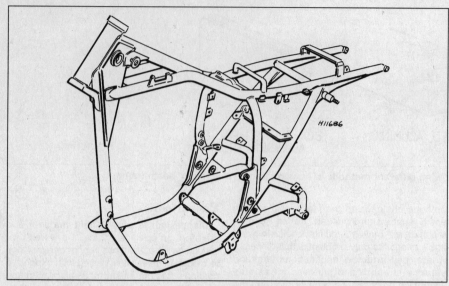

**9.4a  A cradle frame**

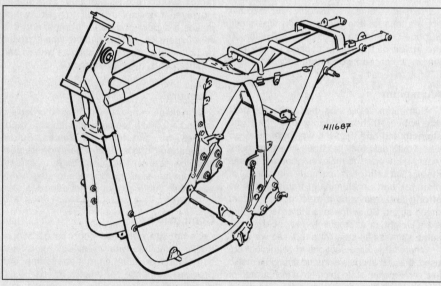

**9.4b  A duplex cradle frame**

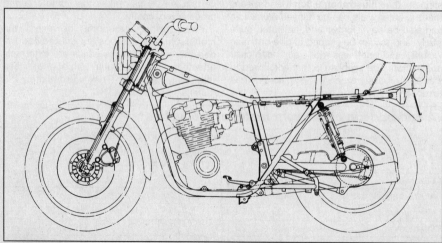

**9.4c  Side view of a typical tubular steel duplex cradle frame showing engine and suspension location points**

## 4  Frame types

### Cradle frames

The frame tubes form a cradle below the engine unit. The engine/transmission unit sits inside the cradle area and is bolted to the frame via brackets and lugs **(see illustration 9.4a)**. On larger and more powerful machines the cradle and top tubes are paired for greater strength in torsion, and this results in a duplex cradle frame **(see illustration 9.4b)**. In the case of the cradle frame, the engine/transmission assembly is a passive element and merely sits inside the frame loop(s) **(see illustration 9.4c)**. Cradle frames are usually constructed in tubular steel, though there are also many examples in box-section steel.

### Trellis frames

The tubes can be either round or square, as long as they are straight **(see illustration 9.4d)**. The frame consists of many small sections welded together to form triangles. The engine is used as a stressed member to form a very rigid and lightweight structure.

### Beam frames

Beam frames basically comprise two large beams extending from the steering head back to the swingarm pivot (unless the swingarm pivots on the engine itself) **(see illustration 9.4e)**. They all use the engine as a stressed member. There are many variations on the theme, and consequently many brand names associated with them, such as the perimeter or pentagon frame and the deltabox frame.

Most beam frames are constructed in box-section aluminium, though some use steel. An interesting departure is the oval section aluminium tubing in a twin spar arrangement as used by Triumph **(see illustration 9.4f)**.

In the case of aluminium frames, the material can be either cast, extruded, or laminated, and often one frame will contain examples of each process, the best process being used for the purpose of the particular section.

### Spine frames

The spine frame is used extensively on a number of scooters and mopeds and is well suited to mass production techniques. The main frame section is sometimes a T-shape formed by two pressed steel halves welded together along the centreline **(see illustration 9.4g)**. The effective diameter of the spine is quite large, providing good resistance against twisting.

In addition, the spine can be used to form or to house such things as the fuel tank, toolbox, air filter and the electrical fittings, to produce a clean and uncluttered machine. The initial design of the frame is often more

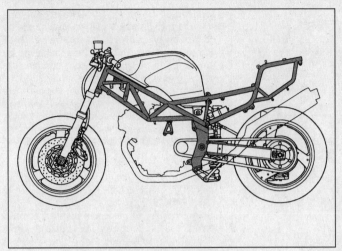

9.4d A trellis type frame

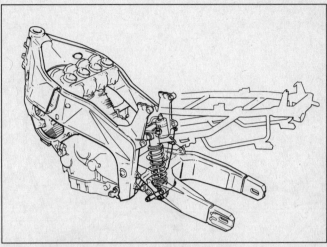

9.4e Yamaha's Deltabox beam frame - with the engine in place it is easy to see how it is used as a stressed member

difficult to finalise than an equivalent tubular version (see illustration 9.4h), but once it has been established it can be produced cheaply and quickly from the two basic steel pressings.

In the past there have been a number of larger machines built around a central spine section, but these were not generally well received by the public, who seem to prefer a 'proper' tubular steel frame. The technique itself has survived, however, and almost all current models feature small pressed steel sections and gussets in some areas of the frame. This is usually due to manufacturing considerations where an all-tubular construction would be prohibitively labour intensive; it is much easier to robot-weld a hybrid frame than to hand-assemble a collection of individual tubes.

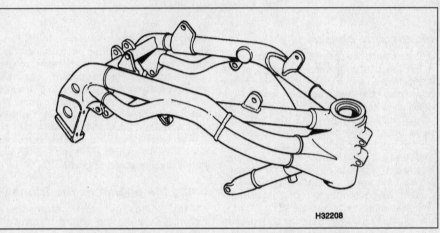

H32208

9.4f Triumph's twin spar oval section aluminium beam frame

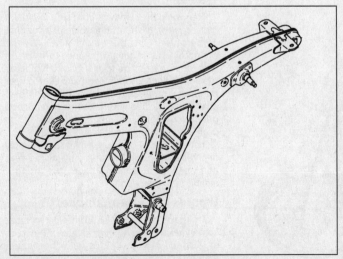

9.4g Typical fabricated spine frame

*The T-shaped frame is made up from two sheet steel pressings welded together along the centre line. The designs allows the battery, air filter and other minor components to be housed inside the frame.*

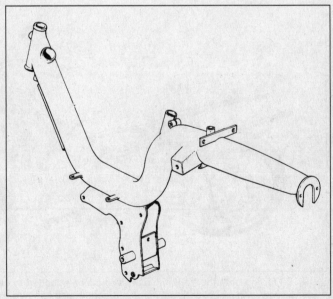

9.4h Tubular spine frame

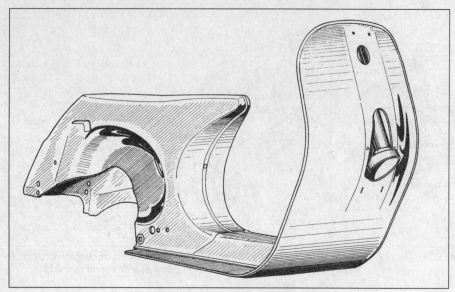

**9.4i  A monocoque chassis**

### Monocoque chassis

The monocoque chassis or body is a logical extension of the welded pressings of the spine frame, and can be found on a few production machines **(see illustration 9.4i)**. It is the same technique that has been adopted almost exclusively on post-war cars, and relies on a number of sheet steel pressings welded together to form a stiff and lightweight structure. This provides the structural equivalent of a frame and also any bodywork.

The best known example is the metal-bodied Vespa scooter which has survived with few fundamental changes since just after the second World War. The main body section is formed by two large steel pressings welded together along the centre line, much like a large spine frame. This is extended with further pressings to form the steering column, legshields and the footboard area. The various pressings are combined to give a fairly light structure, but with immense rigidity. The alternative approach, using a tubular frame clad with steel body panels, would be both weaker and heavier, and in practice the only non-structural panels are items like the side panels and the front mudguard.

### Using the engine as the frame

While there are many examples of motorcycles using the engine to pivot the swingarm, so doing away with the side sections of the frame, BMW have gone one stage further on their 4-valve Boxer range by doing away with a main frame **(see illustration 9.4j)**. This has been achieved by the adoption of Telelever front suspension, which pivots on the engine, and two sub-frames, one at the front to support the steering arrangement and the fuel tank, and one at the rear for the seat. Both sub-frames bolt to the engine and each other, and it is the engine that takes all the stress, not just part of it.

### 5  Handling

The parameters which define the handling characteristics of a motorcycle are all determined on the drawing board at the design stage. The type of bike determines how it will be used, and steering geometry and wheelbase are set to give it handling that suits its purpose. A sports bike will be set up with a narrow rake angle and a short wheelbase so that it will turn quickly. A touring bike will have a longer wheelbase, giving it straight line stability. Once all these parameters are set it is very difficult to alter them in any influential way, with the exception of minor changes through suspension pre-load adjustments.

In use the way a bike handles is influenced by many other things, including suspension settings, tyre choice and pressures, after-market fairings, panniers and top boxes, poor weight distribution of luggage, the addition of a passenger, and so on.

So what causes a bike to misbehave and what can be done about it?

### Weave

The whole bike weaves from side to side at high speed, more noticeably in sweeping corners than in a straight line. Weight distribution is often the cause – too much luggage, too high and too far back. Handlebar mounted fairings, top fairings and even empty panniers can also upset things. Even changing to a different make tyre can upset a previously good set-up, especially if the profile isn't perfectly suited to the bike.

Increasing tyre pressures by one or two psi or increasing rebound damping at the rear and maybe the front will help, but fitting a steering damper won't.

### Wobble (aka 'tankslapper')

The handlebars shake from side to side, sometimes increasing in amplitude if it occurs at a speed that coincides with the natural frequency of the steered mass. Often caused by hitting a bump, especially exiting a corner under acceleration. Incorrect damping set-up at the rear combined with a steering or frame problem may also have an influence.

**9.4j  By having both the front and rear suspension attached to the engine, BMW have done away with a conventional frame altogether, and use sub-frames to support the steering, fuel tank and seat**

The front tyre may not be running true or the wheel could be out of balance. Otherwise there may be too much weight over the steering (instruments, headlight etc). A good fork brace or a stiffer axle may also cure the problem. A steering damper will reduce the effects, but only masks the problem without solving it.

### Wallow

The bike alternately sinks and rises when exiting a corner with the power on. Subtly different from a weave, though sometimes difficult to tell the difference.

A rear suspension problem, usually too little damping and possibly too low a spring rate. Increasing rebound damping is the first step. Increasing spring pre-load is unlikely to improve things without upsetting other things unless the suspension has a steep rising rate. It is better to change the spring itself to one of a different rate but keep the same amount of sag. If it only happens at speed and under hard acceleration increasing the rear tyre pressure may help.

### Patter

Patter can be a problem on almost every bike – the wheel is unable to react quickly enough to a succession of small bumps due to the inertia of the unsprung mass. Instead of following the contours the wheel jumps off the top of one bump and hits the next one half way up. In a corner the rear wheel will patter going in under braking, and the front wheel will patter coming out under acceleration.

Too much stiction in the rear shock or forks may be the problem, but there is little you can do about that except clean and lubricate the sliding parts. It is more likely that there is too much compression damping or too high a spring rate. Reducing unsprung mass makes the problem easier to cure, especially if it is add-on components that have caused the increase.

### Understeer

This is when the bike doesn't want to go round the corner. The front tyre is operating at a higher slip angle (the angle between where the tyre is pointing and where it is going) than the rear, making it slide or drift more than the rear – the bike must be steered more into the corner to hold the line.

Increasing the weight over the front wheel, either by redistributing it or adding some, will reduce it, as will reducing tyre pressure slightly or fitting a tyre with more grip. Opening the throttle earlier in the corner should also help.

### Oversteer

The opposite of understeer, where the bike drops into the corner due to the rear tyre doing what the front tyre does in understeer.

More weight at the rear, a lower rear tyre pressure, or a tyre with more grip, will reduce oversteer.

### Bottoming out

The suspension runs out of travel under compression and results in a large bang or thump through the frame. Whether at the front or the rear, it means there is no suspension left. If it happens occasionally over very large bumps when laden it is not too much of a problem, and in some ways to be expected on a softly sprung bike. If it is happening over small bumps when unladen then a stiffer spring and more compression damping is needed.

Bottoming out could be indicative of damping valve failure. The worst case scenario is if you bottom out at the front through excessive fork dive under heavy braking, and then hit a bump – jarred wrists are a certainty.

### Topping out

The opposite of bottoming out, where the suspension runs out of travel on extension. Either too much pre-load or not nearly enough rebound damping are likely causes.

## 6  Bodywork

### The purpose of bodywork

Bodywork serves many purposes. On a scooter, it protects the rider from wind and rain; it also keeps vital electrical components protected and hides other components to improve aesthetics.

On a sports bike it enhances the aerodynamics of the machine and so improves performance; it reduces the wind blast on the rider which makes it easier to ride the bike; it can improve handling by having a downforce effect to improve traction; it can also enhance the looks of a bike which helps the manufacturer make sales, and provides a platform for paintwork and advertising.

On a touring bike it does all of the above things to extremes, providing the ultimate in weather protection and so giving maximum rider comfort; it also provides storage capacity for luggage and accessories.

### Types of bodywork

All motorcycles have bodywork of some description, varying from a simple plastic mudguard to a fully enclosed fairing system.

Mudguards over the front and rear wheels are standard, with the rear mudguard often forming a mounting platform for electrical components on its topside, which are then covered by the seat. Side panels are also standard, and vary from simple plastic panels to a moulded one piece 'seat cowling' that extends around the rear light unit.

Fairings vary from the small 'cockpit' or 'bikini' fairing to the large 'barn door' type. Small fairings serve more of a cosmetic purpose than an aerodynamic or protective one; they usually fit around the headlight unit and have a small screen which extends over the instrument panel and not much further; they can be either frame or handlebar mounted.

Medium size fairings offer more in the way of weather protection and aerodynamics, having a bigger screen which can be hidden behind to eliminate wind blast. On most sports bikes which have full bodywork the fairing will include air scoops and ducts to direct air under pressure into the airbox **(see illustration 9.6a)**.

The large touring fairings are designed to completely isolate the rider from all weather effects, allowing all-day riding at high speed in an upright and comfortable position. But they

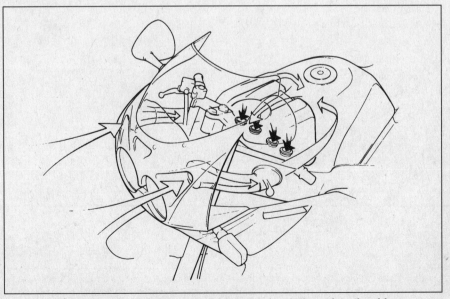

**9.6a The use of air scoops in the fairing to force air through to the airbox**

must do this without increasing drag and weight and without upsetting the handling.

Fairings are often extended around and under the engine in the form of fairing side panels and belly-pans, giving an all-enclosed racing look. These are primarily designed for aerodynamics **(see illustration 9.6b)**. But also protect the engine from dirt and corrosion. They do restrict the cooling effect of the air, though this is not a problem on liquid-cooled machines.

Any other bodywork is usually in the form of cosmetic panels shaped and finished to enhance the overall looks of the machine. Large tourers such as Honda's Goldwing and Pan European have many such panels covering most of the working systems of the bike.

## Construction and materials

The material used depends mainly on the intended use of the bike the bodywork is for, and therefore the purpose of the bodywork itself.

Body panels on early machines were made from pressed steel. Pressed steel, often chromed, is heavy and prone to corrosion from the underside, especially on the mudguards. This gave way to the use of glass fibre, which enabled the manufacture of more complex body panels and fairings. Glass fibre is quite strong, much lighter than steel, and is cheap to produce once the initial mould has been formed. It is also easy to repair and paint.

ABS (acrylonitrile - butadiene - styrene) plastics are now commonplace. They are lighter, easier to mould, and have a smoother finish than glass fibre. Plastics are not easy to repair, although 'plastic welding' kits permit

**9.6b Vents in the fairing channel air to cool the engine and help direct engine heat away from the rider**

the repair of small areas of damage and cracks.

Carbon fibre provides the lightest and strongest form of bodywork and its use is increasing in sporting applications, despite its higher manufacturing cost.

# Chapter 10
## Electrics

---

# Contents

## 1 Introduction

Every motorcycle, moped or scooter is equipped with some sort of electrical system. Most are battery powered and cater for the machine's lighting, signalling and instrumentation requirements.

This Chapter covers the components that make up a motorcycle electrical system and how the system as a whole works. For further details, readers are referred to the **Haynes Motorcycle Electrical Techbook**. Electrics is not an easy subject for many people, and some get put off too early by the 'physics' involved. But a logical application of a few basic rules will make them a lot easier to understand, and make fault-finding a much easier task.

## 2 The electrical circuit

The electrical system on any motorcycle is made up of many different circuits, all of which start and finish in the same place – the power source. Within the electrical system are many sub-systems (the number depending on the machine itself and its complexity). The main circuits that can be found on the majority of motorcycles are the starting circuit (unless kickstart only), the charging circuit, the ignition circuit (see Chapter 3), the lighting circuit and the signalling/warning circuit. Other circuits include fuel injection control and engine management (see Chapter 2), security (in-built or add-on alarm systems), and on a few big tourers, heating, accessory and entertainment circuits (yes, it's true!).

### What is a circuit?

For any electrical system to work, electricity must be able to flow in a complete circuit from the power source via the components and

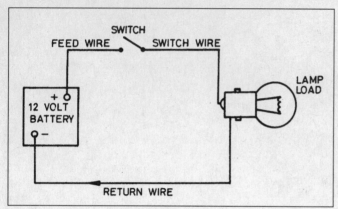

10.2a  A simple circuit

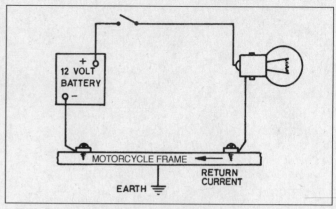

10.2b  The metal structure of a motorcycle becomes part of the wiring circuit

back to the power source, thus completing the circuit **(see illustration 10.2a)**. No circuit – no flow.

Once the power has left the positive side of the battery and run through its component it must then complete the circuit by returning to the battery, on its negative side, and this is known as the earth or ground. To save on wiring, connectors and space, the earth side of the battery is connected directly either to the metal frame of the motorcycle or to the engine **(see illustration 10.2b)**. Around the frame and engine will be various other points to which the wiring coming from the components is connected. In the case of the starter motor it bolts directly onto the engine, which is bolted to the frame. The frame and/or engine therefore form the path to earth.

### What is electricity?

Electricity is the flow of electrons through a conductor. A conductor already contains many free electrons, what they need is a pump or power source (i.e. a generator or battery) to get them moving. There are a number of ways of creating or generating this power, namely heat, light, friction, pressure, chemical reaction and magnetism. Motorcycles incorporate two of these methods, chemical reaction (the battery) and magnetism (the generator).

In contrast to a conductor, an insulator has no free electrons in it, so it doesn't matter how much power you give it, no electrons and therefore no electricity will flow through it.

Therefore electricity is created when there is a power source on one end of the conductor which creates a flow of electrons through it. One school of thought suggests that electricity flows from negative to positive, but for the sake of automotive and most other electrics it is always assumed that the flow is the other way round, from positive to negative.

It is important to understand that a battery does not create electricity any more than a pump creates a liquid. The electrons and the liquid must be there in the first place. The

battery and the pump are merely the means of getting the electrons or the liquid to move. And it is not necessarily the pump which gets the liquid moving, but the pressure it creates, and when there is a pressure difference between two points, there will be flow between them to even the pressure.

The ability of the battery to move electrons is known as its potential difference (pd) (similar to the ability of a pump to create a pressure difference) or electromotive force (emf), and is measured in volts (hence the pd or emf is also called the voltage). The flow of electrons is called the current and is measured in amperes or amps. The rate of flow or size of the current depends on two things, the amount of voltage (potential

difference or electromotive force) driving it and the resistance to it (measured in ohms) that occurs along the conductor. A circuit with little or no resistance will create a large current flow, whereas a high resistance will create a small current flow.

As the current flows, the battery uses up its voltage and so the voltage drops. The higher the current flow, the quicker the voltage will drop. This is why batteries run down and need to be recharged. In the case of a motorcycle the battery needs to be constantly charged during use, which is where the generator comes in. In fact it is the generator that is powering the electrical system when the engine is running, at the same time as recharging the battery.

## Ohm's law

The relationship between voltage, current and resistance is defined by Ohm's law (see illustration 10.2c).

The resistance in a circuit can be determined by dividing the voltage by the current.

The voltage in a circuit can be determined by multiplying the current by the resistance.

The current in a circuit can be determined by dividing the voltage by the resistance.

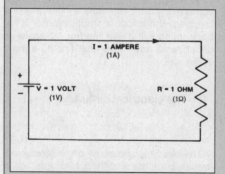

10.2c  Ohm's law defines the relationship between voltage, current and resistance

## The Watt – unit of power

The power that a component needs to make it work is measured in Watts. The power used by a component can be measured by multiplying the voltage in the system by the current it is drawing. Therefore a 60 W bulb working in a 12 V system will be drawing a 5 A current. This also means that the bulb has a resistance of 2.4 Ohms. A 300 W starter motor will be drawing 25 A and has a resistance of 0.48 Ohms.

## ac/dc

There are two types of current, direct current and alternating current. Direct current shows a square wave which has a positive peak only. Alternating current shows a curved 'sine' wave which flows from a positive peak to a negative peak and back to a positive peak and so on. In each case the peak of the wave indicates the voltage which produces the current. The type of current produced depends on the power source that is producing it. The majority of motorcycle electrical systems run on direct current.

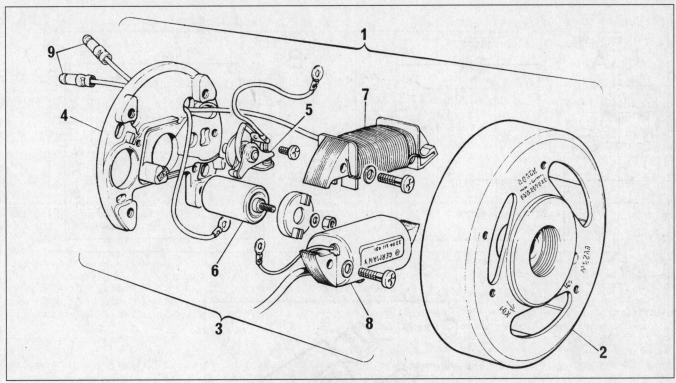

**10.4 Typical moped-type flywheel generator**

*Note that in this example the generator includes the ignition coil as part of the stator assembly (8). On other machines an external coil may be used, in which case this would be replaced by an ignition source coil, similar in appearance to the lighting coil (7).*

| | | |
|---|---|---|
| 1  Flywheel generator assembly complete | 3  Stator assembly | 6  Condenser (capacitor) | 8  Ignition coil |
| 2  Flywheel rotor | 4  Stator plate | 7  Lighting coil | 9  Bullet terminals |
| | 5  Contact breaker assembly | | |

## 3  Generating power

On all motor vehicles, a proportion of the power from the engine is converted into electrical energy to run the various electrical components. The amount of electrical power produced in the system is dependent on two factors: the amount of power needed and the amount of power that can be spared to provide this. In other words, the complexity of the system is generally decided by the size and type of machine. A simple moped or a small motorcycle or scooter needs only basic lighting and a horn, and may not have a battery. In this case a simple flywheel generator will suffice, as we will see below.

Until about 1960, almost all larger motorcycles were fitted with a direct current (dc) generator, or dynamo, which, unlike the flywheel generator, had the advantage of direct current output. A battery can only store dc electricity, and so if only ac current is available, it has to be converted to dc in order to recharge the battery. The main drawback of the dynamo was that it was complicated, and

thus expensive to produce and needing a good deal of maintenance. It was also unable to provide a high power output, especially at low engine speeds, which made them unsuitable for maintaining power output in slow and stop-go riding situations.

The alternator, despite its ac output, is a far simpler, more reliable and more powerful device for the generation of electricity than was the dynamo. For this reason it has more or less replaced the latter on all modern machines.

## 4  Flywheel generators

Flywheel generators, or 'flywheel magnetos' as they are sometimes known, are simple alternators used mainly on mopeds, scooters and lightweight motorcycles **(see illustration 10.4)**. In addition to generating power for the lights and horn they incorporate a separate source coil to power the ignition system, and occasionally the ignition coil itself.

The flywheel generator comprises a fixed

baseplate known as the stator, and a rotating flywheel with permanent magnets embedded in its outer rim. The stator is attached to one side of the crankcase and carries one or more generating coils. Machines using this system sometimes have a full alternating current electrical system, and consequently there is no provision for rectifying (converting to direct current, or dc) the output. This means that the output from the generating coil is carefully chosen to match the demands of the lighting circuit at maximum engine speed. Where there are transistorised components in the system that require dc power, a rectifier is fitted

Power is generated by induction, a principle discussed in the ignition Chapter. To recap briefly, if a wire is passed through a magnetic field, a current is induced in the wire. This flows in one direction as the field builds up, and then reverses as the field decays. In a generator, the field is created by the permanent magnets which sweep past the wire, which is wound into coils to maximise the effect. As each of the magnets passes the coil the current flows first one way, and then the other, hence the term alternating current, or 'ac' for short.

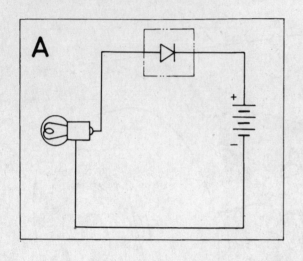

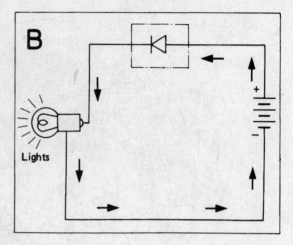

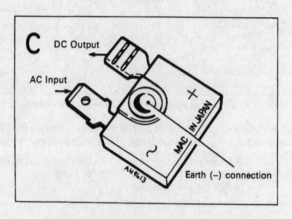

**10.5 How a silicon rectifier (diode) works**

**A**   *If we connect a silicon rectifier as shown, the current flow from the positive terminal (+) to the negative terminal is blocked, and the lamp does not light.*

**B**   *If we turn the rectifier round, current can now flow, and the bulb is lit.*

*If we replace the battery in the above circuit with an alternator the output will attempt to flow first in one direction and then the other. The one-way flow through the diode means that alternate cycles will be blocked, leaving half the output flowing in one direction only. Because half the output wave is lost this is known as half-wave rectification.*

**C**   *This is what most simple half-wave silicon rectifiers look like. The small resin-encapsulated unit is bolted to the frame, often below the seat or side panels.*

When the machine's lighting system is turned off, the coil is earthed, and no current flows around the lighting circuit. When the lights are switched on the current is obliged to flow through the bulbs in the head and tail lamps, illuminating them. At low engine speeds, the power output is limited and the lights will tend to be rather dim. There is also a noticeable flickering as the current alternates rapidly back and forth through a 'dead point'. As the engine speed rises, so too does the output of the generator, but only to a certain level due to what is known as the 'terminal voltage' of a particular generator.

We need not go into this aspect too deeply here; suffice it to say that the internal losses of the coils means that the output curve gradually tails off after a certain engine speed, and this makes the generator more or less self-regulating. In practice this means that the lights become brighter, and the flickering effect is no longer noticeable.

## 5   Flywheel generator/battery systems

The simple flywheel generator system described in Section 4 works well enough for some purposes, but if, for example, turn signals are incorporated in the system, it is no longer adequate. This is mostly because conventional turn signal relays are designed for dc operation from a stable power supply. To get round this problem, many manufacturers fitted a hybrid system, where the necessary power for the turn signals is derived from a separate generating coil. The output from this coil is fed through a rectifier, in the form of a single diode, to a small battery. This is then used to supply the turn signals and also parking lights if these are fitted. The rest of the lighting system is supplied directly from the generator and is ac.

The rectifier, as mentioned above, is a single diode encapsulated in a resin block. The diode acts as a one-way valve, allowing current to flow in one direction only **(see illustration 10.5)**. This means that half the output is lost as the diode clips away one side of the output

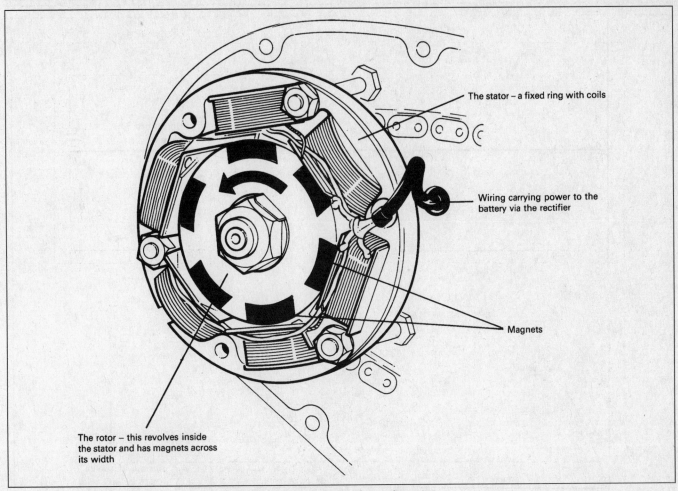

The stator – a fixed ring with coils

Wiring carrying power to the battery via the rectifier

Magnets

The rotor – this revolves inside the stator and has magnets across its width

**10.6a  Typical single-phase alternator**

wave, and this gives the system its name; half-wave rectification. Whilst this is not an efficient way to use the coil's output, it is simple, cheap and adequate for the purpose. The system is most often found on mopeds and on small trail bikes where low weight is an important factor.

## 6  Alternator systems – single phase types

A full alternator system is used where a battery is required to supply the entire electrical system. The alternator itself is like a heavy-duty flywheel generator **(see illustration 10.6a)**. In its simplest form, an 'internal permanent magnet single phase alternator' is used. This unwieldy term can be unravelled as follows:

The rotor consists of a drum-shaped unit keyed to the end of the crankshaft. Embedded in the alloy casting are (normally) six permanent magnets, and these are visible in the form of their laminated pole tips. Fitted around the rotor is the stator assembly comprising six generating coils mounted on a

stator. The latter often takes the form of laminated iron rings, and the whole assembly is sometimes encapsulated in resin for protection.

By using much more powerful magnets in the rotor, and bigger coils positioned outside the rotor, a lot more power can be obtained. In the early days of alternators, this was controlled by switching combinations of coils in or out to suit the demands of the system, and as such the system was only very roughly regulated. The more important requirement was that the output be converted to direct current (dc) so that the battery could be charged. The single diode rectifier described in Section 5 is a simple device, but as we saw it wastes half the output **(see illustration 10.6b overleaf)**. Given that the object of the alternator is to produce a lot more power, we cannot afford to lose half of it, and so a more sophisticated rectifier is required.

The answer to the problem is the bridge, or full-wave rectifier. This device comprises four diodes connected in such a way that the output from the rectifier is dc, irrespective of the changing phases of the alternator. The

accompanying diagram shows this process more clearly than a verbal description, and should be studied before reading further **(see illustration 10.6c overleaf)**.

Physically, the bridge rectifier is a small, heavily finned device which is bolted to a sound earth point on the frame. The finning (or heatsink) allows the heat generated in the device to be dispersed by the airflow past the machine, and by conduction to the frame. The use of a full-wave rectifier makes a lot of difference to the final output of the alternator. In the case of a halfwave (single diode) device, only about 37% of the unrectified current is available. With full-wave rectification, this figure rises to about 63%.

## 7  The zener diode and electronic voltage regulators

With the demand on the electrical system continuing to rise as machines became more sophisticated, the method of controlling the alternator by switching its coils in and out soon proved inadequate. In the case of

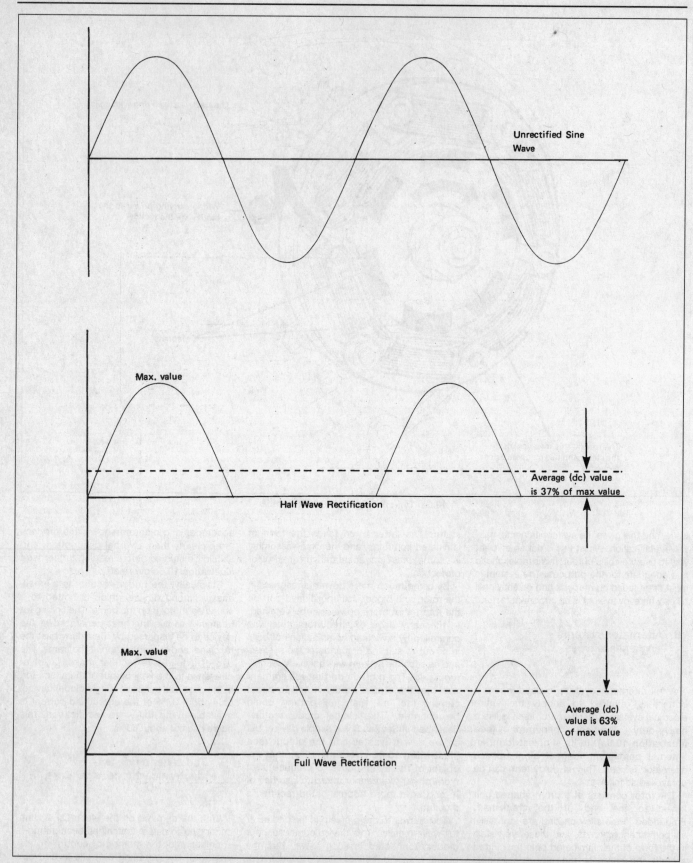

**10.6b Comparison of half-wave and full-wave rectification**

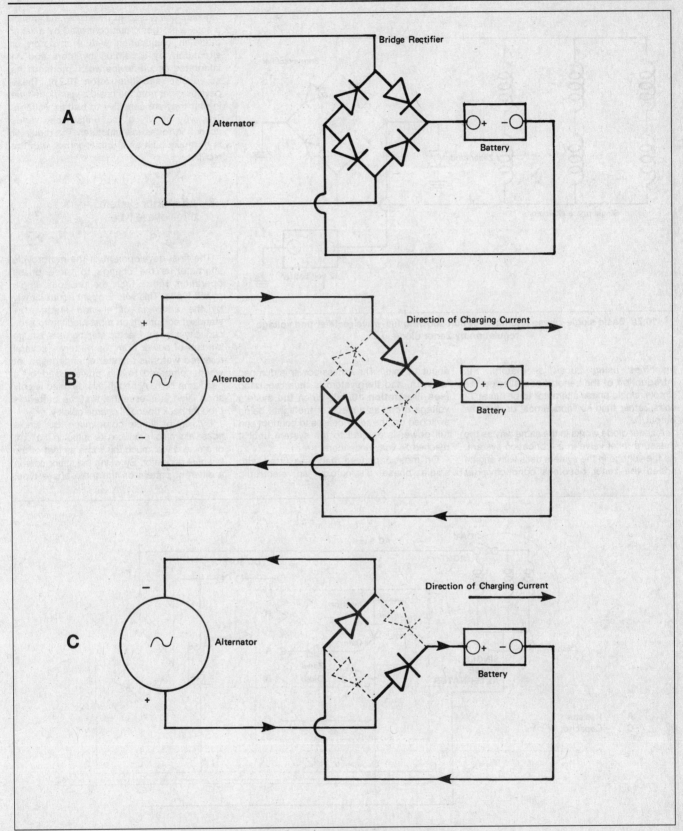

**10.6c How a full wave rectifier works**

*The full wave rectifier circuit (A). Note how first one pair of diodes allow current to pass (B) and then the opposite pair (C) so that the direction of current remains the same.*

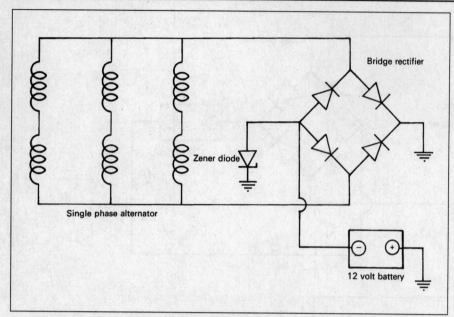

**10.7a Basic single-phase alternator circuit showing full-wave rectifier and voltage regulation by Zener diode**

regulator unit was used. This takes the form of a sealed electronic unit controlled by a zener diode in conjunction with a thyristor, or alternately by a pair of thyristors and an integrated circuit device which monitors the ac voltage **(see illustration 10.7b)**. These devices differ from the basic zener diode type in that they are sensitive to battery voltage. The way in which the units work varies according to the manufacturer. The regulator is normally built as a unit together with the rectifier.

## 8 Alternator systems – three phase types

The final development of the motorcycle alternator is the change to three phase operation, rather than the previous single phase types. This was brought about largely by the adoption of electric starters as standard equipment on most medium to large capacity models. Electric starting uses a huge amount of power from the battery – several hundred watts as the starter engages, a lot when compared to the power used by a headlamp bulb. Although this demand is only short lived, it is essential that the battery is brought back up to full charge quickly.

By way of simple comparison, the single phase alternator produces its output in the form of a sine wave, much the same as that of the flywheel generator. By wiring the stator coils in a different pattern on the three phase type,

machines using Lucas alternators, the introduction of the zener diode allowed the simple, single phase alternator to be run at 12 volts, rather than six, and almost doubled its output.

A zener diode works in the same way as the pressure relief valve in a lubrication system. As the voltage in the system rises with engine speed the zener becomes conductive (at

about 14 volts). The excess power is dumped to earth, and the system is thus regulated **(see illustration 10.7a)**. When the system voltage drops as a result of the lights being switched on, the zener ceases to conduct and full power is applied to the system until it reaches 14 volts once more.

On most Japanese machines fitted with single phase alternators, an electronic

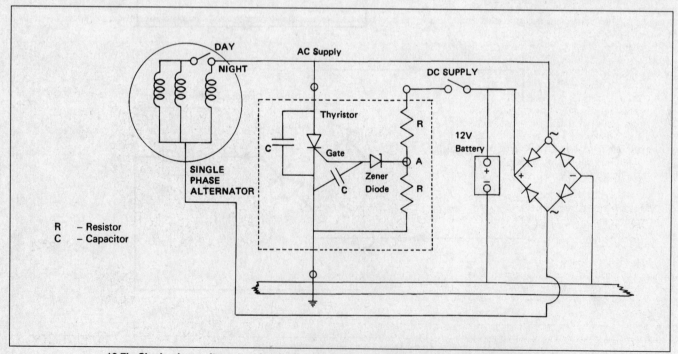

**10.7b Single phase alternator circuit showing full-wave rectifier and electronic voltage regulator**

*The dotted line encloses the voltage regulator components. In practice these are built into a sealed unit mounted on the frame.*

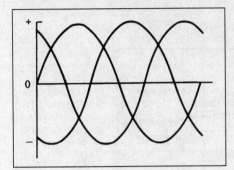

**10.8a The overlapping output waves from a three phase alternator**

three overlapping output waves, or phases, can be obtained **(see illustration 10.8a)**. These are spaced at 120° intervals, and in this way the output is much smoother and more consistent. This and physical considerations allow a much higher output to be obtained from a unit of a given size.

A permanent magnet three phase alternator often looks very much like a heavy duty flywheel generator **(see illustration 10.8b)**. The stator takes the form of a ring with the generating coils arranged radially around its outer edge. The rotor runs outside the coils, with its magnetic poles embedded in the alloy rotor casting.

Other three phase alternator units use electromagnets in place of the permanent magnets so far discussed **(see illustration 10.8c)**. The rotor consists of a central core upon which is wound a single excitor coil. Around this is fitted the two-claw pole assemblies in which alternate magnetic polarity is induced. The rotor is normally fed by the battery to start with, until the output rises sufficiently for the unit to become self-generating, though on some types, residual magnetism in the poles is sufficient to get the process going. One type of three-phase alternator used has been borrowed from the car industry – it uses a wound rotor and incorporates the regulator and rectifier **(see illustration 10.8d)**. It is usually mounted on top of the crankcase and is run off the crankshaft via a chain and sprockets or gears. This enables it to be geared so that it runs faster than the crankshaft.

## 9 Three phrase rectifiers and regulators

As might be expected, a three phase rectifier is a good deal more complex than a single phase type. In practice, six diodes are used in place of four to achieve full-wave rectification of the three phases. Each phase, or wave is rectified separately, giving six output 'ripples' rather than the two found in single phase types. The resulting dc output is much smoother and more powerful.

With an electromagnetic three phase unit it

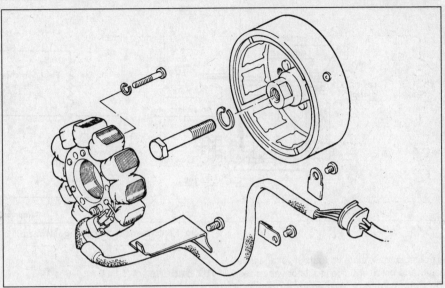

**10.8b Permanent magnet three-phase alternator**

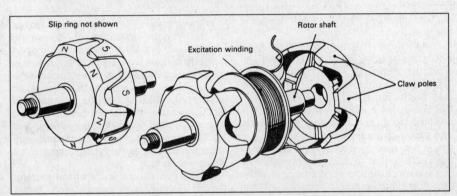

Slip ring not shown     Rotor shaft

Excitation winding

Claw poles

**10.8c Claw pole (electromagnetic) three-phase alternator**

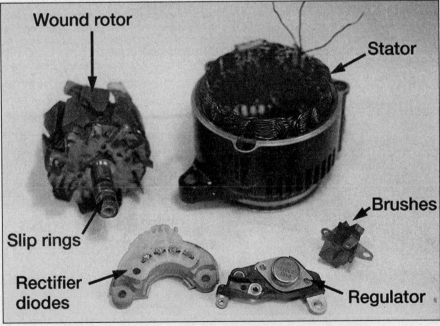

Wound rotor

Stator

Brushes

Slip rings

Rectifier diodes

Regulator

**10.8d Car-type alternator with integral regulator and rectifier**

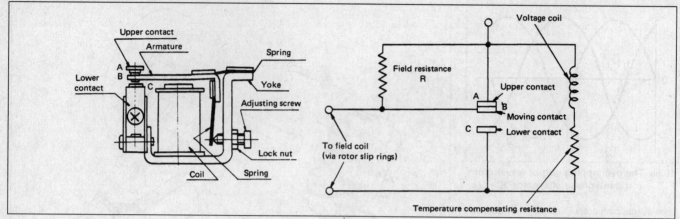

10.9a Electro-mechanical regulator unit

is possible to regulate the output voltage quite easily and precisely. The regulator unit senses the output voltage, and when it reaches a predetermined level, cuts the dc supply to the rotor. This in turn reduces the alternator ac output, and the voltage is thus stabilised at this level.

Early three phase regulators work electromechanically. In a typical regulator, an electromagnetic coil is connected to the dc output and is used to operate switch contacts (see illustration 10.9a). As the voltage rises, the coil opens a pair of contacts, and this switches the dc current through a resistance. The supply to the rotor is thus reduced, and this in turn reduces the output. If the voltage rises still further, a second connection is made in which the rotor is earthed completely. This cuts off the output completely until the system voltage drops to a safe level.

Later three phase regulators are electronically operated (see illustration 10.9b). Thyristors are used to shunt excess current to earth, either from one phase or from all three. Like the single phase equivalent, these regulators usually appear in the form of a resin-encapsulated unit.

## 10 Batteries

In the preceding Sections we have looked at the various methods of generating electricity. If we consider a simple moped electrical system with direct lighting, there is no need to store electrical power because the electrical requirements are so basic that an ac supply will suffice. A bulb, for example, will function whether the current flows through it in one direction or rapidly alternates to and fro. The same applies to the horn; it may vary in pitch according to the system output, but it works well enough.

As soon as we ask more of the system, things become more complicated. Some electrical components are polarity sensitive and thus require a dc supply. In some cases, this supply must be kept at a constant voltage, irrespective of engine speed, and this necessitates rectification to dc, regulation to a set voltage, and ultimately, some way of storing a reserve of power.

The lead/acid battery used on almost every

motorcycle represents a way of storing power in the form of a reversible chemical reaction. When a current is passed into the battery, a chemical reaction takes place, stopping when the reaction becomes exhausted (the battery is fully charged) or the current stops flowing. Given the opportunity, the reaction will reverse and current will flow out of the battery. In this way the battery offers a reserve of electrical power which will keep the system going even when the generator output is less than that required by the system. For example, it will allow the headlamp to maintain its output when the engine is idling or not running, and will permit an electric starter motor to be used.

### The conventional lead-acid battery

The lead acid battery is used almost universally on all motor vehicles for the simple reason that it is the best type available for this application at the moment. It has been in use for decades, and will continue to be used until a better type can be found – a line of research being pursued vigorously in almost every country in the world.

As this might suggest, the lead acid battery

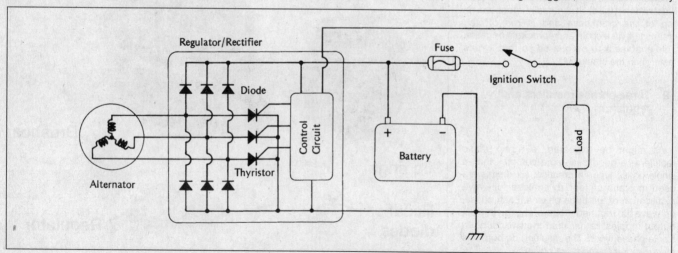

10.9b Three-phase charging circuit showing the electronic regulator/rectifier unit

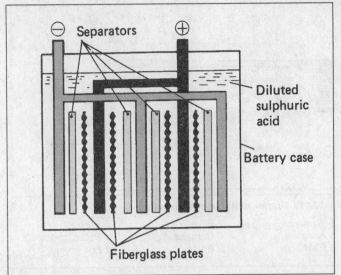

Separators

Diluted sulphuric acid

Battery case

Fiberglass plates

10.10a Battery construction

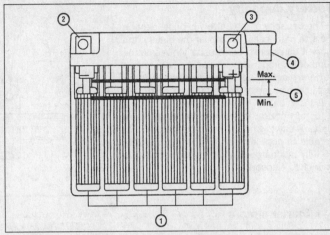

10.10b Cell arrangement and main components of a 12V battery

1  Cells
2  Negative terminal
3  Positive terminal
4  Vent hose connection
5  Electrolyte level markings

is not without its problems. For a start it is heavy and bulky, neither of which are particularly welcome features for motorcycle use. It does not cope well with heavy charging or discharging. This is because it causes the plates to heat up, and if this becomes excessive they will disintegrate. This means that the battery is being sorely tried every time the starter is used. It will cope with this treatment, but only just.

It is also a surprisingly fragile item, and is easily damaged by excessive vibration. This can dislodge the lead sulphate from the plates. The resulting debris at the bottom of each cell can then cause internal shorting. For a combination of the above reasons, coupled with a good measure of neglect and abuse, the battery on any motorcycle has a limited life. If maintained properly, this may average about three years or so, but it is shortened drastically through neglect and damage.

Lead-acid batteries suffer from 'sulphation' when discharged. Under normal use the fine lead sulphate crystals that are produced are converted back by charging. But if the battery is not charged they convert to coarse crystals which build-up on the plates. This reduces

capacity and slows the charging process, and in some cases will render the battery useless.

## Construction

The battery consists of a plastic casing, divided up into compartments called cells **(see illustration 10.10a)**. Each cell houses a number of separate plates connected together in alternating layers. The plates are made from an antimony-lead compound in the form of a grid, the holes in which are filled with a lead oxide paste. Chemically inert separators and glass fibre matting are fitted between each plate to prevent physical contact between them. The cell is filled with a conducting liquid called an electrolyte which in the case of a lead/acid battery is dilute sulphuric acid.

When a current is applied to the two terminals, the resulting chemical reaction converts the lead oxide of the positive plate into lead peroxide, leaving a spongy lead layer in the negative plate. If the current is stopped, the reaction ceases, but if we now connect a load such as a bulb, the reaction will reverse. This causes current to flow out of the cell, lighting the bulb until the reaction becomes exhausted and the cell is discharged, or 'flat'. Each cell

produces a voltage of about 2.2 volts, so a six volt battery has three cells and a twelve volt battery has six cells **(see illustration 10.10b)**.

Because the battery is constantly subjected to charging and recharging cycles the water in the electrolyte evaporates. This means it needs to be regularly maintained by topping it up with distilled water to keep the electrolyte level above the plates.

## Maintenance-free (MF) batteries

The maintenance-free battery was introduced by Yuasa in 1983. Once it has been initially filled with acid it is sealed for life, and thereafter will not require topping up. It has the added advantage of not being able to leak, and due to the construction of the separators is able to withstand the effects of vibration much better than the conventional type **(see illustration 10.10c)**.

The plates are made from a lead-calcium alloy and the separators are made of an absorbent glass mat. The separators soak up the acid so there is no liquid inside the battery. Under charging the chemical reaction between the oxygen produced and the lead on the negative plate forms a layer of lead oxide. The lead oxide reacts with the sulphuric acid and produces water as a by-product, which keeps the battery replenished, and is why it doesn't need topping up. Gel type maintenance-free batteries are often used where the battey position is tilted back rather than upright.

MF batteries do not have a breather tube to vent gases and pressure to the air. To avoid any pressure build-up due to overcharging there are one-way safety valves which open at a certain pressure.

One disadvantage of the MF battery is that it sulphates more than a conventional one when discharged. This requires a much higher initial voltage boost when it is charged to break down the sulphation. Otherwise it simply will not charge up.

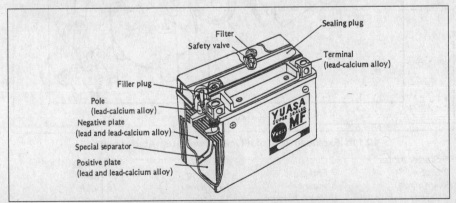

Sealing plug

Filter

Safety valve

Terminal (lead-calcium alloy)

Filler plug

Pole (lead-calcium alloy)

Negative plate (lead and lead-calcium alloy)

Special separator

Positive plate (lead and lead-calcium alloy)

10.10c Maintenance-free battery construction

## Battery capacity

The capacity of the battery is dependent on the size of its cells; the bigger the battery, the more it can store. This is usually given as the number of amperes available per hour from a battery discharged over a ten hour period, and is expressed as ampere-hours, or Ah.

A 12 Ah battery would be able to supply 1.2 A for ten hours. If the discharge rate were higher – say 2.4 hours, the battery would not be able to cope as well, and would probably be fully discharged before the expected five hours had elapsed.

## 11 Starter motors

Electric starting systems can now be found on most types of motorcycle, from the smallest scooter upwards. Only off-road motorcycles do not use them as standard because of the weight and added complexity. Many small motorcycles and scooters are fitted with kickstarts as well as starter motors, probably because they only have room for small batteries. But larger motorcycles have done away with the kickstart completely.

## How they work

An electric motor works in very much the same way as a dc generator, but the other way round. A generator has mechanical energy as its input and electrical energy as its output, whereas a motor has electrical input and mechanical output. In fact any dc motor will generate electrical power if it is spun mechanically, and any dc generator can be run as a motor.

At the heart of the motor is the armature, a series of coils built around the rotating central shaft **(see illustration 10.11a)**. At one end is a drum-shaped section composed of numerous copper segments separated by mica insulators. This is known as the commutator, and its purpose is to allow power to be applied to successive armature coils, via the carbon brushes which rub against its surface. Attached to the motor casing are the field windings which remain stationary and produce the magnetic field which turns the armature.

The motor works by using the magnetic field generated by the field coils to push away the adjacent set of armature windings. As the armature turns in response to this pressure, the brushes apply power to the next pair of commutator segments, and thus the next set of armature windings repeat the process. As the speed of rotation increases, the motor begins to generate its own internal power (called back-emf) in opposition to the supply. This effectively limits the speed of the motor, but gives it high initial torque characteristics; ideal for the purpose of cranking the engine.

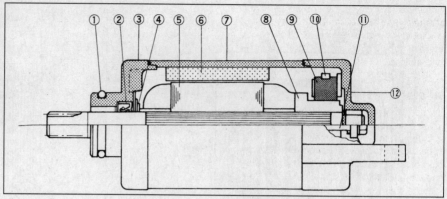

**10.11a  Starter motor in cross section**

| | | | |
|---|---|---|---|
| 1 O-ring | 4 Shims | 7 Body | 10 Spring |
| 2 Oil seal | 5 Armature | 8 Commutator | 11 Retaining bolt |
| 3 End cover | 6 Field coils | 9 Brush | 12 End cover |

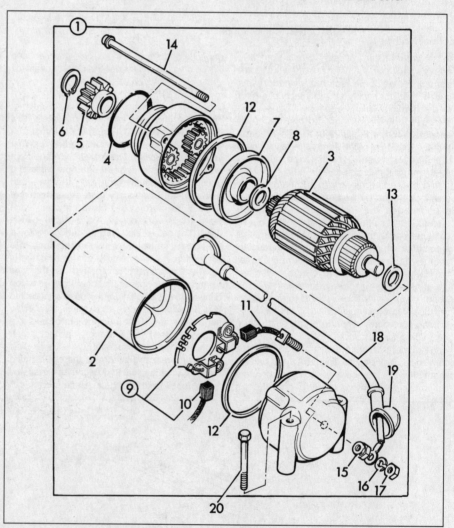

**10.11b  Exploded view of a typical two-brush starter motor**

| | | | |
|---|---|---|---|
| 1 Starter motor | 6 Circlip | 11 Brush | 16 Spring washer |
| 2 Stator | 7 End plate | 12 O-ring | 17 Nut |
| 3 Armature | 8 Washer | 13 Washer | 18 Cable |
| 4 O-ring | 9 Brush holder | 14 Bolt | 19 Boot |
| 5 Pinion | 10 Brush | 15 Nut | 20 Bolt |

Some starter motors use two brushes and others use four, depending on the load being transmitted **(see illustrations 10.11b and c)**. Generally four brush motors are used on larger engines.

## The starter drive train

To use the motor for starting purposes it must be connected to the crankshaft in such a way that once the engine starts, the connection can be broken to avoid damage to the starter motor. This is most often done by incorporating a one-way clutch in the starter drive train (see Chapter 4, Section 4). A reduction gear is also incorporated in the train so that by the time the rotation of the starter motor reaches the crankshaft the overall reduction is in the region of 14:1. This provides the level of torque required to make the system work.

A few machines (Moto Guzzi and BMW) use a car-type pre-engaged starter as an alternative to the one-way clutch arrangement described above. With this system, the starter electromagnetic coil (see Section 13) is fitted on the outside of the starter motor casing and is used to throw a drive pinion into mesh with the starter gear before the motor begins to turn **(see illustration 10.11d)**. When the engine begins to run faster than the starter motor, the drive pinion is forced out of engagement down a spiral thread in the armature end, and this protects the motor from damage.

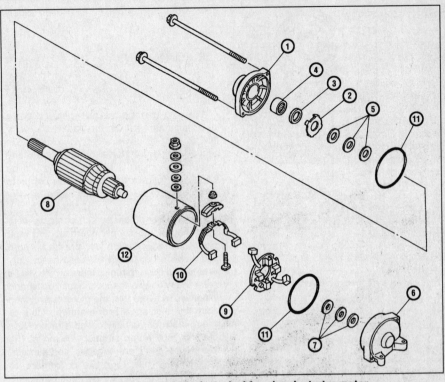

**10.11c Exploded view of a typical four-brush starter motor**

| | | | |
|---|---|---|---|
| 1 Front cover | 5 Washer and shims | 9 Brushplate assembly | 11 Sealing ring |
| 2 Tabbed washer | 6 Rear cover | 10 Brush holder, | 12 Main housing |
| 3 Oil seal | 7 Shims | terminal bolt and | |
| 4 Needle bearing | 8 Armature | insulator piece | |

**10.11d Exploded view of a typical pre-engaged starter motor**

| | | | | | |
|---|---|---|---|---|---|
| 1 Bush | 6 Spring | 11 Washers | 16 Brush holder | 20 Starter motor | 24 Washer |
| 2 Front cover bolts | 7 Solenoid | 12 Rear cover | 17 Seal | assembly/armature | 25 Bolt |
| 3 Front cover | 8 Washer | 13 Rubber plug | 18 Brushes | 21 Starter pinion | 26 Retaining clip |
| 4 Pivot pin | 9 Nut | 14 Brush spring | 19 Screw | 22 Bush | 27 Shims(s) |
| 5 Solenoid lever arm | 10 Rear cover nuts | 15 Spacer | | 23 Retaining clip | |

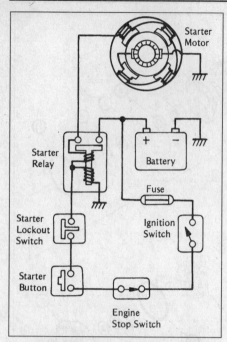

**10.13 Typical starter motor circuit**

## 12 The starter-dynamo

Given the similarity between the starter motor and the dc generator, it is not too surprising that the two units have been amalgamated into a single dual-purpose device, the starter dynamo. These units are not used on current machines, but have been fitted to a few lightweight two-stroke engines in the past (Yamaha RD200). Their main drawback is that they cannot produce a high cranking force, and are rather inefficient as generators, and so have never been widely used.

## 13 Starter relays

When the starter is first operated, it draws a high initial current from the battery. To carry this amount of power a very thick cable is needed and if the starter motor lead on any motorcycle or car is examined this will be evident. It follows that the switch contacts which operate the motor must also be very heavy.

If normal handlebar switch contacts were used they would simply overheat and melt when the starter button was pressed. And if heavy switch contacts were used heavy duty wires would have to run to them, which would make the wiring to the switchgear bulky and unsightly. To avoid this, the motor is switched indirectly via an electromagnetic coil or solenoid switch, usually called a relay. Note that this is a much simpler version of the solenoid used in a pre-engaged starter motor, as it merely has to make a contact to complete a circuit, rather than having to mechanically operate the engagement device; but the principle of operation is the same.

Pressing the starter button supplies power to the relay windings. The relay armature is energised, drawing only a light current, and thus not overloading the button contacts. This closes the heavy starter contacts which draw power from the battery and supply it to the starter motor **(see illustration 10.13)**. The heavy current used does not require a fuse in the starter circuit for protection, so the thick starter motor lead runs directly to the appropriate battery terminal.

## 14 Lighting systems

Every motorcycle has a lighting system of some description, which can be sub-divided into two functions, namely illumination and signalling/warning.

The illumination function is catered for by one or two sidelights, headlights and tail lights, and instrument lights. A simple signalling/warning system consists of brake lights, turn signals, oil pressure or level light, a neutral light for the gearbox, and sometimes a charging light; these lights are usually incorporated in the instrument cluster. More complicated systems may include a hazard warning function, low fuel warning, temperature warning, electronic fault warning, and so on.

Lighting regulations differ between countries, and so the same model of motorcycle sold in two different countries will have two different lighting systems **(see illustrations 10.14a and b)**. The best example is that of the lighting regulations in the US, where there is no lighting switch as such. The lights come on automatically with the ignition switch, and cannot be isolated, which means they are always on. Also the front turn signals often double as riding lights, having dual filament bulbs. The low power filament remains on during use, and when the turn signal is operated the high power filament flashes on and off.

## 15 Bulbs –
### tungsten filament types

Bulbs produce light by allowing an electrical current to flow through a very thin

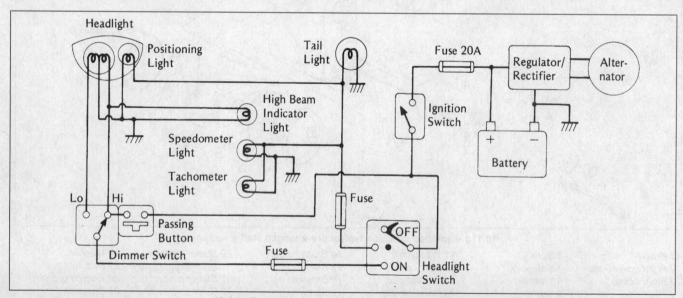

**10.14a Typical lighting circuit for UK/Europe models**

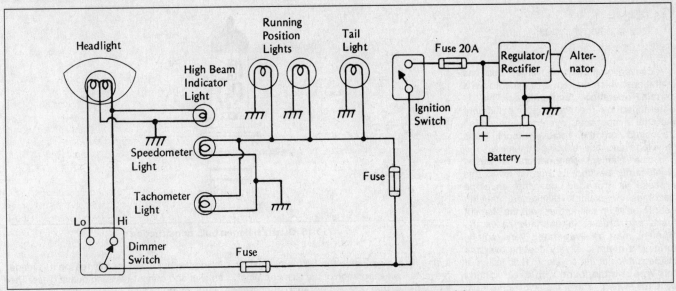

**10.14b Typical lighting circuit for US/Canada models**

wire, usually made from tungsten, called a filament. The resistance of the filament causes heat to build up until it glows white hot and thus gives off light.

To fit a lot of filament into a small space it is wound into a tight coil, and this also increases the heating effect in this area. If the filament were heated in air it would simply burn up and break. This is caused by the presence of oxygen, so the problem is avoided by putting the filament in a sealed glass 'envelope' and surrounding it with an inert gas at low pressure. Add to this the brass cap to which the ends of the filament are connected, and you have a bulb.

Headlight bulbs are usually located in the back of the headlight reflector unit by metal tabs which locate in cutouts; these are often offset to ensure the bulb is always fitted in the correct position **(see illustration 10.15a)**.

Other bulbs are located in their holders by locating their pins into slots in the holder (bayonet type) which are a push and twist fit, or by pressing their wire terminals into corresponding holes in the bulb holder (capless type). Dual filament bulbs, such as used for the brake/tail light have offset pins to ensure they are fitted the correct way around in the bulbholder. A further development of bulb fitting is the plug connection which simply fits into a connector in the wire harness.

The wattage, and thus the brightness of the bulb, is determined by the thickness of the wire and the number of turns in the filament coils, and this allows bulbs of various types to be made to suit different purposes. Some bulbs do more than one job – the stop/tail lamp for example, and these have two separate filaments of different wattage. The same applies to the headlamp bulb, but the second filament has a special role in this case.

In the headlamp, the filaments are very carefully positioned so that on main beam the light is focused by the reflector into a narrow beam. This is further directed by the fluted patterns of the glass front of the headlamp unit to illuminate the road ahead. When dip beam is selected, the main filament goes out and the second filament is lit. This is positioned so that the light is deflected downwards and to one side to avoid dazzling oncoming traffic **(see illustration 10.15b)**.

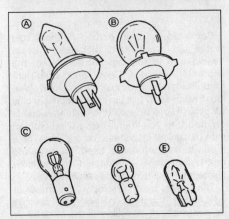

**10.15a Bulb types**

A  Halogen headlight bulb
B  Tungsten headlight bulb
C  Turn signal, brake/tail light bulb
D  Instrument light bulb (bayonet fitting)
E  Instrument light bulb (capless fitting)

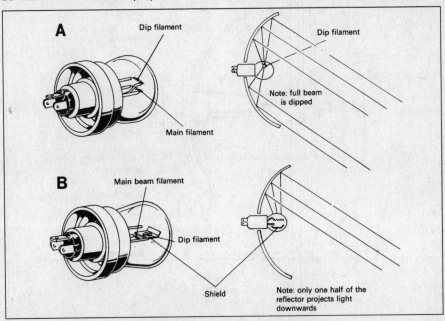

**10.15b Comparison of headlamp bulbs**

A  Offset dip filament     B  Shield dip filament

## 16 Bulbs –
### quartz halogen types

A conventional tungsten filament bulb has limitations which prevent it running above a certain operating temperature. This is determined by the way that the filament material evaporates, eventually becoming deposited on the relatively cool glass 'envelope' and thus reducing brightness.

If the filament temperature is raised significantly beyond its normal level, this process is speeded up; the envelope becomes increasingly blackened, causing heat to build up still further until the element melts and breaks. In dramatic cases the filament may be evaporated very rapidly, forming a metallic silvery coating over the inside surface of the envelope. Bulb failure of this type is often found with direct lighting systems where the failure of one bulb overloads the remainder, usually at high engine speeds. So next time you find a bulb that appears to have been silvered, you will know that it failed through sudden overloading, rather than by the filament fracturing due to vibration.

If a gas of the halogen group, such as

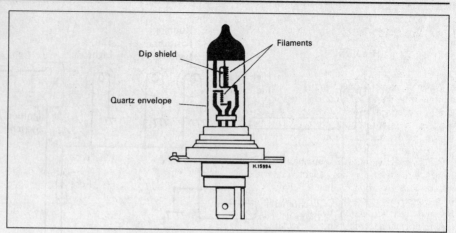

**10.16 Quartz halogen bulb construction**

iodine, is sealed inside the bulb envelope, it prevents the evaporation of the filament. What happens is that the evaporating tungsten combines with the halogen gas to form tungsten halide. This compound will then diffuse back towards the filament instead of depositing on the envelope. As it reaches the filament area, it breaks down once more, and a circulation is maintained. The process requires careful control of the temperatures

inside the bulb, and for this reason it is made smaller and of heat-resisting quartz glass. The resulting bulb runs much hotter, and thus much brighter than a conventional tungsten filament type.

The so-called quartz halogen bulb provides a brighter and whiter light output for a given wattage than a conventional bulb, but is much more sensitive to changes of temperature **(see illustration 10.16)**. In particular, if its running temperature is lower than normal, the service life is drastically reduced, so voltage drop due to corrosion in the wiring and connectors can cause problems.

Another point worth noting is that the quartz envelope is easily etched and marked by acids in perspiration. For this reason the envelope must never be handled without a clean cloth or tissue. If it is touched, it should be carefully cleaned whilst cold, using methylated spirit.

## 17 Sealed beam units

Some older models, particularly those sold in the US, were fitted with sealed beam headlamps. In this type of headlamp, the separate reflector, lens and bulb are combined into a single sealed unit **(see illustration 10.17)**. In the case of conventional tungsten filament types, the bulb envelope is omitted, the whole unit being filled with an inert gas at low pressure to do this job. Where a quartz halogen unit is used, the separate quartz envelope is retained to maintain filament temperature at the required level.

The sealed beam unit offers a number of advantages, the main one being that there is no possibility of corrosion of the reflector or misalignment of the bulb filaments. The main drawback is that the whole unit must be renewed in the event of a filament failing, and this is rather more expensive than just renewing a bulb. The sealed beam unit is really a thing of the past on motorcycles.

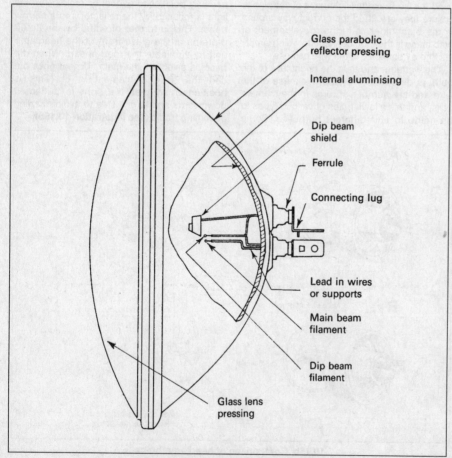

**10.17 Sealed beam unit construction**

## 18 Turn signal systems

With the exception of off-road motorcycles, all new machines are sold with turn signals. On some larger and more sophisticated models, a separate switch allows all four lamps to be flashed simultaneously as a hazard warning.

A standard system comprises two pairs of lamps, a turn signal relay or 'flasher unit', and a three-way switch to control it. The inclusion of a hazard warning function adds another relay and switch **(see illustration 10.18a)**. The lamps are usually mounted on stalks which position them well out from the centre line of the machine; this makes the direction of the intended turn clear to other road users. On faired machines the front turn signals are often incorporated in the fairing itself. Each lamp is fitted with an amber coloured lens to avoid confusion with any of the other lights on the vehicle.

The relay is a device which switches either pair of lamps on and off at regular intervals. In the UK, the relevant traffic laws require the flash rate to be between 60 and 120 cycles per minute, and this frequency is almost universal throughout the world. The handlebar switch has a left and right position with a central 'off' setting. Some machines incorporate a self-cancelling device (see Section 19).

### Capacitor relays

Many systems are controlled by a capacitor type relay. The relay unit takes the form of a cylindrical aluminium alloy canister with two spade, or Lucar, terminals at the base **(see illustration 10.18b overleaf)**. Inside the canister is the capacitor, the solenoid assembly and contacts, and a small resistor. The relay solenoid has two sets of windings; the voltage coil comprising several thousand turns of thin wire and connected across the supply, and the current coil which has a few hundred turns of thicker wire wound on top of the voltage coil and is connected in series with the supply.

When the ignition switch is on and the turn signal switch is at its central 'off' position, current flows through the voltage coil and charges the capacitor. If the switch is moved to the left or right position, current now flows through the current coil, the warning lamp and the turn signal lamps, to earth. This small current is enough to light the warning lamp, but not the two turn signal lamps at this stage. The current flow through the current coil produces a magnetic field which attracts the armature to the core, opening the contacts. This cuts off the supply to the relay, but the capacitor now discharges through the windings to keep the contacts open and to light the turn signal lamps. Once the capacitor is discharged (its capacity determines the

duration of each flash) the contacts close again.

Until the capacitor is recharged, the current flows in opposite directions in the two sets of windings. This means that the magnetic flux is inhibited and the contacts remain closed, with the turn signal lamps lit by battery current. As the capacitor nears full charge, the current flowing through the current coil ceases and the contacts open once more. This switches off the supply to the relay and the turn signal lamps, and the cycle now repeats.

The working of the capacitor relay may seem rather complicated, but it is designed to take in its stride the voltage fluctuations and the effects of vibration which might otherwise affect the flash rate. By using a capacitor to control the effective timing of the relay, these variations are avoided.

### Bimetal relays

A popular alternative to the capacitor relay relies on the use of two bimetal strips to control its operation. A bimetal strip consists of two dissimilar metals (usually brass and steel) fused together into a thin strip **(see**

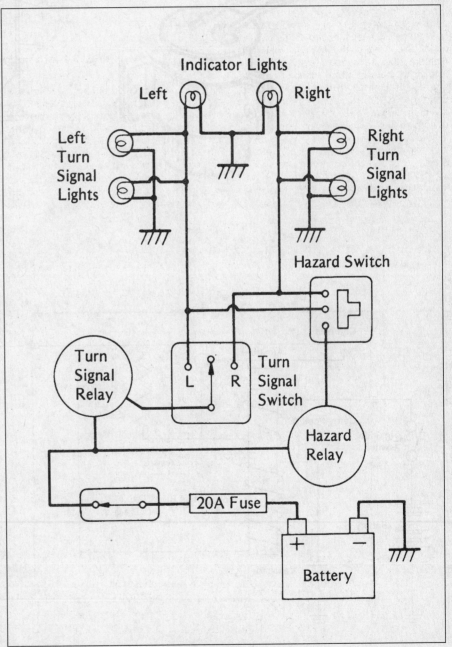

**10.18a Turn signal circuit**

*In this example a second relay is used to flash all four lamps simultaneously for hazard warning purposes.*

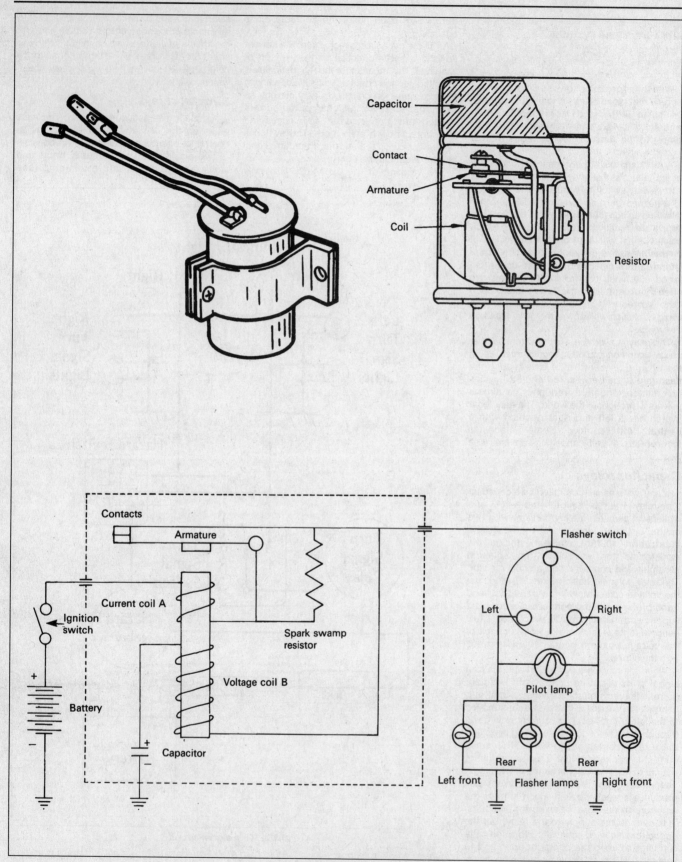

**10.18b Capacitor-type relay and circuit**

**illustration 10.18c)**. If heat is applied to the strip the differing rates of expansion of the two metals cause the strip to bend to one side. In a bimetal relay, the two strips are mounted slightly apart and carry the relay contacts at their free ends.

The voltage coil strip is wound with numerous turns of resistance heating wire, and this coil is connected at one end to the contact, and at the other to the common terminal. The current coil strip is wound with fewer turns of heating wire, again with one end of the coil attached to the contact and the other to the common lamp terminal.

When the turn signal switch is operated, current flows through the voltage coil, which heats up and begins to bend its bimetal strip **(see illustration 10.18d)**. As the contacts close, the turn signal lamps are lit and current ceases to flow in the voltage coil, flowing instead through the current coil. As the first strip cools and begins to bend back, the second strip is heated and bends away. This separates the two contacts, turning off the lamps. The sequence now repeats until the turn signal switch is reset.

## Transistor relays

Fully electronic relays are now standard fitment. They use a multivibrator oscillator to produce ON-OFF pulses which are then directed to a relay via an amplifier **(see**

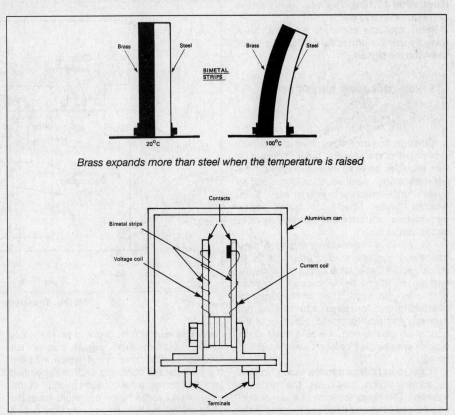

*Brass expands more than steel when the temperature is raised*

**10.18c  Principle and construction of bimetal relay**

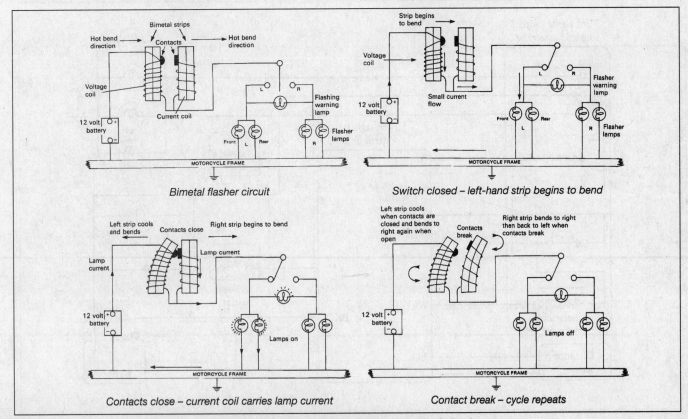

*Bimetal flasher circuit*

*Switch closed – left-hand strip begins to bend*

*Contacts close – current coil carries lamp current*

*Contact break – cycle repeats*

**10.18d  Operation of bimetal relay turn signal circuit**

**illustration 10.18e).** The relay switches the turn signals on and off.

Some systems eliminate the need for a relay by using a power field-effect transistor to switch the signals.

## 19 Self-cancelling turn signals

Although common fitment on cars, where movement of the steering column through a turn provides an easy means of operating a self-cancelling device, adopting such a system on a motorcycle is less easy. Such devices were fitted to many 1980s motorcycles, but there use had now more or less disappeared.

The obvious approach to fitting a self-cancelling system to a motorcycle is to employ some sort of timer circuit to cancel the turn signals after a predetermined amount of time has elapsed. This works fine for overtaking, or for turns where it is not necessary to wait for traffic. However, if the rider is obliged to wait, it would result in the system switching off before it was required to do so.

To get round this problem, a second control is added which measures the distance travelled. This takes the form of a sensor built into the speedometer head and working in the

same way as the pickup coil in an electronic ignition system. The signal pulses are 'counted' by the timer circuit, which will keep the turn signals operating until the specified time and distance have been covered. In this way, when overtaking on a straight road, the distance will have been covered way before

the timer has elapsed. Conversely, when waiting at a road junction the timer will rest, leaving the system running until the correct distance has elapsed. In addition, the rider has the option to override the self-cancelling system and switch the turn signals off manually **(see illustration 10.19)**.

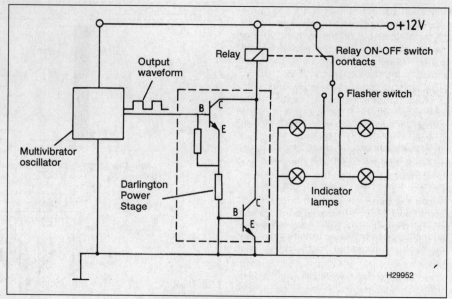

**10.18e  Transistor relay flasher unit**

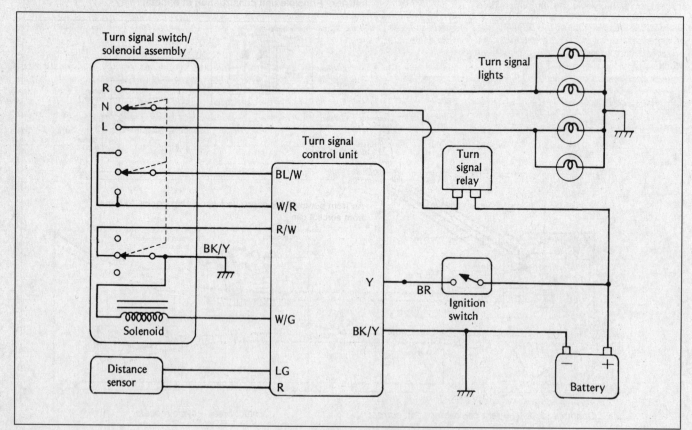

**10.19  Self-cancelling turn signal circuit**

## 20 Horns

### Electromagnetic horns

Most machines are fitted as standard with an electromagnetic horn unit **(see illustration 10.20a)**. This works on the basis of an electromagnetic coil mounted in a circular case, the armature of which is connected to a diaphragm.

When the horn button is pressed, the armature is pulled towards the solenoid core, and the attached moving contact breaks the circuit. The diaphragm returns the armature to its original position, the contacts close, and the cycle is repeated many times each second.

At the front of the diaphragm is a tone disc, which is designed to vibrate at a much higher frequency than the diaphragm. The resulting sound includes both high and low frequencies and is thus more audible than would be the case with the diaphragm alone. A variation of the above is the windtone horn which uses a spiral trumpet section to modify the sound produced by the diaphragm assembly.

### Air horns

Most motorcyclists will be painfully aware that both they and their machine seem to be entirely inaudible as well as invisible to the average car driver. Air horns are often fitted as an accessory and can be an invaluable aid to providing extra safety from cloth-eared, mobile-phone eared or otherwise deaf car drivers **(see illustration 10.20b)**.

They are powered from a remote compressor, itself powered by the battery, which forces air at high pressure through the trumpet-shaped horn. At the back of the horn is a pressure chamber, the outlet of which is closed by a flexible diaphragm. As the pressure rises in the chamber, the diaphragm opens and releases a pulse of air, and then closes until the pressure builds up once more. This cycle repeats many times each second, resulting in a penetrating note from the horn trumpet.

There are versions of the air horn which are operated from an aerosol can of compressed carbon dioxide; useful where the machine's electrical system is not capable of providing enough power to drive a compressor.

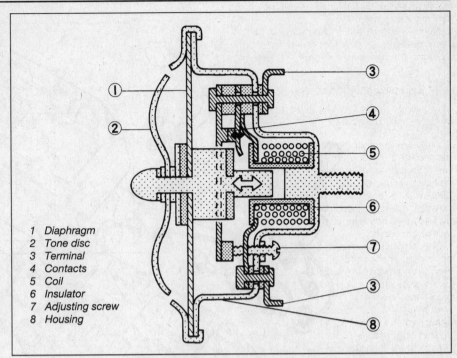

1  Diaphragm
2  Tone disc
3  Terminal
4  Contacts
5  Coil
6  Insulator
7  Adjusting screw
8  Housing

**10.20a  Section through a tone-disc horn**

## 21 Instrumentation and warning systems

Like almost every aspect of motorcycle design, instruments have become increasingly sophisticated. The basic speedometer has been supplemented by a variety of extra instruments, usually electrically or electronically-operated. These include tachometers, voltmeters, ammeters, clocks

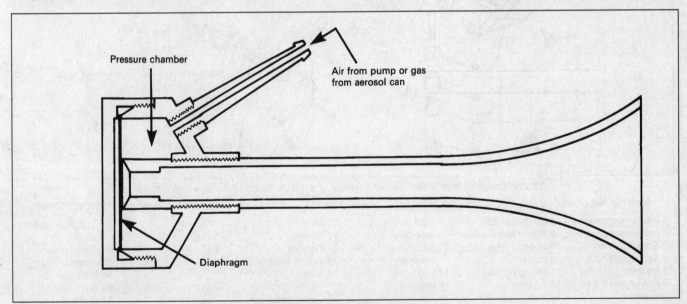

Pressure chamber

Air from pump or gas from aerosol can

Diaphragm

**10.20b  Section through an air horn**

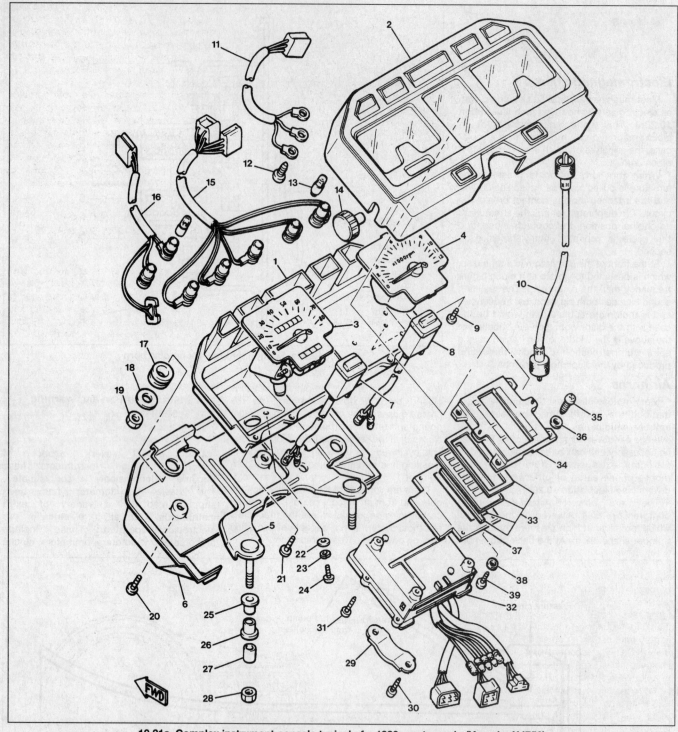

**10.21a Complex instrument console typical of a 1980s motorcycle (Yamaha XJ750)**

*Note the row of warning lamps across the top of the panel, and also the LCD monitor panel between the speedometer and tachometer.*

1 Instrument housing
2 Instrument cover
3 Speedometer
4 Tachometer
5 Mounting bracket
6 Instrument lower
   cover
7 Control switch

8 Control switch
9 Screw and washer
10 Speedometer drive
    cable
11 Wiring harness
12 Screw
13 Bulb
14 Reset knob

15 Bulb holder
    assembly
16 Bulb holder
    assembly
17 Grommet
18 Washer
19 Nut

20 Screw
21 Screw
22 Washer
23 Spring washer
24 Screw
25 Damping rubber
26 Damping rubber

27 Spacer
28 Nut
29 Bracket
30 Screw
31 Screw
32 Computer monitor
   unit

33 Computer monitor
    panel
34 Panel cover
35 Screw
36 Washer
37 Backing plate
38 Washer
39 Screw

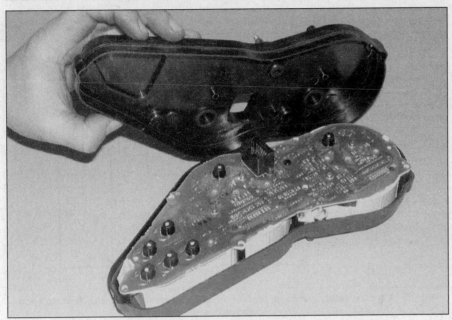

**10.21b Printed circuit board of a fully electronic instrument cluster**

and fuel and temperature gauges **(see illustrations 10.21a and b).**

The array of warning lights has also grown over the years and most current models are fitted with a comprehensive display indicating the status and general condition of the machine. The level of sophistication is, naturally enough, dependent on the type of machine. At one extreme there are the simpler scooters with a speedometer and one or two warning lights, whilst some of the larger capacity machines are equipped with complicated microprocessor-based instrument systems. Electronics and plastics combined make for some extremely light and compact instrument clusters which are ideal for sports bikes.

On some models the instruments are interconnected via a central control unit which monitors all aspects of the engine and electrical functions while the machine is being ridden, and carries out a comprehensive self-checking sequence each time the engine is started. Information is gathered from a variety of switches and sensors and any fault is displayed by warning lights or in some cases, on a liquid crystal display (LCD) panel and/or a meter built into the instrument console. LED's (light emitting diodes) are now also being used in place of standard filament bulbs, especially where the instrument cluster is run using a PCB (printed circuit board).

Speedometers and tachometers can be actuated either by cable or electronically. On the majority of machines the speedometer is cable driven via a drive gear on the front wheel, though sometimes the transmission output shaft is used. On electronic speedometers a sensor pulses a signal for every rotation of either the front sprocket or the output shaft and this is computed into

engine speed and displayed either via a traditional analogue gauge or via a digital display **(see illustration 10.21c).** Tachometers are more often than not driven electronically by the ECU controlling the

ignition system, though older machines may have a cable running off the camshaft or crankshaft and be geared accordingly. Display is analogue, and this is preferable to digital because an analogue gauge depicts rate of change of engine speed much better than a digital display.

As might be expected, the more complex systems use a number of sealed units, and are thus difficult to deal with in the event of a fault. The usual approach in these cases is to substitute new components for those that are suspect until the fault is isolated, though the construction of the control circuits is invariably such that repair is impracticable.

## 22 Warning lamp systems – switches, senders and sensors

A wide variety of switches, senders and sensors are employed to control and/or check the status or condition of the various parts of the engine and electrical system, and also to control safety features like starter interlock circuits. Some of the more common types are discussed below.

Terminology here can be a bit confusing, as there is no clear definition as to the difference between a sensor and a sender. In fact there is no physical or performing parameter that

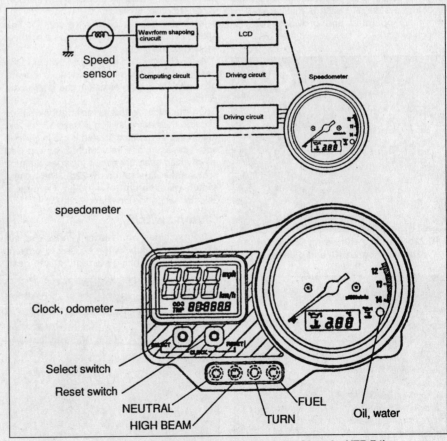

**10.21c Electronic speedometer control circuit (Yamaha YZF-R1)**

**10.22a The neutral switch (arrowed) is set in the crankcase and contacts the selector drum**

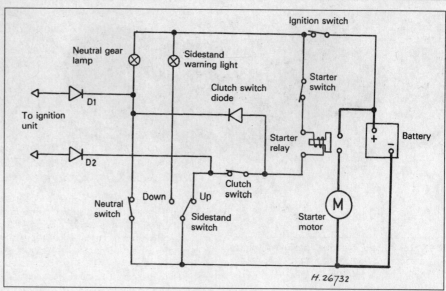

**10.22b A typical safety interlock circuit containing neutral switch, clutch switch and sidestand switch**

defines them, and often manufacturers will have their own preference. In general though, a sender is deemed to be something that sends an unbroken stream of information, usually in the form of a current or voltage, to an instrument that is able to provide a constant and variable readout depicting that information. A sensor is deemed to be something that either creates or cuts an electrical circuit for a warning light and so works in an ON/OFF way only, or something that sends a constant stream of individual signals in the form of electrical pulses to a control unit which reacts separately to each individual signal, such as the crankshaft position sensor in an electronic ignition or fuel injection system. A switch is mechanically or manually operated and provides ON/OFF action only.

**10.22c Clutch swith wiring connector (A), retaining screws (B) and plunger (C)**

### Neutral switch

Almost every machine, other than single-speed or automatic mopeds, has a neutral switch which controls a warning lamp in the instrument panel. On most machines the switch is a simple contact screwed into the transmission casing (see illustration 10.22a). When neutral is selected, a cam on the selector mechanism touches the contact. This allows the neutral warning lamp to be earthed, allowing it to light up.

A development of the neutral switch is the gear position indicator, which powers a digital gear position indicator within the instrument cluster.

On machines with starter interlock safety circuits, the neutral switch is used to prevent the engine from being started if it is in gear, in some cases unless the clutch lever is pulled in, in which case the circuit includes a clutch switch (see illustration 10.22b). The neutral switch will also cut the ignition if a gear is selected when the sidestand is down.

### Clutch switch

On machines with starter interlock safety circuits, the clutch switch is used to prevent the engine from being started if it is in gear,

unless the clutch lever is pulled in. On some machines the clutch must be pulled in even if the gearbox is in neutral.

The clutch switch is of the plunger type and is mounted on the clutch lever bracket (see illustration 10.22c).

### Side stand switch

The side stand switch forms part of a safety circuit designed to prevent the machine being ridden if the side stand is inadvertently left down. The switch is connected either to a warning lamp or to a starter interlock circuit or both.

In the case of the starter interlock circuit, the switch is either connected to the starter relay so that the engine cannot be started until the stand has been retracted, or it is used in conjunction with the neutral switch to stop the engine if a gear is selected with the stand down. On some systems the side stand switch is wired in conjunction with a relay mounted on the frame.

The switch itself is either of the plunger or rotary type and is mounted on the side stand bracket (see illustrations 10.22d and e).

### Brake light switch

The main function of these switches is, of course, to operate the brake lamp when the

**10.22d Plunger type side stand switch**

**10.22e Rotary type side stand switch**

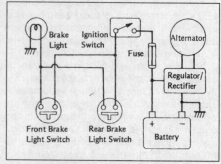

**10.22f Brake light circuit**

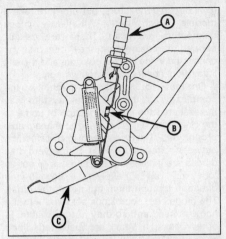

10.22g  Plunger type rear brake switch (A) and its connecting spring (B) to brake pedal (C)

10.22h  Hydraulic type rear brake switch

10.22i  Oil pressure switch

10.22j  Oil level switch as used in a two-stroke oil tank

front or rear brakes are applied (see illustration 10.22f). On scooters the brake switches are often wired into the starter circuit, necessitating the brake to be applied as a safety measure, before the starter can be operated.

Front brake lamp switches are usually small plunger-type units fitted into the lever stock (see illustration 10.22c), though on some models a pressure switch is operated by the front brake hydraulic system. The rear brake switch is usually operated via a spring from the rear brake pedal (see illustration 10.22g), and is adjustable to allow for pedal height and brake free play adjustments, though again some machines use a switch actuated by hydraulic pressure (see illustration 10.22h).

### Oil pressure switch

These are pressure actuated switches designed to warn of low oil pressure in four-stroke engines by lighting the appropriate warning lamp in the instrument panel (see illustration 10.22i). The switch has one fixed contact and a moving contact. When the engine is off and there is no oil pressure, the contacts are together so the switch is closed and completing the circuit to earth via the engine, and therefore the warning light is on. When the engine is started and oil pressure builds up it forces the moving contact off the fixed one and so the switch opens, cutting the circuit to earth and thus extinguishing the warning light.

The circuit normally consists of a power feed through the warning light and to the switch, which when closed completes the circuit to the engine and earth.

### Fluid level switches

These are float-type switches designed to warn of low fluid levels by lighting the appropriate warning lamp in the instrument panel. The switch has one fixed contact and a moving contact fitted to the base of the float. As the level drops, the contacts close, earthing the warning lamp.

Oil level switches are usually found in two-stroke oil tanks (see illustration 22.10j), while four-strokes usually rely on the pressure

switch in the engine itself. An exception to the rule can be found on four-stroke Yamaha models where an oil level switch is fitted in the bottom of the sump.

Similar arrangements have been used in the past for warning the rider of low brake fluid and low battery electrolyte levels.

### Fuel level senders and sensors

A float-operated sender unit is used in conjunction with a fuel gauge to give a precise indication of the amount of fuel remaining in the tank (see illustration 10.22k). A float is

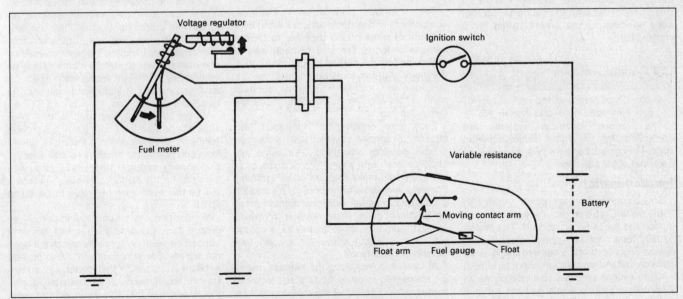

10.22k  Typical fuel gauge circuit

attached to the end of a wire arm and moves up and down with the fuel level. As it does so it operates a variable resistor known as a rheostat. This comprises a number of turns of resistance wire wound round a flat former. The moving contact blade sweeps along the windings, thus determining the overall resistance in the circuit.

The gauge has a scale printed on it, and is calibrated so that when the tank is full the resistance in the circuit places the needle by the FULL mark on the gauge, and as the resistance changes with the amount of fuel left, the needle reacts accordingly.

A fuel level sensor is an on/off switch rather than a variable sender, and operates a warning light in the instrument panel that indicates when only a certain amount of fuel remains in the tank. Fuel level switches are usually mounted in the base of the fuel tank and are often wired through a resistor to prevent the warning light flickering when cornering or during severe acceleration or braking.

### Coolant temperature senders and sensors

Liquid-cooled machines are equipped with temperature gauges and sometimes warning lights. The gauge is actuated by a sender known as a thermocouple which has a resistance that varies according to its temperature. The changes are depicted by the gauge which has a scale printed on it, and is calibrated so that when the engine is cold the resistance in the circuit places the needle by the 'C' mark on the gauge, and as the resistance changes with the temperature, the needle reacts accordingly.

The warning light is used to indicate when the engine temperature is too high. It is sometimes used in conjunction with a gauge, but where space and weight are a concern is used by itself. The sensor unit is a thermocouple as with the gauge set-up, but here operates as an on/off switch for a warning light.

### 23 Control switches

The various electrical systems are controlled from the main switch (ignition switch) in conjunction with switch clusters on each end of the handlebar.

### Ignition switch

This combines the main power switch with some security so that only the keyholder can switch the machine on and off. The switch usually incorporates a mechanical locking device which extends a bar into the steering head so that the handlebars cannot be turned.

Many ignition switches now incorporate an immobiliser system which requires a signal transmitted from the transponder in the ignition key to be sent to a receiver unit in the switch body, thus enabling the starter and ignition systems to function.

The ignition switch controls the main power feed to the wiring loom, and also allows certain circuits to work according to the position of the key. For example most machines incorporate a park facility whereby the sidelight and tail light can be illuminated, the key removed, the ignition circuit and all other circuits switched off, and the steering lock on.

### Handlebar switches

These vary according to the make and model of the machine, but in general the various switches are either of the momentary, or non-latching push-button type (the starter, horn and headlamp flasher buttons) or the lever or rocker type for the lights and turn signals.

Problems are sometimes experienced with switches which could easily be avoided with a little maintenance. Most switch problems are due to corrosion of the contacts, and this is often caused by water getting into the switch in bad weather. The switches (and the various wiring connectors on the machine) can be made virtually impervious to water by packing them with silicone grease. Given the cost of renewing a switch cluster in the event of total failure, this is well worth doing; it is not normally possible to purchase the individual switches. In emergencies, the electrical system can usually be restored after swamping with water by spraying it with a maintenance aerosol spray, such as WD40 or similar.

### 24 The wiring loom and connectors

### Wiring and connectors

The various individual electrical components and systems are connected by a network of wires bound together to form a harness or loom. The size of each wire is determined by the current it must carry, thus the majority of the wires on the machine are fairly thin and flexible. A few wires, such as earth cables and the starter motor leads are very much heavier.

Each wire consists of numerous fine strands of copper covered with a flexible plastic insulator sheathing. The same job could be done with a single, thick conductor, but this would make the wire rather stiff and inflexible, and liable to fracture. The insulator is coloured to permit individual identification. To colour-code a large number of wires without repetition, most have a base colour with a contrasting stripe, or 'tracer' line running along its length.

At various points along the harness, leads are connected to other leads or to electrical components. On earlier machines this was done using individual Lucar (spade) or bullet (cylindrical) connectors, but on more recent models much better multi-way block connectors are used. These are usually handed to ensure that they can only be connected in the correct position, and there is little risk of connecting things wrongly.

On many of the larger machines, the complexity of the electrical system has necessitated the interconnection of some of the circuits to keep the wiring to manageable proportions. This could lead to backfeeding between circuits, and so to prevent this diodes are included in the harness to act as 'one way valves', allowing a flow in one direction through them but not in the other. The diodes are sometimes soldered into the harness itself and so may not be visible. In other cases, a small encapsulated diode block is plugged into the system via a two or three pin block connector.

### Wiring and routing diagrams

Wiring diagrams are created to provide a picture of the electrical system and identify the route taken by each individual wire through the system, to identify which components it feeds and which connectors the wire runs through.

Wiring diagrams are an essential tool for fault-finding, as it is possible to locate start and finish points for a circuit without having to manually trace the wire through the machine itself. They may all look confusing at first, but when they are studied closely and the basic rules mentioned in Section 2 are applied, they become logical. The entire wiring for the machine will usually be presented on a single diagram with the components laid out in their logical locations, i.e. headlight at the front and left and right components on the correct side. Occasionally, the wiring diagram may be split into separate circuits for ignition and starting, charging, lighting and instrumentation.

One of the problems is that manufacturers often have their own set of symbols for identifying components that differ not only from other manufacturers, but also from standards. For example the symbol used by one manufacturer to identify a battery may be completely different from that used by another, and so it is important to get used to and remember all types.

Wiring diagrams also depict the inner workings of a switch housing (i.e. which wire connects to which when a switch is turned from one position to another) so that a test of that switch can be made using the wire terminals in the switch connector, meaning the switch itself does not have to be taken apart.

Wire routing is particularly important to ensure that the wiring does not become trapped between components and that it does not impede steering movement. All wires, and all hoses and pipes for that matter, are cut to a specific length before they are installed, and this is because they are designed to take a specific route through the machine. Taking a different route will mean they are either too long or too short. Too long and they may become kinked or bent sharply, which can fracture a wire or block a hose. Too short and they can become stretched and detached, or can be cracked or rubbed by being tight around a metal bracket. In the case of wiring this is highly undesirable as a rubbed insulator will expose the conductor to the metal of the frame or bracket and create a short circuit to earth. At best this will blow a fuse, and at worst will ruin electronic components or drain the battery extremely quickly.

## 25 Fuses and relays

### Fuses

The purpose of a fuse is to provide a breakable safety link in a circuit to prevent too much current entering a component **(see illustration 10.25a)**. The fuse is a cheap and disposable component. There are many types available, but they all work on the same principle **(see illustration 10.25b, c and d)**.

A wire is held in a body, and that wire is rated to carry a particular current and no more. Therefore if a slightly higher current than desired is being sent to a component, the fuse will 'blow' (the wire in the fuse burns and breaks) and isolate that component from the battery so that it cannot be damaged. Fuses are normally housed together in a fusebox.

### Relays

A relay is basically an electromagnetic switch that uses a low current feed from a manual switch to actuate it and turn a high current circuit on or off. The advantage of using a relay is that it eliminates the need to run a high current, and therefore a thick wire, to the switch itself which would make for a heavy and bulky wiring loom with a large voltage drop. The use of relays means that high current cables can be kept as short as possible.

Relays are used for the starter motor circuit (see Section 13), headlights, cooling fans, fuel pumps, sidestand switches, and in electronic control and management systems for power switching.

Relays are equipped with numbered terminals that either plug into a wiring connector on the loom, or plug into a relay connector block that houses a number of different relays, much like a fusebox **(see illustration 10.25e)**.

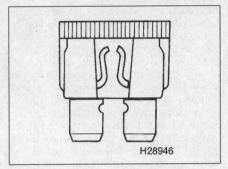

10.25a **A blown fuse can be identified by a break in its element**

10.25b **Flat blade or plug-in fuses**

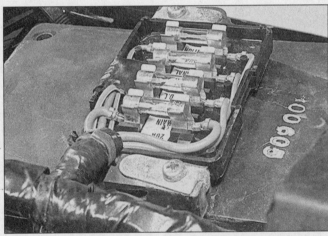

10.25c **Glass cartridge fuses**

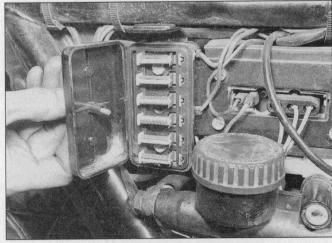

10.25d **Ceramic fuses**

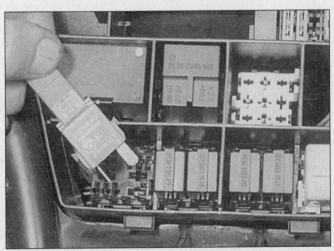

10.25e **Relays are a plug-in fit and often grouped together**

# Notes

# Technical Terms Explained

## A

**Accelerator pump** A carburettor device for temporarily increasing the amount of fuel delivered (i.e. for richening the mixture) so as to improve acceleration.

**Air filter** Either a paper, fabric, felt, foam or gauze element through which the engine draws its air. It traps dirt and debris which might otherwise block carburettor jets or cause wear to the moving parts.

**Air/fuel ratio** Proportions in which air and fuel are mixed to form a combustible gas.

**Alternating current** Electricity varying in polarity and potential (voltage), reversing direction regularly. The kind generated in an alternator. Abbreviated to a.c. (compare with **direct current**).

**Alternator** A generator of alternating current (a.c.) electricity.

**ABS (Anti-lock braking system)** A system, usually electronically controlled, that senses incipient wheel lockup during braking and relieves hydraulic pressure at wheel which is about to skid.

**Ampere (amp)** A unit of measurement for the flow of electrical current. Amps (current) = Volts (voltage) ÷ Ohms (resistance).

**Ampere-hour (Ah)** Measure of battery capacity.

**Antifreeze** A substance (usually ethylene glycol) mixed with water, and added to the cooling system, to prevent freezing of the coolant in winter. Antifreeze also contains chemicals to inhibit corrosion and the formation of rust and other deposits that would tend to clog the radiator and coolant passages and reduce cooling efficiency.

**Anti-dive** System attached to the fork lower leg (slider) to prevent fork dive when braking hard.

**API** American Petroleum Institute. A quality standard for 4-stroke motor oils.

**Armature** That part of an electrical apparatus such as a solenoid, dynamo or magnet, which comprises the electrical windings in which a current flow or a magnetic field is generated or excited (see **magnet**).

**Aspect ratio** With a tyre, the ratio of the section's depth to its width. Old tyres had an aspect ratio of 100% (as fat as they were deep) but modern motorcycle tyres are flatter with an aspect ratio of say 80%.

**ATF** Automatic Transmission Fluid. Often used in front forks.

**ATU** Automatic Timing Unit. Mechanical device for advancing the ignition timing on early engines.

**ATV** All Terrain Vehicle. Often called a Quad.

**Axle** A shaft on which a wheel revolves. Also known as a spindle.

## B

**Backlash** The amount of movement between meshed components when one component is held still. Usually applies to gear teeth.

**Ball bearing** A bearing consisting of a hardened inner and outer race with hardened steel balls between the two races.

**BDC** Bottom Dead Centre - denotes that the piston is at the lowest point of its stroke in the cylinder.

**Bearings** Used between two working surfaces to prevent wear of the components and a build-up of heat. Five types of bearing are commonly used on motorcycles: plain bearings, shell bearings, ball bearings, tapered roller bearings and needle roller bearings.

**Belt drive** Drive by a belt. Typical applications are for drive to the camshafts and transmission, and sometimes to the rear wheel.

**Bevel gear** Gear with slanted teeth, a pair of such gears turning the drive through ninety degrees.

**BHP** Brake Horsepower. The British measurement for engine power output. Power output is now commonly expressed in kilowatts (kW).

**Bias-belted tyre** Similar construction to radial tyre, but with outer belt running at an angle to the wheel rim.

**Big-end** The larger end of a connecting rod and the one mounted on the crankpin. Usually fitted with shell bearings or caged ball bearings.

**Bi-metallic** Made of two metals.

**Bobweight** A countershaft weight on a crankshaft offsetting piston and con-rod mass.

**Bore** Diameter of a cylinder. Often refers to the cylinder itself. In some senses, the surface of a hole.

**Bore: stroke ratio** The ratio of cylinder diameter to stroke. When these are equal the engine is said to be square.

**Boss** A raised area on a component, the thickness being provided for more strength.

**Bottom Dead Centre (BDC)** Denotes that the piston is at the lowest point of its stroke in the cylinder.

**Bottom-end** A description of an engine's crankcase components and all components contained there-in.

**Brake disc** The component of an hydraulic brake system that rotates with the wheel.

**Brake drum** The component of a drum brake system that rotates with the wheel.

**Brake pads** The components which carry the friction material in an hydraulic brake system and which contact the brake disc when the brake is applied.

**Brake shoes** The components which carry the friction material on a drum brake system and which contact the brake drum when the brake is applied.. The friction material (often called lining) is bonded to the shoes.

**BTDC** Before **Top Dead Centre** in terms of piston position. Ignition timing is often expressed in terms of degrees or millimetres BTDC.

**Bush** A cylindrical metal and/or rubber component used between two moving parts.

# C

**Caliper** In an hydraulic brake system, the component spanning the disc and housing the pistons and brake pads.

**Cam chain** The chain which takes drive from the crankshaft to the camshaft(s).

**Cam follower** A component in contact with the camshaft lobes, transmitting motion to the valve gear. Followers often house the shim in a DOHC arrangement.

**Camplate** A flat (or slightly bowed) plate in which are formed slots in which pegs may move for converting complete rotary motion into a sliding mode for the operation of, say, control gear (such as selector forks for controlling gearbox ratio choice).

**Camshaft** A rotary shaft equipped with lobes for converting rotary into linear movement, generally for the operation of valve gear in poppet valve engines.

**Canister** The main component in an evaporative emission control system (California market only); contains activated charcoal granules to trap vapours from the fuel system rather than allowing them to vent to the atmosphere.

**Capacitor** Strictly, a condenser. But, by convention, often one of considerably larger capacity than a normal condenser and able to perform a smoothing role in battery-less current generation.

**Carburettor** Component for mixing variable volumes of air and fuel in the correct ratio to form a combustible mixture for variable speeds and loads.

**Catalytic converter** A device in the exhaust system of some machines which converts certain pollutants in the exhaust gases into less harmful substances.

**Centre of gravity** The point from which a mass could be suspended so that it would be in 'all round balance' and would remain in any attitude in which it was placed. The 'centre of its mass' so to say.

**Centrifugal** To be thrown outwards. An outward force on an object moving around a point. The opposite – the force tending inwards – is centripetal.

**Charging system** Description of the components which charge the battery, i.e. the alternator, rectifier and regulator.

**Clearance volume** The space inside the combustion chamber when the piston is at the top of its stroke (top dead centre), and extending half way up the spark plug threads. Sometimes called the trapped volume.

**Clutch** A device for engaging or disengaging the engine from the driving wheel and so designed that connection may be smooth and progressive at any time.

**Coefficient** The reduction of a characteristic to a numeral value and related to basic units (e.g. per degree Celsius).

**Coil spring** A spiral of elastic steel found in various sizes throughout a vehicle, for example as a springing medium in the suspension and in the valve train.

**Collet** A ring-shaped device, usually divided into two segments, for wedging a component on to a rod, shaft, spindle, etc. Especially to be found on valve and suspension units to enable the spring retainer to lock itself against the valve stem or damper rod.

**Commutator** Part of a rotating armature, against which the pick-up brushes rub, so that electricity generated in the spinning armature may be collected.

**Compression** Squeezing smaller, particularly a fresh charge of mixture in the cylinder by the rising piston.

**Compression damping** Controls the speed the suspension compresses when hitting a bump.

**Compression ratio** The extent to which the contents of the cylinder are compressed by the rising piston. The ratio of the swept volume (cubic capacity) plus the clearance volume (combustion chamber space) in relation to the clearance volume alone.

**Concave** Curved inwards. Hollow or cave-like. Opposite to convex.

**Concentric** Tending to a common centre.

**Condenser** Electrical device able to store electricity and particularly to release it very rapidly. Can assist in the control of arcing in a make-and-break system. Properly called a capacitor.

**Connecting-rod** The rod, commonly known as a con-rod, in a reciprocating engine connecting the piston to the crankshaft via the big and small ends.

**Constant rate** A spring is this when each equal increment in load produces an equal change in length. (Contrast with **multi-rate** and **progressive rate**.)

**Contact breaker** An electrical switch designed to permit a field-producing current to flow in an HT coil and then to abruptly cut the current so that the rapid inward collapse of the magnetic flux produces a strong, high voltage current in the secondary windings.

**Continuity** The uninterrupted path in the flow of electricity. Little or no measurable resistance.

**Cradle** A support, usually designed to embrace components. A type of frame in which the bottom tubes embrace the engine.

**Crankcase** The structurally-strong chamber in which is carried the crankshaft. The singular and plural forms are used indiscriminately as, in much motorcycle design, this component is made in two non-mirror images to form a pair.

**Crankshaft** A forged component, using the principle of the eccentric (crank) for converting the reciprocating piston engine's linear power pulse into rotary motion.

**Cross-ply tyre** Form of tyre construction in which the wraps of fabric in the tyre carcass are laid over each other diagonally instead of radially (see **radial ply**).

**Cross valve** A rotary valve placed above the cylinder and handling exhaust as well as inlet gases on the four-stroke cycle. Permits high compression ratios with a good resistance to detonation and yields excellent fuel consumption.

**Crownwheel** The larger of the two gear wheels in the reduction (or final drive) pair at the axle of a shaft-drive motorcycle. The smaller is called the pinion.

**Cruciform** Cross-shaped.

**Current** The amount of flow in an electrical circuit, measured in Amps or Amperes. Amps (current) = Volts (voltage) ÷ Ohms (resistance).

**Cush drive** A shock-absorbing component in a transmission system. In the rear wheel, cush drive rubber dampers are usually incorporated between the hub and the sprocket carrier to absorb transmission shock. In some engines, a sprung cam that locates against a similar solid cam on a joining shaft is used to absorb sudden surges in power and so smooth delivery to the rear wheel.

**Cylinder** A parallel-sided circular cavity, usually containing a piston.

**Cylinder head** Component closing the blind end of the cylinder. Houses the valve gear on a four-stroke engine.

# D

**Damper** A device for controlling and perhaps eliminating unwanted movement. In suspension systems, for quickly arresting oscillations, and for absorbing unwanted energy to release it as heat.

**Decarbonise** To remove accumulated carbon and other deposits from the combustion chamber, inlet tract and exhaust system.

**Decompressor** A small valve, usually manually operated, to release above-piston compression for kickstarting purposes.

**Deflector crown** A raised part or hump on the piston crown of some two-strokes to deflect the incoming fresh charge away from the exhaust port.

**Depression** The amount of partial vacuum in the inlet manifold.

**Desmodronic** A method of operating poppet valves so that they are positively closed by a rocker arm as well as opened. Design used by Ducati.

**Detent** A mechanical device to lock a movement, in particular the selector system of a gearbox.

**Detonation** Explosion of the mixture in the combustion chamber, instead of controlled burning. May cause a tinkling noise, known as **pinking**, under an open throttle. Intensely destructive.

**Diaphragm** The rubber membrane in a master cylinder or carburettor which seals the upper chamber.

**Diaphragm spring** A single sprung plate often used in clutches.

**Diode** An electrical device which allows a current to flow in one direction only. See also **zener diode**.

**Direct current** Electricity of constant polarity (direction) which may or may not fluctuate in potential (voltage). The kind of electricity produced by a dynamo or stored in a battery. Abbreviated to d.c. (compare with **alternating current**).

**Disc brake** A brake design incorporating a rotating disc onto which the brake pads are squeezed. The resulting friction converts the energy of a moving vehicle into heat.

**Disc valve (or rotary valve)** A induction control system used on some two-stroke engines.

**Displacement** The amount of volume displaced by the piston of an engine on rising from its lowest position to its highest. In some cases may be marginally different from the cubic capacity calculated from the bore and the crankshaft's eccentricity (throw).

**Dog** A projection from a moving part, mating with another dog or a slot, on another part, so that the two components may be locked together or left free of each other. Used in gearboxes to connect two pinions on a shaft.

**Double-overhead camshaft (DOHC)** An engine that uses two overhead camshafts, one for the intake valves and one for the exhaust valves.

**Downdraught** Downward inclination of the induction tract, usually the carburettor too.

**Drum brake** One with a rotating chamber (of drum shape) attached to a wheel and inside which are held 'shoes' carrying friction material (**brake shoes**) which are forced outwards against the inner periphery of the chamber.

**Drivebelt** A toothed belt used to transmit drive to the rear wheel on some motorcycles. A drivebelt has also been used to drive the camshafts. Drivebelts are usually made of Kevlar.

**Driveshaft** Any shaft used to transmit motion. Commonly used when referring to the final driveshaft on shaft drive motorcycles.

**Dry liner** Cylinder liner not in contact with water (see **wet liner**) .

**Dry sump** Four-stroke lubrication system in which the oil is carried in a separate oil tank and not in the sump. Drainage into the sump is removed by a scavenge pump so that the sump is kept dry.

**Duplex** Two. A duplex frame has two front down tubes. A duplex chain has two rows of rollers (a simple chain has but one).

**Dwell** That period of rotation of a valve or contact breaker cam in which the valve is closed or the breaker open.

**Dynamic** Moving, in action – the opposite of lifeless or static.

**Dynamo** A generator of direct current (d.c.) electricity.

# E

**Earth** The negative terminal of a battery, or part of the **earth return**. A connection to earth (or ground). By definition, of zero potential (voltage).

**Earth return** The path of an electrical circuit that returns to the battery, utilising the motorcycle's frame.

**Eccentric** Not central. An offset pin used to drive or be driven.

**ECU (Electronic Control Unit)** A computer which controls (for instance) an ignition system, or an anti-lock braking system.

**EGO** Exhaust Gas Oxygen sensor. Sometimes called a Lambda sensor.

**Electrode** A conductor with an end from which electricity can be taken.

**Electrolyte** The liquid in a battery, usually an acid but sometimes an alkali.

**Electro-magnet** A magnet, strongly excited by an electric current, used to create a local field by means of flowing the current in windings. Has the quality of losing virtually all magnetism practically instantaneously the moment the current flow ceases.

**EMS (Engine Management System)** A computer controlled system which manages the fuel injection and the ignition systems in an integrated fashion.

**Energy transfer** A system of ignition in which closed contact breaker points allow energy to build up in the alternator windings, point opening resulting in a rush of current to an external HT coil which transforms its low voltage into high voltage for the spark plug.

**EP (Extreme Pressure)** Oil type used in locations where high loads are applied, such as between gear teeth.

**Evaporative emission control system** Describes a charcoal filled canister which stores fuel vapours from the tank rather than allowing them to vent to the atmosphere. Usually only fitted to California models and referred to as an EVAP system.

**Expansion chamber** Section of two-stroke engine exhaust system so designed to improve engine efficiency and boost power.

# F

**Ferrous** Containing iron.

**Filament** Electrical resistance wire incandescing (glowing) when made to pass an adequately heavy current and thus yielding light.

**Final drive** Description of the drive from the transmission to the rear wheel. Usually by chain or shaft, but sometimes by belt.

**Finning** A thin but wide plate-like projection, usually arranged in multiples, and generally functioning for the dissipation of heat. Fins are sometimes used for strengthening and often for appearance.

# Technical Terms Explained

**Firing order** The order in which the engine cylinders fire, or deliver their power strokes, beginning with the number one cylinder.

**Flat head** An engine with a flat cylinder head instead of curved internal contours. The valve arrangement may be **sv** or **ohv**.

**Flat top** Piston with a flat top, in contrast to one with a concave (hollow) or convex (domed) crown.

**Flat twin (or four/six)** An engine with horizontal adjacent or opposed cylinders, thereby having a flat configuration.

**Float** A buoyant object. Used in a carburettor to open and close the fuel inlet valve to maintain a constant **fuel level**. Also used in fluid gauge senders.

**Float chamber** A carburettor component used to stabilise the fuel level regardless of the head of fuel supplied by gravity flow from an overhead tank or by a pump. It uses a **float** to operate the fuel inlet valve.

**Float level** The height at which the float is positioned in the float chamber, so determining the **fuel level**.

**Flywheel** A rotating mass of considerable weight and radius, used to smooth out power impulses and to store energy to assist clutch engagement.

**Four-stroke** An operating cycle for an internal combustion engine in which combustion takes place on every other ascent of the piston. The four events (induction, compression, ignition, exhaust) in the engine cycle are thus completed in four strokes (two up, two down) of the piston. See also **Two-stroke**.

**Freeplay** The amount of travel before any action takes place. The looseness in a linkage, or an assembly of parts, between the initial application of force and actual movement. For example, the distance the rear brake pedal moves before the rear brake is actuated.

**Friction** The resistance between two bodies moving in contact with each other and relatively to each other.

**Front fork** Telescopic tubes incorporating springs and dampers used to provide a **suspension** system for the front of a motorcycle. Conventional forks have the outer tube at the bottom, connected to the wheel axle, and acting as the slider, moving over the inner tube, which is secured at the top in the yokes. See also **Upside-down forks**.

**Fuel injection** The fuel/air mixture is metered electronically and directed into the engine intake ports (indirect injection) or into the cylinders (direct injection). Sensors supply information on engine speed and conditions.

**Fuel/air mixture** The charge of fuel and air going into the engine. See **Stoichiometric ratio**.

**Fuel level** The level of fuel in a float chamber. Can be altered by changing the **float level**.

**Fulcrum** The point about which a leverage system pivots (see **lever**).

**Fuse** An electrical device which protects a circuit against accidental overload. The typical fuse contains a soft piece of metal which is calibrated to melt at a predetermined current flow (expressed as amps) and break the circuit.

# G

**Gaiter** A rubber tube, usually corrugated and always flexible, around a sliding or otherwise moving joint, and used for protection of working components.

**Gasket** Any thin, soft material - usually cork, cardboard, asbestos or soft metal - installed between two metal surfaces to ensure a good seal. For instance, the cylinder head gasket seals the joint between the block and the cylinder head.

**Gassing** The giving-off of gas from the cells of a battery due to excessive charging. Explosive hydrogen oxygen mixture is released. Gassing does not commence prior to the achievement of full charge.

**Gear** A component, often circular, with projections for the positive transmission of movement to a companion gear which may, or may not be, of the same shape and size.

**Gearbox** An assembly containing the transmission components used in varying the ratio of the gearing. Even when this is effected by short chains and sprockets, and other methods of ratio variation, the term gearbox is still used.

**Gear ratio** The ratio of turning speeds of any pair of gears or sprockets, derived from their number of teeth. Particularly the total drive ratio of each set of gears in a gearbox or the overall transmission ratio.

**Grease** A stabilised mixture of a metallic soap and a lubricating oil. Lime (calcium) and lithium are both used as base soaps.

**Gudgeon pin** The pin, usually made of hardened steel, linking the piston to the small end of the connecting rod. Possibly the most high stressed bearing of an engine. Often called a **piston pin** or wrist pin.

# H

**Helical gears** Gear teeth are slightly curved and produce less noise that straight-cut gears. Often used for primary drives.

**Helicoil** A thread repair system using an insert to replace damaged threads. Commonly used as a repair for stripped spark plug threads.

**Hertz** A measurement of frequency. A Hertz is a movement of one cycle per second of an alternating waveform.

**HT High Tension** Description of the electrical circuit from the secondary winding of the ignition coil to the spark plug.

**HT lead** A heavily insulated wire carrying the high tension current from the coil to the spark plug.

**High tensile** Material of high tensile (or 'stretch' strength). Tough.

**Honing** Achieving a good finish and precision control of size, to better than one ten thousandth part of an inch in, say, cylinders, by a slowly-proceeding abrasion process. Similar to grinding, but done slowly. A cylinder honing tool can be used to deglaze the cylinder, leaving a fine cross-hatch pattern designed to trap oil to lubricate the piston rings.

**Horizontally-opposed** A type of engine in which the cylinders are opposite to each other with the crankshaft in between.

**Hub** The centre part of a wheel.

**Hub centre steering** Motorcycle steering modified to car practice so that the lock to lock axis lies within the hub itself.

**Hydraulic** A liquid filled system used to transmit pressure from one component to another. Common uses on motorcycles are brake and clutch actuating mechanisms. Sometimes used in the valve train to eliminate clearance.

**Hydrocarbon** Hydrogen and carbon compound forming the basis of all lubricants and oils formed from crude oil.

**Hydrometer** A device for measuring the specific gravity (S.G.) of a liquid, and in particular of battery acid so to assess the state of charge.

**Hygroscopic** Water absorbing. In motorcycle applications, braking efficiency will be reduced if DOT 3 or 4 hydraulic fluid absorbs water from the air - care must be taken to keep new brake fluid in tightly sealed containers.

**Hypoid oil** An extreme-pressure oil formulated to stand up to severe and unique conditions in hypoid transmission gears.

# I

**lbf ft** Pounds-force feet. An imperial unit of torque. Sometimes written as ft-lbs.

**lbf in** Pounds-force inch. An imperial unit of torque, applied to components where a very low torque is required. Sometimes written as in-lbs.

**IC** Abbreviation for Integrated Circuit.

**Idler** Gear interposed between two others so the direction of rotation of the other gears is the same. An idler does not alter the ratio between the proper gears.

**Ignition advance** Means of increasing the timing of the spark at higher engine speeds. Done by mechanical means (ATU) on early engines or electronically by the ignition control unit on later engines.

**Ignition timing** The moment at which the spark plug fires, expressed in the number of crankshaft degrees before the piston reaches the top of its stroke, or in the number of millimetres before the piston reaches the top of its stroke.

**Impeller** A powered device used to impel coolant through an engine and radiator to assist natural thermo-syphon action. Usually a rotary vane-type pump.

**Inertia** The property of matter by which it wants to continue at rest, or in motion, without change of direction or velocity (See **Momentum**).

**Infinite resistance (∞)** Description of an open-circuit electrical state, where no **continuity** exists.

**Injector** Equipment for squirting a fluid. Used for both fuel and oil.

**Insulator** Substance or component for handicapping the transfer of heat or entirely preventing the transmission of electricity.

**Interference fit** Two parts so sized that the inner is minutely larger than the outer. When forced together they jam in place, grasping each other to obstruct separation.

**Inverted forks (upside down forks)** The sliders or lower legs are held in the yokes and the fork tubes or stanchions are connected to the wheel axle (spindle). Less unsprung weight and stiffer construction than conventional forks.

# J

**JASO** Quality standard for 2-stroke oils.

**Jet** A hole through which air, fuel or oil passes, the size of the jet determining the quantity.

**Jockey** A wheel placed between the centres of a belt or chain, engaging with one run of it, and used to adjust tension.

**Joule** The unit of electrical energy.

**Journal** The bearing surface of a shaft.

# K

**Kickstart** A crank, operated by foot, for starting an engine.

**Kilovolt** One thousand volts, abbreviated to Kv.

**Kinetic energy** The energy of motion, and not that of position.

**Knock** Similar to **detonation**, with same end results, but only the end gases in the far reaches of the combustion chamber ignite. The knocking sound, also known as pinking, occurs when the central and outer flame fronts meet.

# L

**Lambda (λ) sensor** A sensor fitted in the exhaust system to measure the exhaust gas oxygen content (excess air factor).

**Land** The raised portion between two grooves (e.g. between the ring grooves in a piston).

**Latent heat** The amount of heat input needed to change a solid to its liquid state, or a liquid to a gas, without change of temperature.

**Layshaft** In a 'direct top gearbox' a gearbox shaft parallel to the mainshaft and carrying the laygears with which the mainshaft gears mesh to achieve ratio change.

**LCD** Abbreviation for Liquid Crystal Display.

**Leading link** A form of front suspension using a pivoting link – approximately horizontal – with the axle in front of the pivot.

**LED** Abbreviation for Light Emitting Diode.

**Liner** A detachable insert in a component used either to reduce size or to provide a better working surface or to restore a working surface (see **sleeve**). Often a steel liner in an aluminium cylinder block.

**Lobe** The total part of a cam that is eccentric to its centre, the part not on the base circle, and that is used to intermittently actuate another component, such as a valve, as it rotates.

**LT Low Tension** Description of the electrical circuit from the power supply to the primary winding of the ignition coil.

**Lubricant** A substance, usually an oil, interposed between rubbing surfaces to decrease friction.

# M

**Magnetism** A force invested in magnetic situations or substances, having the quality of attraction and repulsion depending on polarity, and of some similarity to electricity.

**Magneto** A self-contained ignition spark generating instrument featuring primary and secondary (HT) windings and requiring no external power source.

**Main bearing** The principal bearing(s) on which a component is carried but usually reserved exclusively for the crankshaft.

**Mainshaft** A principal shaft, as in an engine or a gearbox.

**Maintenance-free (MF) battery** A sealed battery which cannot be topped up.

**Master cylinder** The operator end of an hydraulic control system, so called because (on cars) it operates several slave cylinders.

**Mesh** The closeness of fit of the teeth of gears and similar articles. Gears which run together all the time, irrespective of whether drive is being transmitted through them (i.e. can be freewheeling) are referred to as being in 'constant mesh'.

**Momentum** The desire of a moving object to continue in motion (see **Inertia**).

**Monograde oil** An oil, the viscosity of which is within the limits set for a single SAE number.

**Monoshock** A single suspension unit linking the swingarm or suspension linkage to the frame.

**Multigrade oil** Having a wide viscosity range (e.g. 10W40). The W stands for Winter, thus the viscosity ranges from SAE10 when cold to SAE40 when hot.

**Multi-rate** A spring which changes length unequally for equal increments of load. (Contrast with **constant rate** and **progressive rate**.)

# N

**Needle roller bearing** A bearing made up of many small diameter rollers of hardened steel, usually kept separated by a cage. Often used where lubrication is poor.

**Negative earth** Using the negative or minus pole of the battery as the earth.

**Nm** Newton metres used to measure torque.

**Non-ferrous** Compounds which do not contain iron.

# O

**Octane** A colourless inflammable hydrocarbon that is a constituent of fuel (petrol).

**Octane rating** Defines the amount of octane in a fuel, and used as a measure of the **knock** resistance of the fuel. The larger the number, the more knock resistant the fuel.

**Odometer** A mileage recorder.

**Ohm** The unit of electrical resistance. Ohms (resistance) = volts (voltage) ÷ amps (current).

**Oil cooling** The use of oil as a cooling medium to transfer heat from a hot component to the environment (atmosphere or even a cooler part of the engine).

**Oil injection** A system of two-stroke engine lubrication where oil is pump-fed to the engine in accordance with throttle position.

**Oil pump** A mechanically-driven device for distributing oil around a four-stroke engine or pumping oil into a two-stroke engine.

**Otto cycle** The cycle of operation of a four-stroke engine, namely induction, compression, ignition and exhaust. See also **Two-stroke** and **Four-stroke**.

**Overhead valve (OHV)** A four-stroke engine with the poppet valves in the cylinder head and operated by pushrods.

**Overhead cam (OHC)** As above but with the camshaft contained in the cylinder head and operated by chain, gear or belt from the crankshaft. (See also **SOHC** and **DOHC**).

**Overlap** The duration of crankshaft rotation during which the inlet and exhaust valve are open at the same time.

**Oversize (OS)** Term used for piston and ring size options fitted to a rebored cylinder.

**Oxygen sensor** A device installed in the exhaust system which senses the oxygen content in the exhaust and converts this information into an electric current. Also called a Lambda sensor.

# P

**Pawl** A catch to mesh with a ratchet wheel, sometimes to prevent reverse motion.

**Permanent magnet** A magnet made of very retentive steel alloy which holds its magnetism well, in contrast to soft iron and electro-magnets.

**Petroil** Lubrication mixture for two-strokes. Oil is mixed with the petrol prior to the mixture's induction to the engine.

**Pinion** In transmission terms, strictly the smaller of a pair of gears but colloquially any gear. The larger gear (or sprocket) is termed the wheel.

**Pinking** The noise arising from **Detonation** and **Knock**.

**Piston** A moving plunger in a cylinder, intended to seal the cylinder and to accept or deliver thrust.

**Piston boss** The material below the piston crown (and also joined to the skirt) which carries the gudgeon pin.

**Piston pin** The pin, usually made of hardened steel, linking the piston to the small end of the connecting rod. Possibly the most high stressed bearing of an engine. Often called a **gudgeon pin** or wrist pin.

**Pitch** The nominal distance between two specified points such as gear teeth, spring coils or chain rollers.

**Planetary** A system of gears in which two or more wheels orbit round a central sun wheel. Found in some transmission systems and starter motor drives.

**Plug cap** A cover over the top of a spark plug that transmits the HT voltage from the coil and lead to the plug. Also incorporates a suppressor.

**Plug lead** A heavily insulated wire carrying the high tension current from the coil to the spark plug.

**Plunger pump** An oil pump consisting of a reciprocating plunger in a chamber, and provided with ports.

**Polarity** The electrical condition of a pole - either positive or negative.

**Pneumatic** Utilising or pertaining to air or another gas.

**Poppet valve** The conventional type of valve used in almost all cylinder heads. In simple terms, a disc on the end of a rod which pops open and shut to open or close valve ports in the head.

**Port** Strictly, a hole or opening but also used to described the transfer ports in a two-stroke engine.

**Positive earth** Using the positive or plus pole of the battery as the earth.

**Power band** The band of rpm in which the engine produces really useful power in contrast to the speeds outside of it in which disproportionately much less power is available.

**Pre-ignition** Auto-ignition taking place before the desired moment and happening, not by sparking, but by incandescence.

**Pre-load (suspension)** The amount a spring is compressed when in the unloaded state. Pre-load can be adjusted by gas, spacer or mechanical adjuster. Determines ride height.

**Premix** The method of engine lubrication on older two-stroke engines. Engine oil is mixed with the petrol in the fuel tank in a specific ratio. The fuel/oil mix is sometimes referred to as 'petroil'.

**Pressure** The exerting of a pushing force. Expressed in psi (pounds per square inch) or Bars.

**Pre-unit engine** Engine and gearbox as separate entities. Compare with **unit engine**.

**Primary chain** Heavy duty chain joining the engine to the gearbox on a pre-unit engine, or the crankshaft to the clutch on a unit construction engine.

**Primary current** see **LT Low Tension**.

**Primary gears** The pair of gears connecting the crankshaft to the clutch in a unit construction engine.

**Printed circuit** A route for electricity to flow impressed on to insulating material, instead of actual wires being used to join the terminals involved. A printed circuit board (PCB) contains many printed circuits.

**Progressive rate** A spring that progressively deflects less for equal increments in load (see **Constant rate** and **Multi-rate**).

**PSI** Abbreviation for pounds per square inch, an imperial unit of pressure.

**Pulse secondary air injection system** An emission control system. A process of promoting the burning of excess fuel present in the exhaust gases by routing fresh air into the exhaust ports.

**Pump** Component for propelling oil, coolant or fuel through a circuit at high pressure.

**Pushrod** A stout rod used to transmit a push as in clutch or overhead-valve operation.

# Q

**Quadrant** A selector piece, usually provided with gear-like teeth for driving purposes, and strictly occupying a fourth part of a circle (namely 90°). Found in kickstarters and gearchange mechanisms.

**Quartz halogen bulb** A tungsten filament bulb with a halogen gas filling. Used for headlights because of the high efficiency in lumens per watt, long life and absence of blackening of the glass.

# R

**Radial ply tyre** Form of tyre construction in which the wraps of fabric in the tyre carcass are laid over each other radially, and not diagonally.

**Radiator** Device for losing heat. Heat from hot oil or coolant is transferred to the atmosphere via a large surface area mounted in the airstream.

**Rake** The angle of the steering axis from the vertical.

**Ratchet** Wheel or quadrant with inclined or castellated teeth into which a pawl can notch to prevent reverse movement or to achieve one-way drive with an over-running capacity as in a kickstarter.

**Ratio** The proportion of one thing to another, in terms of quantity. Often reduced to a comparison against unity (one) as a base figure. (See **gear ratio** and **compression ratio**.)

**Rebore** Removing the worn surface of a cylinder to create a new working surface. Such a bore is then larger than before, and is termed 'oversize'. Similarly oversize pistons and pistons rings must then be used.

**Rebound damping** A means of controlling the oscillation of a suspension unit spring after it has been compressed. Resists the spring's natural tendency to bounce back after being compressed.

**Reciprocating weight** The mass of parts that reciprocate. In the case of a piston and con-rod assembly, all of the piston, ring and gudgeon pin mass, plus half the mass of the rod.

**Recoil** The bouncing backwards, towards its static position, of a spring as it asserts itself.

**Rectifier** Electrical device passing current in one direction only (and thus a wave), used to convert alternating current into direct current.

**Reed valves** A valve functioning like a reed, with pressure causing the 'flap' to open or close. Capable of working at extremely high speeds.

**Regulator** Device for maintaining the charging voltage from the generator or alternator within a specified range.

**Relay** An electrical device used to switch heavy current on and off using a low current auxiliary circuit. Relays are used to switch heavy currents such as for the starter motor. Eliminates the need to have heavy duty wires and switches on the handlebar.

**Resistance** Measured in ohms. An electrical component's ability to pass electrical current. Ohms (resistance) = volts (voltage) ÷ amps (current).

**Reverse flow** Control of the fresh charge into the two-stroke combustion space by oblique and upward angling of the transfer ports, so directing the new charge that it drives the burnt gases out before it.

**Rim** The edge, margin or periphery. In the case of a wheel, the part that carries the tyre.

**Rising rate** Condition set up using a three-way linkage between the swingarm and the shock absorber to give progressive suspension action.

**Rocker** A device pivoting between its ends and transmitting a push on one end in the opposite direction at the other. Rockers can also handle pulling forces. Some rockers (e.g. in some valve gear) lack the true rocking action and are pivoted at one end and so do not reverse motion.

**Rocking couple** The tendency of some kinds of reciprocating engine to generate a rocking effect on the machine.

**Roller bearing** One containing rollers as the support medium, and not balls. The rollers run in specially prepared tracks and are kept clear of each other by a cage. Rollers are usually of hardened steel.

**Rotary** Capable of rotation. Spinning. An engine, the principal components of which spin instead of reciprocate.

**Rotary valve** A valve for two-stroke or four-stroke which, by rotation, opens and closes gas passageways at the appropriate times and usually disc, conical or cylindrical in shape. Normally found on inlet systems.

**rpm** revolutions per minute.

**Runout** Wobble. Out of truth. Total runout is the full measurement from one extreme to the other. Sometimes referred to as total indicator reading. Confusion occurs when runout is measured from the midpoint, which is actually half the total runout.

# S

**SAE** Abbreviation for Society of Automotive Engineers. SAE numbers form a system for classifying lubricating oils into viscosity ranges at prescribed temperatures.

**Scavenge** To clear away, particularly exhaust gas from the cylinder and oil from a dry sump.

**Schnurle loop scavenging** Scavenging system used in two-stroke engines with flat-top pistons. The incoming mixture, so directed by the transfer port, loops up the cylinder, across the head, and down towards the exhaust port, propelling burnt gas residues before it.

**Secondary current** That flowing, at high voltage (or **high tension, HT**) in the coil secondary windings, HT lead and across the spark plug electrodes.

**Seizure** The binding together of two moving parts through pressure, temperature or lack of lubrication, and often all three. Also called freezing up.

**Selector fork** A forked-shaped prong, mating with the track of a gearbox pinion or dog, for the purpose of sliding that component from side to side.

**Shaft drive** A method of transmitting drive from the transmission to the rear wheel.

**Shock absorber** A device for ironing out the effects of riding over bumps in the road to give a smooth ride - commonly a spring used in conjunction with an hydraulic damper fitted between the swingarm and frame. Also used in engines for ironing out minute irregularities in power delivery to smooth the transmission of power in the engine.

**Shoe** A rigid component able to press against another, sometimes, as with brake shoes, being faced with a friction material.

**Side valve (SV)** An engine having its valve gear at the side of the cylinder and not overhead.

**Sidewall** The part of a tyre between the bead and the tread. On this part is moulded the maker's name, sizing, etc.

**Silencer** Device to quieten the exhaust note.

**Single-overhead camshaft (SOHC)** An engine that uses one overhead camshaft to operate both intake valves and exhaust valves via **rockers**.

**Skimming** Machining operation involving the removal of the minimum amount of metal for the purpose of straightening or flattening.

**Skirt** On a piston that part below the gudgeon pin and ring belt areas.

**Slave cylinder** The equipment end of an hydraulic control system. Usually referred to as a caliper in a brake system.

**Sleeve** Very similar to a **liner,** but used more as an insert to restore a worn component to its original size.

**Slider** A part that moves up and down. On telescopic front forks the moving bottom leg, which slides over or in the fixed top tube.

**Small-end** The smaller end on a connecting rod to which the piston is attached. Usually fitted with a plain bearing or a needle-roller bearing.

**Solenoid** An electrically operated device consisting of a soft iron core drawn into an electro-magnetic field by magnetic suction. Commonly used as starter motor relays.

**Spark plug** Device for arcing an electric current, as a spark, between two electrodes inserted in the combustion space.

**Specific gravity (SG)** The state of charge of the electrolyte in a lead-acid battery. A measure of the electrolyte's density compared with water.

**Spindle** The fixed rod about which an article turns or perhaps swings in an arc.

**Spoke** A wire rod, hooked at one end and threaded at the other, uniting a wheel rim to the hub. A sturdy, integral part of a wheel, joining centre to periphery.

**Sprag** A jamming device. Often used in a starter clutch.

**Spring** A deformable component used to permit a movement but to provide a positive return. Springing mediums may be metal, rubber or even gas.

**Sprocket** Toothed wheel used in chain drive.

**Stanchion** A strong, rigid, structural member. In a telescopic front fork, that tubular part attached to the fork yokes and on or in which travels the moving slider.

**Steering head** The part of the frame which houses the steering stem, which links the handlebars to the front wheel and acts as the steering pivot point.

**Stiction** Initial resistance to movement. When once overcome, the item moves more readily. Mainly used in respect of suspension systems. Not to be confused with friction – a rubbing resistance – stiction exists only when movement is absent.

**Stoichiometric ratio** The optimum chemical air/fuel ratio for a petrol engine, said to be 14.7 parts of air to 1 part of fuel.

**Stroke** The linear travel of a component. In a reciprocating engine, the distance between the highest and lowest points of the piston, i.e. the distance between **top dead centre** (TDC) and bottom dead centre (BDC).

**Sub-frame** The rear part of a motorcycle frame which carries the seat, rear lighting and electrical components. The sub-frame is often detachable from the main frame.

**Sulphuric acid** The liquid (electrolyte) used in a lead-acid battery. Poisonous and extremely corrosive.

**Sump** A well, hollow or reservoir for excess fluid. Detachable chamber on the bottom of a four-stroke engine that contains the oil.

**Supercharger** A rotating pump for increasing the quantity of mixture delivered to an engine. In slang, a blower.

**Suspension** The means of creating a flexible link, commonly using springs and hydraulic dampers (see **telescopic fork** and **shock absorber**), between the wheels and the frame to iron out bumps in the road surface and so create a smooth ride.

**Suspension linkage** Components linking the swingarm and the shock absorber so arranged to provide progressive or **rising rate** suspension.

**Swept volume** The volume of an engine as swept by the piston.

**Swingarm** Moveable joint between the motorcycle's frame and rear end. Supports the rear wheel and rear suspension.

**Swirl** Rotary or swirling motion given to a charge mixture as it enters the cylinder by offsetting the inlet tract.

**Switch** A device for making or breaking an electrical circuit, often mechanical.

# T

**Taper** A narrowing width along the length.

**Taper pin** A tapered pin of metal driven through two or more components until it jams in the hole thus locking all together.

**Taper rollerbearing** A hardened steel roller, being tapered instead of cylindrical, and able to take heavy axial as well as radial loads.

**Tachometer** Rev-counter. An instrument for measuring engine speed, normally showing revolutions per minute (rpm).

**Tappet** A cylindrical component which transmits motion from the cam to the valve stem, either directly or via a pushrod and rocker arm. Also called a cam follower.

**Telescopic** Two tubes, one fitting snugly inside the other, which are able to slide in and out like a telescope. Widely used in conjunction with a spring and hydraulic mechanism to provide the front suspension, and known as telescopic forks.

**Thermal efficiency** The ratio of useful work available from an engine to the heat supplied from the fuel in question.

**Thermo-syphon** Natural cooling, utilising the fact that two columns of liquid at different temperatures possess natural circulation because the hotter weighs less on account of its lower density.

**Thermostat** A temperature sensitive device used to control the flow of engine coolant into the radiator, thus stabilising engine temperature.

**Throttle** A valve in the inlet tract, designed to provide control of power output by limiting the amount of fresh mixture induced. Literally, a throttling.

**Throw** The amount the crankpin is eccentric (offset) from the crankshaft's rotational centre and, in a conventional engine, equal to half the stroke.

**Thrust face** A working surface of a piston, bearing, shim, etc., which takes the thrust and any rubbing action. The 'active' face in contrast to the 'passive' one.

**Timing** The opening and closing points of valves and the moment of ignition in the engine cycle. Usually expressed in degrees of crankshaft rotation or in linear piston movement.

**Timing chain** The chain driving the camshaft(s) – usually called the 'cam chain'.

**Top Dead Centre (TDC)** Denotes that the piston is at the highest point of its stroke in the cylinder.

**Top-end** A description of an engine's cylinder block, head and valve gear components.

**Torque** A twisting force about a shaft, measured in Nm, kgf m or lbf ft. Used to express the tightening force required to secure fasteners at the correct tightness.

**Torque converter** An hydraulic device, such as in an automatic gearbox, for varying the relative speeds of input and output shafts.

**Total loss** A system of lubrication in which the oil is lost after its one and only delivery to the working surfaces. Thus two-stroke engine lubrication is total loss.

**Traction Control System (TCS)** An electronically-controlled system which senses wheel spin and reduces engine power to eliminate it.

**Trail** The distance between the point where a vertical line through the wheel axle touches the ground, and the point where a line through the steering axis touches the ground.

**Trailing link** A form of front suspension using a pivoting link with the axle behind the pivot.

**Transfer port** The port (or passageway) through which the fresh mixture, in a two-stroke, is transferred from the crankcase to the cylinder

**Transistorised ignition** A system in which all switching is done by transistorised circuiting.

**Turbocharger** A centrifugal device, driven by exhaust gases, that pressurises the intake air. Normally used to increase the power output from a given engine displacement.

**Turbulence** Agitation in a liquid or gas and especially in the fresh charge inside a cylinder. Adequate turbulence may assist good combustion.

**Twistgrip** Rotary throttle control on the right handlebar, operated by twisting.

**Two-stroke** An operating cycle for an internal combustion engine in which combustion takes place on every ascent of the piston. The four events (induction, compression, ignition, exhaust) in the engine cycle are thus completed in two strokes (one up, one down) of the piston. See also **Four-stroke**.

# U

**Unit construction** Engine and transmission manufactured as one single unit, sharing a common crankcase.

**Universal joint or U-joint (UJ)** A double-pivoted connection for transmitting power from a driving shaft to a driven shaft through an angle. Typically found in shaft drive assemblies.

**Unsprung weight** Anything not supported by the bike's suspension (i.e. the wheel, tyres, brakes, final drive and bottom (moving) part of the suspension).

**Upside down forks (inverted forks)** In contrast to conventional forks, these have the inner tube at the bottom, connected to the wheel axle, and acting as the slider, moving in the outer tube, which is secured at the top in the yokes. Less unsprung weight and stiffer construction than conventional forks.

# V

**Valve** A device through which the flow of liquid, gas or vacuum may be stopped, started or regulated by a moveable part that opens, shuts or partially obstructs one or more ports or passageways. The intake and exhaust valves in the cylinder head are of the poppet type.

**Valve bounce** Occurs when a poppet valve crashes on to its seat too hard for the spring to hold it down, so that it bounces off that seat.

**Valve clearance** The clearance between the valve tip (the end of the valve stem) and the rocker arm, or between the tappet/follower and the camshaft lobe, depending on the valve train arrangement. The valve clearance is measured when the valve is closed and the engine is cold, and is adjustable. The correct clearance is important - if too small the valve won't close fully when it is hot and will burn out, whereas if too large noisy operation will result. Incorrect clearance also affects the running of the engine at idle speed.

**Valve lift** The amount a valve is lifted off its seat when opened.

**Valve seat** That part of the cylinder head against which the valve face seats and seals. Many seats are renewable or can be re-cut.

**Valve timing** The exact setting for the opening and closing of the valves in relation to piston position.

**Valve train** The components that make up the valve actuating mechanism.

**Variable transmission** A system of gearing which adjusts itself, within limits, to load and speed, and without steps. Also called CVT (constantly variable transmission).

**V-belt** A flexible belt, usually of rubber and canvas, having a V-like section.

**V-engine** A motor with its cylinders arranged in V formation. Can be either transverse (across the frame) like a Moto Guzzi, or longitudinal (in line with the frame) like a Harley Davidson.

**Velocity** Speed, gait, rate of movement.

**Venturi** A narrowing down of a gas passage intended to cause a pressure reduction. Found in carburettors and used to create the suction needed to lift fuel from a jet.

**Viscosity** The thickness of a liquid or its resistance to flow. Indicated by an SAE number. The higher the numerical figure the thicker (or more viscous) the fluid.

**Volt** A unit for expressing electrical 'pressure' in a circuit. Volts (voltage) = amps (current) x ohms (resistance).

**Volume** Space occupied by gas or liquid, usually measured in cubic centimetres (cc).

# W

**Wankel engine** A type of engine, invented by Felix Wankel, containing one or more three-sided inner rotors in one or more specially shaped chambers which create three compression and combustion spaces to each rotor.

**Watercooling** Engine cooling system which uses a recirculating liquid coolant which passes through channels in the engine castings and externally through a radiator matrix, to transfer heat away from the engine.

**Water pump** A mechanically-driven device for moving coolant around the engine. See **impeller**.

**Watt** A unit for expressing electrical power. Watts (power) = volts (voltage) x amps (current).

**Wet liner** A liner inserted into a cylinder block so that cooling water is in direct contact with the liner's outer surface.

**Wet sump** Conventional four-stroke engine lubrication system in which the oil is carried in a pan (**sump**) bolted to the bottom of the crankcase.

**Wheelbase** The distance, measured lengthways, between the axles of the front and rear wheels.

**Windings** Coils of wire for generating a magnetic field in which electricity is generated, and wound around a former or core.

**Wiring harness or loom** Describes the electrical wires running the length of the motorcycle and enclosed in tape or plastic sheathing. Wiring coming off the main harness is usually referred to as a sub harness.

# Y

**Yoke** A component that connects two or more others. The top and bottom yokes connect the steering stem to the front forks on a conventional steering and front suspension arrangement.

# Z

**Zener diode** An electrical component allowing a controlled leak to earth above a specified voltage, surplus current appearing as heat.

# Index

# Haynes Motorcycle Manuals – The Complete List

| Title | Book No |
|---|---|
| APRILIA RS50 (99 – 06) & RS125 (93 – 06) | 4298 |
| Aprilia RSV1000 Mille (98 – 03) ♦ | 4255 |
| Aprilia SR50 | 4755 |
| BMW 2-valve Twins (70 -96) ♦ | 0249 |
| BMW F650 ♦ | 4761 |
| BMW K100 & 75 2-valve models (83 - 96) ♦ | 1373 |
| BMW F800 (F650) Twins (06 - 10) ♦ | 4872 |
| BMW R850, 1100 & 1150 4-valve Twins (93 – 06) ♦ | 3466 |
| BMW R1200 (04 – 09) ♦ | 4598 |
| BMW R1200 dohc Twins (10 - 12) ♦ | 4925 |
| BSA Bantam (48 – 71) | 0117 |
| BSA Unit Singles (58 – 72) | 0127 |
| BSA Pre-unit Singles (54 – 61) | 0326 |
| BSA A7 & A10 Twins (47 – 62) | 0121 |
| BSA A50 & A65 Twins (62 – 73) | 0155 |
| CHINESE, Taiwanese & Korean Scooters | 4768 |
| Chinese, Taiwanese & Korean 125cc motorcycles | 4781 |
| DUCATI 600, 620, 750 & 900 2-valve v-twins (91 – 05) ♦ | 3290 |
| Ducati Mk III & Desmo singles (69 – 76) ◇ | 0445 |
| Ducati 748, 916 & 996 4-valve V-twins (94 – 01) ♦ | 3756 |
| GILERA Runner, DNA, Ice & SKP/Stalker (97 – 11) | 4163 |
| HARLEY-DAVIDSON Sportsters (70 – 11) ♦ | 2534 |
| Harley-Davidson Shovelhead & Evolution Big Twins (70 -99) ♦ | 2536 |
| Harley-Davidson Twin Cam 88, 96 & 103 models (99 – 10) ♦ | 2478 |
| HONDA NB, ND, NP & NS50 Melody (81 -85) ◇ | 0622 |
| Honda NE/NB50 Vision & SA50 Vision Met-in (85-95) ◇ | 1278 |
| Honda MB, MBX, MT & MTX50 (80 – 93) | 0731 |
| Honda C50, C70 & C90 (67 – 03) | 0324 |
| Honda XR50/70/80/100R & CRF50/70/80/100F (85 – 07) | 2218 |
| Honda XL/XR 80, 100, 125, 185 & 200 2-valve models (78 – 87) | 0566 |
| Honda H100 & H100S Singles (80 – 92) ◇ | 0734 |
| Honda 125 Scooters (00 – 09) | 4873 |
| Honda ANF125 Innova Scooters (03 -12) ♦ | 4926 |
| Honda CB/CD125T & CM125C Twins (77 – 88) ◇ | 0571 |
| Honda CBF125 (09 – 12) | 5540 |
| Honda CG125 (76 – 07) ◇ | 0433 |
| Honda NS125 (86 – 93) ◇ | 3056 |
| Honda CBR125R (04 – 10) | 4620 |
| Honda MBX/MTX125 & MTX200 (83 – 93) | 1132 |
| Honda XL125V & VT125C (99 – 11) | 4899 |
| Honda CD/CM185 200T & CM250C 2-valve Twins (77 – 85) | 0572 |
| Honda CMX250 Rebel & CB250 Nighthawk Twins (85 – 09) ◇ | 2756 |
| Honda XL/XR 250 & 500 (78 – 84) | 0567 |
| Honda XR250L, XR250R & XR400R (86 – 03) | 2219 |
| Honda CB250 & CB400N Super Dreams (78 – 84) ◇ | 0540 |
| Honda CR Motocross Bikes (86 – 07) | 2222 |
| Honda CRF250 & CRF450 (02 – 06) ♦ | 2630 |
| Honda CBR400RR Fours (88 – 99) ◇♦ | 3552 |
| Honda VFR400 (NC30) & RVF400 (NC35) V-Fours (89 – 98) ◇♦ | 3496 |
| Honda CB500 (93 – 02) & CBF500 (03 – 08) ◇ | 3753 |
| Honda CB400 & CB550 Fours (73 – 77) | 0262 |
| Honda CX/GL500 & 650 V-Twins (78 – 86) | 0442 |
| Honda CBX550 Four (82 – 86) ◇ | 0940 |
| Honda XL600R & XR600R (83 – 08) ♦ | 2183 |
| Honda XL600/650V Transalp & XRV750 Africa Twin (87 – 07) ♦ | 3919 |
| Honda CB600 Hornet, CBF600 & CBR600F (07 – 12) ♦ | 5572 |
| Honda CBR600F1 & 1000F Fours (87 – 96) ♦ | 1730 |
| Honda CBR600F2 & F3 Fours (91 – 98) ♦ | 2070 |
| Honda CBR600F4 (99 – 06) ♦ | 3911 |
| Honda CB600F Hornet & CBF600 (98 – 06) ◇♦ | 3915 |
| Honda CBR600RR (03 – 06) ♦ | 4590 |
| Honda CBR600RR (07 -12) ♦ | 4795 |
| Honda CB650 sohc Fours (78 – 84) | 0665 |
| Honda NTV600 Revere, NTV650 & NT650V Deauville (88 – 05) ◇♦ | 3243 |
| Honda Shadow VT600 & 750 (USA) (88 – 09) | 2312 |
| Honda NT700V Deauville & XL700V Transalp (06 -13) ♦ | 5541 |
| Honda CB750 sohc Four (69 – 79) | 0131 |
| Honda V45/65 Sabre & Magna (82 – 88) | 0820 |
| Honda VFR750 & 700 V-Fours (86 – 97) ♦ | 2101 |
| Honda VFR800 V-Fours (97 – 01) ♦ | 3703 |
| Honda VFR800 V-Tec V-Fours (02 – 09) ♦ | 4196 |
| Honda CB750 & CB900 dohc Fours (78 – 84) | 0535 |
| Honda CBF1000 (06 -10) & CB1000R (08 – 11) ♦ | 4927 |
| Honda VTR1000 Firestorm, Super Hawk & XL1000V Varadero (97 – 08) ♦ | 3744 |
| Honda CBR900RR Fireblade (92 – 99) ♦ | 2161 |
| Honda CBR900RR Fireblade (00 – 03) ♦ | 4060 |
| Honda CBR1000RR Fireblade (04 – 07) ♦ | 4604 |
| Honda CBR1100XX Super Blackbird (97 – 07) ♦ | 3901 |
| Honda ST1100 Pan European V-Fours (90 – 02) ♦ | 3384 |
| Honda ST1300 Pan European (02 -11) ♦ | 4908 |
| Honda Shadow VT1100 (USA) (85 – 07) | 2313 |
| Honda GL1000 Gold Wing (75 – 79) | 0309 |
| Honda GL1100 Gold Wing (79 – 81) | 0669 |
| Honda Gold Wing 1200 (USA) (84 - 87) | 2199 |
| Honda Gold Wing 1500 (USA) (88 – 00) | 2225 |
| Honda Goldwing GL1800 ♦ | 2787 |
| KAWASAKI AE/AR 50 & 80 (81 – 95) | 1007 |
| Kawasaki KC, KE & KH100 (75 – 99) | 1371 |
| Kawasaki KMX125 & 200 (86 – 02) ◇ | 3046 |
| Kawasaki 250, 350 & 400 Triples (72 – 79) | 0134 |
| Kawasaki 400 & 440 Twins (74 – 81) | 0281 |
| Kawasaki 400, 500 & 550 Fours (79 – 91) | 0910 |
| Kawasaki EN450 & 500 Twins (Ltd/Vulcan) (85 – 07) | 2053 |
| Kawasaki ER-6F & ER-6N (06 -10) ♦ | 4874 |
| Kawasaki EX500 (GPZ500S) & ER500 (ER-5) (87 – 08) ♦ | 2052 |
| Kawasaki ZX600 (ZZ-R600 & Ninja ZX-6) (90 – 06) ♦ | 2146 |
| Kawasaki ZX-6R Ninja Fours (95 – 02) ♦ | 3451 |
| Kawasaki ZX-6R (03 – 06) ♦ | 4742 |
| Kawasaki ZX600 (GPZ600R, GPX600R, Ninja 600R & RX) & ZX750 (GPX750R, Ninja 750R) (85 – 97) ♦ | 1780 |
| Kawasaki 650 Four (76 – 78) | 0373 |
| Kawasaki Vulcan 700/750 & 800 (85 – 04) ♦ | 2457 |
| Kawasaki Vulcan 1500 & 1600 (87 – 08) ♦ | 4913 |
| Kawasaki 750 Air-cooled Fours | 0574 |
| Kawasaki ZR550 & 750 Zephyr Fours (90 – 97) ♦ | 3382 |
| Kawasaki Z750 & Z1000 (03 – 08) ♦ | 4762 |
| Kawasaki ZX750 (Ninja ZX-7 & ZXR750) Fours (89 – 96) ♦ | 2054 |
| Kawasaki Ninja ZX-7R & ZX-9R (94 – 04) ♦ | 3721 |
| Kawasaki 900 & 1000 Fours (73 – 77) | 0222 |
| Kawasaki ZX900, 1000 & 1100 Liquid-cooled Fours (83 – 97) ♦ | 1681 |
| KTM EXC Enduro & SX Motocross (00 – 07) ♦ | 4629 |
| LAMBRETTA Scooters (58 – 00) ♦ | 5573 |
| MOTO GUZZI 750, 850 & 1000 V-Twins (74 – 78) | 0339 |
| MZ ETZ models (81 – 95) | 1680 |
| NORTON 500, 600, 650 & 750 Twins (57 – 70) | 0187 |
| Norton Commando (68 – 77) | 0125 |
| PEUGEOT Speedfight, Trekker & Vivacity Scooters (96 – 08) ◇ | 3920 |
| PIAGGIO (Vespa) Scooters (91 – 09) ◇ | 3492 |
| SUZUKI GT, ZR & TS50 (77 – 90) ◇ | 0799 |
| Suzuki TS50X (84 – 00) ◇ | 1599 |
| Suzuki 100, 125, 185 & 250 Air-cooled Trail bikes (79 – 89) | 0797 |
| Suzuki GP100 & 125 Singles (78 – 93) ◇ | 0576 |
| Suzuki GS, GN, GZ & DR125 Singles (82 – 05) ♦ | 0888 |
| Suzuki Burgman 250 & 400 (98 – 11) ♦ | 4909 |
| Suzuki 250 & 350 Twins (68 – 78) | 0120 |
| Suzuki GT250X7, GT200X5 & SB200 Twins (78 – 83) ◇ | 0469 |
| Suzuki DR-Z400 (00 – 10) ♦ | 2933 |
| Suzuki GS/GSX250, 400 & 450 Twins (79 – 85) | 0736 |
| Suzuki GS500 Twin (89 – 08) ♦ | 3238 |
| Suzuki GS550 (77 – 82) & GS750 Fours (76 – 79) | 0363 |
| Suzuki GS/GSX550 4-valve Fours (83 – 88) | 1133 |
| Suzuki SV650 & SV650S (99 – 08) ♦ | 3912 |
| Suzuki GSX-R600 & 750 (96 – 00) ♦ | 3553 |
| Suzuki GSX-R600 (01 – 03), GSX-R750 (00 – 03) & GSX-R1000 (01 – 04) ♦ | 3986 |
| Suzuki GSX-R600/750 (04 – 05) & GSX-R1000 (03 – 06) ♦ | 4382 |
| Suzuki GSF600, 650 & 1200 Bandit Fours (95 – 06) ♦ | 3367 |
| Suzuki Intruder, Marauder, Volusia & Boulevard (85 – 09) ♦ | 2618 |
| Suzuki GS850 Fours (78 – 88) | 0536 |
| Suzuki GS1000 Four (77 – 79) | 0484 |
| Suzuki GSX-R750, GSX-R1100 (85 – 92) GSX600F, GSX750F, GSX1100F (Katana) Fours (88 – 96) ♦ | 2055 |
| Suzuki GSX600/750F & GSX750 (98 – 02) ♦ | 3987 |
| Suzuki GS/GSX1000, 1100 & 1150 4-valve Fours (79 – 88) | 0737 |
| Suzuki TL1000S/R & DL V-Strom (97 – 04) ♦ | 4083 |
| Suzuki GSF650/1250 (07 – 09) ♦ | 4798 |
| Suzuki GSX1300R Hayabusa (99 – 04) ♦ | 4184 |
| Suzuki GSX1400 (02 – 08) ♦ | 4758 |
| TRIUMPH Tiger Cub & Terrier (52 – 68) | 0414 |
| Triumph 350 & 500 Unit Twins (58 – 73) | 0137 |
| Triumph Pre-Unit Twins (47 – 62) | 0251 |
| Triumph 650 & 750 2-valve Unit Twins (63 – 83) | 0122 |
| Triumph 675 (06 – 10) ♦ | 4876 |
| Triumph 1050 Sprint, Speed Triple & Tiger (05 -13) ♦ | 4796 |
| Triumph Trident & BSA Rocket 3 (69 – 75) | 0136 |
| Triumph Bonneville (01 – 12) ♦ | 4364 |
| Triumph Daytona, Speed Triple, Sprint & Tiger (97 – 05) ♦ | 3755 |
| Triumph Triples & Fours (carburetor engines) (91 – 04) ♦ | 2162 |
| VESPA P/PX125, 150 & 200 Scooters (78 – 12) | 0707 |
| Vespa GTS125, 250 & 300 (05 – 10) | 4898 |
| Vespa Scooters (59 – 78) | 0126 |
| YAMAHA DT50 & 80 Trail Bikes (78 – 95) ◇ | 0800 |
| Yamaha T50 & 80 Townmate (83 – 95) | 1247 |
| Yamaha YB100 Singles (73 – 91) ◇ | 0474 |
| Yamaha RS/RXS 100 & 125 Singles (74 – 95) | 0331 |
| Yamaha RD & DT125LC (82 – 87) ◇ | 0887 |
| Yamaha TZR125 (87 – 93) & DT125R (88 – 07) | 1655 |
| Yamaha TY50, 80, 125 & 175 (74 – 84) ◇ | 0464 |
| Yamaha XT & SR125 (82 – 03) ◇ | 1021 |
| Yamaha YBR125 & XT125R/X (05 – 13) | 4797 |
| Yamaha YZF-R125 (08 – 11) ♦ | 5543 |
| Yamaha Trail Bikes (81 – 00) | 2350 |
| Yamaha 2-stroke Motocross Bikes (86 – 06) | 2662 |
| Yamaha YZ & WR 4-stroke Motocross Bikes (98 – 08) | 2689 |
| Yamaha 250 & 350 Twins (70 – 79) | 0040 |
| Yamaha XS250, 360 & 400 sohc Twins (75 – 84) | 0378 |
| Yamaha RD250 & 350LC Twins (80 – 82) | 0803 |
| Yamaha RD350 YPVS Twins (83 – 95) | 1158 |
| Yamaha RD400 Twin (75 – 79) | 0333 |
| Yamaha XT, TT & SR500 Singles (75 – 83) | 0342 |
| Yamaha XZ550 Vision V-Twins (82 – 85) | 0821 |
| Yamaha FJ, FX, XY & XV600 Radian (84 – 92) | 2100 |
| Yamaha XT660 & MT-03 (04 – 11) ♦ | 4910 |
| Yamaha XJ600S (Diversion, Seca II) & XJ600N Fours (92 – 03) ♦ | 2145 |
| Yamaha YZF600R Thundercat & FZS600 Fazer (96 – 03) ♦ | 3702 |
| Yamaha FZ-6 Fazer (04 – 08) ♦ | 4751 |
| Yamaha YZF-R6 (99 – 02) ♦ | 3900 |
| Yamaha YZF-R6 (03 – 05) ♦ | 4601 |
| Yamaha YZF-R6 (06 – 13) ♦ | 5544 |
| Yamaha 650 Twins (70 – 83) | 0341 |
| Yamaha XJ650 & 750 Fours (80 – 84) | 0738 |
| Yamaha XS750 & 850 Triples (76 – 85) | 0340 |
| Yamaha TDM850, TRX850 & XTZ750 (89 – 99) ◇♦ | 3450 |
| Yamaha YZF750R & YZF1000R Thunderace (93 – 00) ♦ | 3720 |
| Yamaha FZR600, 750 & 1000 Fours (87 – 96) ♦ | 2056 |
| Yamaha XV (Virago) V-Twins (81 – 03) ♦ | 0802 |
| Yamaha XVS650 & 1100 Drag Star/V-Star (97 – 05) ♦ | 4195 |
| Yamaha XJ900F Fours (83 – 94) ♦ | 3239 |
| Yamaha XJ900S Diversion (94 – 01) ♦ | 3739 |
| Yamaha YZF-R1 (98 – 03) ♦ | 3754 |
| Yamaha YZF-R1 (04 – 06) ♦ | 4605 |
| Yamaha FZS1000 Fazer (01 – 05) ♦ | 4287 |
| Yamaha FJ1100 & 1200 Fours (84 – 96) ♦ | 2057 |
| Yamaha XJR1200 & 1300 (95 – 06) ♦ | 3981 |
| Yamaha V-Max (85 – 03) ♦ | 4072 |

## ATV's

| Title | Book No |
|---|---|
| Honda ATC 70, 90, 110, 185 & 200 (71 – on) | 0565 |
| Honda Rancher, Recon & TRX250EX ATVs | 2553 |
| Honda TRX300 Shaft Drive ATVs (88 – 00) | 2125 |
| Honda Foreman (95 – 11) | 2465 |
| Honda TRX300EX, TRX400EX & TRX450R/ER ATVs (93 – 09) | 2318 |
| Kawasaki Bayou 220/250/300 & Prairie 300 ATVs (86 – 03) | 2351 |
| Polaris ATVs (85 – 97) | 2302 |
| Polaris ATVs (98 – 07) | 2508 |
| Suzuki/Kawasaki/Artic Cat ATVs (03 – 09) | 2910 |
| Yamaha YFS200 Blaster ATV (88 – 06) | 2317 |
| Yamaha YFM350 & YFM400 (ER & Big Bear) ATVs (87 – 09) | 2126 |
| Yamaha YFZ450 & YFZ450R (04 – 10) | 2899 |
| Yamaha Banshee and Warrior ATVs (87 – 10) | 2314 |
| Yamaha Kodiak and Grizzly ATVs (93 – 05) | 2567 |
| ATV Basics | 10450 |

## TECHBOOK SERIES

| Title | Book No |
|---|---|
| Twist and Go (automatic transmission) Scooters Service and Repair Manual | 4082 |
| Motorcycle Basics Techbook (2nd edition) | 3515 |
| Motorcycle Electrical Techbook (3rd edition) | 3471 |
| Motorcycle Fuel Systems Techbook | 3514 |
| Motorcycle Maintenance Techbook | 4071 |
| Motorcycle Modifying | 4272 |
| Motorcycle Workshop Practice Techbook (2nd edition) | 3470 |

◇ = not available in the USA   ♦ = Superbike

The manuals on this page are available through good motorcycle dealers and accessory shops.
In case of difficulty, contact: **Haynes Publishing**
(UK) +44 1963 442030    (USA) +1 805 498 6703
(SV) +46 18 124016
(Australia/New Zealand) +61 2 8713 1400

MCL 30.09.13

# Preserving Our Motoring Heritage

> The Model J Duesenberg Derham Tourster. Only eight of these magnificent cars were ever built – this is the only example to be found outside the United States of America

Almost every car you've ever loved, loathed or desired is gathered under one roof at the Haynes Motor Museum. Over 300 immaculately presented cars and motorbikes represent every aspect of our motoring heritage, from elegant reminders of bygone days, such as the superb Model J Duesenberg to curiosities like the bug-eyed BMW Isetta. There are also many old friends and flames. Perhaps you remember the 1959 Ford Popular that you did your courting in? The magnificent 'Red Collection' is a spectacle of classic sports cars including AC, Alfa Romeo, Austin Healey, Ferrari, Lamborghini, Maserati, MG, Riley, Porsche and Triumph.

## A Perfect Day Out

Each and every vehicle at the Haynes Motor Museum has played its part in the history and culture of Motoring. Today, they make a wonderful spectacle and a great day out for all the family. Bring the kids, bring Mum and Dad, but above all bring your camera to capture those golden memories for ever. You will also find an impressive array of motoring memorabilia, a comfortable 70 seat video cinema and one of the most extensive transport book shops in Britain. The Pit Stop Cafe serves everything from a cup of tea to wholesome, home-made meals or, if you prefer, you can enjoy the large picnic area nestled in the beautiful rural surroundings of Somerset.

> John Haynes O.B.E., Founder and Chairman of the museum at the wheel of a Haynes Light 12.

> The 1936 490cc sohc-engined International Norton – well known for its racing success

The Museum is situated on the A359 Yeovil to Frome road at Sparkford, just off the A303 in Somerset. It is about 40 miles south of Bristol, and 25 minutes drive from the M5 intersection at Taunton.

Open 9.30am - 5.30pm (10.00am - 4.00pm Winter) 7 days a week, *except Christmas Day, Boxing Day and New Years Day*
Special rates available for schools, coach parties and outings  Charitable Trust No. 292048